Adventuring with Books

NCTE Bibliography Series

Adventuring with Books

A Booklist for Pre-K–Grade 6

1997 Edition

Wendy K. Sutton, Editor,

and the Committee to Revise the Elementary School Booklist

With a Foreword by

Patricia MacLachlan

National Council of Teachers of English
1111 W. Kenyon Road, Urbana, IL 61801-1096

Prepress: Precision Graphics

Production Editor: Rona S. Smith

Interior Design: Doug Burnett

Series Cover Design: R. Maul

Cover Illustration: Front cover artwork © 1995 by Leo and Diane Dillon from *Her Stories: African American Folktales, Fairy Tales, and True Tales*, by Virginia Hamilton, illustrated by Leo and Diane Dillon, published by The Blue Sky Press, an imprint of Scholastic Inc. Used with permission.

NCTE Stock Number: 00805-3050

Permissions acknowledgments for photographs appear on p. 396.

About the Cover

The painting on our cover is from the front cover of *Her Stories: African American Folktales, Fairy Tales, and True Tales*, by Virginia Hamilton. It was painted by Leo and Diane Dillon, who have won numerous awards for their illustrations of children's books. Like *Her Stories, Adventuring with Books* includes a wealth of poetry and stories, fictional, nonfictional, mythic, adventurous, courageous, and inspiring. The storytellers in *Her Stories* saw their tales as gifts they could hand down to the next generation, gifts that reflect all the elements of life that the Dillons have so vividly and imaginatively portrayed. So, too, would we like to give to our students a love for stories—of all kinds. We hope that in these pages they will find the inspiration for a lifetime of reading.

We are grateful to Leo and Diane Dillon and Scholastic Inc. for allowing us to reprint this art on our cover. We are pleased to be able to feature the work of the Dillons and of Virginia Hamilton, all of whom have done much over the years to foster a love of literature among young people.

ISSN 1051-4740

ISBN 0-8141-0080-5

About the NCTE Bibliography Series

The National Council of Teachers of English is proud to be part of a tradition that we want to share with you. In our bibliography series are four different booklists, each focused on a particular audience, each updated regularly. These are *Adventuring with Books* (pre-K through grade 6), *Kaleidoscope* (multicultural literature, grades K through 8), *Your Reading* (middle school/junior high), and *Books for You* (senior high). Together, these volumes list thousands of recent children's and young adult trade books. Although the works included cover a wide range of topics, they all have one thing in common: They are good books that students and teachers alike enjoy.

How are these volumes put together? The process begins when an educator who knows literature and its importance in the lives of students and teachers is chosen by the NCTE Executive Committee to serve as booklist editor. That editor works with teachers and librarians who review, select, and annotate hundreds of new trade books sent to them by publishers. It is a complicated process, one that can last three or four years. But because of their dedication and strong belief in the need to let others know about the good literature that is available, these professionals volunteer their time in a way that is commendable and serves as an inspiration to all of us. The members of the committee that compiled this volume are listed in the front of the book, and we are truly grateful for their hard work.

As educators know, no single book is right for every reader or every purpose, so inclusion in this booklist is not necessarily an endorsement from NCTE. But it does indicate that the professionals who make up the booklist committee feel that the work in question is worthy of teachers' and students' attention, whether for its informative or aesthetic qualities. Similarly, exclusion from an NCTE booklist is not necessarily a judgment on the quality of a given book or publisher. Many factors—space, time, availability of certain books, publisher participation—may influence the final shape of the list.

We hope that you will find this booklist a useful resource in discovering new titles and authors, and we hope that you will want to collect other booklists in the series. Our mission is to help improve the teaching and learning of English and the language arts, and we hope you will agree that the quality of our booklists contributes substantially toward that goal.

Michael Greer
Director of Acquisitions and
Development in Publications

Contents

Acknowledgments

This edition of *Adventuring with Books* reflects the constant goodwill and expertise of university colleagues, teachers, teacher librarians, and graduate students. I am immensely indebted to each of them—those who contributed at important stages of the book's development and those whose involvement was ever-present throughout the three years of the project. Of the latter, I would like to acknowledge particularly the contributions of Richard Beaudry, Sally Clinton, Sheila Egoff, Morag Macdonald, and Renee Norman, who were always unconditionally there when needed. I am also grateful to the Department of Language Education at the University of British Columbia and to Dr. Victor Froese and Dr. Marion Crowhurst, past and current heads of the department, respectively, for their encouragement and support.

My very first thanks must go to the many publishers whose generous and continuous contributions of review materials made possible this valuable record of quality literature for children. A special thank you goes to Patricia MacLachlan. I am honored to have such a distinguished author write the foreword to this edition of *Adventuring with Books.* Also, although I have not had the pleasure of meeting either of them, I would like to thank Rona Smith, Production Editor at NCTE, and Kirsten Dennison, Director of Full Service and Composition at Precision Graphics in Champaign, Illinois, for their expertise and personal commitment during the production of *Adventuring with Books.*

Wendy K. Sutton

Foreword: From Reader to Writer

I really don't remember *learning* to read. I remember always being able to do it. What I do remember, as if it were yesterday, is my mother introducing me to the library. She had a mysterious, excited look about her, the same kind of look she got before we would begin a long journey.

"Imagine, a building full of books—*free* books to borrow and bring back and take out to read again!" my mother said.

Imagine! I remember my first day at the library; the shelves and shelves and shelves of books. I remember signing out a stack of eight books that first day. I read the first book, *The Story of Ferdinand*, as my mother and I walked home, her hand on my shoulder, guiding me across streets, around dogs sleeping on the sidewalk, up the stairs to my house where my mother discovered that I had read all eight books! From that day on, I was allowed to take out as many books as I wished, a reward for being a great reader. From that day on I not only loved books, I loved librarians who would suggest books to me. I decided that I would be a librarian when I grew up, and for years afterward I made my parents check out their own books at home!

My father loved books, and he and I acted out the plots of our favorites. I remember acting out *Peter Rabbit* with him again and again, changing or adding to the plot as we went along. I believe that this is how books became real to me, sometimes more real than my daily life.

"Books have all the answers you need," said my father once. "Don't forget that."

It is no surprise to me that in my novel *Baby*, Ms. Minifred, a teacher and lover of books, says much the same thing when she tells her class "all you need to see and hear is in poetry." I think that all the characters in my books who love stories are modeled after my mother and father, and then much later after my husband—another great reader— and my children.

When I was in the fourth grade we moved to the country. I was very excited to see that the library (I called it "my" library) was across the road and down the hill from my house. My library building was a small formal building with a little dome on the top. There was no other building in town like it. Inside there were seven rows of children's books. I read all those books, some of them twenty times.

I still have favorite books that I read again and again. And when my writing is not going well, when I see no way to go in a book, I sometimes take a book I admire down from my shelves and begin reading.

"Now that's the way words go together!" I say to myself. "That's the way a character comes alive or surprises the reader."

I close the book, put it back on the shelf for next time, and go back to my writing. It always goes better, reassuring me that a good book is a good model. Just as we need heroes in our lives, we need great books, too.

It is no surprise to those who know me well that all of my books come from a personal connection. Quite simply, I cannot write about anything that doesn't concern me, interest me, trouble me. Often my books have a lot to do with what is happening to me in real life. Looking back, it is obvious to me that I wrote *Journey*, a book about a mother leaving a family, at a time when my own mother was leaving me because of Alzheimer's disease. *Baby*, a story about a baby left with a family who doesn't even know how much this baby will heal them, was written at a time when all of my children had left to go off to college or work, my oldest as far as Africa. It was my great desire then to have a baby left at my house to help fulfill that need in me to care for something other than myself. It did not happen, of course, but as a writer I could create the experience.

The older I get the more I write about place, my own personal landscape. I am connected to my landscape now, my mountain home with its herd of wild turkeys, deer, bobcats, and bear that come up on my deck and look in my window. But mostly I am connected to the place I knew as a child. My memories of childhood include the fields where I played, the stone walls we walked on, the prairie with its grasses that rippled in the wind. I carry a little bag of prairie dirt with me everywhere I go to remind me of where I was a child. That bag of prairie dirt has its own life, finding its way into the screenplay of *Skylark*, and into my picturebook *What You Know First*. Place or the setting of a story has, for me, always been the first character in any book I write.

Most of all, however, we the writers are always in our own stories whether we realize it or not. Long after a book is published I begin to understand where my story life and my personal life merge; I begin to understand exactly where a story begins. This is one of the true surprises, I suppose, of my work. I do not always control the story. The story leads me, and I have to be brave enough to follow. Most often I am, though if you were to peek in my writing room you would see me grumbling and grousing all the way.

This leads me to the one true thing I can say about writing; sometimes I love writing, sometimes I hate it. Rarely do I feel hohum about it. Never neutral. But however difficult it may be, there is an indescribable excitement when it works. Out of twenty-six letters of the alphabet— just twenty-six!—comes a story that is being written down for the first time. It may be read for the first time by someone out there, maybe someone being walked home from the library. Someone led home by a mother's hand on the arm, across streets, around sleeping dogs on the sidewalk, past buildings, up the stairs; read by someone who may one day be a writer, too.

Patricia MacLachlan

Patricia MacLachlan is the author of more than fifteen critically acclaimed books for young readers, among them the 1986 Newbery Medal winner, Sarah, Plain and Tall, *and its continuation,* Skylark. Skylark *and three other titles by MacLachlan—*What You Know First, All the Places to Love, *and* Baby*—are featured in this edition of* Adventuring with Books.

Introduction

The Process

Imagine the pleasure of receiving boxes and boxes of brand-new books, week after week, for more than three years. Now imagine the challenge of organizing and evaluating this abundance of riches. We began the process by categorizing each book as fiction, nonfiction, or poetry, and entering its bibliographic information into a database. The books were read and annotated by the committee, the annotations were entered into the database, and the database files were used to generate the four indexes and the manuscript. In addition to the pleasure of discovering exciting new literature, we treated ourselves to an evening program, "The Best of the Best," during which the annotators introduced some of their favorite books.

Although we relied on the generosity of the publishers for the majority of the books, we also included other titles that we felt should be represented in this collection in order to offer an array of titles by authors and illustrators from the United States, Canada, Great Britain, Europe, Australia, and New Zealand.

Contents and Organization of the Book

Our literary choices were guided by the interests of children in kindergarten to grade 6, ages 5 to 12. We also organized the contents by beginning with a focus on the youngest readers. Books for Young Children, Poetry, and Traditional Literature start the collection, followed by Fantasy, Contemporary Realistic Fiction, and Historical Fiction serving as a transition to the nonfiction or information chapters, Biography, Social Studies, and Science: Pure and Applied. Fine Arts, Crafts and Hobbies, and Celebrations: Fiction and Nonfiction complete the collection.

In the Table of Contents, each of the twelve chapters has a number of subheadings to help locate specific types of literature or topics more easily. For example, the annotation for Courtni Wright's *Journey to Freedom: A Story of the Underground Railroad* is in Chapter 6, Historical Fiction, under Nineteenth Century, United States. However, recognizing that the complexity of fine literature mitigates against assigning a book to a single category, we organized the Subject Index so that the many facets of a book are represented. Thus, Wright's *Journey to Freedom* can also be found in the Subject Index under *African Americans, African American history, Harriet Tubman, slavery,* and *Underground Railroad.*

Although a deliberate attempt was made to represent as many authors, poets, and illustrators as possible, the breadth of the work of specific individuals had to be acknowledged. For example, Stephen Biesty is featured for his fascinating compilations of detailed information, Jim Brandenburg for his amazing photography, Jean Craighead George for her carefully researched fiction and nonfiction, Lee Bennett Hopkins for his sensitivity as a selector of poems, Eric Kimmel for his skill as a reteller of folk and fairy tales, Myra Cohn Livingston for her wealth of poetry, Lynn Munsinger for the mischievous fun of her illustrations, Laurence Yep for his insight into the past and present lives of Chinese Americans, and Jane Yolen for the richness and diversity of her writing.

The Nineties: A Few Observations

Publishers continue to challenge the traditional form of the book with their production of CD-ROMs, audiotapes, books with sound and music, interactive books with pull-tabs and movable pieces, wheels, flap pages, fold-outs, pop-ups, overlays, and holograms. Fortunately, in the midst of these innovations, the integrity of the story usually remains intact. Other changes in form and content are also apparent, particularly in paperback publishing, with a shift from sweet and comic stories to tales of horror and the supernatural. Since the last edition of *Adventuring with Books,* writers of horror such as Christopher Pike and R. L. Stine, whose *Goosebumps* series is produced for and avidly read by primary children, have emerged. Spinoffs from movies and television shows such as *Batman, Star Wars,* and *The X-Files* are also becoming more prevalent and new books in familiar series, including Nancy Drew and the Hardy Boys, appear monthly. However, coinciding with what some may see as alarming changes is a gratifying emphasis on the arts, poetry, folk and fairy tales, and captivating nonfiction. Environmental concerns and endangered species, presented in increasingly sophisticated books, continue to be recognized as important topics to young people. And books featuring the ever-popular dinosaurs and bears, penguins and pigs, whales and sharks, and of course cats and dogs, are being produced in astonishing numbers.

The Annotations and the Subject Index

Clearly the annotations are the heart of the book. Of the more than 10,000 books we received over three years, 1,200 were chosen. Each of the books presented in this collection exemplifies the high-quality literature being published for young people today.

Because of the growing recognition of the contribution literature can make to all of the subject areas of the elementary school curriculum, suggestions detailing a book's specific strength are often provided, such as its potential for reading aloud, readers' theater, drama, or science, art, or timeline projects. The medium used by an illustrator is also described and listed in the Subject Index under entries such as *collage, oil paintings, scratchboard art, watercolors,* and *woodcuts.* A specific format or type of text can be located through entries in the Subject Index, such as *atlases, dictionaries, story collections, diaries, audiotapes, CD-ROMs, cumulative text, rhyming text, Spanish text, riddles,* and *tricksters.* The Table of Contents and Subject Index can help a teacher or librarian expand a child's enthusiasm for a topic by identifying related fiction, nonfiction, and poetry.

Cultural Diversity

A glance at the Subject Index will quickly reveal the many cultures and their histories, folklore, and contemporary lives that are represented in this collection. In addition to the exciting diversity of the many cultural and ethnic groups living in North America, peoples of Australia, the Caribbean, China, Egypt, Ethiopia, India, Italy, Japan, Lithuania, Mongolia, Norway, Russia, Sudan, Tanzania, and Zimbabwe are all found in this edition.

An Invitation

All of us who have devoted countless hours to the preparation of the 1997 edition of *Adventuring with Books* hope you will find this collection stimulating and rewarding. We are confident that the annotations will entice you to find the books described, both for your own reading pleasure and for that of the young people with whom you work. We invite you to mine this treasury of fine literature for children. Enjoy!

1 Books for Young Children

Alphabet Books

1.3 Alys-Browne, Philippa. **African Animals ABC.** Illustrated by Philippa Alys-Browne. Sierra, 1995. ISBN 0-87156-372-X. 32p. 5–7.

Twenty-six paintings of African animals use bold tribal patterns to portray insects and mammals such as the little-known xoona moth and the African elephant. Two-word sentences such as "Anteater naps," "Bushbaby blinks," and "Crocodile snaps" accompany each painting. Bright colors, patterns, and textures are visually stimulating. A detailed glossary provides interesting facts about each of the animals and denotes those that are endangered, vulnerable, or specially protected. This is a very useful book for language instruction, research projects, and art projects.

1.1 Bernhard, Durga. **Alphabeasts: A Hide & Seek Alphabet Book.** Illustrated by Durga Bernhard. Holiday House, 1993. ISBN 0-8234-0993-7. 32p. 5–7.

This beautifully illustrated alphabet book will delight preschool readers. An animal is named for each letter of the alphabet and the reader must find the animal camouflaged in its natural surroundings. The warm, vibrant colors of the bold artwork are inviting. Two large pages at the end hide all twenty-six animals and letters for the reader to find. This is a worthwhile addition to alphabet collections.

1.2 Brown, Margaret Wise. **Sleepy ABC.** Illustrated by Esphyr Slobodkina. HarperCollins, 1994. ISBN 0-06-024284-1. 16p. 5–6.

The rich, rhythmic language patterns, together with the patchwork-quilt motif art, give this alphabet book its special appeal for young children. Parents will appreciate the soothing rhymes that are just right for bedtime and teachers will want to choose this book for transition to quiet times in their classrooms. Reissue.

1.4   Grover, Max. **The Accidental Zucchini: An Unexpected Alphabet.** Illustrated by Max Grover. Harcourt Brace, 1993. ISBN 0-15-276716-9. 34p. 5–7.

"Apple autos," "bathtub boats," and "cupcake canyon" are just some of the whimsical word combinations in this brightly illustrated alphabet book that is bound to stimulate the imagination of young readers and give teachers plenty of opportunity to enrich the vocabulary of elementary students. Children will delight in creating their own alliterative alphabet patterns and pictures.

1.5   Johnson, Stephen T. **Alphabet City.** Illustrated by Stephen T. Johnson. Viking, 1995. ISBN 0-670-85631-2. 32p. 5–8.

Just when you thought you have seen every possible variation of the basic alphabet book, Stephen T. Johnson shows how innovative children's illustrators can be. This Caldecott Honor Book presents commonplace urban images that suddenly become letters. The illustrations use a variety of techniques: pastels, watercolors, gouache, and even charcoal on hot pressed watercolor paper. There is an *E* in a traffic light, a *G* in a lamppost, and a *Z* in a fire escape. The result is a brilliant alphabet book that guarantees that you will never see a traffic light in quite the same way again.

1.6   Kaye, Buddy, Fred Wise, and Sidney Lippman. **A You're Adorable.** Illustrated by Martha Alexander. Candlewick, 1994. ISBN 1-56402-237-4. 25p. 5–6.

This rendition of a popular 1940s song is a unique alphabet book of words and phrases that express feelings of love and delight toward another person (in this instance, a child). The delicate illustrations show young children, babies, and assorted pets climbing over and under and through the letters *A* to *Z*. Complete with sheet music, this book may be used for language, music, and social studies programs.

1.7   Kunin, Claudia. **My Hanukkah Alphabet.** Photographs by Claudia Kunin. Golden, 1993. ISBN 0-307-13719-8. unpaged. 5–6.

This preschool alphabet book contains many realistic photographs of objects and traditions that relate to the Hanukkah holiday. Uppercase and lowercase letters of the English alphabet appear on the page with an accompanying sample word for that letter, a brief statement of text, and the photograph. Mothers, fathers, children, grandparents, and holiday objects such as dreidls, stars of David, latkes, and menorahs abound. Those who are familiar with the many alphabet books in print may be amused that even in this subject-specific book, *z* is for *zebra*, *x* is for *xylophone*, and *u* is for *umbrella*. Kunin has also written a counting book, *My Hanukkah Book of Numbers*.

1.8   Lobel, Anita. **Pierrot's ABC Garden.** Illustrated by Anita Lobel. Artists and Writers Guild, 1993. ISBN 0-307-17551-0. 24p. 5–7.

Pierrot the clown gathers gifts from his garden to take to Pierrette. The fruits and vegetables are huge and their names are arranged in alphabetical order, starting with asparagus, beets, and celery and ending with the basket being carried by a zebra. This zany, appealing book could be used to reinforce alphabet skills and to initiate a discussion about nutritious fruits and vegetables.

1.9   Mahurin, Tim. **Jeremy Kooloo.** Illustrated by Tim Mahurin. Dutton, 1995. ISBN 0-525-45203-6. 32p. 5–6.

A big white cat named Jeremy Kooloo is the subject of this original ABC story. "A Big Cat Drank . . ." begins Jeremy's attempt to drink all four glasses of milk he spots high on the table. Large, colorful, and expressive illustrations provide readers with the opportunity to fill the narrative gaps between pages. Highlighted in blue, the letters of the alphabet are emphasized as Jeremy's adventure progresses from *A* through *Z*. Readers of all ages will enjoy Tim Mahurin's playful cat.

1.10   Marshall, Janet. **Look Once, Look Twice.** Illustrated by Janet Marshall. Ticknor & Fields, 1995. ISBN 0-395-71644-6. 56p. 5–7.

Patterns and alphabet letters are combined in this intriguing alphabet book to create a unique guessing game. The reader must look carefully at the patterns on the letters to determine what object in nature is represented. For example, the letter *d* is covered with black and white blotches. On the next page is a dalmatian. The letter *h* is covered with hexagons; the picture following is a honeycomb.

1.11   Maurer, Donna. **Annie, Bea, and Chi Chi Dolores: A School Day Alphabet.** Illustrated by Denys Cazet. Orchard, 1993. ISBN 0-531-05467-5. 32p. 5–6.

In this humorous alphabet book, the illustrations are cartoonlike portrayals of various animals at school. Unconventional words such as *icky* under the letter *I* help to bring the text closer to children's language and experience. This book is particularly useful for exploring school, preschool, or daycare life with children before and during attendance.

1.12   Metaxas, Eric. **The Birthday ABC.** Illustrated by Tim Raglin. Simon & Schuster, 1995. ISBN 0-671-88306-2. 26p. 5–8.

Animals from Alligator to Zebra come together for a birthday party, addressing the young reader with short, poetic rhymes to celebrate his or her birthday. Read aloud, the humorous verses let children appreciate language and sound patterns and learn about animals as they move through the alphabet.

1.13   Mullins, Patricia. **V for Vanishing: An Alphabet of Endangered Animals.** Illustrated by Patricia Mullins. HarperCollins, 1994. ISBN 0-06-023556-X. 32p. 5–7.

This alphabet book about endangered animals from all over the world captivates young readers with its message about the threat of extinction. The elaborate collage art sets the animals in their natural habitats and enhances the author's message with stunning images. This content-related book helps children think about the importance of conservation while letting them enjoy the beauty of the world's rare creatures.

1.14   Onyefulu, Ifeoma. **A Is for Africa.** Illustrated by Ifeoma Onyefulu. Dutton, 1993. ISBN 0-525-65147-0. 26p. 5–8.

The author/photographer based this stunning alphabet book on her favorite images of her homeland, Nigeria. Each letter introduces a key word, which is used in a description of some aspect of Nigerian life. The photographs are rich with warm, vibrant colors and add many details that elaborate on the text. This book is excellent for early reading activities and for older students interested in Nigerian culture.

1.15   Tapahonso, Luci, and Eleanor Schick. **Navajo ABC: A Dené Alphabet Book.** Illustrated by Eleanor Schick. Simon & Schuster, 1995. ISBN 0-689-80316-8. 32p. 5–8.

Color pencil drawings of objects and ideas from Navajo daily life, such as arroyo, fried bread, keyah, and turquoise, are featured in this unique alphabet book. Some of the alphabet words are in English and some in Dené. A glossary is provided to help readers translate the words from Dené into English and vice versa.

1.16   Whatley, Bruce, and Rosie Smith. **Whatley's Quest: An Alphabet Adventure.** Illustrated by Bruce Whatley. HarperCollins, 1995. ISBN 0-06-026291-5. 52p. 5–7.

This elaborately illustrated alphabet book lets readers of all ages delight in finding words, objects, animals, and people; each page is devoted to a letter of the alphabet. The young child is taken on a treasure hunt that gets better as the imagination takes flight in creating new words, sentences, and stories. As the author's notes point out, teachers can take advantage of this open-ended word play to stimulate students' oral language and creative writing skills. Children will enjoy the humor of the complex and crafty pictures that let them search for hidden treasures in the words and illustrations.

Color Books

1.17   Baker, Alan. **White Rabbit's Color Book.** Illustrated by Alan Baker. Kingfisher, 1994. ISBN 1-85697-953-9. 24p. 5–6.

Part of the Little Rabbit Books series, this beautifully illustrated picture book introduces young children to the concepts of primary colors and their combinations. Through simple motivating sentences, the author relates the adventures of a white rabbit who discovers the fun of playing with colors and the effects of mixing them and becoming immersed in them. With outstanding watercolor art, this book is an excellent example of literature integrated into the content areas of science. A good read-aloud.

1.18   Charles, N. N. **What Am I? Looking through Shapes at Apples and Grapes.** Illustrated by Leo Dillon and Diane Dillon. Scholastic, 1994. ISBN 0-590-47891-5. 40p. 5–6.

Standard colors and shapes are brightly displayed in this attractive concept book. In the form of a simple question and answer game, each question spread shows different shades of a color on one page and a cutout and rhyme on the next; a beautiful spread follows with the answer. The closing rhyme, "make the world a better place, a rainbow of the human race," is accompanied by a painting of the hands of children of different races.

Counting Books

1.19   Baker, Alan. **Gray Rabbit's 1, 2, 3.** Illustrated by Alan Baker. Kingfisher, 1994. ISBN 1-85697-952-0. 24p. 5–6.

Another one in the series of Alan Baker's Little Rabbit Books, this counting book lets young readers accompany the gray rabbit on a discovery of numbers from one to ten. The author's beautiful illustrations of whimsical clay art animals, along with the alliterative rhyme of the simple yet rich language, provide teachers of young primary-level children with an excellent opportunity to teach language and early number concepts at the same time. A good read-aloud.

1.20   Baker, Barbara. **One Saturday Morning.** Illustrated by Kate Duke. Dutton, 1994. ISBN 0-525-45262-1. 48p. 7–10.

This visual feast of a picture book uses the popular counting rhyme of "1, 2, buckle my shoe" as the pattern for Big Fat Hen and her friends to count from one to ten. The acrylic paint illustrations are bright, and the print is bold and easy to read. Children will delight in counting and chanting along as well as discovering the richness of numbers and objects in the barnyard scenes.

1.21   Cherrill, Paul. **Ten Tiny Turtles: A Crazy Counting Book.** Illustrated by Paul Cherrill. Ticknor & Fields, 1995. ISBN 0-395-71250-5. 32p. 5–6.

Colorful cartoons showing all kinds of animals, from a water-squirting dog to ten tiny turtles in T-shirts, illustrate the numbers one to ten. The slimy worms wearing sunglasses, the spotted fishes playing hockey, and the chickens drinking pop will captivate the interest of beginning readers and counters. They will want to read this book again and again.

1.22   Dale, Penny. **Ten out of Bed.** Illustrated by Penny Dale. Candlewick, 1993. ISBN 1-56402-322-2. 28p. 5–7.

In this richly illustrated counting book based on the traditional rhyme "Ten out of bed," one little boy and nine toys take young readers through a fun-filled countdown to bedtime in different fantasy and realistic play settings. They get to play at the beach and in the air, go camping, and hop on a train; they act, dance, and pretend they are pirates, ghosts, and monsters—until everybody happily falls asleep.

1.23   Falwell, Cathryn. **Feast for 10.** Illustrated by Cathryn Falwell. Clarion, 1993. ISBN 0-395-62037-6. 32p. 5–7.

In this action-filled counting book, children can count along as a family goes grocery shopping and cooks a feast. Cathryn Falwell, creator of the popular Nicky books, uses color, line, and collage to make vibrant and engaging pictures.

1.24   Halpern, Shari. **Moving from One to Ten.** Illustrated by Shari Halpern. Macmillan, 1993. ISBN 0-02-741981-9. 32p. 5–6.

Moving can be both exciting and stressful for young children. Using paint and cut-paper collages, Shari Halpern tells a simple story that expresses what it can be like to move. David embarks on one long car ride with two angry cats, three worried sisters, and four handy tools. Once at their new house, everyone feels better and celebrates.

1.25 Harshman, Marc. **Only One.** Illustrated by Barbara Garrison. Dutton, 1993. ISBN 0-525-65116-0. 32p. 5–7.

This delightful counting book is set at the county fair. A set of objects is counted, and these objects are shown as part of one whole object: "There may be 500 seeds, but there is only one pumpkin." Collage and graphic techniques are combined for a unique effect called *collagraph* that is reminiscent of old etchings. Young readers will quickly learn the predictable pattern of the book and be able to read it on their own. They may also be inspired to write their own examples.

1.26 Hunt, Jonathan, and Lisa Hunt. **One Is a Mouse.** Illustrated by Jonathan Hunt and Lisa Hunt. Macmillan, 1995. ISBN 0-02-745781-8. 24p. 5–6.

Ten animals create a precarious pyramid that eventually collapses. As each creature piles on top of the others, number concepts are introduced and then reinforced. One is a mouse that carries a rose, two is a bear, three is a cat, four is a dog, five is a toucan, and so on up to ten, a ladybug. As the animals build the pyramid, each page invites counting and re-counting. It also provides opportunities for predictions . . . and laughter!

1.27 Jackson, Woody. **Counting Cows.** Illustrated by Woody Jackson. Harcourt Brace, 1995. ISBN 0-15-220165-3. 30p. 5–6.

Cows are a familiar farm animal to many children, and holsteins in particular are well-loved. Counting cows while in a car can be a favorite pastime, so a book that counts cows seems most fitting. Brilliant blues, greens, reds, blacks, and whites create distinctive images. The gouache pictures are simple but striking. The countdown begins with ten cows and by the time there are zero cows, such words as *heifers, bovines, cattle, holsteins,* and *bossies* have been introduced. This book is suitable for developing math concepts and vocabulary.

1.28 Loomis, Christine. **One Cow Coughs: A Counting Book for the Sick and Miserable.** Illustrated by Pat Dypold. Ticknor & Fields, 1994. ISBN 0-395-67899-4. 32p. 5–7.

Counting from one to ten and back again, this hilarious picture book uses rich rhyming language and the bright colors of cut-paper collage to delight young children. Farm animals go from feeling miserable in some way to being on the mend. This delightful book lets teachers and young elementary students playfully work with the concepts of minor illnesses and injuries as well as language concepts and forms. A good read-aloud.

1.29   McKellar, Shona, selector. **Counting Rhymes.** Dorling Kindersley, 1993. ISBN 1-56458-309-0. 29p. 5–8.

This is a good resource for children who are learning to count. The book combines rhymes and songs, along with clear photographs displaying the corresponding number of objects and in some cases the Arabic numerals as well. Classic rhymes such as "One, two, buckle my shoe" are included, as well as less familiar verse, totaling twenty-five rhymes, riddles, and songs. The large size and format of the book are helpful for classroom and library activities.

1.30   Merriam, Eve. **Twelve Ways to Get to Eleven.** Illustrated by Bernie Karlin. Simon & Schuster, 1993. ISBN 0-671-75544-7. 34p. 5–7.

In a colorful and engaging format, this book presents twelve combinations of numbers that add up to eleven. For example, you can pick up nine pinecones and two acorns from the forest floor or count a sow and her ten piglets. This imaginative book provides fun for early counting and addition activities.

1.31   Micklethwait, Lucy, compiler. **I Spy Two Eyes.** Greenwillow, 1993. ISBN 0-688-12640-5. 48p. 5–8.

This variation on the "I spy" game is a counting book in which the reader examines twenty well-known paintings to find the number of objects named. "I spy four fish" in Matisse's *Goldfish* and "I spy seventeen birds" in Picasso's *The New Year* are examples of how the counting is linked to looking at art. Readers must look carefully at the painting, moving their eyes all over the surface, which encourages a closer exploration. The author makes these paintings accessible and helps children build stores of images in their minds. This book is a pleasure on its own and could be useful for art appreciation and simple counting activities. It also complements Micklethwait's first book, *I Spy: An Alphabet in Art.*

1.32   Olyff, Clotilde. **123.** Illustrated by Clotilde Olyff. Ticknor & Fields, 1994. ISBN 0-395-70736-6. 22p. 6–9.

This pop-up book features the digits one to ten with a difference. Each spread offers a graphically styled number that is individually conceived, with ten typeface renditions of the number lined up vertically along the left. The book concludes with a list of typeface names, including "Moonbase Alpha" and "Variex Bold." Such artistic, graphic features make this book more suitable for older primary students because no pictorial sets appear by the numbers.

1.33 Pace, David. **Shouting Sharon: A Riotous Counting Rhyme.** Illustrated by David Pace. Artists and Writers Guild, 1995. ISBN 0-307-17518-9. 32p. 5–6.

Mischievous Sharon causes all kinds of unexpected events to happen when she shouts at the top of her lungs and fills the pages of this hilarious counting book with more and more people, creatures, and objects. Young readers get to predict her exclamations and will enjoy the alliterations in the language as the story climbs toward a surprising end with the number ten. The bright watercolor illustrations reinforce the whimsical and dramatic effect of Sharon's counting capers. A fun-filled book to read aloud.

1.34 Rocklin, Joanne. **Musical Chairs and Dancing Bears.** Illustrated by Laure de Matharel. Holt, 1993. ISBN 0-8050-2374-7. 32p. 5–7.

A birthday party is the premise for this counting book. Ten dancing bears count backward as they are eliminated from a game of musical chairs. The bright illustrations and distinct rhythms of the polka will engage young listeners and readers.

1.35 Schaefer, Jackie Jasina (translated by Alberto Blanco). **Miranda's Day to Dance/El dia de Miranda para bailar.** Illustrated by Jackie Schaefer. Four Winds, 1994. ISBN 0-02-781111-5 (English); 0-02-781112-3 (Spanish). 32p. 5–7.

In this counting book with a strong South American flavor, the text is complemented well by color illustrations that swirl with animals, birds, and fruits from the jungle. A postscript gives a brief illustrated description of all the animals introduced in the body of the text. Miranda is named for the famous dancer Carmen Miranda. Editions are available in both English and Spanish.

1.36 Sturges, Philemon. **Ten Flashing Fireflies.** Illustrated by Anna Vojtech. North-South, 1995. ISBN 1-55858-421-8. 32p. 5–7.

While catching fireflies, two young children delight in counting from ten to one and back again as they put the luminous creatures into a jar one by one and then release them. The rhyming pattern and repetitive, rhythmic chant of the language make this picture book a good read-aloud to young children. Children will enjoy the bright colors of the fireflies against the dark, mysterious scenery of the night.

1.37   Tryon, Leslie. **One Gaping Wide-Mouthed Hopping Frog.** Illustrated by Leslie Tryon. Atheneum, 1993. ISBN 0-689-31785-9. 32p. 5–6.

Engaging visuals make this an entertaining cumulative counting rhyme for young children. Two birthday cakes for a very old dog and three monkeys dancing the clog captivate the imagination. Watercolor and color pencil drawings illustrate individual numbers, but the cumulative drawings showing one to five and finally one to ten invite readers to take a second look. Whether alone or in a group, with a parent or a friend, children can count, read, and reread this rhyme.

1.38   Wise, William. **Ten Sly Piranhas: A Counting Story in Reverse (A Tale of Wickedness—and Worse!)** Illustrated by Victoria Chess. Dial, 1993. ISBN 0-8037-1201-4. 32p. 5–7.

The subtitle explains the contents of this book succinctly. Ten piranhas gradually diminish in number. The story is told in verse as well as reverse. This counting book is a delightfully wicked but realistic look at piranhas for very young children. The illustrations of South American jungles and rivers are ablaze with color and animal life, and the piranhas take on a certain individuality.

1.39   Wormell, Christopher. **A Number of Animals.** Illustrated by Christopher Wormell. Creative Education, 1993. ISBN 0-88682-625-X. 32p. 5–6.

This stunningly illustrated counting book for very young children tells the story of a little chick in search of her mother. On her journey she encounters all kinds of barnyard animals in numbers from one to ten. The simple sentences that accompany the boldly outlined engravings use onomatopoeic sounds and alliterations to capture the interest of the young reader. Teachers and parents will find this book a visual and verbal feast to be shared with and read aloud to young children.

Nursery Rhymes

1.40   Hale, Sarah Josepha. **Mary Had a Little Lamb.** Illustrated by Sally Mavor. Orchard, 1995. ISBN 0-531-06875-7. 26p. 5–6.

Fabric relief illustrations make this familiar nursery rhyme come to life. Applique, embroidery, wrapping, dying, and soft sculpture are all used to create scenes of Mary, her family, the lamb, and school. The lamb is soft and cute. The illustrations not only enhance the verse, but would inspire fabric art creations.

1.41   Hannant, Judith Stuller. **The Doorknob Collection of Bedtime Rhymes.** Illustrated by Judith Stuller Hannant. Little, Brown, 1993. ISBN 0- 316-34366-8. unpaged. 5–6.

This is a collection of four bedtime nursery rhymes: "Hey Diddle Diddle," "Come Let's to Bed," "Diddle Diddle Dumpling," and "Star Light, Star Bright." The board books fit into a container that can be hung on a doorknob, and the cover of each book cleverly builds on the preceding cover illustration. Engaging artwork in soft, warm colors matches the traditional nighttime rhymes.

1.42   Manson, Christopher. **The Tree in the Wood: An Old Nursery Song.** Illustrated by Christopher Manson. North-South, 1993. ISBN 1-55858-192-8. 26p. 5–8.

Reminiscent of picture books at the turn of the century, this adaptation of the nursery song familiar to many as "The Green Grass Grew All Around" is peaceful and comforting. The woodcut illustrations lead from a fine oak tree to the bird that builds a nest in it, to a baby who grows up and plants an acorn, and finally to the oak tree grown from the acorn. The rhythm and circular rhyme make this a good participatory read-aloud for young children.

1.43   Marks, Alan. **Over the Hills and Far Away: A Book of Nursery Rhymes.** Illustrated by Alan Marks. North-South, 1994. ISBN 1-55858-285-1. 97p. 5–8.

In this companion volume to *Ring-a-Ring O'Roses and a Ding Dong Bell*, Alan Marks has achieved the perfect balance between richly colored, action-filled illustrations and striking black-on-white silhouettes. Each of the sixty classic rhymes remains timeless and appealing, making this a treasured addition to any nursery rhyme collection and one that begs to be shared with young children.

1.44   Paparone, Pamela. **Five Little Ducks: An Old Rhyme.** Illustrated by Pamela Paparone. North-South, 1995. ISBN 1-55858-473-0. 32p. 5–6.

This traditional nursery rhyme is also a counting book as, one by one, the five little ducks disappear. Children will delight in the repetition, the colorful and appealing illustrations, and rhythmic text. Young readers will rejoice when all five ducklings finally return to their cozy home.

1.45   Rader, Laura. **Mother Hubbard's Cupboard: A Mother Goose Surprise Book.** Illustrated by Laura Rader. Tambourine, 1993. ISBN 0-688-12562-X. 48p. 5–8.

Eleven well-known Mother Goose rhymes, including such traditionals as "Jack and Jill," "Humpty Dumpty," "Little Miss Muffet," and "Hey Diddle Diddle," are included in this collection. There is certainly no dearth of nursery rhyme books, but Laura Rader's split pages add an element of surprise to this brightly illustrated edition.

1.46   Slier, Debby, selector. **The Real Mother Goose Book of American Rhymes.** Illustrated by Bernice Loewenstein and Nan Pollard. Scholastic, 1993. ISBN 0-590-50955-1. 124p. 5–9.

With the look and feel of a very early American collection of nursery rhymes, this anthology includes such well-known verses as "Hush Little Baby," "Eency, Weency Spider," and "The Duel." The illustrations are reminiscent of Kate Greenaway's work and the old-fashioned style is appealing. An alphabetical list of first lines and titles serves as a guide to the poetry.

Other Concept Books

1.47   Agee, Jon. **Flapstick: Ten Ridiculous Rhymes with Flaps.** Illustrated by Jon Agee. Dutton, 1993. ISBN 0-525-45124-2. 24p. 5–8.

This delightful flapbook includes ten humorous rhymes in ABCA meter. A picture representing the last word of each rhyme is hidden under the flap. The back cover of the book displays the ten "answers" with both pictures and words. Children will delight in this imaginative guessing game. The original rhymes and large, colorful illustrations could encourage children to write and illustrate their own "flap rhymes."

1.48   Aliki. **Tabby: A Story in Pictures.** Illustrated by Aliki. Harper-Collins, 1995. ISBN 0-06-024915-3. unpaged. 3–6.

This wordless story begins with a little girl and her father selecting a pet tabby kitten and continues to chronicle the growing bond between the child and the cat during its first year of life. The colored pencil, pastel, and ink-outlined pictures with large, round-faced characters will appeal to young children. The small format makes this an ideal book for preschoolers to look at on their own.

1.49   Banyai, Istvan. **Zoom.** Illustrated by Istvan Banyai. Viking, 1995. ISBN 0-670-85804-8. 64p. 6–9.

This wordless book explores perspective by moving from an illustration of farm animals to a child playing with the farm animal toys to a photograph of a child playing with the farm animal toys, onward to the planet and a spot of light in space. Opposite each illustration is a page of solid black, adding to the sense of movement through space. This intriguing book will be returned to and shared again and again.

1.50   Blackstone, Margaret. **This Is Baseball.** Illustrated by John O'Brien. Holt, 1993. ISBN 0-8050-2390-9. 32p. 5–8.

This simple introduction to baseball covers the basic equipment, the players, and the key plays in this national pastime. The lively pictures take the reader through the excitement of a game. Beginning readers will enjoy the simple text and humorous artwork.

1.51   Boyd, Lizi. **Mouse in a House.** Illustrated by Lizi Boyd. Little, Brown, 1993. ISBN 0-316-10444-2. 26p. 5–7.

This fold-out cardboard mouse house comes with a cuddly mouse and felt for making mouse clothes. A small book of directions offers advice for simple cutting and assembling of the mouse couture. Simple rhyming text borders the floor of each of the four sections of the house. Although there is little to the story, the house is brightly illustrated and full of play possibilities. This interactive book will draw both younger and older readers into the illustrations.

1.52   Breathed, Berkeley. **Goodnight Opus.** Illustrated by Berkeley Breathed. Little, Brown, 1993. ISBN 0-316-10853-7. 32p. 5–7.

Opus the penguin, dressed in his bunny jammies, suddenly rebels against his grandma's gentle and traditional goodnight moon story, which she is reading to him for the two hundred ninth time. Opus departs from the text and indulges in a glorious nighttime romp. The illustrations follow the mood of the story, moving from soft grays to riotous color and action, and then back to peace and quiet, with Grandma receiving the final burst of color as she slyly enjoys the departure from the text. This imaginative goodnight book would be fun to read at any time.

1.53   Brown, Margaret Wise. **The Summer Noisy Book.** Illustrated by Leonard Weisgard. HarperCollins, 1993. ISBN 0-06-020855-4. 34p. 5–6.

This reissue of Margaret Wise Brown's classic story about little dog Muffin's adventures continues to delight young readers with its rich onomatopoeic language. The story and pictures— evocative illustrations contrasting bright and dark colors—let children imagine and participate in the everyday sounds and events in their environment, guessing about what might create the sounds. The visual variety with which the text is displayed on the different pages sustains young children's interest and gives teachers plenty of ideas for creatively using and displaying the written word. Also available as reissues are *The Quiet Noisy Book* and *The Seashore Noisy Book.*

1.54   Brown, Margaret Wise. **A Pussycat's Christmas.** Illustrated by Anne Mortimer. HarperCollins, 1994. ISBN 0-06-023532-2. 32p. 5–7.

Acclaimed as one of the finest contemporary painters of cats, Anne Mortimer's newly illustrated version of Margaret Wise Brown's delightful 1949 tale of a curious Pussycat enjoying the traditions of Christmas is richly colored and appealingly realistic. Brown's mastery of repetition and rhythm, making this an excellent read-aloud book, is further enhanced by the creative arrangement of text on each page.

1.55   Brown, Margaret Wise. **The Winter Noisy Book.** Illustrated by Charles G. Shaw. HarperCollins, 1994. ISBN 0-06-020865-1. 42p. 5–7.

This reprint of a 1947 picture book should find a place in every collection for preschoolers. Children will become more aware of winter noises while guessing the answers to the questions. It is a useful text for exploring children's sensory skills, especially listening skills and sound identification.

1.56   Bunting, Jane. **Children's Visual Dictionary.** Illustrated by David Hopkins. Dorling Kindersley, 1995. ISBN 1-56458-881-5. 64p. 5–10.

Arranged into general themes such as "Towns and Cities," "Food and Eating," and "Birds," this large reference book provides an introduction to using dictionaries and grouping related topics. Colorful photographs and illustrations are clearly labeled and grouped with similar subjects. An extensive index makes this an excellent resource for finding clear pictures of objects, animals, and activities. Invaluable in any classroom, this visual dictionary would be useful in teaching vocabulary to both English-speaking students and ESL students.

1.57   Burningham, John. **First Steps.** Illustrated by John Burningham. Candlewick, 1994. ISBN 1-56402-205-6. unpaged. 2–6.

In this reissue of John Burningham's book about numbers, colors, letters, and opposites, the popular children's author delights young elementary and preschool children with humorous illustrations that accompany the bold, big print. Teachers can use this book to foster and reinforce emerging literacy skills through basic concept words.

1.58   Burns, Marilyn. **The Greedy Triangle.** Illustrated by Gordon Silveria. Scholastic, 1994. ISBN 0-590-48991-7. 34p. 5–8.

In this delightfully humorous story about a very busy and very greedy triangle, the author teaches children about concepts of geometric shapes while entertaining them with the adventures of a triangle who is not satisfied to be just a triangle. The accompanying author's notes about mathematics and extending children's learning make this brightly illustrated book an excellent teaching tool. Children can easily see how these shapes can be transferred to everyday objects in their environment; for extra fun, they can act out the shapes. A good read-aloud.

1.59   Burstein, Chaya M. **Jewish Kids' Hebrew-English Wordbook.** Illustrated by Chaya Burstein. Jewish Publication Society, 1993. ISBN 0-8276-0381-9. 40p. 6–10.

In charming illustrations, a monkey named Kofee hides in each picture spread. Various familiar settings such as home, school, and playtime are depicted, complete with borders that portray the English word, the word in Hebrew, and a very readable Hebrew pronunciation printed in English letters. Words and phrases describing more specific cultural and traditional themes such as the synagogue, Jewish holidays, and Israel are also included. This book is a useful resource for learning Hebrew vocabulary and Judaic rituals through the interactive sharing of a book. Words specific to contemporary Israeli life—soldier, tank, and Arab—also make the book a forum for discussion.

1.60   Cameron, Alice. **The Cat Sat on the Mat.** Illustrated by Carol Jones. Houghton Mifflin, 1994. ISBN 0-395-68392-0. 32p. 5–6.

This book repeats the phrase "The cat sat on the . . ." with fourteen different objects and displays the corresponding word. The illustrations are comical and the design makes use of windows to build suspense. This creative and interesting resource could be used to help children learn the connection between objects and words.

1.61   Carlstrom, Nancy White. **How Does the Wind Walk?** Illustrated by Deborah Kogan Ray. Macmillan, 1993. ISBN 0-02-717275-9. 32p. 5–7.

How Does the Wind Walk? is a poem about experiencing the seasons. A series of rhythmic responses to questions about the wind, the poem is rich in imagery of movement and seasonal change. This poem appeals to all of the senses and is best read aloud to children. The language is supported by evocative full-page illustrations by Deborah Ray.

1.62   Chapman, Cheryl. **Snow on Snow on Snow.** Illustrated by Synthia Saint James. Dial, 1994. ISBN 0-8037-1457-2. 32p. 5–7.

Patterned after a poem by Christina Rossetti, this preschool picture book begins with a small boy waking in the morning to discover that the world is enveloped in snow. He goes out to play, and the text moves from his relationship with his mother to his friendships with other children and his dog. The repetition of words creates a melodic, poetic effect.

1.63   Chermayeff, Ivan. **Fishy Facts.** Illustrated by Ivan Chermayeff. Harcourt Brace, 1994. ISBN 0-15-228175-4. 30p. 6–8.

This compact, uncomplicated book is brightened by colorful, collagelike illustrations. Yellows, blues, reds, and grays are splashed generously across the pages as various fish are introduced with succinct, well-written facts. The language is as interesting as the pictures. Both work well to convey information and images.

1.64   Coffelt, Nancy. **The Dog Who Cried Woof.** Illustrated by Nancy Coffelt. Harcourt Brace, 1995. ISBN 0-15-200201-4. 32p. 5–8.

In another one of Nancy Coffelt's delightful tales for young readers, Ernie the dog annoys people with his very loud, nonstop barks. When a slinky orange cat moves in next door and steals Ernie's food, Ernie finally loses his voice from too much barking. In the end he learns a lesson about "crying woof" too many times and about how and when to bark more appropriately. The large, boldly colored oil pastel illustrations are bound to attract young readers' attention. Teachers will be delighted to discover that young children recognize this retelling of the original "Cry Wolf" story.

1.65   Conrad, Pam. **Animal Lingo.** Illustrated by Barbara Bustetter Falk. HarperCollins, 1995. ISBN 0-06-023401-6. 32p. 5–6.

Large, appealing illustrations of various animals around the world are accompanied by brief text identifying a country and a corresponding animal sound. Children will enjoy realizing that animals have a language that is specific to where they live. Perhaps the principal value of this book is its implicit invitation to explore language.

1.66   Cooper, Helen. **The Bear under the Stairs.** Illustrated by Helen Cooper. Dial, 1993. ISBN 0-8037-1279-0. 32p. 5–7.

William is afraid of the hungry bear who he imagines is living in the closet under the stairs. To keep the bear happy, William decides he must feed it. Every day the little boy musters up enough courage to open the closet door a crack and toss in some food. Eventually his mother notices the terrible smell creeping out from under the door. William shares his fear with his mother and together they confront and overcome it. Helen Cooper's gentle, soft-hued illustrations complement this engaging, comforting tale. A story-time must for young children.

1.67   Crimi, Carolyn. **Outside, Inside.** Illustrated by Linnea Asplind Riley. Simon & Schuster, 1995. ISBN 0-671-88688-6. 36p. 5–8.

Molly wakes up indoors while a storm builds and erupts outside. Each page contrasts what Molly does to occupy herself on the rainy day with the progressive stages of the storm. In the end, the storm dissipates and Molly welcomes the outside in! The text is complemented by paper appliqué illustrations, which create a three-dimensional effect.

1.68   Ehlert, Lois. **Snowballs.** Illustrated by Lois Ehlert. Harcourt Brace, 1995. ISBN 0-15-200074-7. unpaged. 5–6.

What is most memorable about this book is its visual appeal. The collages are striking and include the seeds of winter: sunflower seeds, peanuts, popcorn, birdseed, raisins, and corn. These seeds help feed birds, but they can also create snow dad, snow man, snow boy, snow girl, snow baby, and snow cat. The full-spread collages must be presented vertically and are well suited for preschool and kindergarten story times. They could promote discussions about such things as family, winter, birds, and the environment.

1.69   Fanelli, Sara. **My Map Book.** Illustrated by Sara Fanelli. Harper-Collins, 1995. ISBN 0-06-026455-1. unpaged. 5–8.

A map of your tummy, a map of a face, a map of my day, a book jacket that unfolds into a poster-size personal map—Sara Fanelli offers an unconventional, childlike view of the world. This is an excellent book for exploring maps, drawing, labeling, and new vocabulary with children. The fact that the author/illustrator is a child herself makes the book even more useful for encouraging children to publish. It has a postmodern feel, representing unconventional geographies important to children.

1.70   Feder, Jane. **Table, Chair, Bear: A Book in Many Languages.** Illustrated by Jane Feder. Ticknor & Fields, 1995. ISBN 0-395-65938-8, unpaged. 6–8.

This is a good resource for demonstrating the diversity of written and spoken languages. Various objects are presented with a simple illustration and an accompanying English word and pronunciation. The page is bordered with the word in Korean, French, Arabic, Vietnamese, Japanese, Portuguese (Brazilian), Lao, Spanish (Mexican), Chinese (Mandarin), Tagalog, Cambodian, and Navajo. Both the actual script of the language and the anglicized transliteration (pronunciation) are included. The book concludes with the phrases "my room" and "please come in."

1.71   Fowler, Richard. **Honeybee's Busy Day.** Illustrated by Richard Fowler. Harcourt Brace, 1994. ISBN 0-15-200055-0. unpaged. 5–6.

This delightful interactive book comes with a cardboard honeybee who resides in a handy plastic pocket on the front cover until it's time to slide the bee through the slots. Then each spread tells the story of Honeybee's work gathering nectar from the flowers to make into honey. The words swirl in flight across the pages, roller-coaster style, interspersed with ellipses, pointing the way to the next slot. Honeybee flies through each slot, meeting various animal friends on the way to her hive.

1.72 Fox, Mem. **Time for Bed.** Illustrated by Jane Dyer. Harcourt Brace, 1993. ISBN 0-15-288183-2. 32p. 5–6.

Baby animals are soothed to sleep by their parents. The simple chant begins, "It's time for bed . . ." and the full-spread watercolor illustrations evoke a sleepy mood. A foal settles down in a moonlit meadow, a pair of fish blow bubbles underwater, and a kitten is groomed by its mother. The repetitive text is soothing and conveys the strong feelings of love and security in a family.

1.73 Fox, Mem. **Tough Boris.** Illustrated by Kathryn Brown. Harcourt Brace, 1994. ISBN 0-15-289612-0. 32p. 5–8.

The spare, engaging text and illustrations rich with story and emotion present pirates as having characteristics other than evil ones. Children will delight in the rhythmic text, respond to the pathos and humor, and be eager to share the discovery of the additional story found only in the illustrations.

1.74 Gerstein, Mordicai. **The Story of May.** Illustrated by Mordicai Gerstein. HarperCollins, 1993. ISBN 0-06-022288-3. 48p. 6–8.

In this exuberantly illustrated story about the twelve months, "Little May" travels through the year and meets all her relatives, including her father, the month of December, whom she has not met before. May learns about the months' and seasons' unique gifts and characteristics while members of her family, from her mother, April, to her grandmother, November, teach her about both humorous and serious aspects of family relationships. Children will enjoy the rich text, with its detailed dialogue and narrative, and delight in the positive messages about the rhythms and patterns of life. Teachers will treasure this book as a valuable allegoric portrayal of the interrelatedness of humans with nature. An excellent read-aloud book.

1.75 Gray, Libba Moore. **Small Green Snake.** Illustrated by Holly Meade. Orchard, 1994. ISBN 0-531-06844-7. 32p. 5–7.

In this playfully written story about a young garter snake whose curiosity leads him to numerous adventures beyond the garden wall, the author uses alliterative and onomatopoeic language patterns as well as creative print arrangements to capture children's interest. The artwork, done in a torn-paper collage with bold colors, enhances the appeal of this picture book to young readers.

1.76 Grejniec, Michael. **Good Morning, Good Night.** Illustrated by Michael Grejniec. North-South, 1993. ISBN 1-55858-173-1. 32p. 5–6.

Brightly colored, crayonlike drawings depict a single day, from morning to night, for a girl and boy. In the process, word opposites are introduced such as inside/outside, hiding/seeking, one/many, low/high, quiet/noisy, far/close, and morning/night. The use of familiar objects such as butterflies, swings, snails, and goldfish invites children to talk about their days, making this book a valuable language teaching resource.

1.77 Grisewood, John, and Angela Crawley, editors. **My First Incredible, Amazing Dictionary.** Dorling Kindersley, 1995. ISBN 1-56458-902-1. CD-ROM. 5–8.

This is a highly intuitive, graphic, interactive dictionary for young readers. Students can start by clicking on alphabet letters and pictures, or on icons located at the bottom of the screen. Textual definitions are supported by full sound and some animation. Clicking on the trumpet at the beginning of a definition allows the child to hear a word pronounced or an entire sentence spoken in a child's voice. The content of this dictionary is appropriate for children aged four to six. Teachers can use this CD-ROM book to promote mouse skills, teach the alphabet, and begin teaching researching skills at an early age. The CD-ROM comes in both Mac and PC formats.

1.78 Hall, Donald. **I Am the Dog, I Am the Cat.** Illustrated by Barry Moser. Dial, 1994. ISBN 0-8037-1505-6. 32p. 5–7.

The essence of what it is to be a dog or a cat is emphasized in this picture book through large, realistic watercolor illustrations. The text is composed of alternating voices: The cat reveals a private, impersonal, and fearless nature, and the dog is a slightly neurotic yet wholly lovable creature who shudders at the sound of thunder and sniffs out telephone poles. The poetic, simple text makes the book ideal for reading aloud.

1.79 Hayes, Ann. **Meet the Marching Smithereens.** Illustrated by Karmen Thompson. Harcourt Brace, 1995. ISBN 0-15-253158-0. 34p. 5–8.

A parade with its bands is always fun to watch and the parade in Ann Hayes's book is no exception. The rhythmic text and rollicking illustrations capture the excitement of the musical celebration. The specialized vocabulary and facts about each instrument are valuable but may be challenging for young children, who will need help with the explanations of the musical instruments.

1.80   Hess, Debra. **Wilson Sat Alone.** Illustrated by Diane Greenseid. Simon & Schuster, 1994. ISBN 0-671-87046-7. 32p. 5–7.

Wilson is a loner. He never laughs or becomes involved with the other children at school. It takes a new girl in the class to show him how to break out of his shell. Young children will relate to the emotions in this delightful story. Diane Greenseid's pictures capture the loneliness and then the joy of Wilson as he joins the fun with his classmates.

1.81   Jaspersohn, William. **My Hometown Library.** Photographs by William Jaspersohn. Houghton Mifflin, 1994. ISBN 0-395-55723-2. 48p. 6–9.

In this detailed information book, children are introduced to the way the library system works by taking a tour of the author's hometown library in Guildford, Connecticut. Through elaborate color photographs, drawings, and text that introduces key vocabulary in simple yet engaging captions and sentences, young elementary students can explore the detailed world of books within a historical and contemporary framework. Teachers and librarians can use this book to introduce students to the public library system.

1.82   Jenkins, Steve. **Biggest, Strongest, Fastest.** Illustrated by Steve Jenkins. Ticknor & Fields, 1995. ISBN 0-395-69701-8. 32p. 5–8.

Through full spreads and paper collages, some of the "world record holders" of the animal kingdom are represented. Children will be fascinated by the colors and designs in the art and the small inserts of factual information that accompany each animal. They will discover who holds the record for the tallest, smallest, and best jumper. A chart at the end of the book lists all of the included animals and provides facts about their size, diet, and range.

1.83   Jenkins, Steve. **Looking Down.** Illustrated by Steve Jenkins. Houghton Mifflin, 1995. ISBN 0-395-72665-4. 32p. 6–9.

This wordless picture book begins far out in space and steadily zooms closer to the earth. Each successive paper-cut collage moves from an aerial view of a city, community, neighborhood, house, or yard, and finally to a magnified view of a ladybug.

This may be a very useful book for introducing mapping skills and for inspiring art projects.

1.84 Kharms, Daniil, translated by Jamey Gambrell. **The Story of a Boy Named Will, Who Went Sledding down the Hill.** Illustrated by Vladimir Radunsky. North-South, 1993. ISBN 1-55858-214-2. 27p. 5–7.

This entertaining cumulative tale involves a boy named Will, a sled, and a hill. Will swiftly descends the hill on his sled. First, he runs into a hunter, then a dog, fox, hare, and finally a bear. The illustrations succeed in visually portraying the speeding calamity from several viewpoints. Finally, when the bear is revealed in the eyes of the panic-stricken sledders, you feel their fear of the impending impact.

1.85 Kozikowski, Renate. **Special Street.** Illustrated by Renate Kozikowski. Artists and Writers Guild, 1993. ISBN 0-307-17604-5. p. 5–8.

This interactive book unfolds into a street that stands up, ready for play. The panels contain pop-up stores such as toy and grocery stores, complete with cut-out animal figures that can be manipulated for role play. The rhyming text on the back of the panels is rather simple, but the illustrations are clever.

1.86 Kulman, Andrew. **Red Light, Stop, Green Light, Go.** Illustrated by Andrew Kulman. Simon & Schuster, 1993. ISBN 0-671-79493-0. 26p. 5–7.

When the traffic lights turn red, everyone comes to a stop and waits. Here at the red light the reader meets all sorts of cars and drivers. Such concepts as size, speed, color, and kinds of cars are developed. The illustrations are vibrant and energetic, encouraging several readings. Young children will delight in this witty, exuberant concept book.

1.87 Kuskin, Karla. **City Noise.** Illustrated by Renée Flower. Harper-Collins, 1994. ISBN 0-06-021076-1. 32p. 5–8.

City sounds and urban life are explored in a simple, alliterative text with bright, stylized illustrations. A little girl holds a tin can up to her ear like a conch shell and hears squalling/calling, crashing/rushing, honking/joking, and belching/smoking. In addition to serving as a good introduction to simple vocabulary words for new speakers and readers, the book is also useful for reading aloud with young children to encourage them to explore sounds and reflect on urban environments.

1.88   Kuskin, Karla. **James and the Rain.** Illustrated by Reg Cartwright. Simon & Schuster, 1995. ISBN 0-671-88808-0. 32p. 5–7.

This rainy day book, which lends itself to being read aloud, introduces counting, patterns, and poetry. James begins a search for rainy games. Each animal he meets loves the rain and tells him why. First published and illustrated by Karla Kuskin in 1957, this new colorful edition has great visual appeal. The ducks, cow, toads, dogs, rabbits, and birds are striking. Viewed from a distance they are clear and easy to see and would give young listeners a chance to actively participate in the story.

1.89   Lillie, Patricia. **When This Box Is Full.** Illustrated by Donald Crews. Greenwillow, 1993. ISBN 0-688-12016-4. 24p. 5–7.

"This box is empty, but not for long." As each month of the year is introduced, a familiar object associated with that month is placed in the box: a snowman's scarf for January, a red foil heart for February, a robin's feather for March. Young children can share their own experiences and ideas about the objects and the months. Concepts such as empty/full, inside/outside, seasons, counting, and time can also be discussed.

1.90   Ling, Mary. **Wild Animal Go-Round.** Dorling Kindersley, 1995. ISBN 0-7894-0213-0. unpaged. 5–7.

Penguins, zebras, parrots, snakes, ostriches, giraffes, tigers, and elephants are interesting at any time. In this fun book, the young reader turns a revolving disk to see such creatures grow from baby to adult. Attractive photographs combined with large, easy-to-read print make this an excellent book for beginning readers.

1.91   London, Jonathan. **Into This Night We Are Rising.** Illustrated by G. Brian Karas. Viking, 1993. ISBN 0-670-84905-7. 32p. 5–7.

This picture book is a welcome addition to other bedtime "mood" books such as *Goodnight Moon.* Here a dream sequence is depicted, with the children of the earth dreaming wonderful, playful scenes. Their awakening is also happy: "Back in our beds the day is a flower. There are petals of soft light in our hair."

1.92   Maass, Robert. **When Summer Comes.** Illustrated by Robert Maass. Holt, 1993. ISBN 0-8050-2087-X. 32p. 5–7.

This colorful photoessay will evoke many familiar feelings among students who remember that perfect time when school is out and they are able to enjoy the pleasures of summer. The special foods, events, places, and family occasions are shared through a simple text and beautifully composed photographs. This book will be enjoyable during science units on the seasons or as students anticipate the end of school and summer vacation. Maass has also written *When Winter Comes.*

1.93   MacDonald, Margaret Read. **Parent's Guide to Storytelling: How to Make Up New Stories and Retell Old Favorites.** Illustrated by Mark T. Smith. HarperCollins, 1995. ISBN 0-06-446180-7. 118p.

Margaret Read MacDonald has created another excellent resource for ideas and tips on storytelling. Tales arranged by themes such as "Bedtime Stories," "Family Stories," and "Stories You Create" are presented, along with suggestions for developing your own stories. Included is a bibliography of stories and storytelling books arranged by themes such as "Multicultural Folktales" and "Audience Participation." Notes about the stories and their sources are included in a section at the end of the book, making it possible to trace the origins of these stories. Readers will be inspired and encouraged by the easy-to-use format.

1.94   Mahy, Margaret. **The Christmas Tree Tangle.** Illustrated by Anthony Karins. McElderry, 1994. ISBN 0-689-50616-3. 32p. 5–7.

This whimsical Christmas rhyme is set in a very large tree in the center of a town square. Young children will enjoy the cumulative action: One animal after another attempts to rescue a mewing kitten who has found adventure on the topmost branch and clings to the Christmas star. All attempts to rescue the kitten fail, including those of a well-prepared team of pigs in climbing gear. Each animal becomes entangled in the bushy branches of the tree. Astonishingly realistic artistry carries the story, which concludes imaginatively as a small girl buys four balloons from a vendor.

1.95   Maisner, Heather. **Find Mouse in the Yard.** Illustrated by Charlotte Hard. Candlewick, 1994. ISBN 1-56402-350-8. 20p. 5–6.

A mouse is hidden behind one of the flaps in this hide-and-seek book. Each charmingly illustrated page offers two possible choices, with directions under the flaps that send the reader to another page and location. The book is organized with tabs that match the picture clues under the flaps. Although there is only one correct solution to the mystery, there are many routes to follow during subsequent rereadings. Children will also enjoy *Find Mouse in the House.*

1.96   Markle, Sandra. **A Rainy Day.** Illustrated by Cathy Johnson. Orchard, 1993. ISBN 0-531-05976-6. 32p. 5–8.

A young girl's observations during a summer rainstorm are the focus of this preschool introduction to the science of rain. Information on how animals react to rain, what effect rain has on the soil, how we keep ourselves dry, how rainbows are formed, and how the water cycle works is embedded in the text. This clear text draws the reader into the magic of a rainy day. Preschool programs could use this as a read-aloud or as the start to a rainy day walk.

1.97   Martin, Linda. **Watch Them Grow.** Dorling Kindersley, 1994. ISBN 1-56458-458-5. 45p. 5–8.

Attractive endpapers lead into this presentation of the development from baby to adult of sixteen animals and plants. Four general sections ask questions that actively involve the reader. Familiar domestic animals such as cat, dog, and horse and familiar plants such as apple and bean are shown in four large boxed and numbered sections on a full spread. Large print, a table of contents, clear organization, and familiar research subjects will make this a popular book.

1.98   Marzollo, Jean. **I Spy Fantasy: A Book of Picture Riddles.** Photographs by Walter Wick. Scholastic, 1994. ISBN 0-590-46295-4. 35p. 5–7.

This book, suitable for home, school, or library, uses two-page photographs of cleverly arranged toys and trinkets. A rhymed "I spy" riddle accompanies each photograph to encourage children to find various articles hidden in the images. For instance, Saturn, complete with rings of spinning plastic toys and moons of marbles, carries the riddle, "I spy a magnet, a fork, a kazoo, / A blue Scottie dog, a soccer ball, too." The task is to find these items in the photograph.

1.99   Marzollo, Jean. **I Spy Mystery: A Book of Picture Riddles.** Photographs by Walter Wick. Scholastic, 1993. ISBN 0-590-46294-6. 37p. 5–8.

This book contains fascinating two-page photographs of objects with "I spy" rhyming riddles. The riddles challenge readers to find the items listed, serving as coordinated reading and visual discrimination tasks. The book's large size makes it easy to use in classrooms and libraries.

1.100   Mazzone, Kelly. **A House for Hickory.** Illustrated by Pat Reynolds. Mondo, 1995. ISBN 1-57255-027-9. 16p. 5–7.

Hickory Mouse goes in search of a house. He finds several possibilities in a snail's shell, knitting basket, beehive, nest, and cave. However, once readers look under the lift-up flaps, they discover that each house already has an occupant. When the mouse discovers an empty slipper, he is relieved and falls asleep in the slipper. The brightly colored drawings and subject matter make this an ideal book for a unit on homes and shelter.

1.101   McGuire, Richard. **Night Becomes Day.** Illustrated by Richard McGuire. Viking, 1994. ISBN 0-670-85547-2. 34p. 5–7.

This simply yet effectively illustrated picture book uses the concepts of evolving events and themes that children can find all around them to help them understand the rhythm and sequence of change over time. A stream becomes a river, then an ocean, for example, or a cloud becomes rain, and rain becomes a tree. With its universal concepts evolving into a cyclical story line, this book is fun to read aloud to children in early primary classrooms and lends itself to further creative brainstorming of more such concepts.

1.102   McMillan, Bruce. **Mouse Views: What the Class Pet Saw.** Photographs by Bruce McMillan. Holiday House, 1993. ISBN 0-8234-1008-0. 32p. 5–7.

Readers are challenged to identify common classroom objects seen from the point of view of the class pet, a tiny golden mouse. This concept story about visual perception will appeal to children about to start school and to kindergartners and first-graders who delight in trying to solve picture puzzles. A map at the end of the book retraces the trip that the mouse took while the students were at home.

1.103   McMillan, Bruce. **Puffins Climb, Penguins Rhyme.** Photographs by Bruce McMillan. Harcourt Brace, 1995. ISBN 0-15-200362-2. 34p. 5–6.

In this very attractive book, two-word rhyming sentences compare puffins of the North Atlantic with penguins of the Antarctic. The bold, color photographs are appealing and instructive as they present details of behavior associated with each of these birds. The book ends with a spread contrasting the characteristics of the two birds and an author's note providing additional facts.

1.104 McPhail, David. **Pigs Aplenty, Pigs Galore!** Illustrated by David McPhail. Dutton, 1993. ISBN 0-525-45079-3. 32p. 5–7.

As he sits quietly in his house, the narrator hears a small sound. He investigates and finds . . . pigs! Dressed in very imaginative costumes, they take over the house, to the despair of the owner. What will he do? In the end peace is restored and they learn to accept each other. McPhail's boisterous, flamboyant pictures capture the fun of the story and children will be delighted by the antics of the visiting pigs.

1.105 Melmed, Laura Krauss. **I Love You as Much.** Illustrated by Henri Sorensen. Lothrop, 1993. ISBN 0-688-11718-X. 24p. 5–7.

In this charmingly simple lullaby, animal mothers and their babies depict the theme of motherly love, linked to something special they share: "Said the mother bear to her child, 'I love you as much as the forest has trees.'" Geese, elephants, camels, mountain goats, and mice are shown with their young in beautiful watercolor illustrations that will be enjoyed and revisited by children and adults.

1.106 Miller, Margaret. **My Five Senses.** Photographs by Margaret Miller. Simon & Schuster, 1994. ISBN 0-671-79168-0. 24p. 5–6.

Margaret Miller's wonderful photography heightens the senses she explores in this attractive book. Practical, straightforward photos and simple text make this a useful language teaching tool. The book could be used one-on-one with young children and children learning English as a second language. The photographs reinforce basic concepts related to how we use our senses in the world around us, but could also evoke ideas for writing.

1.107 Mora, Pat. **Pablo's Tree.** Illustrated by Cecily Lang. Macmillan, 1994. ISBN 0-02-767401-0. 32p. 5–8.

Every year Pablo's grandfather uses different artful objects, such as streamers, balloons, and paper lanterns to decorate the tree he planted when Pablo was adopted into the family. Once again it is Pablo's birthday and he can't wait to visit his grandfather to see what is on the tree this year. This warm intergenerational and intercultural story about the love between a boy and his grandfather in a Mexican American setting interweaves Spanish and English and is greatly enhanced by the brilliantly dyed cut-paper collage.

1.108   Mullins, Patricia. **Dinosaur Encore.** Illustrated by Patricia Mullins. HarperCollins, 1993. ISBN 0-06-021069-9. 24p. 5–7.

Patricia Mullins's vivid torn-tissue collage illustrations, enhanced by fold-out pages and innovative questions about dinosaurs—a subject most young children are fascinated with—make this picture book a delight for young readers. The comparisons of dinosaurs with familiar present-day animals, as well as the information provided in the back of the book by paleontologist Alex Ritchie, add to the value of this book and make it interesting to a broader audience.

1.109   Murphy, Chuck. **One to Ten: Pop-up Surprises!** Illustrated by Chuck Murphy. Simon & Schuster, 1995. ISBN 0-671-89908-2. unpaged. 5–6.

In this wordless pop-up book the numbers one to ten, illustrated in bold, black-and-white shapes, hide nine different colorful and elaborately drawn animals and leave the reader with a surprise inside the number ten. This beautifully crafted book allows scope for the imagination and provides ample opportunities for language development when shared with young children.

1.110   Novak, Matt. **Mouse TV.** Illustrated by Matt Novak. Orchard, 1994. ISBN 0-531-06856-0. 32p. 5–7.

When a mouse family gets together to watch television, each has a different opinion as to which shows should be viewed. When the TV set stops working one night, the fighting ends and they learn to have fun as a family by getting involved in different activities such as playing games and singing songs. The story with its subtle moral is engagingly presented through clever, distinctive illustrations.

1.111   Owens, Mary Beth. **Counting Cranes.** Illustrated by Mary Beth Owens. Little, Brown, 1993. ISBN 0-316-67719-1. 32p. 5–9.

With its beautiful language reminiscent of haiku poetry and its delicate and intricate watercolor illustrations, this counting book pays tribute to the survival of the whooping crane in a series of fifteen stunning images, masterfully blending text and art. The book also includes author notes on this species, whose world population in 1941 was only fifteen. Now there are many more cranes; they "test the winds and leave for northern marshes, where spring awaits."

1.112   Patron, Susan. **Dark Cloud Strong Breeze.** Illustrated by Peter Catalanotto. Orchard, 1994. ISBN 0-531-06815-3. 32p. 5–7.

Young children will enjoy the clever rhymes and word plays used to tell the story of a young girl's efforts to help her daddy recover the keys he has accidentally locked in his car. This modern cumulative tale could be used as a model to help older elementary school students understand the structure of this type of folktale and to compose stories of their own. Peter Catalanotto's watercolors add to the West Coast rainy day atmosphere evoked by the text.

1.113   **P.B. Bear's Birthday Party.** Dorling Kindersley, 1995. ISBN 0-7894-0043-X. CD-ROM. 5–7.

An excellent introduction for children to the world of CD-ROM books, *P.B. Bear's Birthday Party* is an interactive story of a stuffed bear who receives a package on his birthday. During the party, an intriguing mystery surfaces as P.B.'s friends discover that the package does not come from them. As the story is read, the pictures are replaced by text. Students can stop and start the story at any time, proceed to particular parts of the book, and click on highlighted words to check pronunciation. The story is supported by sound and animation. Early readers (four to six years) will enjoy the funny animation and simple point-and-click approach to reading. This CD-ROM can purchased for Mac or PC computers.

1.114   Poltarnees, Welleran. **A Most Memorable Birthday.** Illustrated by Paul Cline and Judythe Sieck. Green Tiger, 1993. ISBN 0-671-77862-5. 26p. 5–8.

When a messenger arrives with a mysteriously wrapped box, it can only mean that Uncle Andrew's annual birthday gift has arrived! The birthday boy and his guests watch in amazement as the box unwraps itself and out marches a miniature traveling circus, entertaining the children with delightful and funny tricks, clown acts, and acrobats. Children delight in the sheer magic of the unfolding center page, the rich details of the illustrations and the characters, and the surprising finale.

1.115   Preller, James. **Wake Me in Spring.** Illustrated by Jeffrey Scherer. Scholastic, 1994. ISBN 0-590-47500-2. unpaged. 5–6.

Mouse loves winter, and he is looking forward to sharing it with his best friend, Bear. However, Bear yawns, stretches, and prepares to hibernate, but before he settles down for his long winter's nap, he gives Mouse a big hug to let him know that they are still special friends. This is a heartwarming story for beginning readers. The story would complement a teaching unit on winter, mammals, and friendship.

1.116   Raschka, Chris. **Yo! Yes?** Illustrated by Chris Raschka. Orchard, 1993. ISBN 0-531-05469-1. 32p. 5–8.

Although this book contains only thirty-four words, barely one to a page, it is a picture book for all. A boy offers his friendship to another who has courageously acknowledged his own loneliness. Joyfully, the second boy accepts. With a "Yow!" and a grand leap into the air, the two embark on a new future. Posture, expression, and movement in the bold, painted text create a book that grows with each reading.

1.117   Reid, Barbara. **Two by Two.** Illustrated by Barbara Reid. Scholastic, 1993. ISBN 0-590-45869-8. 30p. 5–10.

In a stunning rendering of the Noah's Ark story, this Canadian author/illustrator has created a version that will delight young readers and make them eager to emulate the art form. Her distinctive three-dimensional effect is achieved through the use of plasticine to create intricately sculptured scenery, animals, and human figures, making each page rich with detail, color, and humor. The lyrical rhyming couplets make this a book that demands to be read aloud again and again.

1.118   Riley, Linda Capus. **Elephants Swim.** Illustrated by Steve Jenkins. Houghton Mifflin, 1995. ISBN 0-395-73654-4. 38p. 5–7.

Creatures of all kinds need, use, and enjoy water. Elephants, kangaroos, armadillos, jaguars, squids, pelicans, and wildebeests are among the wide array of wildlife from around the world shown in this book. Each full-spread collage vividly portrays an animal in relation to water. Caribou cross a river in search of food, a platypus swims using its flat tail as a rudder, a tiger escapes the heat by relaxing in water, and a sea otter anchored by seaweed drifts off to sleep. Notes at the end of the book provide valuable background information for the teacher. This book would promote discussion about water, animals, habitats, and environment.

1.119 Robbins, Ken. **Power Machines.** Photographs by Ken Robbins. Holt, 1993. ISBN 0-8050-1410-1. 32p. 5–8.

This striking photographic picture book takes a close-up look at thirteen powerful machines such as a crane, a bulldozer, and a backhoe. Robbins blends a simple text with graphic vocabulary words children will enjoy and hand-colored photographs to give the reader a vivid sense of the impressive might of these huge machines. Children fascinated with big machines will be keenly interested in this book.

1.120 Rockwell, Anne. **Pots and Pans.** Illustrated by Lizzy Rockwell. Macmillan, 1993. ISBN 0-02-777631-X. 24p. 5–6.

This preschool concept book focuses on the many wonderful objects found in most kitchens. Two children explore their kitchen and find all sorts of colorful, interesting things. The book uses simple text with big, bold pictures of pots, pans, plastic containers, and measuring items. Beginning readers will recognize many of the items and will want to join in the reading.

1.121 Roddie, Shen. **Chicken Pox!** Illustrated by Frances Cony. Little, Brown, 1993. ISBN 0-316-75347-5. unpaged. 5–6.

This "touch and feel, pull-tab, pop-up book" deals humorously with an itchy subject. Baby Chick wakes up with chicken pox and the young reader can pull the tab and scratch along. As Baby Chick tries to get rid of the spots, a lovely, wacky series of scenes unfolds. Be warned that the humorous ending—Mother gets the chicken pox next—is more realistic than Baby Chick's bout with chicken pox (his spots disappear after a good night's sleep).

1.122 Rodgers, Richard, and Oscar Hammerstein. **In My Own Little Corner.** Illustrated by Katherine Potter. Simon & Schuster, 1995. ISBN 0-671- 79458-2. 28p. 5–6.

This is a lyrical piece taken from the 1957 musical *Cinderella* by Richard Rodgers (music) and Oscar Hammerstein II (lyrics). The song "In My Own Little Corner" reveals the secret dreams a young girl enjoys when she curls up in her "own little chair" and can be whatever she wants to be: a Norwegian princess, a milkmaid, a prima donna, or a mermaid. Katherine Potter's pastel illustrations are cheerful and bold. The endpapers contain the musical score and lyrics.

1.123 Root, Betty. **My First Dictionary.** Illustrated by Jonathan Langley. Dorling Kindersley, 1993. ISBN 1-56458-277-9. 96p. 7–9.

This picture dictionary for young readers is a stimulating introduction to words and their meanings. It is ledger-size and has one thousand headwords in large print, defined in simple language and illustrated with full-color photographs and drawings. It has an index of over 150 additional words that appear in bold type in the text. The words have been carefully selected from words commonly used by young children and the pages have been tested in schools. A section of dictionary games allows children to practice dictionary skills. This book would be useful in the home and in the classroom, as well as in public and school libraries.

1.124 Ruschak, Lynette. **One Hot Day.** Illustrated by May Rousseau. Artists and Writers Guild, 1994. ISBN 0-307-17607-X. 22p. 5–6.

A surprise ending concludes this bright flap book, but do not be surprised if some children dislike the fact that the "shiniest bug" in the story, who sports a sparkly, touchable silver casing, gets eaten! The text is made up of very long sentences with "who" clauses that build to the climax. This book is an excellent vocabulary builder and uses many comparative words such as *skinniest, ugliest, biggest,* and *darkest.*

1.125 Scamell, Ragnhild. **Buster's Echo.** Illustrated by Genevieve Webster. HarperCollins, 1993. ISBN 0-06-022883-0. 26p. 5–8.

Buster the dog and his companions, the rooster, the cow, and the mouse, set out to find out about the mysterious and annoying creatures across the valley who keep imitating their barks, crows, moos, and squeaks. Young children will enjoy the onomatopoeic language and bold colorful illustrations built around the concept of echo.

1.126 Schotter, Richard, and Roni Schotter. **There's a Dragon About: A Winter's Revel.** Illustrated by R. W. Alley. Orchard, 1994. ISBN 0-531-06858-7. 32p. 5–7.

A troupe of child actors arrives at a house one snowy night to enact a play in exchange for warmth. The lyrical verse of this tale takes us through scenes of a traditional king's court and the slaying of a dragon. In the end, one actor appears as a doctor to cure the ailing creature. This provides a useful introduction to poetry, theater, and dragons!

1.127 Schotter, Roni. **When Crocodiles Clean Up.** Illustrated by Thor Wickstrom. Macmillan, 1993. ISBN 0-02-781297-9. 32p. 5–7.

Naughty crocodiles continue to play and eat even when issued a motherly ultimatum to clean their messy room. The large-print story text is juxtaposed with comic-strip balloons containing the young crocodiles' unrepentant dialogue. The busy illustrations are full of fun as the crocodiles finally clean up in their own way.

1.128 Schwartz, Amy. **A Teeny Tiny Baby.** Illustrated by Amy Schwartz. Orchard, 1994. ISBN 0-531-06818-8. 32p. 5–6.

"I'm a teeny tiny baby and I know how to get anything I want." So begins the humorous story of a baby who enjoys his special position as the center of attention. Much loved and thoroughly entertained by life in the city, this little baby provides a humorous look at a baby's perception of his busy life. Told in first person, the short and simple text is coupled with large, colorful, and funny illustrations. Anyone with young children will laugh at the self-centered voice of this teeny baby. Children will get a kick out of reliving how they behaved as babies.

1.129 Serfozo, Mary. **Joe Joe.** Illustrated by Nina S. Montezinos. Macmillan, 1993. ISBN 0-689-50578-7. 32p. 5–6.

Joe Joe goes out to play. He bangs a stick along a fence, bongs the garbage can lids, clangs his fire engine, and claps at birds. Words describing the sounds and action are printed twice on each full-spread illustration—once in easy-to-read black type and the other in a bright, expressive style. Early readers and young children will enjoy the pictures; for teachers working with beginning ESL students this would be a rich teaching aid.

1.130 Shecter, Ben. **When Will the Snow Trees Grow?** Illustrated by Ben Shecter. HarperCollins, 1993. ISBN 0-06-022897-0. 32p. 5–8.

A young boy meets a wise bear who explains the meaning of autumn and Thanksgiving. Together they drink hot chocolate, bake a pumpkin pie, and bring out quilts and sweaters in preparation for the coming of winter. When the snow begins to fall, the boy, dressed for winter, waves goodbye to the bear, who leaves to hibernate. The rich autumnal colors of the illustrations and the charm of the bear greatly enhance this simple, lyrical story.

1.131 Shephard, Jeff. **Full Moon Birthday.** Illustrated by S. D. Schindler. Atheneum, 1995. ISBN 0-689-80321-4. 32p. 3–7.

It is Owl's birthday and his friends try to get him the moon as a present. Their amusing efforts will please young readers, who will rejoice at their final solution. S. D. Schindler's pictures convey the antics of Owl's friends as they try to capture the perfect birthday gift.

1.132 Skofield, James. **'Round and Around.** Illustrated by James Graham Hale. HarperCollins, 1993. ISBN 0-06-025746-6. 32p. 3–8.

A father and his young son spend an evening doing the things parents and their children enjoy together as part of everyday life, such as going for a walk, observing nature, and having a snack. They encounter circle shapes everywhere around them and realize the importance of things that go "round and round." Through delightful pictures and easy descriptive language, young readers can share in discovering the magic of circles as part of our world. An excellent and delightful read-aloud that actively involves students in reading and in learning about a concept.

1.133 Stickland, Henrietta. **Dinosaur Roar!** Illustrated by Paul Stickland. Dutton, 1994. ISBN 0-525-45276-1. 26p. 5–6.

This book for preschoolers and young readers introduces new vocabulary in conjunction with colorful illustrations of dinosaurs of different sizes, shapes, and positions. The humorous images are delightful, making learning new words more fun.

1.134 Sturges, Philemon. **Rainsong Snowsong.** Illustrated by Shari Halpern. North-South, 1995. ISBN 1-55858-471-4. 32p. 5–7.

Philemon Sturges's rhythmical, somewhat predictable rhyming text celebrates the summer rain and winter snow. The seemingly simple collages by Shari Halpern are well-designed, effective, and skillfully executed. This book would have special appeal for the young reader.

1.135 Teichman, Mary. **Merry Christmas: A Victorian Verse.** Illustrated by Mary Teichman. HarperCollins, 1993. ISBN 0-06-022889-X. 32p. 5–8.

Brightly colored illustrations reminiscent of Victorian Christmas cards attract attention. Poetic lines are rendered for each letter in the words *Merry Christmas.* Each page has its own old-fashioned Christmas border of leaves, holly, and berries.

1.136 Tompert, Ann. **Just a Little Bit.** Illustrated by Lynn Munsinger. Houghton Mifflin, 1993. ISBN 0-395-51527-0. 32p. 5–7.

The familiar theme that everyone has a contribution to make is delightfully interpreted by Lynn Munsinger's humorous and appealing illustrations. This is a cumulative tale in which the attempts of the elephant and the mouse to play on a seesaw are unsuccessful until a small, brown beetle lands on top of the many other animals who have joined the mouse's side and finally tips the balance, lifting the elephant in the air. The hilarious scenes of the animals trying to resolve the problem will be revisited again and again.

1.137 Van Laan, Nancy. **Sleep, Sleep, Sleep: A Lullaby for Little Ones around the World.** Illustrated by Holly Meade. Little, Brown, 1995. ISBN 0-316-89732-9. 32p. 5–6.

In rhythmic verse, mothers around the world, both human and animal, lull their babies to sleep. Each culture is represented by a mother and child and two examples of animals with their young from the same continent. The endpages have outline maps of the seven continents and the universality of a mother's love is presented with brightly colored collages.

1.138 Walsh, Ellen Stoll. **Pip's Magic.** Illustrated by Ellen Stoll Walsh. Harcourt Brace, 1994. ISBN 0-15-292850-2. 32p. 5–8.

Little salamander Pip is afraid of the dark. He hunts for old Abra, the wizard whose magic will help him overcome his fear. Pip's search for the wizard takes him into the shadowy woods, through a dim tunnel, and into the black night. He never does find the wizard, but by sunrise his fear has disappeared, with the help of no magic but his own. Walsh's cheerful and bold cut-paper collage illustrations give her story special appeal.

1.139 Wick, Walter, and Jean Marzollo. **I Spy Fun House: A Book of Picture Riddles.** Scholastic, 1993. ISBN 0-590-46293-8. 33p. 5–8.

This book contains colorful and cleverly arranged photographs with a fun-house theme. Images of distorting mirrors, illusory doors, magic hats, clowns, and puppets with an accompanying rhyming riddle challenge the reader to discover the objects listed. The book can be used in conjunction with a circus or magic theme. The book's large size makes it suitable for classroom and library use.

1.140 Wilkes, Angela. **See How I Grow.** Dorling Kindersley, 1994. ISBN 1-56458-464-X. 32p. 5–8.

"My first smiles," "It's my bath time," "I can feed myself," and eleven other events are shown in full-spread photos; borders of smaller photos depict a baby's development over a period of eighteen months. Large text, written from a baby's perspective, and colorful photographs make this a perfect book for sharing aloud with young children and older siblings.

1.141 Wolff, Ashley. **Stella & Roy.** Illustrated by Ashley Wolff. Dutton, 1993. ISBN 0-525-45081-5. 24p. 5–6.

The famous fable of the hare and the tortoise is reprised as a sister and her younger brother have a race on their bikes. This simple, pleasant story could be useful in the classroom for discussing the original fable and its moral.

1.142 Wood, Audrey. **The Napping House Wakes Up.** Illustrated by Don Wood. Harcourt Brace, 1994. ISBN 0-15-200890-X. 22p. 5–7.

The cumulative story told in a predictable pattern is a sequel to *The Napping House.* This pop-up book relies on visual humor and details that invite the reader to return to each page for another look. The illustrations move from blue to yellow tones as the napping house occupants wake up. The book repeats much of the content of its predecessor.

1.143 Wormell, Mary. **Hilda Hen's Happy Birthday.** Illustrated by Mary Wormell. Harcourt Brace, 1995. ISBN 0-15-200-299-5. 32p. 5–6.

Hilda the hen is delighted to discover a trail of birthday gifts for her as she makes her way through the farmyard. What she does not understand is that none of the gifts were meant for her. The resulting irony makes a humorous story for children. Illustrated with bright linocut prints, this book is useful for themes ranging from birthdays to farmyard life and is an effective text to help children appreciate different points of view. Young children will also enjoy *Hilda Hen's Search* (1994), in which Hilda looks for a place to lay her eggs.

1.144 Wu, Norbert. **Fish Faces.** Photographs by Norbert Wu. Holt, 1993. ISBN 0-8050-1668-6. 32p. 5–8.

Wu uses stunning underwater photographs to bring the reader close to hundreds of fish. Readers see fish with stripes, spikes, spines, and spots, or fish with winglike fins or long, flat noses. The book is a great introduction to the wide variety of fish and their ways of camouflaging and protecting themselves. The rich but simple, predictable text invites reader participation and the large, clear, color photographs will spark reader interest.

1.145 Yee, Wong Herbert. **Big Black Bear.** Illustrated by Wong Herbert Yee. Houghton Mifflin, 1993. ISBN 0-395-66359-8. 31p. 5–7.

When Big Black Bear smells something delicious coming from the city, he decides to visit Little Girl at her house. The chaos caused by his visit turns the house upside down. In the end Mother Bear saves the day and a valuable lesson about manners is learned. This delightful story will amuse young readers and the illustrations are lighthearted and fun.

1.146 Zimmerman, Andrea, and David Clemesha. **The Cow Buzzed.** Illustrated by Paul Meisel. HarperCollins, 1993. ISBN 0-06-020808-2. 32p. 5–7.

A simple sneeze by a bee turns the farm animals' lives upside down. If only they had listened to the sensible rabbit. In the end, life on the farm returns to normal. This is a great book to read aloud in class. Children will delight in repeating the various animal sounds, particularly as they do not match up with the right animals. Paul Meisel's hilarious pictures bring the right touch to this amusing story.

Question and Answer Books

1.147 Lovell, Scarlett, and Diane Snowball. **Is This a Monster?** Mondo, 1995. ISBN 1-57255-018-X. 24p. 5–7.

The question "Is this a monster?" accompanies a close-up view of a particular feature of an animal or insect, making the creature seem like a monster. The following page contains the answer and presents a picture of the entire creature. Children will enjoy quizzing themselves and others and will gain an awareness of how pictures can deceive when they isolate and enlarge only a part of the whole.

1.148 McMillan, Bruce. **Sense Suspense: A Guessing Game for the Five Senses.** Photographs by Bruce McMillan. Scholastic, 1994. ISBN 0-590-47904-0. 32p. 5–8.

This photo-illustrated concept book will intrigue young children as they explore a Caribbean island with two engaging inhabitants. As each page is turned, a new setting is revealed. This game continues as decisions are made about which of the five senses is used in each photo. Sense choices are depicted symbolically on each page.

1.149 Miller, Margaret. **Can You Guess?** Photographs by Margaret Miller. Greenwillow, 1993. ISBN 0-688-11180-7. 40p. 5–6.

The author asks nine questions arising from the everyday life experiences of preschool children (for example, "What do you comb in the morning?"). Once the question is asked, four wrong answers are suggested and the reader turns the page for the correct answer. The questions and answers are supported by large color photographs of children in their home environment. This highly predictable text will engage young readers, encouraging them to read the book themselves. This book is suitable for parent-and-child reading, reading aloud in school, and independent reading for beginners.

Songs and Music

1.150 Halpern, Shari. **What Shall We Do When We All Go Out? A Traditional Song.** Illustrated by Shari Halpern. North-South, 1995. ISBN 1-55858-425-0. 33p. 4–6.

Brightly colored collages answer the question, "What shall we do when we all go out to play?" Children ride bikes, play on seesaws, somersault, roller skate, fly kites, climb trees, and much more. This book uses a traditional song, making it popular circle-time fare that can be read, sung, discussed, and dramatized in a variety of ways. The musical score for the song is included at the end of the book.

1.151 Manushkin, Fran. **My Christmas Safari.** Illustrated by R. W. Alley. Dial, 1993. ISBN 0-8037-1295-2. 32p. 5–7.

Look carefully at the frontispiece and title page. A little girl opens a Christmas gift from her father: a set of African animals. While the girl sleeps under the Christmas tree, her dreams are rendered to the tune of "The Twelve Days of Christmas": "On the first day of Christmas, my father showed to me, a nice green truck for our safari." The twelve days proceed with two leopard cubs, three wildebeest, four shy giraffes, five big baboons, and so on. The lyrics are interesting and the colored drawings detailed enough to invite close scrutiny. Music for the song is found on the back cover. Young writers may be inspired to create their own versions of familiar Christmas carols.

2 Poetry

Anthologies

2.1   Begay, Shonto. **Navajo: Visions and Voices across the Mesa.** Illustrated by Shonto Begay. Scholastic, 1995. ISBN 0-590-46153-2. 48p. 9–12.

This stunning collection of paintings by Navajo artist Shonto Begay is augmented by his own poetry. Together, text and illustration provide an eloquent panorama of the Navajo tradition. As his text clearly suggests, Begay has tried both to pay homage to his past and to recognize and accept his present—to strike a "balance in living between the 'New World' and the ancient world of my people." This is a world of ancient chants and pickup trucks, of legends of the coyote and tales of next-door neighbors. Begay concludes by asking us to appreciate this beautiful and mysterious land and culture, for they will "reveal themselves and their stories / if you look very carefully and listen."

2.2   Benjamin, Floella, collector. **Skip across the Ocean: Nursery Rhymes from around the World.** Illustrated by Sheila Moxley. Orchard, 1995. ISBN 0-531-09455-3. 45p. 5–8.

Thirty-three nursery rhymes and lullabies have been collected from countries all over the world—Australia, Canada, China, Germany, India, Japan, Nigeria, Peru, Sweden, Trinidad, and the United States—and many have the original language as well as the English translation. Finger game ideas are also included for a number of rhymes. The bold and colorful illustrations by Sheila Moxley are a perfect accompaniment to this delightful international collection.

2.3   Bierhorst, John, editor. **On the Road of Stars: Native American Night Poems and Sleep Charms.** Illustrated by Judy Pedersen. Macmillan, 1994. ISBN 0-02-709735-8. 32p. 5–9.

"How shall I begin my song in the / blue night that is settling? / I will sit here and begin my song." Over twenty Native American tribes are represented in this tender collection of fifty-one sleep songs. Comforting poems, lullabies, dreams, charms, and night voices soothe the listener and invite sleep. The mixed-media illustrations beautifully complement the text.

2.4   Booth, David, selector. **Doctor Knickerbocker and Other Rhymes.** Illustrated by Maryann Kovalski. Ticknor & Fields, 1993. ISBN 0-395-67168-X. 71p. 8–11.

This comprehensive collection of 157 street and playground rhymes includes autograph verses, ball-bounce chants, counting-out rhymes, nonsense verses, skipping songs, taunts, tongue twisters, and many other rhymes. Rhymes are arranged in sections: contemporary, yesterday, and long ago. The clever illustrations combine nineteenth-century woodcuts, pen-and-ink drawings, and hand-lettered text to provide witty and irreverent images that flow across the pages. An index of first lines and an index of rhymes by type are helpful additions.

2.5   Brenner, Barbara, editor. **The Earth Is Painted Green: A Garden of Poems about Our Planet.** Illustrated by S. D. Schindler. Scholastic, 1994. ISBN 0-590-45134-0. 82p. 9–11.

This beautifully illustrated collection of ninety-one poems from around the world celebrates diverse aspects of our green earth. S. D. Schindler's rich watercolors enhance the wonders of nature depicted in the poetry. Indexes include authors, titles, and first lines. A must-have for any library, this anthology offers curricular connections to art, science, and social studies.

2.6   Brent, Isabelle, illuminator. **All Creatures Great and Small.** Illustrated by Isabelle Brent. Little, Brown, 1994. ISBN 0-316-10869-3. 24p. 5–11.

Beautifully illuminated gold leaf illustrations complement the timeless text. Ten poems by familiar poets such as Edward Lear, Lewis Carroll, A. A. Milne, and Hilaire Belloc are included. This is a classic book of text and illustration for all ages.

2.7   Cecil, Laura, compiler. **A Thousand Yards of Sea: A Collection of Sea Stories and Poems.** Illustrated by Emma Chichester Clark. Greenwillow, 1993. ISBN 0-688-11437-7. 77p. 5–8.

This collection of sea stories and poems by authors such as Edward Lear, Margaret Mahy, and Rudyard Kipling is accompanied by bold watercolors of both realistic and fanciful representations of people and sea creatures. This would be a supportive selection for a study or unit on pirates, chanteys, and folklore of the sea.

2.8 Demi, compiler. **Demi's Secret Garden.** Illustrated by Demi. Holt, 1993. ISBN 0-8050-2553-7. 40p. 9–11.

Demi has created an exquisite garden where the reader can delight in small creatures such as the grasshopper, dragonfly, ant, cicada, treehopper, and walking stick. The rich text includes the poetry of classic writers such as Keats, Shelley, Basho, Li Po, Shakespeare, Blake, and Rossetti. Liberal use of gold embellishment enhances the stunning collages of designed papers and paints. Many of the intricate illustrations open out into three- and four-page spreads. Information on each insect is presented on the last two pages. Sure to intrigue and delight, this book is a must in a school or public library.

2.9 Feelings, Tom, selector. **Soul Looks Back in Wonder.** Illustrated by Tom Feelings. Dial, 1993. ISBN 0-8037-1001-1. 34p. 5–10.

In this magnificently illustrated book, the overall collage effect beautifully enhances poems by such renowned African American writers as Langston Hughes, Lucille Clifton, Walter Dean Myers, and Maya Angelou. This collection contains the first publication of the poem "To You" by Langston Hughes. Dramatic endpapers add to the beauty of this book, and biographical notes on each poet represented in the collection are also included. This book provides a rich experience through both visuals and text.

2.10 Glaser, Isabel Joshlin, selector. **Dreams of Glory: Poems Starring Girls.** Illustrated by Pat Lowery Collins. Atheneum, 1995. ISBN 0-689-31891- X. 47p. 8–10.

Under the headings "Sports," "Power," and "Dreams of Glory," thirty poems celebrating girls are featured. Well-known poets such as Myra Cohn Livingston, Gertrude Stein, Jean Little, Gwendolyn Brooks, and Lillian Morrison are included. Poems that are rich in hope, powerful in their determination, and sensitive about fears help make this small anthology a special creation. Three illustrations by Pat Lowery Collins enhance the title pages.

2.11 Gordon, Ruth, selector. **Pierced by a Ray of Sun: Poems about the Times We Feel Alone.** HarperCollins, 1995. ISBN 0-06-023613-2. 107p. 11–12.

Poems of loneliness, alienation, stress, and survival are represented in this collection of seventy-three poems. Ruth Gordon has selected traditional poetry ("In Memoriam" by Alfred, Lord Tennyson) as well as contemporary poetry ("Elegy for John, My

Student Dead of AIDS" by Robert Cording). Fifty-two poets from around the world make this an anthology of international and universal vision. This outstanding collection includes indexes of authors, titles, and first lines.

2.12   Hoberman, Mary Ann, selector. **My Song Is Beautiful.** Little, Brown, 1994. ISBN 0-316-36738-9. 32p. 5–8.

Japanese, African American, Korean, and Mexican are a few of the cultures represented in this delightful book of fourteen simple poems. Poems are accompanied by illustrations done by different artists using a variety of techniques: painted fabric, watercolor, silk-screen printing, colored pencils, wood-block carving, and acrylics. This creative combination of international artwork and text emphasizes how children are alike and how they are different. Helpful information on the featured poets and illustrators is included on the last page.

2.13   Hopkins, Lee Bennett, selector. **Blast Off! Poems about Space.** Illustrated by Melissa Sweet. HarperCollins, 1995. ISBN 0-06-024260-4. 48p. 5–8.

In his fifth I Can Read book, Lee Bennett Hopkins has selected twenty poems celebrating the sun, moon, planets, and stars. Well-known poets such as Barbara Juster Esbensen, Ashley Bryan, Aileen Fisher, and Eve Merriam are included in this delightful collection. Engaging, warm illustrations by Melissa Sweet complement the text. The book includes an index of authors and titles.

2.14   Hopkins, Lee Bennett, selector. **Extra Innings: Baseball Poems.** Illustrated by Scott Medlock. Harcourt Brace, 1993. ISBN 0-15-226833-2. 40p. 9–13.

Nineteen poems capture the thrill, hope, intensity, and excitement of baseball, from backyard pickup games to professional competition. Expressive, energetic oil paintings vividly reflect the mood of each poem.

2.15   Hopkins, Lee Bennett, selector. **Hand in Hand: An American History through Poetry.** Illustrated by Peter M. Fiore. Simon & Schuster, 1994. ISBN 0- 671-73315-X. 144p. 9–12.

This superb collection of seventy-eight poems offers the reader a sweeping panorama of the history of the United States. Poets of the past (Carl Sandburg, Walt Whitman, Langston Hughes, Robert Frost, and Henry Wadsworth Longfellow) and modern poets (Cynthia Rylant, Paul Janeczko, Gwendolyn Brooks, Myra Cohn Livingston, and Lucille Clifton) are included. The book is divided into nine sections encompassing the nation's beginnings, the Great Depression, wars, modern issues, and even space exploration. Peter M. Fiore's watercolor paintings are as expressive as the rich textual mixture of poetic voices. Indexes by title, first line, and author are a helpful addition.

2.16 Hopkins, Lee Bennett, selector. **It's about Time!** Illustrated by Matt Novak. Simon & Schuster, 1993. ISBN 0-671-78512-5. 36p. 5–9.

Sixteen poems capture the pleasure of a child's activities throughout the day, starting with Harry Behn's "All Kinds of Time" and concluding with Ilo Orleans's "Time Passes." This delightful collection contains works by such renowned poets as Eleanor Farjeon, Aileen Fisher, Gwendolyn Brooks, Bobbi Katz, Karla Kuskin, and Jack Prelutsky. This is an excellent book for encouraging an awareness of time; each drawing contains a clock appropriate to the accompanying poem. Finely executed colored pencil illustrations enhance the text.

2.17 Hopkins, Lee Bennett, selector. **Questions: Poems of Wonder.** Illustrated by Carolyn Croll. HarperCollins, 1994. ISBN 0-06-444181-4. 64p. 5–8.

In this inviting collection, thirty poems ask Who? What? Where? When? How? and Why? Poets such as Aileen Fisher, Felice Holman, Bobbi Katz, Karla Kuskin, Eve Merriam, and Christina Rossetti are included in this attractive, small volume. Carolyn Croll's cheerful illustrations are full of charm.

2.18 Hopkins, Lee Bennett, selector. **Ragged Shadows: Poems of Halloween Night.** Illustrated by Giles Laroche. Little, Brown, 1993. ISBN 0-316-37276-5. 32p. 6–12.

Although libraries abound with books featuring Halloween poetry, *Ragged Shadows* is a marvelous collection and contains fourteen poems by such notable poets as Karla Kuskin, Valerie Worth, Barbara Juster Esbensen, Jane Yolen, and Aileen Fisher. The wealth of detail included in the unique cut-paper illustrations will intrigue and inspire children. This collection is an exciting collaboration of artwork and poetry.

2.19 Hopkins, Lee Bennett, selector. **Small Talk: A Book of Short Poems.** Illustrated by Susan Gaber. Harcourt Brace, 1995. ISBN 0-15-276577-8. 48p. 5–8.

This selection includes thirty-three short poems from such diverse sources as Mother Goose, Christina Rossetti, Robert Frost, and Jane Yolen. The poems include examples of haiku, rhymed verse, and free-form verse. In this regard, the book is an excellent introduction to poetic forms for children. Although the poems are loosely organized by the seasons of the year, the content is sufficiently varied to make them amenable to a wide range of themes and interests. Each poem is illustrated with delicate, small pictures conveying some aspect or affective quality of the verse.

2.20   Hopkins, Lee Bennett, selector. **Weather.** Illustrated by Melanie Hall. HarperCollins, 1994. ISBN 0-06-021463-5. 64p. 5–8.

Noted poets such as Barbara Juster Esbensen, Aileen Fisher, Langston Hughes, Myra Cohn Livingston, Christina Rossetti, and Valerie Worth are included in this appealing collection of poems thematically linked by the weather. Melanie Hall's whimsical illustrations complement the lyrics. The collection is part of the I Can Read series.

2.21   Huck, Charlotte, selector. **Secret Places.** Illustrated by Lindsay Barrett George. Greenwillow, 1993. ISBN 0-688-11669-8. 32p. 4–10.

Each poem describes a special, secret place in this magnificent collection of nineteen poems, including such favorites as David McCord's "This is My Rock," A. A. Milne's "Solitude," Rachel Field's "If Once You Have Slept on an Island," and Myra Cohn Livingston's "There Was a Place." The beautiful gouache paintings feature a wealth of detail and are rich in color—an ideal accompaniment to the text.

2.22   Hudson, Wade, selector. **Pass It On: African-American Poetry for Children.** Illustrated by Floyd Cooper. Scholastic, 1993. ISBN 0-590-45770-5. 32p. 6–12.

Nineteen poems express the joys, hurts, discoveries, and pride centered around the African American experience. Well-known African American poets such as Langston Hughes, Nikki Giovanni, Eloise Greenfield, Countee Cullen, and Lucille Clifton are included in this collection. Rich, warm paintings are a wonderful visual accompaniment to the poetry. The book concludes with a short biography of each poet.

2.23   Hudson, Wade, and Cheryl Hudson. **How Sweet the Sound.** Illustrated by Floyd Cooper. Scholastic, 1995. ISBN 0-590-48030-8. 48p. 8–10.

A companion book to *Pass It On: African-American Poetry for Children,* this collection of twenty-three African American songs depicts key periods in the history of the culture through its rich legacy of music. Well-known spirituals, freedom songs, jazz, chants, and contemporary works are included in this volume, a picture book that illustrates songs. The rich, colorful paintings are a beautiful expression of the text they accompany. The music, information about the songs and composers, and a recommended reading and listening list are included. The index is extensive.

2.24   Hughes, Langston. **Sweet and Sour Animal Book.** Oxford, 1994. ISBN 0-19-509185-X. 48p. 5–8.

This is an alphabetical collection of twenty-seven poems about animals. These short, clever verses have never been published before. For the young reader, they offer a rich and varied menagerie of animals. For the perceptive reader, these poems reflect the ambiguity and complexity of daily existence: "A lion in a zoo. / Shut up in a cage, / Lives a life / of smothered rage." Hughes would describe these poems as serious fun. The children of the Harlem School of the Arts—mostly first, second, and third graders—created the charming and fresh artwork. Biographical details about the poet are offered in George P. Cunningham's afterword. Photographs of the artists are also included.

2.25   Jones, Hettie, selector. **The Trees Stand Shining: Poetry of the North American Indians.** Illustrated by Robert Andrew Parker. Dial, 1993. ISBN 0- 8037-9084-8. 32p. 5–10.

These brief songs, lullabies, and chants celebrate the rich oral tradition of the North American Indians. Each of the thirty-two poems mirrors a closeness and sensitivity to nature, and the brilliant, impressionistic paintings beautifully enhance the text. Reissue.

2.26   Kennedy, Dorothy M., selector. **I Thought I'd Take My Rat to School: Poems for September to June.** Illustrated by Abby Carter. Little, Brown, 1993. ISBN 0-316-48893-3. 63p. 8–12.

In this broad collection, life at school is vividly depicted through poems by such writers as Myra Cohn Livingston, Eve Merriam, David McCord, Carl Sandburg, Karla Kuskin, and Jack Prelutsky. Everything from "Homework" to "Cruel Boys" is represented in these fifty-seven poems. The energetic and expressive black-and-white illustrations capture the mood of each poem.

2.27   Livingston, Myra Cohn, selector. **Animal, Vegetable, Mineral: Poems about Small Things.** HarperCollins, 1994. ISBN 0-06-023008-8. 69p. 9–12.

Fifty excellent poems are grouped into three sections: Animal, Vegetable, and Mineral. This fine collection includes traditional and contemporary poets such as William Shakespeare, D. H. Lawrence, Langston Hughes, Lilian Moore, Valerie Worth, John Keats, Walter de la Mare, Barbara Juster Esbensen, and Karla Kuskin. The book is not illustrated, but readers could create their own imaginative pictures. Indexes of author, translator, first line, and title are included.

2.28   Livingston, Myra Cohn, selector. **Call Down the Moon.** McElderry, 1995. ISBN 0-689-80416-4. 170p. 10–12.

From the tremendously rich body of poems composed to celebrate music, Myra Cohn Livingston has chosen 135 by such poets as Walter de la Mare, Langston Hughes, Karla Kuskin, Edward Lear, Li Po, Eve Merriam, Plato, William Shakespeare, and Valerie Worth. A wide variety of poetic forms is represented, ranging from traditional rhyme patterns in Edward Lear's limericks to the concrete poetry of Anita Wintz. The book is divided into twelve sections, including "The Singers," "The Woodwinds," and "Time to Practice." Indexes to authors, titles, first lines, and translators are appended. This book contains a wealth of poetry and is an inspiring tribute to the world of music.

2.29   Livingston, Myra Cohn, compiler. **Riddle-Me Rhymes.** Illustrated by Rebecca Perry. McElderry, 1994. ISBN 0-689-50602-3. 90p. 9–11.

Myra Cohn Livingston has compiled a broad, appealing collection of eighty-six riddles, divided into six sections: "Alive, Alive, Oh!" "In or Out, Up or Down," "Mostly Inside," "Mostly Outside," "A Mixed Bag," and "Some with Answers." Well-known poets such as Lewis Carroll, Emily Dickinson, Robert Frost, David McCord, Eve Merriam, Christina Rossetti, and Carl Sandburg are included in the collection. Rebecca Perry's lively pen-and-ink drawings appear on the title page of each section. Indexes by author, translator, and title or first line are included in this engaging anthology.

2.30   Marshall, James. **Pocketful of Nonsense.** Illustrated by James Marshall. Artists and Writers Guild, 1993. ISBN 0-307-17552-9. 28p. 5–8.

Traditional rhymes such as "Teddy Bear, Teddy Bear, Turn Around" and "Fuzzy Wuzzy Was a Bear" are included in this collection, along with limericks (old and new), nonsense verse, and poems. The selections are illustrated with colorful, bold cartoon figures of children and animals.

2.31 Nye, Naomi Shihab, selector. **The Tree Is Older Than You Are.** Simon & Schuster, 1995. ISBN 0-689-80297-8. 112p. 8–12.

Sixty-four Mexican poets and painters are represented in a wonderful collaboration of art and text. Naomi Shihab Nye has compiled a fascinating collection of poems written by Mexican writers, and has included the Spanish text. The art is vivid and compelling. In her lyrical introduction, she states that she prefers "to imagine cultures trading invisible riches. The stories and songs and ripe images of Mexico are a gift to our lives and hearts." This marvelous anthology can also be placed in collections dealing with Mexican culture.

2.32 Paladino, Catherine, selector. **Land, Sea, & Sky: Poems to Celebrate the Earth.** Photographs by Catherine Paladino. Little, Brown, 1993. ISBN 0-316-68892-4. 32p. 5–8.

Nineteen poems, including works by David McCord, Langston Hughes, Emily Dickinson, Lilian Moore, and Myra Cohn Livingston, offer thoughtful images that celebrate Earth's beauty. Each poem is illustrated by a vivid and sensitively composed photograph. The poems encourage children to appreciate the wonder and fragility of their environment.

2.33 Philip, Neil, editor. **Singing America: Poems That Define a Nation.** Illustrated by Michael McCurdy. Viking, 1995. ISBN 0-670-86150-2. 153p. 9–11.

Walt Whitman's *Leaves of Grass* (1855) "encouraged American poets to speak up and speak out," marking the emergence of the American poetic voice. Neil Philip has compiled ninety-three poems that capture the American voice and celebrate the American identity. Poems of historical significance ("Buffalo Dusk" by Carl Sandburg) and poems of America's self-image today ("A Supermarket in California" by Allen Ginsberg) are included. The black-and-white illustrations are beautifully designed and executed, reminiscent of great engravings of the past. Indexes of poets, titles/first lines, subject, and further readings are included.

2.34   Philip, Neil, editor. **Songs Are Thoughts: Poems of the Inuit.** Illustrated by Maryclare Foa. Orchard, 1995. ISBN 0-531-06893-5. 25p. 9–11.

Folklorist Neil Philip selected these poems from a collection by Danish ethnologist Knud Rasmussen and Peter Freuchen, his colleague, in the course of their 1921–1924 expedition to Greenland, Northern Canada, and Alaska. The poetry in this short volume is spare and speaks of individual triumphs, joys, mysteries, and hardships. This starkness is echoed in the vigorous, colorful imagery of Maryclare Foa's oil paintings.

2.35   Robb, Laura, selector. **Snuffles and Snouts.** Illustrated by Steven Kellogg. Dial, 1995. ISBN 0-8037-1597-8. 40p. 8–10.

Steven Kellogg's illustrations in this book are superb. The twenty-five poems, presenting vintage pigs at their best, are by such well-known poets as Ogden Nash, Lewis Carroll, Eleanor Farjeon, Jane Yolen, Myra Cohn Livingston, and Walter de la Mare. This imaginative and witty collaboration of text and artwork will delight both young and old.

2.36   Robinson, Fay, compiler. **A Frog inside My Hat: A First Book of Poems.** Illustrated by Cyd Moore. Bridgewater, 1993. ISBN 0-8167-3129-2. 64p. 5–8.

These thirty-seven poems are the best of the best for very young readers. Poets such as Edward Lear, Lilian Moore, Myra Cohn Livingston, R. L. Stevenson, Eve Merriam, John Ciardi, and Langston Hughes are represented in this collection of brief, whimsical poems. The expressive illustrations capture the delight and humor of the poems. This book is a must for the primary classroom.

2.37   Rogasky, Barbara, selector. **Winter Poems.** Illustrated by Trina Schart Hyman. Scholastic, 1994. ISBN 0-590-42872-1. 40p. 8–11.

The voices of great poets, including William Shakespeare, Robert Frost, Thomas Hardy, Carl Sandburg, Lilian Moore, and even an anonymous tenth-century Japanese poet, ring throughout this remarkable collection. The exquisite text and beautiful illustrations make this book a must for every library.

2.38   Rosen, Michael, selector. **The Kingfisher Book of Children's Poetry.** Illustrated by Alice Englander. Kingfisher, 1993. ISBN 1-85697-909-1. 255p. 9–14.

This extensive cross-cultural collection of 250 poems includes American, Arabic, Australian, British, Chinese, French, German, Greek, Guyanese, Polish, and Swedish poetry. Works by renowned writers such as Blake, Chaucer, Dickinson, Farjeon, Merriam, Sandburg, Shakespeare, Silverstein, and Wordsworth appear in this anthology along with poems written by children. A wide variety of poetic forms are represented: free verse, concrete verse, ballads, limericks, riddles in rhyme, and nonsense verse. The book contains indexes of titles and first lines, subjects, and poets. Black-and-white illustrations complement the text. Reissue.

2.39 Rosen, Michael, selector. **Poems for the Very Young.** Illustrated by Bob Graham. Kingfisher, 1993. ISBN 1-85697-908-3. 77p. 5–6.

From the opening poem "Wakey, wakey, rise and shine, / Make your bed, / And then make mine" to the final poem "Brighter, brighter, shine yon moon," Rosen has collected a broad range of poetry intended for the young child. Poems from Australia, Canada, Great Britain, Japan, the Philippines, and the United States are represented, as well as original poetry written by children. Bob Graham's bright, cheerful pictures match the playful poems in this collection.

2.40 Slater, Teddy, selector. **Eloise Wilkin's Babies: A Book of Poems.** Illustrated by Eloise Wilkin. Golden, 1993. ISBN 0-307-15864-0. 32p. 5–6.

Teddy Slater has selected twenty-seven poems from works by such well-known poets as Rossetti, Stevenson, Longfellow, and Browning, and includes ten of her own original rhymes. Eloise Wilkin's easily recognizable full-color illustrations of cherubic babies accompany these short poems.

2.41 Soto, Gary. **Canto Familiar.** Illustrated by Annika Nelson. Harcourt Brace, 1995. ISBN 0-15-200067-4. 79p. 9–12.

Gary Soto's gentle wit and insight are evident in these twenty-five poems depicting the everyday activities and feelings of a little Mexican American girl. All children are sure to relate to many of the "familiar songs" expressing their emotions and experiences. With its inclusion of Spanish words, Mexican American children will find this book particularly appealing. Bold, colorful, full-page illustrations effectively complement the text.

2.42 Westcott, Nadine Bernard, selector. **Never Take a Pig to Lunch and Other Poems about the Fun of Eating.** Illustrated by Nadine Bernard Westcott. Orchard, 1994. ISBN 0-531-06834-X. 65p. 9–11.

Over sixty poems dedicated to the joys and trials of eating appear on these pages. Well-known poets such as David McCord, Mary Ann Hoberman, Jack Prelutsky, Lilian Moore, Myra Cohn Livingston, Hilaire Belloc, and Eve Merriam contribute to this poetry feast. The humorous verses are energetically interpreted with bright, lively illustrations. This book includes a table of contents listing "Poems about Eating Silly Things," "Poems about Eating Foods We Like," "Poems about Eating Too Much," and "Poems about Manners at the Table." Indexes of titles and poets are included.

2.43   Yolen, Jane, selector. **Weather Report: Poems.** Illustrated by Annie Gusman. Wordsong, 1993. ISBN 1-56397-101-1. 64p. 7–12.

Weather poems forecasting a good read are found in this delightful anthology. Over three dozen traditional and modern poets are represented, including R. L. Stevenson, Myra Cohn Livingston, Eve Merriam, Shakespeare, John Ciardi, Lilian Moore, and even an anonymous ancient Egyptian poet. Every aspect of weather is described in this thoughtful and witty collection. Annie Gusman's black, grey, and white illustrations sail through the book and cleverly complement the theme of the text.

Collections by a Single Poet

2.44   Adoff, Arnold. **Street Music: City Poems.** Illustrated by Karen Barbour. HarperCollins, 1995. ISBN 0-06-021522-4. 32p. 5–8.

Arnold Adoff's symphony of sound captures the cityscape and its people. His fifteen free-verse poems explore the life and excitement found on city streets. The vivid illustrations enhance the text and give a sophisticated feel to the book. Each new page excites the eye with a bold new color scheme.

2.45   Altman, Susan, and Susan Lechner. **Followers of the North Star.** Illustrated by Byron Wooden. Children's Book Press, 1993. ISBN 0-516-05151-2. 48p. 7–12.

This collection of twenty-six poems depicts courageous experiences in the lives of prominent African American heroes. Arranged chronologically from American patriot Crispus Attucks (1723–1770) to astronaut Guion Stewart Blueford, Jr. (born 1946), each poem describes a historical event or experience. The metered rhyme of the text is successfully interpreted by the bold illustrations. A tape accompanies the book, combining narrative reading of the poems and African American music.

2.46   Bagert, Brod, editor. **Edgar Allan Poe: Poetry for Young People.** Illustrated by Carolynn Cobleigh. Sterling, 1995. ISBN 0-8069-0820-3. 48p. 10–12.

Thirteen of Poe's original poems are included in this collection, plus eight prose passages rearranged into verse form (from "The Fall of the House of Usher" and "The Pit and the Pendulum," for instance). Poems such as "To Helen" and "For Annie" reveal the tender side of Poe's character, but there is a dark sadness that runs throughout most of Poe's work. His writing can be gruesome, creepy, spine-chilling, and gloomy. The eerie illustrations vividly portray the images. This fascinating book includes biographical information, commentaries, definitions, and an index.

2.47   Bolin, Frances Schoonmaker, editor. **Carl Sandburg: Poetry for Young People.** Illustrated by Steven Arcella. Sterling, 1995. ISBN 0-8069-0818-1. 48p. 10–12.

Part of the Poetry for Young People series, this collection presents thirty-three of Carl Sandburg's poems, including perennial favorites such as "Fog," "Arithmetic," "Phizzog," and "Buffalo Dusk." The poet's view of the world is strikingly illustrated. Additional features such as extensive biographical information, helpful definitions, and an index enhance this fine book.

2.48   Bolin, Frances Schoonmaker, editor. **Emily Dickinson: Poetry for Young People.** Illustrated by Chi Chung. Sterling, 1994. ISBN 0-8069-0635-9. 48p. 9–11.

The first in a new series, Poetry for Young People, this book is a delight for both children and adults. Emily Dickinson's poems celebrate the gentle beauty and wonder found in the everyday world. Chi Chung's enchanting illustrations, full of color and whimsical imagery, capture the spirit of the text. Biographical information, informative definitions, and helpful commentaries add to the pleasure of this volume.

2.49   Cassedy, Sylvia. **Zoomrimes: Poems about Things That Go.** Illustrated by Michele Chessare. HarperCollins, 1993. ISBN 0-06-022632-3. 51p. 8–12.

The author has created an imaginative collection of poems about movement and "things that go." The twenty-six poems, arranged alphabetically from Ark to Zeppelin, display a great variety of poetic forms and techniques. The poetry contains clever twists and subtleties, encouraging readers to look closely in order to appreciate the word play: "A satisfying boat is the kayak. / Each end the same. / How very like its name / is this palindrome / afloat." Black-and-white pen-and-ink illustrations complement the imaginative text.

2.50 Chandra, Deborah. **Rich Lizard and Other Poems.** Illustrated by Leslie Bowman. Farrar, Straus, 1993. ISBN 0-374-36274-2. 45p. 9–11.

In this beautiful volume, twenty-four poems, rich in imagery, evoke delight and wonder: "I was surprised, / I didn't know / my own breath / could be a thing / so marble-round, / and glistening" (a bubble). The wonderfully expressive scratchboard black-and-white illustrations interpret the subject matter perfectly. This is a stimulating and insightful collection of poems.

2.51 Chandra, Deborah. **Who Comes?** Illustrated by Katie Lee. Sierra, 1995. ISBN 0-87156-407-6. 32p. 5–10.

A waterhole in the African savanna is the setting for this book of poetry. The animals come to quench their thirst—the wildebeest, waterbucks, giraffe, zebra—and all the time they are being watched: "The lion sees with golden eyes someone move among the reeds." The complex world of survival and death is vividly portrayed in Chandra's text. Katie Lee's expressive and stunning illustrations beautifully capture the mood of this wild, cool, moonlit scene.

2.52 Esbensen, Barbara Juster. **Dance with Me.** Illustrated by Megan Lloyd. HarperCollins, 1995. ISBN 0-06-022793-1. 32p. 7–10.

In the beautiful balletic rhythms of Esbensen's poetry emerge such dancers as raindrops, bubbles, a basketball player, the garden hoe, lightning, and waves. The poet's ability to capture the world of motion is exquisitely evident in each of her fifteen poems. The conté crayon and soft pastel illustrations are a visual delight and effectively complement the poems.

2.53 Farber, Norma. **When It Snowed That Night.** Illustrated by Petra Mathers. HarperCollins, 1993. ISBN 0-06-021707-3. 32p. 6–9.

In this book of poetry, the animals of the kingdom travel from afar to view the infant Jesus. Three kings arrive, and so do three queens. They bring Mary a "homespun gown of blue, / and chicken soup—with noodles, too— / and a lingering, lasting cradle-song." This enchanting collection of fifteen Nativity poems is exquisitely illustrated by Petra Mathers. Her richly colored artwork beautifully enhances the text.

2.54   Florian, Douglas. **Beast Feast.** Illustrated by Douglas Florian. Harcourt Brace, 1994. ISBN 0-15-295178-4. 48p. 5–8.

Douglas Florian has written twenty-one delightful animal poems: "The rhea rheally isn't strange— / It's just an ostrich, rhearranged." The bright illustrations capture the levity of Florian's gentle wit as he reveals the intriguing natures of both obscure and familiar animals.

2.55   Graham, Joan Bransfield. **Splish Splash.** Illustrated by Steve Scott. Ticknor & Fields, 1994. ISBN 0-395-70128-7. 32p. 5–8.

Twenty-one playful poems explore the wonders of water in a rhythmic text. Steve Scott's bold, playful images are an invitation to share in the delights of concrete poetry. This is a fresh look at water in its many forms.

2.56   Harter, Penny. **Shadow Play: Night Haiku.** Illustrated by Jeffrey Greene. Simon & Schuster, 1994. ISBN 0-671-88396-8. 32p. 5–9.

"At dusk a cloud / of fireflies rises— / the Milky Way." Through the exquisite haiku form, Penny Harter has created an intimate world of night. Her thirty-nine verses are richly enhanced by the atmospheric and powerful pastel illustrations.

2.57   Holbrook, Sara. **Nothing's the End of the World.** Illustrated by J. J. Smith-Moore. Wordsong, 1995. ISBN 1-56397-249-2. 48p. 9–11.

Forty poems recount the emotional upheavals involved in coping with troublesome siblings, grown-ups, young love, exam panic, and forgetfulness. Life's little bothers are aptly illustrated by the pen-and-ink drawings.

2.58   Hopkins, Lee Bennett. **Good Rhymes, Good Times.** Illustrated by Frané Lessac. HarperCollins, 1995. ISBN 0-06-023499-7. 32p. 5–8.

This collection of original poems includes poems that have been published elsewhere. Such well-known favorites as "Good Books, Good Times!" and "This Tooth" are included here. The genuine naïveté of Frané Lessac's illustrations is charming and complements the text.

2.59   Hughes, Langston. **The Block.** Illustrated by Romare Bearden. Viking, 1995. ISBN 0-670-86501-X. 32p. 8–12.

There is an intriguing touch of mystery in Romare Bearden's powerful artwork. Imaginative use of collage evokes a sense of time and place, offering the reader immediate identification with the environment. The artwork is a perfect match for the poetry of Langston Hughes. The thirteen poems by this poet of the Harlem Renaissance vividly explore neighborhood life in a Harlem street—the friendships, dreams, loneliness, fears, and hopes. This is a fascinating book to share. Biographies of the poet and the artist are included.

2.60   Jacobs, Leland B. **Is Somewhere Always Far Away? Poems about Places.** Illustrated by Jeff Kaufman. Holt, 1993. ISBN 0-8060-2677-0. 32p. 5–7.

"Is somewhere / Always far away? / In other lands? / Beyond today?" Leland Jacobs has written twenty-five whimsical poems about special places in the country, city, make-believe, and at home. The selections are in metered rhyme and describe such things as bridges, stores, bus stops, shoelaces, pigeons, and waves. Cut-and-dyed paper collages are a bold and bright addition to this book.

2.61   Jacobs, Leland B. **Just around the Corner: Poems about the Seasons.** Illustrated by Jeff Kaufman. Holt, 1993. ISBN 0-8050-2676-2. 32p. 5–7.

This collection of poems captures the special characteristics of each season. The text is illustrated with brightly colored cut-and-dyed paper collages.

2.62   Kennedy, X. J. **Drat These Brats.** Illustrated by James Watts. McElderry, 1993. ISBN 0-689-50589-2. 44p. 6–8.

This is the third in X. J. Kennedy's "Brats" and "Fresh Brats" series. The "brattiest brats" ever are depicted in this collection. Clever black-and-white pencil drawings are wittily interspersed throughout the poems and reinforce the offbeat, outrageous humor of the verses.

2.63   Lear, Edward. **The Pelican Chorus and Other Nonsense.** Illustrated by Fred Marcellino. HarperCollins, 1995. ISBN 0-06-205062-1. 40p. 5–10.

Three of Lear's best-loved nonsense rhymes—"The Pelican Chorus," "The Owl and the Pussycat," and "The New Vestments"—

are given a fresh and exuberant rendering with wildly humorous illustrations. The title rhyme has a Victorian setting with stuffy pelican parents giving a coming-out ball for their daughter on the banks of the Nile. "The New Vestments" is reminiscent of H. C. Andersen's "The Emperor's New Clothes," with the hero arriving home divested of his unusual clothes but no doubt a wiser man. The familiar "The Owl and the Pussycat" is also delightfully presented and will be happily revisited by children.

2.64   Levy, Constance. **Tree Place and Other Poems.** Illustrated by Robert Sabuda. McElderry, 1994. ISBN 0-689-50599-X. 40p. 9–11.

The wonders of nature are explored through forty gentle, thoughtful poems. Levy's brief, evocative poems resonate with rich images and phrases. The carefully cadenced text contains interesting internal and end rhymes, reminiscent of Valerie Worth's poetry. The book design is simple and uncluttered, with pencil drawings carefully placed throughout the text.

2.65   McNaughton, Colin. **Making Friends with Frankenstein.** Illustrated by Colin McNaughton. Candlewick, 1994. ISBN 1-56402-308-7. 93p. 5–8.

Disgusting, witty, quirky, unrepentant, tasteless, offbeat—the contemporary playground culture comes alive in this book of poems. This lively volume, packed with fifty-six grossest-of-the-gross poems, cheerfully offers children rhymes not usually heard in the story hour. Colin McNaughton's amusing pen-and-watercolor illustrations make vigorous statements in themselves.

2.66   Moore, Lilian. **I Never Did That Before.** Illustrated by Lillian Hoban. Atheneum, 1995. ISBN 0-689-31889-8. 31p. 5–7.

Young children will take great delight in Lilian Moore's inviting book of poetry. Fourteen poems are thematically linked by the idea of discovery—a child doing something for the very first time. The perfectly cadenced poems are enhanced by the warm, whimsical illustrations.

2.67   Morgenstern, Christian (translated by Anthea Bell). **Christian Morgenstern: Lullabies, Lyrics and Gallows Songs.** Illustrated by Lisbeth Zwerger. North-South, 1995. ISBN 1-55858-365-3. 42p. 5–9.

Reminiscent of the nonsense poetry of Lewis Carroll and Edward Lear, Christian Morgenstern's imaginative verse can be explored on many levels. The Munich-born poet (1871–1914) was a keen observer of human nature and a poem such as "Song of the Gallows Birds" reflects his fascination with the human condition: "How strange is life! How full of dread! / Here we all dangle from red thread." Morgenstern was an early experimenter with the concrete poetry form ("Fish's Night Song") and with nonsense verse in its purest form of sound play ("Gruesong" and "A Gallows Child's Calendar"). The illustrations are imaginative and witty. Most require careful study to appreciate the subtleties. The captivating visual details by illustrator Lisbeth Zwerger, a Hans Christian Andersen Medal Winner, enrich each poem.

2.68   Olaleye, Isaac. **The Distant Talking Drum: Poems from Nigeria.** Illustrated by Frané Lessac. Wordsong, 1995. ISBN 1-56397-095-3. 33p. 6–9.

Fifteen poems depict everyday happenings in a Nigerian village: collecting water in gourds, dancing to a distant drummer, grinding peas, or beating laundry on the rocks by a stream. Isaac Olaleye's free verse poetry is colorfully illustrated by full-page gouache paintings.

2.69   Paraskevas, Betty. **Junior Kroll.** Illustrated by Michael Paraskevas. Harcourt Brace, 1993. ISBN 0-15-241497-5. 34p. 5–10.

This lively collection of fifteen story-poems describes different experiences in the life of a young boy, Junior Kroll. Events such as rescuing lobsters from a pot of boiling water, lessons in card skills, and landing in a chicken pot pie are depicted. The gouache illustrations are full of color, humor, and action.

2.70   Paraskevas, Betty. **Junior Kroll and Company.** Illustrated by Michael Paraskevas. Harcourt Brace, 1994. ISBN 0-15-241497-5. 34p. 5–8.

The Paraskevas team has produced another irresistible Kroll book to follow their original collection, *Junior Kroll.* Thirteen playful story-poems relate the adventures of Junior Kroll. He acquires a macaw that recites Rupert Brooke's poetry. His grandfather's cousin, Blanche, teaches him to dance. A mosquito invades his bedroom. The poet's humor is matched by the artist's exuberant, witty illustrations. Kroll fans will delight in this latest offering.

2.71   Paraskevas, Betty. **A Very Kroll Christmas.** Illustrated by Michael Paraskevas. Harcourt Brace, 1994. ISBN 0-15-292883-9. 34p. 5–8.

In this third book of Junior Kroll's adventures, Junior celebrates Christmas in his own inimitable way. He visits the Christmas Bazaar, experiments with Christmas baking, encounters trouble in Toyland, and attempts a recreation of Bethlehem—all of which add up to a very Kroll kind of Christmas. Bold, colorful illustrations capture the levity of these ten entertaining story-poems.

2.72 Pomerantz, Charlotte. **Halfway to Your House.** Illustrated by Gabrielle Vincent. Greenwillow, 1993. ISBN 0-688-11804-6. 32p. 5–7.

Thirty short poems capture whimsical moments in the life of a young child. The poems are warm and appealing, as are the gentle illustrations.

2.73 Pomerantz, Charlotte. **The Tamarindo Puppy.** Illustrated by Byron Barton. Greenwillow, 1993. ISBN 0-688-11902-6. 31p. 6–8.

Charlotte Pomerantz intermingles English and Spanish throughout her thirteen poems. No translations are given; the two languages blend and meaning emerges through context, as in the following poem: "My friend's name is Marisol. / Mar is the sea. / Sol is the sun. / I dream, I dream of Marisol. / Sueno del Mar, / De Mar y sol, / When the golden day is done." The bright, warm paintings have a childlike quality. Reissue.

2.74 Prelutsky, Jack. **The Dragons Are Singing Tonight.** Illustrated by Peter Sis. Greenwillow, 1993. ISBN 0-688-09645-X. 40p. 6–10.

Here is an irresistible Prelutsky collection of dragon poems with magnificent oil and gouache illustrations by Peter Sis. Written in the narrative voice, these seventeen poems create exuberant images of various dragons: the amiable kind who "have no wish to scare," the mechanical dragon who "rolls on irregular wheels," the computer dragon with "eyes of malevolent green," and operatic dragons who "sing in cacophonous chorus." Strong rhythms and witty rhymes unite with magical artwork to produce a spectacular book.

2.75 Prelutsky, Jack. **Rolling Harvey Down the Hill.** Illustrated by Victoria Chess. Mulberry, 1993. ISBN 0-688-12270-1. 47p. 7–11.

In Prelutsky's playful and entertaining style, the narrator describes his four friends: "There's Tony and there's Lumpy / and There's Harvey and there's Will, / and we all hang out together / in the middle of the hill." Fifteen poems expand on the antics of this hilarious group of "best friends"—including rolling Harvey down the hill. The black-and-white illustrations provide an amusing accompaniment to Prelutsky's colorful text.

2.76   Prelutsky, Jack. **Tyrannosaurus Was a Beast.** Illustrated by Arnold Lobel. Greenwillow, 1993. ISBN 0-688-12613-8. 32p. 5–7.

In keeping with the subject matter, this collection works especially well as a big book. Jack Prelutsky's fourteen rhythmical, rhymed poems will delight dinosaur fans. Arnold Lobel's accompanying watercolors are detailed and colorful. Information on the period, location, and size of each dinosaur is included in the table of contents. Reissue.

2.77   Schertle, Alice. **How Now, Brown Cow?** Illustrated by Amanda Schaffer. Harcourt Brace, 1994. ISBN 0-15-276648-0. 32p. 5–8.

This is a delightful collection of fifteen excellent poems about the thoughts and feelings of cows: "Taradiddle / She landed hard, / they say, / and afterward was slightly lame. . . . / She never tried to jump again, / but gazed for hours at the moon. / They never found the dish and spoon." Deliciously humorous, these thematically-linked poems offer an interesting variety of forms, including the cinquain and the seldom-used triolet. The poet's wit is matched by Amanda Schaffer's lively, colorful paintings.

2.78   Shields, Carol Diggory. **Lunch Money and Other Poems about School.** Illustrated by Paul Meisel. Dutton, 1995. ISBN 0-525-45345-8. 40p. 5–9.

These twenty-four poems present scenes of school in contagiously rhythmic and rhymed verse. Topics such as math, book reports, recess rules, and clock-watching are included in this lively, child-centered collection. The text relates to easily identifiable childhood experiences. Cheerful and colorful illustrations reflect the mood of the poems.

2.79   Singer, Marilyn. **Family Reunion.** Illustrated by R. W. Alley. Macmillan, 1994. ISBN 0-02-782883-2. 32p. 5–8.

This wonderful collection of fourteen poems describes a magical day in August when a reunion takes place in Small Park, "big enough to hold" the various members of an extended family. Marilyn Singer's lilting verse captures the delightful and varied personalities of this large family. R. W. Alley's engaging pen, ink, and watercolor artwork provides the ideal accompaniment. His detailed illustrations invite the reader to linger and explore.

2.80 Singer, Marilyn. **It's Hard to Read a Map with a Beagle on Your Lap.** Illustrated by Clement Oubrerie. Holt, 1993. ISBN 0-8050-2201-5. 32p. 6–10.

A lively, humorous collection of canine verse, with witty illustrations, celebrates the world of dogs. The twenty-six rhymed poems often wind across pages or appear in small circular inserts, adding a playful element to the book's design. A readers' theater presentation, featuring the essence of doghood, could be staged around these poems.

2.81 Singer, Marilyn. **Sky Words.** Illustrated by Deborah Kogan Ray. Macmillan, 1994. ISBN 0-02-782882-4. 32p. 5–8.

Marilyn Singer's verbal skills are evident in this collection of fifteen poems. These poems elicit images of changes in the sky. In "Fog," "Steeples rise like silent rockets"; in "Meteor," "This rock / as heavy as five thousand smashed cars / Whooshless / it fell / through the blacky black"; and in "Monarch Migrating," "I thought some tall tree / had gotten tired of summer early / and sent its orange leaves / into the sky." Singer's lyrical and imaginative poetry is beautifully complemented by the illustrations.

2.82 Spires, Elizabeth. **With One White Wing.** Illustrated by Erik Blegvad. McElderry, 1995. ISBN 0-689-50622-8. 32p. 6–10.

Elizabeth Spires has created twenty-six picture and word puzzles to tempt young riddle fans. The poetic imagery is delightful. The expressive and beautifully detailed watercolors are a visual treat. Here is a perfect way for adults to enjoy riddles with the young.

2.83 Spooner, Michael. **A Moon in Your Lunch Box.** Illustrated by Ib Ohlsson. Holt, 1993. ISBN 0-8050-2209-0. 63p. 6–12.

This appealing collection of forty-three seasonal poems seldom uses traditional rhyme patterns and shows variety in rhythm and form. Imagery is imaginative: "The mud is alive today, / and its grubby slurping lips / smooch with the soles of my shoes." Fresh insights surprise the reader, as in "Cat's Cradle" where the twisting and patterning of a loop of string is compared to a life "always turning over, always changing shape . . . we need some tension on the string / a little stress to keep / our lives true, the pattern clear." Poems are linked by the moon symbol and are complemented by Ohlsson's whimsical sketches.

2.84   Turner, Ann. **Christmas House.** Illustrated by Nancy Edwards Calder. HarperCollins, 1994. ISBN 0-06-023429-6. 31p. 5–8.

Ann Turner has created thirteen poems that will appeal to adults as well as children. Each poem creates a special Christmas mood: Mother's search for Christmas meaning in her walk in the snowy woods, Grandfather's memories of a Christmas past, Nicky's curiosity about what his gifts will be, the cat's distress at the noise and confusion—even the dining room table has an opinion. The sensitive and evocative poetry is enhanced by Nancy Edwards Calder's beautiful artwork. Her richly detailed pictures are a visual delight. This is much more than a December book.

2.85   Turner, Ann. **Moon for Seasons.** Illustrated by Robert Noreika. Macmillan, 1994. ISBN 0-02-789513-0. 40p. 5–8.

These twenty-eight brief poems describe the changing seasons. Each seasonal cycle is thematically linked by the symbol of the moon; in "Fall Moon," "The leaves are down, / the colors gone, / except where the hill / wears the orange moon / like a bright jewel / on its shoulder." This appealing collection of poems is enhanced by exquisite watercolor illustrations. Vibrant colors compel the eye to linger over details and images of nature.

2.86   Viorst, Judith. **Alphabet from Z to A (with Much Confusion on the Way).** Illustrated by Richard Hull. Atheneum, 1994. ISBN 0-689-31768-9. 32p. 7–11.

Judith Viorst takes the reader on a backwards romp through the alphabet. Her verse playfully exposes some of the intricacies of the English language: "S is for SURE and for SHORE, / And for SUN and for SEA, / And for SEE and for SON." The book ends with a challenge for readers to compare their alphabet lists with the author's and the illustrator's.

2.87   Viorst, Judith. **Sad Underwear and Other Complications.** Illustrated by Richard Hull. Atheneum, 1995. ISBN 0-689-31929-0. 78p. 6–11.

These forty-four poems for children (and their parents) are a companion collection to Judith Viorst's well-known volume *If I Were in Charge of the World and Other Worries*. Poems for every kind of reader abound in this witty volume, conveniently divided into chapters with such titles as "Stuff You Shouldn't Know," "Pals and Pests," "Adventurers," "Moms and Dads," and "When I Grow Up." Richard Hull's pen-and-ink drawings scattered through the book delightfully capture the mood of the poetry.

2.88 Wong, Janet S. **Good Luck Gold and Other Poems.** McElderry, 1994. ISBN 0-689-50617-1. 42p. 9–11.

This small collection addresses difference and diversity through poems about growing up as the child of Asian immigrant parents. Janet Wong writes about traditions such as good luck gold and bonsai with insight and irony. Her narrative poems also speak of experiences at school, in the neighborhood, and at home, and will resonate with children of any background. Many of these poems explore multiculturalism and prejudice and could promote important discussions in classrooms.

2.89 Worth, Valerie. **All the Small Poems and Fourteen More.** Illustrated by Natalie Babbitt. Farrar, Straus, 1994. ISBN 0-374-30211-1. 194p. 9–12.

In addition to the ninety-nine poems published in the celebrated Small Poems collections, this award-winning poet has added fourteen new poems dealing with such topics as garage sales, skeletons, books, and autumn geese. These new poems are as richly crafted as their predecessors, but sadly will be our last poems by Valerie Worth, who died in 1994.

2.90 Yolen, Jane. **Animal Fare.** Illustrated by Janet Street. Harcourt Brace, 1994. ISBN 0-15-203550-8. 32p. 5–8.

Jane Yolen's sixteen nonsense poems bring to life such beasts as the Blimpanzee, the Hippotanoose, the Mustanks, and the Anteloop. Word plays abound in this collection, an imaginary menagerie of strange and colorful creatures. Janet Street's lively artwork adds to the fun of this appealing volume.

2.91 Yolen, Jane. **Raining Cats and Dogs.** Illustrated by Janet Street. Harcourt Brace, 1993. ISBN 0-15-265488-7. 32p. 5–8.

This collection is a warm and witty compilation of nine cat and nine dog poems, cleverly bound together in a front-to-back, back-to-front, upside-down format. Jane Yolen's poems often parallel each other, as in the opening (or closing) poem: "I am Cat— / I am silk and velvet, / I am spit and squall, / I am stretch of moonlight, / I am river's crawl" and "I am Dog— / I am tweed and carpet, / I am bark and bite, / I am red leaves falling, / I am morning's light." Full-page watercolor illustrations enhance this very original and appealing collection.

2.92   Yolen, Jane. **The Three Bears Holiday Rhyme Book.** Illustrated by Jane Dyer. Harcourt Brace, 1995. ISBN 0-15-200932-9. 32p. 5–8.

Fifteen poems depicting holidays throughout the year are presented from the viewpoint of Goldilocks and the Three Bears. Jane Yolen's rhyming text describes celebrations such as New Year's Eve, Earth Day, Halloween, Christmas, and Hanukkah. Jane Dyer's full-page watercolor illustrations are cheerful and appealing. The colors are well chosen, giving rise to charming imagery.

2.93   Zolotow, Charlotte. **Snippets: A Gathering of Poems, Pictures, and Possibilities.** Illustrated by Melissa Sweet. HarperCollins, 1993. ISBN 0-06-020818-X. 48p. 5–8.

Forty-one winsome poems have been selected by Charlotte Zolotow from a number of her previous books. The warmth and charm found in Melissa Sweet's illustrations greatly enhance this collection.

Individual Poems

2.94   Bates, Katharine Lee. **America the Beautiful.** Illustrated by Neil Waldman. Atheneum, 1993. ISBN 0-689-31861-8. 32p. 5–8.

Neil Waldman illustrates the famous nineteenth-century poem "America the Beautiful" in a series of full-spread acrylic paintings. It is an artistic record of landscapes found across the United States. Such sites as Niagara Falls, the Grand Canyon, Mesa Verde, the Great Plains, and Pikes Peak, where Katherine Lee Bates was inspired to write the words to "America the Beautiful," are included in this book.

2.95   Berry, James. **Celebration Song.** Illustrated by Louise Brierley. Simon & Schuster, 1994. ISBN 0-671-89446-3. 26p. 9–11.

The world celebrates the first birthday of Jesus in this powerful Nativity poem. Mary tells her child the story of his birth: "Your born-day is a happening day. / All day I feel a celebration, / everywhere alive in jubilation." Mary also ponders the future, asking whether his day will be one "LONG LONG celebration day." Louise Brierley's watercolors are as expressive as the text, rich in color and reflective of the exuberant mood of the Caribbean setting.

2.96 Blake, William. **The Tyger.** Illustrated by Neil Waldman. Harcourt Brace, 1993. ISBN 0-15-292375-6. 32p. 5–8.

This is a stylized version of William Blake's poem "The Tyger." Neil Waldman's acrylics on grey-and-black painted backgrounds lead up to a four-page spread containing all the images previously illustrated: the snake, the stars, the lamb, and the tyger. Waldman's illustrations of an "immortal hand or eye" and "dread feet" demonstrate the monumental challenge that faces any artist who attempts to capture Blake's haunting, metaphysical text.

2.97 Bouchard, David. **If You're Not from the Prairie.** Illustrated by Henry Ripplinger. Atheneum, 1995. ISBN 0-689-80103-3. 32p. 6–10.

The text of this book is a poem praising prairie life. Each verse of the poem is framed with "If you're not from the prairie, you don't know . . . ," and what you don't know includes sun, wind, sky, flatness, grass sounds, snow, cold, and the poet. The detailed paintings of figures and landscapes depict the everyday beauty of life on the Canadian prairies. The book is useful for both geography and poetry units.

2.98 Capucilli, Alyssa Satin. **Inside a Barn in the Country.** Illustrated by Tedd Arnold. Scholastic, 1995. ISBN 0-590-46999-1. 30p. 5–6.

Based on the popular cumulative tale *The House That Jack Built,* Capucilli's story-poem tells how, one after another, all the barn animals wake each other up. This playful poem is strong in rhythm and rhyme. Tedd Arnold's colorful illustrations make good use of the rebus device. The images, in their simplicity, make clever use of vibrant line that gives texture to the background and creates a lively feeling throughout the book.

2.99 Child, Lydia Maria. **Over the River and through the Woods.** Illustrated by Christopher Manson. North-South, 1993. ISBN 1-55858-210-X. 32p. 5–8.

"Over the river and through the woods, / To Grandfather's house we go" are the familiar words of Lydia Maria Child's famous Thanksgiving poem, first published in 1844. Christopher Manson's richly painted woodcuts of old rural New England enliven every page. Colorful endpapers are an appealing addition to the book, and the final page contains the musical notation to Child's poem.

2.100   Field, Eugene. **Wynken, Blynken, & Nod.** Illustrated by Johanna Westerman. North-South, 1995. ISBN 1-55858-422-6. unpaged. 5–7.

There have been many illustrated editions of this famous and well-loved poem. This will stand among the best of them because of the illustrator's combination of imagination and childlike simplicity. The children have an ethereal quality, as if cast in the moonlight. It is an excellent bedtime story, both for the dreamlike quality of the illustrations and for the text, which finds the children in their very own beds by the end of the adventure.

2.101   Giovanni, Nikki. **Knoxville, Tennessee.** Illustrated by Larry Johnson. Scholastic, 1994. ISBN 0-590-47074-4. 32p. 5–8.

The gentle narrative of this single-poem book evokes the warmth of friends, family, and loving grandparents as seen through the eyes of a young African American girl. The peaceful mood of summer is reflected in the beautifully expressive, full-spread illustrations.

2.102   Harness, Cheryl. **Papa's Christmas Gift: Around the World on the Night before Christmas.** Illustrated by Cheryl Harness. Simon & Schuster, 1995. ISBN 0-689-80344-3. 32p. 5–10.

This is an imaginative look back to Christmas Eve, 1822, when the family of Clement Clarke Moore gathered to hear his first reading of "A Visit from Saint Nicholas." Intrigued by the fact that people all over the world are "simultaneously engaged in so many different activities," Cheryl Harness has created a series of illustrations that takes the reader around the world on this extraordinary night. The scenes include Beethoven tramping through a snowy Vienna street, pilgrims gathering in Bethlehem, Mexicans reenacting the story of Mary and Joseph, trappers camping in the American West, and English families making merry around the yule log. These scenes are presented in richly detailed pen, ink, and colored-pencil illustrations. The beautifully decorative borders have a unifying effect throughout the book.

2.103   Johnson, James Weldon. **The Creation.** Illustrated by James E. Ransome. Holiday House, 1994. ISBN 0-8234-1069-2. 32p. 5–8.

This African American poem of the biblical creation story uses idiomatic language and imagery from the South reminiscent of southern black country sermons in the 1800s. The oil paintings artfully portray light, shade, and marvelous facial expressions.

The story is told by a preacher-elder to a group of attentive children under a tree. "The Creation" was originally written in 1919, but later appeared in 1927 in *God's Trombones: Seven Negro Sermons in Verse.*

2.104 Johnson, James Weldon. **The Creation: A Poem.** Illustrated by Carla Golembe. Little, Brown, 1993. ISBN 0-316-46744-8. 32p. 5–8.

James Weldon Johnson, a poet and distinguished anthologist of African American literature, was inspired to preserve this adaptation of the creation story after listening to a particularly moving sermon. Johnson's poetic retelling of the biblical story from Genesis was written in 1919 and was later published in *God's Trombones: Seven Negro Sermons in Verse.* Strikingly vivid monotypes completely fill each page and enhance the tone and mood of this poem.

2.105 Keillor, Garrison. **Cat, You Better Come Home.** Illustrated by Steve Johnson and Lou Fancher. Viking, 1995. ISBN 0-670-85112-4. 40p. 6–9.

This book is irresistible. Keillor's wonderfully witty poem is brilliantly illustrated by Steve Johnson and Lou Fancher. The artwork is stylish and bold; each page is beautifully composed. Creative textural techniques are used throughout. The cat's eyes are alive with expression and will charm any cat lover.

2.106 Knutson, Kimberley. **Bed Bouncers.** Illustrated by Kimberley Knutson. Macmillan, 1995. ISBN 0-02-750871-4. 32p. 5–6.

With bouncy rhythm and rhyme, this book of poetry is delightful. Imaginative travels take all the bed bouncers of the world far into the velvety night: "Beginners and experts, / Some fast and some slow, / All bouncing while watching / the cities below." Expressive, motion-filled collage figures sail across the pages. This is an engaging book for the young.

2.107 Lear, Edward. **The New Vestments.** Illustrated by DeLoss McGraw. Simon & Schuster, 1995. ISBN 0-671-50089-9. 40p. 5–8.

Edward Lear's classic verse has been vividly brought to life by DeLoss McGraw's gouache illustrations. The imagery is original and the artist's enthusiasm for splattering paint gives an uninhibited feeling to the book. Brilliant colors and bold shapes have a stimulating visual effect. The wandering text is a welcome change from the traditional straight-line format.

2.108   Lear, Edward. **The Table and the Chair.** Illustrated by Tom Powers. HarperCollins, 1993. ISBN 0-06-020804-X. 32p. 5–6.

The lively, offbeat illustrations in this book highlight Edward Lear's familiar verse. This book of single poems invites the young reader into the wonderful world of nonsense. Large-sized print facilitates reading and sharing.

2.109   Lindbergh, Reeve. **What Is the Sun?** Illustrated by Stephen Lambert. Candlewick, 1994. ISBN 1-56402-146-7. 26p. 5–6.

In this question and answer rhyming poem, a grandmother responds to her grandson's questions about nature. Reeve Lindbergh's soothing text captures the toddler's curiosity. Soft pastel illustrations also capture the curiosity and wonder of a young child. Insets of the boy and his grandmother are cleverly placed within imagined scenes of the child and his dog. This is a delightful bedtime read-aloud book for the preschool child.

2.110   Livingston, Myra Cohn. **Abraham Lincoln: A Man for All the People.** Illustrated by Samuel Byrd. Holiday House, 1993. ISBN 0-8234-1049-8. 32p. 7–12.

The life of Abraham Lincoln is chronicled in this ballad by Myra Cohn Livingston. Scenes from his early childhood to his death by an assassin's bullet are described in narrative form. The detailed illustrations complement the text.

2.111   Livingston, Myra Cohn. **Keep on Singing: A Ballad of Marian Anderson.** Illustrated by Samuel Byrd. Holiday House, 1994. ISBN 0-8234- 1098-6. 32p. 5–8.

"Born in Philadelphia— / Her mother told her true, / Whatever you are doing, / Someone's watching you." These words open and close Myra Cohn Livingston's powerful ballad. This ballad is the story of Marian Anderson's life—how she moves from humble childhood beginnings to world-famous contralto. The story is also about Anderson's dignity, courage, and triumph. Samuel Byrd's confident illustrations are expressive, contributing to a fine collaboration between art and text.

2.112   McLean, Janet. **Dog Tales.** Illustrated by Andrew McLean. Ticknor & Fields, 1995. ISBN 0-395-72288-8. 32p. 5–7.

This poetry book is a delightful romp through the canine world of five dogs and the children who love them. The noisy, naughty, friendly, fighting, paws-and-jaws activities are explored with warmth and humor in the poetry. The playful illustrations are a wonderful visual accompaniment to this text.

2.113 Merriam, Eve. **The Hole Story.** Illustrated by Ivan Chermayeff. Photographs by Ivan Chermayeff. Simon & Schuster, 1995. ISBN 0-671-88353-4. 32p. 5–7.

From cover to cover, innovative color photographs and collages are used in this book to demonstrate the abundance of holes found in nature and everyday objects. Eve Merriam's simple poetic verse is placed on top of full-spread illustrations. The close-up style of these illustrations focuses the eye on the details of such familiar objects as buttons and Swiss cheese. An excellent source for introducing shapes and patterns, this large picture book could also be used to discuss texture and color.

2.114 Moore, Clement C. **The Night before Christmas.** Illustrated by Ted Rand. North-South, 1995. ISBN 1-55858-465-X. 22p. 5–8.

This illustrated interpretation of this famous verse combines the domestic background of 1823 (when the work first appeared in print) with pictures of a modern North American Santa Claus. Despite Moore's description of St. Nicholas, the American picture of Santa Claus did not appear in illustration form until political cartoonist Thomas Nast gave shape to the modern Santa Claus.

2.115 Moss, Lloyd. **Zin! Zin! Zin! A Violin.** Illustrated by Marjorie Priceman. Simon & Schuster, 1995. ISBN 0-671-88239-2. 32p. 5–7.

This poetic verse explores the instruments and sounds of an orchestra. A trombone begins in solo, a trumpet joins in for a duet, and a french horn is added for a trio, until each instrument is introduced in turn. In the end, the entire orchestra is playing in symphony. The illustrations and the curving lines of text give a sense of flowing music. This is a good introduction to orchestral instruments for young children.

2.116 Nash, Ogden. **The Tale of Custard the Dragon.** Illustrated by Lynn Munsinger. Little, Brown, 1995. ISBN 0-316-59880-1. 32p. 5–8.

Ogden Nash's famous text is expressively illustrated by Lynn Munsinger. Her amusing portrayals give a fresh flavor to this nonsense verse of the cowardly dragon and Belinda, who is "brave as a barrelful of bears." This is a delightful edition of the classic story told in verse. The artist brings warmth and humor to the text with her engaging visual details.

2.117 Near, Holly. **The Great Peace March.** Illustrated by Lisa Desimini. Holt, 1993. ISBN 0-8050-1941-3. 32p. 5–8.

In this single-poem text, the words are meant to be sung. Holly Near's poem is presented with music for piano and guitar, plus brief historical notes on the 1986 Peace March for Nuclear Disarmament. Colorful illustrations support the mood of the song and its universal message.

2.118 Numeroff, Laura. **Dogs Don't Wear Sneakers.** Illustrated by Joe Mathieu. Simon & Schuster, 1993. ISBN 0-671-79525-2. 32p. 5–7.

Lively, bright illustrations amplify Laura Numeroff's rhymed text. The text in this collection depicts the many ways in which humans differ from various creatures of the animal kingdom. A playful challenge to the imagination is offered on the last page.

2.119 O'Donnell, Elizabeth Lee. **Sing Me a Window.** Illustrated by Melissa Sweet. Morrow Junior Books, 1993. ISBN 0-688-09500-3. 32p. 5–8.

At the end of the day, a little girl begs her father to "Sing me a night song, / a soft song, / a dream song." Safely tucked in bed, she listens to her father describe the activities they experienced together on their perfect day. This poem contains a strong sense of rhyme and rhythm. Softly hued, full-color artwork in pencil, watercolor, and ink creates a whimsical accompaniment to the text.

2.120 O'Malley, Kevin, reteller. **Who Killed Cock Robin?** Illustrated by Kevin O'Malley. Lothrop, 1993. ISBN 0-688-12430-5. 32p. 5–8.

The traditional nursery rhyme "Who Killed Cock Robin?" is transformed into a delightfully intriguing detective story. Inspector Owl uncovers clues in each of Kevin O'Malley's cleverly detailed illustrations. The villain is eventually apprehended and the mystery of "a deed most foul" is solved.

2.121 Oppenheim, Joanne. **Have You Seen Trees?** Illustrated by Jean Tseng and Mou-Sien Tseng. Scholastic, 1995. ISBN 0-590-46691-7. 40p. 5–8.

This book explores trees with enchanting illustrations and verse. Passages such as "Have you seen summer trees? / Shade-me-from-the-light trees. / Whisper-in-the-night trees. / I can hear the trees." This is an excellent springboard for discussing children's experiences in nature, especially with trees, leading into a more scientific consideration. The concluding pages contain a tree identification guide that invites observation and analysis in the field.

2.122 Pilkey, Dav. **Moonglow Roll-O-Rama.** Illustrated by Dav Pilkey. Orchard, 1995. ISBN 0-531-06876-5. 32p. 5–6.

"Have you ever wondered / Where animals go, / At night when the light / Of the moon is aglow?" In rhyming text, Dav Pilkey captures the imaginative world of animals performing at the Moonglow Roll-O-Rama. The artist's watercolor and pencil illustrations are rich and evocative. The book is a visual delight.

2.123 Sandburg, Carl. **Arithmetic: Illustrated as an Anamorphic Adventure.** Illustrated by Ted Rand. Harcourt Brace, 1993. ISBN 0-15-203865- 5. 32p. 6–10.

Ted Rand creates fascinating anamorphic pictures to illustrate this celebrated poem by Carl Sandburg. Anamorphic pictures are images that have been precisely distorted and must be viewed from a certain angle to appear normal. A Mylar sheet is provided with the book for viewing several of the pictures. The book provides the reader with an intriguing, challenging experience and concludes with information on anamorphic images.

2.124 Scieszka, Jon. **The Book That Jack Wrote.** Illustrated by Daniel Adel. Viking, 1994. ISBN 0-670-84330-X. 32p. 7–11.

Jon Scieszka offers a unique variation of the famous cumulative nursery rhyme. It begins with "The Book That Jack Wrote" and takes the reader through a madcap nursery rhyme journey. The author's humor is matched by Daniel Adel's wonderful framed paintings. Text and illustrations combine wit and imagination that cannot fail to delight. The book is irresistible and of particular interest to sophisticated readers.

2.125 Seymour, Tres. **The Smash-up Crash-up Derby.** Illustrated by S. D. Schindler. Orchard, 1995. ISBN 0-531-06881-1. 32p. 5–7.

A boy and his family attend the demolition derby at the local fair in this single-poem text. Cars come to life and, at one point, take on the shapes of dinosaurs in the lively gouache artwork. The illustrations are full of motion and color, and the characters in them are wonderfully expressive.

2.126 Siebert, Diane. **Plane Song.** Illustrated by Vincent Nasta. HarperCollins, 1993. ISBN 0-06-021464-3. 32p. 5–8.

Different kinds of airplanes and their unique attributes are described in rhyming text. These "birds that human hands have built" include small one-passenger planes, jumbo jets, cargo planes, bombers, spy planes, bush planes, and crop dusters. The detailed paintings show the world of flight from several perspectives. The lyrical poem works well with the realistic paintings to give the reader a feel for flying and information on the many uses of airplanes.

2.127   Sloat, Teri. **The Thing That Bothered Farmer Brown.** Illustrated by Nadine Bernard Westcott. Orchard, 1995. ISBN 0-531-06883-8. 32p. 5–7.

This hilarious continuous rhyming poem about an annoying mosquito that robs Farmer Brown and his farm animals of a good night's sleep is filled with onomatopoeic, repetitive language patterns that will delight young children, especially when read aloud. The bright and humorous watercolor illustrations that accompany the text add to the appeal of this story.

2.128   Stewart, Sarah. **The Library.** Illustrated by David Small. Farrar, Straus, 1995. ISBN 0-374-34388-8. 40p. 5–8.

In a single-poem format, the story of the lady and the library is brought to life by the rhythmic text of Sarah Stewart. Her delightful verse relates the story of Elizabeth Brown, who, as a child, finds herself "adrift in dreams of entering / A reader's olympiad." Detailed watercolors enliven every page. The endpapers are a wonderful addition. The combination of lively text and expressive artwork makes this a warmly appealing book.

2.129   Thayer, Ernest Lawrence. **Casey at the Bat.** Illustrated by Gerald Fitzgerald. Atheneum, 1995. ISBN 0-689-31945-2. 26p. 5–9.

Although this familiar poem was published over a hundred years ago, it still captures the spirit of the game today. Young readers who know baseball will enjoy the jargon and the dramatic conclusion of this sports classic.

2.130   Weiss, George David, and Bob Thiele. **What a Wonderful World.** Illustrated by Ashley Bryan. Atheneum, 1995. ISBN 0-689-80087-8. 25p. 5–6.

The bright, cheerful colors of Ashley Bryan's tempera and gouache paintings add a positive note to the song made famous by Louis Armstrong. Characters from many backgrounds bring the lyrics to life as they present a puppet show. This short, simple book can be enjoyed with young readers.

2.131   Welch, Willy. **Playing Right Field.** Illustrated by Marc Simont. Scholastic, 1995. ISBN 0-590-48298-X. 32p. 5–7.

This delightful, rhymed text follows the bored ruminations of a boy exiled to right field during a baseball game. The boy dreams of becoming someone greater. When the ball is hit in his direction, he inadvertently catches it and becomes an accidental hero before resuming his reveries. The watercolor illustrations capture the dreamlike quality of a hot afternoon of baseball. The story will appeal to Little Leaguers who know what it is like to be exiled to right field.

2.132   Zelinsky, Paul O., adapter. **The Maid and the Mouse and the Odd-Shaped House.** Illustrated by Paul O. Zelinsky. Dutton, 1993. ISBN 0-525-45095-5. 32p. 3–6.

"Once in a funny, odd-shaped house / There lived a wee maid and a mouse. / The mouse was fat, the maid was thin. / The house was new—they'd just moved in." Life is fine in this tiny house until the maid and the mouse begin renovations. Slowly, their little house takes on a life of its own as it develops ears and whiskers through Zelinsky's witty, curvilinear illustrations. This familiar draw-and-tell story is told in rhyming verse that is delightful to read aloud and could be a perfect introduction to participatory storytelling.

3 Traditional Literature

Classic Literature

3.1   McCaughrean, Geraldine. **Stories from Shakespeare.** Illustrated by Antony Maitland. McElderry, 1995. ISBN 0-689-80037-1. 144p. 10–12.

This collection presents ten of Shakespeare's plays in the form of short stories. Illustrations accompany the text, which takes a narrative approach to the plays, integrating some key lines as dialogue. As might be expected in such a project, the stories emphasize plot rather than character development. The collection might serve as an interesting introduction to Shakespeare's dramatic work.

Contemporary Folk Literature

3.2   Andersen, Hans Christian (adapted by Adrian Mitchell). **The Ugly Duckling.** Illustrated by Jonathan Heale. Dorling Kindersley, 1994. ISBN 1- 56458-557-3. 32p. 7–10.

This rich textual adaptation of the story of a young duckling's plight is reminiscent of the oral tradition of storytelling. Complemented by bold, beautiful woodcut illustrations, this retelling of Hans Christian Andersen's classic fairy tale is a textual and visual treat for young and older readers alike. With poignant details and humorous comments in contemporary idiom, this version recreates and expands on the timeless theme of being different and asks "What does it matter if you're born in a Duckyard so long as you're hatched from the egg of a Swan?"

3.3   Armstrong, Jennifer. **Chin Yu Min and the Ginger Cat.** Illustrated by Mary GrandPré. Crown, 1993. ISBN 0-517-58656-8. 32p. 6–8.

This engaging tale takes place in China and recounts the story of a parsimonious and unkind old woman who is transformed by her love for a stray ginger cat. Initially, the cat helps her to fish and thereby to live after her husband's death. Then she inadvertently gives a beggar an old basket without realizing that the cat was napping inside. Deeply distressed, she spends her fortune searching for the basket with the cat inside, only to be left penniless and dejected. Only then does she find an old monk who gives her the basket she is looking for. The illustrations are richly textured, expressive, and whimsical.

3.4   Avi. **The Bird, the Frog, and the Light: A Fable.** Illustrated by Matthew Henry. Orchard, 1994. ISBN 0-531-06808-0. 26p. 5–7.

Avi's delightful fable tells of a mockingbird, loved by the sun, who brings light to a proud frog's underground kingdom, thereby revealing how insignificant the frog's possessions truly are. Matthew Henry's textured illustrations effectively delineate the contrast between light and darkness that the tale evokes as the bird brings light and wisdom to the pompous frog. The tale concludes with the bird convincing the frog that he must learn to read in order to come out of the darkness.

3.5   Babbitt, Natalie. **Bub: or the Very Best Thing.** Illustrated by Natalie Babbitt. HarperCollins, 1994. ISBN 0-06-205044-3. 32p. 5–7.

A dispute arises between a young king and queen over the care of their baby son. Should he be given soft, silly toys or dry, boring lessons? Each tries desperately to find out what would be the very best thing for the young Prince. The combination of Babbitt's elegant writing style with her gentle, appealing illustrations make this a very engaging picture book.

3.6   Banks, Lynne Reid. **The Magic Hare.** Illustrated by Barry Moser. Morrow, 1993. ISBN 0-688-10895-4. 49p. 6–8.

These short stories retold in folktale fashion are reminiscent of the Brer Rabbit tales, for both their trickster antics and the humor. The illustrations are stunning and effectively complement the comedy. Teachers and parents looking for gentle and humorous stories for reading and telling will welcome this collection.

3.7   Carle, Eric. **Walter the Baker.** Illustrated by Eric Carle. Simon & Schuster, 1995. ISBN 0-689-80078-9. 32p. 5–8.

This delightful story is brightly illustrated in Carle's characteristic collage art. Walter the Baker is much loved by everyone in his Duchy for his delicious rolls. One day, his cat spills the milk, forcing Walter to use water instead. The Duke and Duchess detest his rolls and threaten to banish him unless overnight he can produce a good-tasting roll through which the rising sun can shine three times. The next day, Walter accidentally discovers the pretzel and regains the favor of the Duke and Duchess. Reissue.

3.8   Czernecki, Stefan, and Timothy Rhodes. **The Hummingbirds'
Gift.** Illustrated by Stefan Czernecki. Hyperion, 1994. ISBN 1-
56282-605-0. 32p. 5–7.

A Mexican family tries to save the hummingbirds even though
their crop of wheat has been destroyed by a drought. In gratitude, the hummingbirds teach the family how to weave straw
into beautiful figures. The full-page, color illustrations with
Mexican motifs complement the text, but the charm of the book
lies in the simple straw figures that are now well-known Mexican artifacts. The straw weavings are by Juliana Reyes de Silva
and Juan Hilario Silva.

3.9   Derby, Sally. **Jacob and the Stranger.** Illustrated by Leonid Gore.
Ticknor & Fields, 1994. ISBN 0-395-66897-2. 32p. 8–12.

"Work wanted. Not too much and not too hard." In this appealing book Jacob accepts a job minding an unusual plant. A warning accompanies this job: "You must return to me all that is
mine." Jacob returns all the tiny cats that have come from the
plant but is accused of having stolen one's heart. In his confrontation with a wizard, Jacob turns out to be quick, clever, and
wise.

3.10   Field, Susan. **The Sun, the Moon and the Silver Baboon.** Illustrated by Susan Field. HarperCollins, 1993. ISBN 0-06-022990-X.
26p. 5–7.

In this brightly illustrated original tale about a brown baboon
who earns a beautiful silver coat for being the most helpful creature, young children are introduced to many different animals
and their habits and traits. It is the clever baboon who knows
how to solve the problem when a star falls from the sky and gets
tangled in a tree. This is a good read-aloud for primary classrooms that evokes the rhythmic, repetitive language of traditional animal tales.

3.11   French, Vivian. **Red Hen and Sly Fox.** Illustrated by Sally Hobson. Simon & Schuster, 1995. ISBN 0-689-80010-X. 26p. 5–8.

In this story, which is structured like a fairy tale, Sly Fox attempts to have the ever-helpful and friendly Red Hen as his
tasty chicken dinner. Playing on her good character, Sly Fox
manages to bag the hen. Unfortunately for him, he underesti-
mates the cunning of Red Hen and lets his guard down at the
wrong moment. Full-page, stylized oil paintings in bold colors
provide a playful background for this battle between good and

evil. Children will enjoy the tale's familiarity and Red Hen's wit and resourcefulness.

3.12 Gershator, Phillis, reteller. **Tukama Tootles the Flute: A Tale from the Antilles.** Illustrated by Synthia Saint James. Orchard, 1994. ISBN 0-531- 06811-0. 32p. 5–8.

This is a giant story from the Antilles in the tradition of "Jack the Giant Killer," but here the lazy little boy has almost magical musical powers. The repetitive, simple songs call for accompanying music and are well suited to oral interpretation. The stylized illustrations with their strong primary colors are oil paintings but resemble collage.

3.13 Greenfield, Karen Radler. **The Teardrop Baby.** Illustrated by Sharleen Collicott. HarperCollins, 1994. ISBN 0-06-022943-8. 40p. 5–7.

This contemporary fairy tale recounts the story of a young couple who turn to a wizard woman to help them conceive a baby. They are successful, but as payment the wizard demands that they give the baby to her when he reaches age seven. The boy is taken away as foretold, but he learns to use the wizard's own magic to make his way home again. This fairy tale uses enchantment to explore issues of desire, love, and separation.

3.14 Harrison, Michael, and Christopher Stuart-Clark, selectors. **The Oxford Treasury of Children's Stories.** Oxford, 1994. ISBN 0-19-278133-2. 159p. 5–9.

Old and new, long and short, what these twenty-six stories have in common is an element of the fantastic. Philipa Pearce's Mrs. Cockle is carried high over London by a bunch of balloons, where she walks on the clouds to the sea. Joan Aiken's Dan grows glass in place of skin when he swears and must go to the hills to learn the secrets of language. Margaret Mahy's little boy befriends a lion and teaches his mother a lesson. Other characters in the collection include Frog and Toad, the Selfish Giant, Kipling's rhinoceros, and Andersen's soldier, as well as other new inventions. A lovely blend, linked by illustrations and fantasy, this book is an excellent introduction to the short story genre.

3.15 Irving, Washington. **The Legend of Sleepy Hollow.** Illustrated by Robert Van Nutt. Rabbit Ears Books, 1995. ISBN 0-689-80202-1. cassette. 6–10.

Glenn Close brings this classic American ghost story to new life for today's children. With subtle changes in her voice, she creates all of the characters who fill the story of the Headless Horseman with humor, romance, and mystery. Children following along with the book that accompanies the audiotape will find that Robert Van Nutt's illustrations add to the dramatic suspense of Washington Irving's story.

3.16 Myers, Walter Dean. **The Story of the Three Kingdoms.** Illustrated by Ashley Bryan. HarperCollins, 1995. ISBN 0-06-024286-8. 32p. 5–8.

Shark, Elephant, and Hawk each rule their kingdoms of the sea, the forest, and the sky until the people overcome each of them. Then the people say, "We do not need to be masters of the earth. We can share because it is wise to do so." Although not a traditional folktale, this lovely teaching tale for the modern child is told in the style of a folktale. Bryan's beautiful illustrations are highly patterned and call to mind African fabric designs.

3.17 Perlman, Janet. **The Emperor Penguin's New Clothes.** Illustrated by Janet Perlman. Viking, 1994. ISBN 0-670-85864-1. 32p. 5–7.

In this charming sequel to her highly successful *Cinderella Penguin,* Janet Perlman once again adapts a familiar fairy tale to the world of her immediately recognizable penguins. The tale faithfully reproduces the familiar Andersen allegory, always with the realization that the naked king is a penguin.

3.18 Rosen, Michael. **Crow and Hawk: A Traditional Pueblo Indian Story.** Illustrated by John Clementson. Harcourt Brace, 1995. ISBN 0-15-200257- X. 32p. 5–8.

In this traditional Pueblo Indian story, Crow lays a nest full of eggs, then gets bored and flies away. Hawk spots the eggs and decides to sit on them until their mother returns. When no one returns, she ends up hatching and caring for the baby crows. Life gets complicated when Crow returns to claim her children. Colored-paper collage and detailed border designs influenced by Southwestern art are a perfect background for the retelling of this story.

3.19 Rylant, Cynthia. **Dreamer.** Illustrated by Barry Moser. Scholastic, 1993. ISBN 0-590-47341-7. 32p. 5–7.

In this creation story, the world and its flora and fauna were created by the first artist, whom "they have always called God." The people, artists all, were also created to share in the masterpiece and to daydream the most beautiful things in the world. The language in this book is simple and poetic and well supported by the colorful illustrations.

3.20 Stevens, Janet, adapter. **Tops and Bottoms.** Illustrated by Janet Stevens. Harcourt Brace, 1995. ISBN 0-15-292851-0. 32p. 5–8.

With roots in European folktales and the slave stories of the American South, *Tops and Bottoms* celebrates the trickster tradition of overcoming hardship by using one's wits. Bear has wealth and land but he is lazy; Hare has nothing but brains and a hungry family. Equipped with his wits, Hare tricks Bear into relinquishing some of his land and the resulting harvest. The elaborate paintings are reminiscent of the work of E. H. Shepard, the illustrator of A. A. Milne's *Winnie the Pooh.*

3.21 Stevens, Kathleen. **Aunt Skilly and the Stranger.** Illustrated by Robert Andrew Parker. Ticknor & Fields, 1994. ISBN 0-395-68712-8. 32p. 5–7.

A stranger arrives at Aunt Skilly's mountainside cabin and accepts her kind invitation to dinner. Through what appears to be casual conversation, he learns that she lives alone with no hound dog to protect her, no neighbors nearby, and no bar with which to lock her door at night. After dinner, well-fed and seemingly appreciative, the stranger thanks her and rides away on his mule. Later that night, Aunt Skilly awakens to the sound of an intruder: The stranger has returned to rob her. But Aunt Skilly is not as naïve and trusting as the robber assumed. The author captures the flavor of an Appalachian Mountain tale with warmth, good humor, and a clever buildup of suspense.

3.22 Williams, Carol Ann. **Tsubu the Little Snail.** Illustrated by Tatsuro Kiuchi. Simon & Schuster, 1995. ISBN 0-671-87167-6. 32p. 5–7.

The retelling of this Japanese folktale resembles more familiar folktales in which love and faith triumph. Tsubu was a gift from the Water God to a poor rice farmer and his wife, who prayed endlessly for a baby. At age twenty, Tsubu so impresses a wealthy landowner that a marriage is arranged between the snail and the landowner's youngest daughter. Full-page, subdued oil paintings reveal the beauty of the Japanese countryside. An author's note provides information about the origin and meaning of the folktale and could be used in discussing the common elements among folktales from different cultures.

Fables

3.23   Barber, Antonia. **The Monkey and the Panda.** Illustrated by Meilo So. Simon & Schuster, 1995. ISBN 0-02-708382-9. 25p. 5–8.

Panda and Monkey both are loved by the children of a village, but for different reasons. Monkey is jealous of Panda because he thinks the children love Panda more. The fable celebrates the uniqueness of each individual. With its appealing illustrations, this book could also be used with a self-esteem unit.

3.24   Charles, Veronika Martenova. **The Crane Girl.** Illustrated by Veronika Martenova Charles. Orchard, 1993. ISBN 0-531-05485-3. 32p. 5–7.

A Japanese girl chooses to be transformed into a crane rather than live with her parents, who seem to have forgotten her after the birth of a new child. The heroine's return to her family and her final transformation back into a little girl are beautifully rendered by Charles's richly textured illustrations.

3.25   Katz, Avner. **Tortoise Solves a Problem.** Illustrated by Avner Katz. HarperCollins, 1993. ISBN 0-06-020798-1. 34p. 5–7.

Avner Katz offers an original answer to the question of how the tortoise got his shell, a problem considered in pourquoi tales of many cultures. Katz's version has a council of the three wisest tortoises in the land commissioning one particularly creative tortoise to design a home. This tortoise submits one outrageous plan after another before an idea is finally accepted. Katz first wrote and published this story in Hebrew. Children will enjoy the lively, offbeat illustrations, which may inspire them to design tortoise homes of their own.

3.26   van Pallandt, Nicolas. **Troll's Search for Summer.** Illustrated by Nicolas van Pallandt. Farrar, Straus, 1994. ISBN 0-374-36560-1. 25p. 5–8.

Nicolas van Pallandt's story tells of a troll's search for the warmth of summer. He is joined on this journey by a snake and an owl. They discover the various attitudes of traditional winter figures (such as arknarks, hubbins, and Ice Witches) toward the summer. The quest ends when the trio returns to the troll's snug home to fall asleep and await the warm fingers of summer. The author merges the realistic and mythical aspects of winter in rich detail, providing an evocative portrait of the uniqueness of winter in the land of the trolls.

Folk Songs and Ballads

3.27   Berry, Holly. **Old MacDonald Had a Farm.** Illustrated by Holly Berry. North-South, 1994. ISBN 1-55858-281-9. 26p. 5–8.

Brightly colored illustrations accompany the words to this familiar song. Each animal receives a musical instrument until the entire animal band is assembled, singing and dancing in the final picture. The book includes a brief note about the song and a useful musical score.

3.28   Orozco, José-Luis. *De Colores* **and Other Latin-American Folk Songs for Children.** Illustrated by Elisa Kleven. Dutton, 1994. ISBN 0-525-45260-5. 55p. 8–10.

Twenty-seven songs, rhymes, and chants have been selected by José-Luis Orozco. Lyrics are in both Spanish and English with delightful suggestions for group responses, games, and activities to accompany each song. Bright, cheerful, whimsical illustrations are a beautiful complement to the text. Pages containing the musical arrangements for piano, voice, and guitar are enhanced by detailed, colorful borders. This is an inviting book to share.

Folktales and Fairy Tales

3.29   Ada, Alma Flor (translated by Rosa Zubizarreta). **Dear Peter Rabbit/Querido Pedrin.** Illustrated by Leslie Tryon. Atheneum, 1994. ISBN 0-689-31850-2 (English); 0-689-31915-0 (Spanish). 32p. 7–12.

This humorous, metafictive book combines several stories in a unique format. Peter Rabbit, the three little pigs, Goldilocks, Baby Bear, the wolf, and Little Red Riding Hood all correspond back and forth in a series of letters. By the end of the book, all the characters (except the wolf) converge at Goldilocks McGregor's birthday party, held at McGregor's Farm. The various familiar tales emerge through the contents of the letters, interwoven together. The use of several fonts helps in following the shift from one letter-writer to the next. This unusual twist on some well-loved stories cleverly kindles interest in discussion of the plot details and story characters. This book would be useful with letter-writing and drama activities, sparking imaginations. Editions are available in English and Spanish.

3.30   Andersen, Hans Christian. **The Snow Queen.** Illustrated by P. J. Lynch. Harcourt Brace, 1994. ISBN 0-15-200874-8. 48p. 6–10.

P. J. Lynch's gift for bringing the tales of Hans Christian Andersen to life is nowhere more evident than in these stunning illustrations. Lynch returns us to the magnificence of the story collections of the nineteenth century. Andersen's strange tale is about Gerda's rescue of Kay from the sterility of the Snow Queen's world. The focus is on the need for personal growth and the discovery that the wisest adults remain children at heart.

3.31   Andersen, Hans Christian (translated by Anthea Bell). **The Swineherd.** Illustrated by Lisbeth Zwerger. North-South, 1995. ISBN 1-55858- 428-5. 25p. 6–9.

This playful retelling reveals how funny this fairy tale can be. The prince disguises himself as a swineherd to discover the true character of a princess. The expressive lines and wonderful shapes of the amusing illustrations depict the characters in homely detail: A pig enjoys a back-scratch by the prince, and the Emperor holds onto a pageboy for balance while putting on slippers. This reissue was first published in 1982.

3.32   Andersen, Hans Christian. **Twelve Tales: Hans Christian Andersen.** Illustrated by Erik Blegvad. McElderry, 1994. ISBN 0-689-50584-1. 92p. 9–12.

This interesting collection of both familiar and unfamiliar Andersen tales clearly proclaims the pride felt by Danish collector and illustrator Erik Blegvad. His ink-and-watercolor illustrations, clearly indebted to traditional Danish illustrators such as Vilhelm Pedersen and Lorenz Frolich, provide a reassuring sense of authenticity to the often enigmatic and controversial tales that established Andersen as one of the most renowned writers of literature for children. The inclusion of seldom-collected tales such as "Twelve by Coach" and "The Pixie at the Grocer's" make this a welcome addition to Andersen collections.

3.33   Arnold, Katya, reteller. **Baba Yaga: A Russian Folktale.** Illustrated by Katya Arnold. North-South, 1993. ISBN 1-55858-208-8. 26p. 5–8.

Baba Yaga is a familiar figure in Russian folklore, appearing sometimes as a fearsome witch and other times as a caring helper. In this story she is a conniving witch who kidnaps a beloved son from his family and prepares to eat him. She discovers, however, that he has tricked her into eating her own child instead. When she seeks revenge, she is once again outwitted. Katya Arnold's text and illustrations reflect careful research. She based her retelling on her own translation of a story found in nineteenth-century Russian folklorist Aleksandr Afanasev's collection of folktales. Her simple, bold illustrations resemble woodcuts. They are inspired by lubok pictures, a style of Russian folk art originating in the seventeenth century.

3.34   Arnold, Tim. **The Three Billy Goats Gruff.** Illustrated by Tim Arnold. McElderry, 1993. ISBN 0-689-50575-2. 32p. 5–8.

Soft, soothing watercolor backgrounds, carefully detailed pen-and-ink drawings, and a lyrical text distinguish Tim Arnold's gentle interpretation of this much-retold Scandinavian folktale from much rougher and louder versions. This book would be useful in a comparison study of this folktale. It is also a lovely telling to share as a bedtime story.

3.35   Baumgartner, Barbara. **Crocodile! Crocodile! Stories Told around the World.** Illustrated by Judith Moffatt. Dorling Kindersley, 1994. ISBN 1-56458- 463-1. 45p. 5–8.

Cut-and-folded paper art in vibrant colors lends an effective folk tone to this collection of tales from around the world. The book ends with suggestions for dramatization of these tales as well as a list of additional sources for other versions of the tales.

3.36   Bernhard, Emery. **The Girl Who Wanted to Hunt: A Siberian Tale.** Illustrated by Durga Bernhard. Holiday House, 1994. ISBN 0-8234-1125-7. 32p. 6–9.

Collectors Emery and Durga Bernhard base their retelling on versions of this story collected in Siberia over a century ago. It shares many features of the archetypical Cinderella story: Magical helpers free a kind and innocent girl from the abuses of a wicked stepmother. This version is unique in that the heroine is not ultimately rescued by marriage to a handsome prince, nor is she content to pursue the conventionally female tasks her stepmother assigns her, but chooses to fill the traditionally male role of hunter. Durga Bernhard's powerful illustrations reflect the same careful research that informs Emery Bernhard's retelling.

3.37   Birdseye, Tom. **Soap! Soap! Don't Forget the Soap! An Appalachian Folktale.** Illustrated by Andrew Glass. Holiday House, 1993. ISBN 0-8234- 1005-6. 32p. 5–8.

Tom Birdseye's written text remains true to the oral tradition of the Appalachian folktale in this story of a little boy whose poor memory repeatedly gets him in trouble as he tries to run an errand for his mother. The warmth and humor of Birdseye's retelling are reflected in Andrew Glass's charming illustrations. A great read-aloud!

3.38 Bruchac, Joseph, reteller. **The Boy Who Lived with the Bears and Other Iroquois Stories.** Illustrated by Murv Jacob. Harper-Collins, 1995. ISBN 0-06-021287-X. 63p. 6–11.

This collection of Iroquois animal tales is told by acclaimed Native American storyteller Joseph Bruchac. Murv Jacob, a painter and pipemaker of Kentucky Cherokee descent, provides the richly colored tapestries that accompany the legends. Most of the tales are pourquoi tales, telling us how a chipmunk got stripes or how birds got their feathers. All provide a strong sense of the relationship between humankind and the natural world that defines Iroquois culture. Children and teachers are fortunate that Bruchac and Jacob collaborated to share these delightful and timeless tales. This version is also available on audio cassette.

3.39 Bruchac, Joseph, reteller. **First Strawberries: A Cherokee Story.** Illustrated by Anna Vojtech. Dial, 1993. ISBN 0-8037-1332-0. 32p. 5–8.

This book is a charming explanation of how strawberries came to grow on earth. This explanation is combined with a Cherokee Garden of Eden story that does not end in disaster. The portraits of the Cherokee couple have a sculptured, dignified look that contrasts with the paradisiacal natural surroundings.

3.40 Brusca, Maria Cristina, and Tona Wilson. **The Cook and the King.** Illustrated by Maria Cristina Brusca. Holt, 1993. ISBN 0-8050-2355-0. 34p. 5–8.

Maria Cristina Brusca and Tona Wilson base their story on characters and incidents common to Argentinean folklore. In this tale, Florinda, the finest cook in the village, agrees to work for the king if he will grant her one wish. In turn, she must agree not to meddle in the affairs of the kingdom. She minds her own business until she discovers how unfairly the king is treating his subjects. The story unfolds as Florinda uses wit, good humor, and the power of her wish to teach the king some important lessons about justice. An interesting note at the end of this story explains its connection to the traditional Andean tale that inspired it. Readers will enjoy Brusca's amusing, cartoonlike illustrations.

3.41 Bryan, Ashley. **The Story of Lightning and Thunder.** Illustrated by Ashley Bryan. Atheneum, 1993. ISBN 0-689-31836-7. 32p. 5–8.

This West African tale must be read aloud to release the rhythm, rhyme, and alliteration that turn the text into poetry. Unusual and delightful, the brightly colored and highly patterned illustrations are based on African folk art. Ashley Bryan, an African American scholar, has created a beautiful way to bring African folktales to North American children.

3.42   Bull, Emma. **The Princess and the Lord of Night.** Illustrated by Susan Gaber. Harcourt Brace, 1994. ISBN 0-15-263543-2. 32p. 6–8.

This beautifully illustrated princess story is engaging in its message of independence and thoughtfulness. A princess is cursed by the Lord of the Night: If ever she wants something she cannot have, the kingdom will fall into ruin and the king and queen will die. The unspoiled thirteen-year-old princess sets out on her own to resolve the matter. Along the way she gives away all her prized possessions to people in need. She also tricks the Lord of the Night, releasing herself from the curse. This story is laden with lush word images. The main character is refreshingly sensitive to others but also wise and capable of solving her own problems.

3.43   Chang, Margaret, and Raymond Chang, retellers. **The Cricket Warrior: A Chinese Tale.** Illustrated by Warwick Hutton. McElderry, 1994. ISBN 0-689-50605-8. 32p. 5–8.

Margaret and Raymond Chang trace this tale of family loyalty and magical transformation to seventeenth-century Shandong province, China. The emperor is so fond of crickets and cricket fights that he demands that a special tax be paid to him in crickets rather than in cash. Poor farmer Cheng Ming's only hope of saving his farm is to find an expert fighting cricket to offer to the king. Out of love for his father, Cheng Ming's son Wei nian agrees to turn into a cricket himself. The emperor is so impressed with this unusual cricket's fighting skills that he forgives Cheng Ming both his taxes and his large debt. Of course, when all good has been achieved, Wei nian returns in human form to his family. Warwick Hutton's delicate watercolors reflect this story's quiet strength.

3.44   Climo, Shirley. **The Korean Cinderella.** Illustrated by Ruth Heller. HarperCollins, 1993. ISBN 0-06-020432-X. 48p. 5–8.

This interesting variant of the Cinderella story, with its striking and authentic illustrations incorporating ancient Korean patterns, invites comparison with the more familiar story. A frog, sparrows, and an ox replace the traditional fairy godmother but are just as successful in helping Pear Blossom find happiness.

3.45   Cohn, Amy L. **From Sea to Shining Sea: A Treasury of American Folklore and Folk Songs.** Scholastic, 1993. ISBN 0-590-42868-3. 400p. 9–12.

Every child and adult should have an opportunity to experience this unique collection of folktales, folk songs, poems, and essays that celebrate the cultural and historical roots of the American people. The book is organized chronologically into four main sections, with many subsections beginning with traditional Native American stories and ending with the folklore of the twentieth century. A different artist illustrates each subsection. This book invites browsing and the subject guide lists works by ethnic and religious groups, song and story types, and geographical regions. Sources are documented, musical notation is given for the songs, and lists for further reading are provided. Indexes, a chronology of the selections, and biographies of the artists are also included.

3.46   Curry, Jane Louise. **The Christmas Knight.** Illustrated by DyAnne DiSalvo-Ryan. McElderry, 1993. ISBN 0-689-50572-8. 32p. 5–9.

This tale, set in medieval Britain in the days before King Arthur, offers a refreshing change from more familiar Christmas fare. Sir Cleges and his wife, Dame Clarys, have always been generous at Christmas, inviting everyone, rich and poor, to share in a magnificent holiday feast. When hard times come, they sell all that they own in order to provide for others. Left with nothing for themselves, they are rewarded with a magical gift from God. The authenticity of detail in Jane Louise Curry's text reflects her reputation as a scholar of medieval English literature.

3.47   Day, Nancy Raines. **The Lion's Whiskers: An Ethiopian Folktale.** Illustrated by Ann Grifalconi. Scholastic, 1995. ISBN 0-590-45803-5. 32p. 5–8.

This retelling of an Ethiopian folktale is about a loving stepmother who is willing to brave death to gain the love of her reluctant stepson. Ann Grifalconi used textured material and paper to create bold and original illustrations portraying the traditional lifestyle of the Amhara people.

3.48   De Felice, Cynthia, and Mary De Marsh, retellers. **Three Perfect Peaches: A French Folktale.** Illustrated by Irene Trivas. Orchard, 1995. ISBN 0-531-06872-2. 32p. 5–8.

The retellers, also known as the Wild Washerwomen Storytellers, have produced a wonderfully funny and satisfying fairy tale. The youngest son succeeds in wedding the princess as a consequence of very amusing circumstances. The line and wash illustrations enhance the humor surrounding the delightfully silly, flawed, but likable protagonists.

3.49   de Gerez, Tree. **When Bear Came Down from the Sky.** Illustrated by Lisa Desimini. Viking, 1994. ISBN 0-670-85171-X. 32p. 5–8.

Bear lives in the Sky with his family of Stars. But as time passes he becomes increasingly curious and wants to explore the world below him. One day he floats down to discover the delights, and horrors, of life on earth—delights such as honey and horrors such as ants. Lisa Desimini's imaginative oil paintings capture the spirit of this ancient story from Finno-Ugric folklore.

3.50   Deetlefs, Rene. **Tabu and the Dancing Elephants.** Illustrated by Lyn Gilbert. Dutton, 1995. ISBN 0-525-45226-5. 32p. 5–9.

Rene Deetlefs adapted this folktale from a version she was told by a South Sotho woman in South Africa. This is a happy little tale about Tabu, who is such a happy baby that he doesn't mind when his favorite animal, the elephant, borrows him. But his parents do mind and his mother finds a way to get him back. This book is filled with the simple pleasures of life. The illustrations depict authentic African flora and fauna and the traditional ways of village life.

3.51   Diller, Harriett. **The Waiting Day.** Illustrated by Chi Chung. Green Tiger, 1994. ISBN 0-671-86579-X. 34p. 5–8.

This quiet moral tale has a cumulative pattern. A busy ferryman in ancient China learns from an old beggar how to appreciate the beauty of nature. The glowing colored illustrations are in classic Chinese style. This book might be useful for special occasions.

3.52   Fleischman, Susan. **The Boy Who Looked for Spring.** Illustrated by Donna Diamond. Harcourt Brace, 1993. ISBN 0-15-210699-5. 32p. 5–8.

A boy named Ben goes out to look for Spring at the end of a long winter. A white fox guides him to a beautiful woman, Mother Earth, who cannot awake so that Spring can be born. Ben must solve three riddles to help her. This modern fairy tale is beautifully written and illustrated. Rich, subtly lit, full-page pictures face pages of text adorned with bare branches that gradually bud and flower as Mother Earth awakes.

3.53   Gershator, Phillis. **The Iroko-man: A Yoruba Folktale.** Illustrated by Holly C. Kim. Orchard, 1994. ISBN 0-531-06810-2. 32p. 5–8.

This Nigerian folktale is a variation of the German Rumpelstiltskin and the English Tom Tit Tot stories. The ending in this version is more satisfactory: The husband is able to outwit the tree spirit, save his wife and child, and please the Iroko-man. The text is enriched with repetitive verse and the illustrations reflect the colors of Nigeria.

3.54   Gerson, Mary-Joan, reteller. **How Night Came from the Sea: A Story from Brazil.** Illustrated by Carla Golembe. Little, Brown, 1994. ISBN 0-316- 30855-2. 32p. 5–9.

The stunningly bold illustrations in this picture book include oil pastels, colored pencils, and gouache. The effect richly complements this beautiful, traditional Brazilian tale of how one special gift from a sea goddess brought about the earth's rhythm of night and day. With richly detailed and finely narrated text, this new collaboration by the creators of *Why the Sky Is Far Away* is another treasure of the cultural lore of Africa and Brazil.

3.55   Gerson, Mary-Joan. **People of Corn: A Mayan Story.** Illustrated by Carla Golembe. Little, Brown, 1995. ISBN 0-316-30854-4. 32p. 5–9.

This Mayan myth embedded in a modern story describes the rituals, beliefs, and world view of the Mayan people of Guatemala. It would be very useful for an elementary class study of the culture of South America. Carla Golembe incorporates ancient Mayan patterns into the brilliantly colored illustrations. The folk art style of the illustrations and the medium (gouache on black paper) could inspire interesting art projects.

3.56   Ginsburg, Mirra. **The King Who Tried to Fry an Egg on His Head.** Illustrated by Will Hillenbrand. Macmillan, 1994. ISBN 0-02-736242-6. 32p. 5–8.

This is a delightful telling of a Russian folktale. An absurd and unsuccessful king learns some rather impractical lessons from the three bridegrooms (the Sun, the Moon, and a Raven) whom he has allowed to marry his daughters. His attempts to teach his wife this newfound wisdom—for example, how to fry an egg on your head—are amusingly portrayed by Will Hillenbrand's oil pastels. This is a thoroughly engaging parable on the need to learn to live by your own wits.

3.57   Goode, Diane, compiler. **Diane Goode's Book of Scary Stories and Songs.** Illustrated by Diane Goode. Dutton, 1994. ISBN 0-525-45175-7. 64p. 6–10.

The author notes in her introduction that scary stories of ghosts, goblins, and ghouls help to explain the unknown and give one a sense of control over fright. This collection of familiar ("The Green Ribbon") and less familiar ("Dauntless Little John") stories and poems from various cultures will become cozy, shivery favorites. The pastel illustrations by award-winning Diane Goode, with an attractive frame for each page, are gentle enough to share with preschoolers.

3.58   Greaves, Nick. **When Lion Could Fly and Other Tales from Africa.** Illustrated by Rod Clement. Barron's, 1993. ISBN 0-8120-1625-4. 144p. 9–11.

When Lion Could Fly adds to Nick Greaves's earlier collection of African tales, *When Hippo Was Hairy.* This book offers entertaining stories of smaller and lesser-known African animals such as duikers, pangolins, and guinea fowls. Included are many pourquoi tales, such as "Why Python Can Shed His Skin" and "Why Pangolin Has Scales." As in his previous book, Greaves interlaces the stories with factual information about the animals featured in them. Rod Clement's realistic illustrations enrich the interesting fact pages, making this book a useful natural history resource.

3.59   Grimm, Jacob, and Wilhelm Grimm. **The Golden Goose.** Illustrated by Uri Shulevitz. Farrar, Straus, 1995. ISBN 0-374-32695-9. 32p. 5–8.

A golden goose is given to a simpleton. Anyone who touches the goose gets stuck and must follow the simpleton. The more people who get stuck, the sillier the procession. This ridiculous story is retold in the plain, uncomplicated style associated with the oral tradition. Caldecott medal–winning Uri Shulevitz's quirky and unusual illustrations pull one through the book just as the goose pulls those who get too close.

3.60   Grimm, Jacob, and Wilhelm Grimm. **Iron Hans.** Illustrated by Marilee Heyer. Viking, 1993. ISBN 0-670-81741-4. 32p. 6–9.

This meticulous recreation of the Italian Renaissance is a perfect setting for one of the Grimms' most enigmatic characters, the enchanted wildman Iron Hans. The author's technique of alternating text with double-page illuminations may confuse some children, but the overall impact is breathtaking. The final illustration of Iron Hans's entrance at the wedding of the young prince is remarkable, with an attention to detail reminiscent of late medieval paintings.

3.61   Grimm, Jacob, and Wilhelm Grimm. **Little Red-Cap.** Illustrated by Lisbeth Zwerger. North-South, 1995. ISBN 1-55858-382-3. 25p. 5–8.

This is a thoroughly delightful retelling of the folktale with the now-traditional happy ending. Zwerger's watercolor washes bring both humor and freshness to the familiar story. The illustrations show the genius for detail that one always associates with this gifted illustrator. This is a memorable text for children of any age.

3.62   Grimm, Jacob, and Wilhelm Grimm (translated by Anthea Bell). **The Sleeping Beauty: A Fairy Tale.** Illustrated by Monika Laimgruber. North-South, 1995. ISBN 1-55858-399-8. 26p. 5–8.

This retelling of the familiar story recaptures the distinct German flavor of the original Grimm version. The traditional witches are now simply wise women and Beauty is rather plain and actually does grow from a young girl to a mature woman. Monika Laimgruber's illustrations visually reinforce this attractive retelling, providing much for children to discover.

3.63   Hadithi, Mwenye. **Baby Baboon.** Illustrated by Adrienne Kennaway. Little, Brown, 1993. ISBN 0-316-33729-3. 32p. 5–8.

This beautifully illustrated picture story set in Africa takes young readers on a safari among the native animals of that continent. Leopard learns a lesson about trying to take advantage of Baby Baboon and others animals such as Hare and clever Vervet Monkey. A seamless melding of pictures and text, with a rich variety in illustration, characterize this very worthwhile book.

3.64   Hadithi, Mwenye. **Hungry Hyena.** Illustrated by Adrienne Kennaway. Little, Brown, 1994. ISBN 0-316-33715-3. 32p. 5–7.

In yet another delightful tale by this author/illustrator team, children will be enchanted by the tricky and clever dealings of African animal characters such as the fish eagle, the pangolin, and the hyena. Hyena learns a hard lesson about greed and deceit when he tries to be more clever than the eagle and the monkey. The bright, bold watercolor illustrations vividly evoke the beauty of the African landscape.

3.65   Hamada, Cheryl, reteller. **Fourth Question: A Chinese Folktale.** Illustrated by Janice Skivington. Children's Press, 1993. ISBN 0-516-05144-X. unpaged. 6–8.

In this traditional tale a young man learns the rewards of helping others as he journeys across China in search of a solution to his family's poverty. This tale in the Adventures in Storytelling series is presented in wordless picture book form, accompanied by an audio cassette. The book contains an interesting introduction to the art of storytelling and the full text of the story is printed at the back. Janice Skivington's evocative and carefully researched illustrations record critical story events in detailed pencil drawings set into boldly colored landscapes.

3.66   Hamada, Cheryl, reteller. **Kao and the Golden Fish: A Folktale from Thailand.** Illustrated by Monica Liu. Children's Press, 1993. ISBN 0-516- 05145-8. unpaged. 6–8.

This popular Cinderella-type tale involves a young woman who suffers cruel treatment from her stepmother and stepsister. Her dead mother returns in various incarnations to comfort her daughter and lead her to marriage with a handsome prince. This tale in the Adventures in Storytelling series is presented in wordless picture book form, with pleasant Chinese brush illustrations, accompanied by an audio cassette. This is meant to encourage independent storytelling in a child's own words, with only the picture book as a guide. The book contains an interesting introduction to the art of storytelling and the full text of the story is printed at the back.

3.67   Hamanaka, Sheila. **Screen of Frogs: An Old Tale.** Illustrated by Sheila Hamanaka. Orchard, 1993. ISBN 0-531-05464-0. 32p. 5–8.

A wealthy young Japanese man has almost wasted his inheritance when he learns from a human-sized frog, who knew him when he was a boy, how to save his remaining acres: mountains and lakes that are home to wildlife. The story shows children how people in other parts of the world are concerned about the survival of our environment.

3.68   Hamilton, Virginia. **Her Stories: African American Folktales, Fairy Tales, and True Tales.** Illustrated by Leo Dillon and Diane Dillon. Blue Sky, 1995. ISBN 0-590-47370-0. 114p. 8–12.

This exquisite collection of animal stories, fairy tales, myths, legends, folktales, supernatural tales, and autobiographical accounts celebrates the lives of African American women, both fictional and historical. The collection includes stories from the days of slavery in the United States, the Caribbean, and Africa. Each category is introduced with an insightful explanation of the genre. The illustrations are vibrant, rich acrylic compositions that complement the book's design. The concluding section focuses on autobiographical accounts of notable African American women, helping to bridge the rich mythic text with the characters' real-life struggles and accomplishments.

3.69   Harness, Cheryl. **The Queen with Bees in Her Hair.** Illustrated by Cheryl Harness. Holt, 1993. ISBN 0-8050-1715-1. 32p. 5–7.

In this original fairy tale Queen Ruby's selfish desire to rid her kingdom of bees and other "pests" creates an ecological crisis. Disaster is averted when she realizes the necessity of returning things to their natural order, a decision that not only saves her kingdom, but also unites her kingdom with that of the neighboring Hermit King. The author/illustrator's decorative illustrations, influenced by Italian Renaissance paintings, effectively detail this unique tale.

3.70   Haskins, James. **The Headless Haunt and Other African-American Ghost Stories.** Illustrated by Ben Otero. HarperCollins, 1994. ISBN 0-06-022994-2. 116p. 8–12.

This book might be suitably subtitled *Everything You Wanted to Know about Ghosts but Were Afraid to Ask.* This collection includes not only tales of encounters with ghosts and spirits, but also the history of some of the objects and beliefs associated with the supernatural. For example, the author informs us that in African American folklore, *jack-o'-lantern* is the name given to the evil spirit of a dead person who is forbidden to enter Heaven or Hell. Equally interesting is the list of things to do in order to acquire the ability to see ghosts (looking through a mule's ear, wiping off a dusty nail and putting it in your mouth, or breaking a cuckoo's egg into some water and then washing your face in it).

3.71   Hauff, Wilhelm (translated by Anthea Bell). **Dwarf Nose.** Illustrated by Lisbeth Zwerger. North-South, 1994. ISBN 1-55858-261-4. 49p. 6–10.

This delightful story by early-nineteenth-century German storyteller Wilhelm Hauff is the tale of a young villager, Jacob, who unwisely insults an old woman, telling her to get her long, ugly nose out of his way. Of course, she is a wicked fairy who curses Jacob to be Dwarf Nose, a tiny disfigured outcast who must somehow find his way in an alien world. Hauff's thinly disguised parable is not so much about the transformed Jacob as it is about the pettiness of the bourgeois mentality that scorns him. Zwerger's rich yet subtle watercolor illustrations beautifully capture the poignancy of Dwarf Nose's fate as well as the wit and playfulness of Hauff's unique approach to the fairy tale.

3.72 Hobson, Sally. **Chicken Little.** Illustrated by Sally Hobson. Simon & Schuster, 1994. ISBN 0-671-89548-6. 26p. 5–7.

Sally Hobson's beautifully illustrated version of this classic children's story about the silly chicken who thinks the sky is falling when an acorn leaf falls on its head will captivate young readers. Children will delight in the artist's bright contrasting color combinations that set off the bold text pattern of this charming tale. This is an excellent read-aloud that students can compare with other versions of this well-loved story.

3.73 Hunter, Mollie. **Gilly Martin the Fox.** Illustrated by Dennis McDermott. Hyperion, 1994. ISBN 1-56282-518-6. 36p. 5–8.

A benevolent fox with shape-shifting powers is at the center of this Celtic folktale, here retold in picture storybook format. The tale has a rhythmic, repetitive pattern that lends itself to telling aloud and the brilliant pictures feature Celtic motifs.

3.74 Jaffe, Nina. **The Uninvited Guest and Other Jewish Holiday Tales.** Illustrated by Elivia. Scholastic, 1993. ISBN 0-590-44653-3. 72p. 7–12.

This collection of Jewish folktales highlights Jewish holidays such as Rosh Hashanah, Hanukkah, and Purim. Each folktale is preceded by a one-page description of the holiday in which the story is set. The stories are written engagingly, with either humor, mystery, or morality, and retain the spirit of the original source. The book includes a glossary and bibliography.

3.75 Kimmel, Eric A., reteller. **The Adventures of Hershel of Ostropol.** Illustrated by Trina Schart Hyman. Holiday House, 1995. ISBN 0-8234-1210-5. 64p. 8–11.

This is a fine collection of funny stories about the Jewish folk hero Hershel of Ostropol, the same man who saved Hanukkah in Kimmel's earlier, beloved book, *Hershel and the Hanukkah Goblins*. Kimmel's retelling of these stories is witty and Hyman's drawings are charming and full of character. The book would be suitable for children in grades 4 to 6 who enjoy reading jokes. The humor and Jewish cultural content make this a good text for learning and pleasure.

3.76   Kimmel, Eric A. **Anansi and the Talking Melon.** Illustrated by Janet Stevens. Holiday House, 1994. ISBN 0-8234-1104-4. 32p. 5–8.

It is impossible to resist an Anansi story and this retelling is no exception. Here the wily spider tricks several animals in the jungle, including the gorilla king. The text is cumulative, an asset for telling aloud. Huge jungle animals are portrayed realistically but with a lively, cartoonlike quality.

3.77   Kimmel, Eric A. **Asher and the Capmakers: A Hanukkah Story.** Illustrated by Will Hillenbrand. Holiday House, 1993. ISBN 0-8234-1031-5. 32p. 5–7.

Another Hanukkah story from Eric Kimmel combines fairy lore from Ireland, England, and Eastern Europe. A boy named Asher encounters capmakers (Jewish fairies) on his way to the henhouse to get eggs for the family's potato latkes. Asher hides and watches the capmakers fly up the chimney to Jerusalem and then follows them. There he witnesses their wild celebration, but the pasha's soldiers angrily storm the hall. The capmakers fly off and Asher, who loses his magic cap, is left to receive all the blame. Asher manages to trick the pasha and his soldiers and flies back home, only to discover that he has been gone seven years. Vivid illustrations add to the magic and adventure of this original story.

3.78   Kimmel, Eric A., reteller. **The Goose Girl: A Story from the Brothers Grimm.** Illustrated by Robert Sauber. Holiday House, 1995. ISBN 0-8234-1074-9. 32p. 5–7.

Rich illustrations and the language of fairy tales enliven this Brothers Grimm account of a beautiful and good princess forced to trade places with her evil serving maid, who takes her place at the side of a prince. Of course, the true princess's identity is discovered at the end and she and the prince are united. The traditional plot is brought to life by beautifully colored paintings.

3.79   Kimmel, Eric A., reteller. **I-Know-Not-What, I-Know-Not-Where: A Russian Tale.** Illustrated by Robert Sauber. Holiday House, 1994. ISBN 0-8234-1020-X. 64p. 9–11.

This classic Russian fairy tale is in the tradition of stories in which kindness is rewarded. While hunting, a young man injures a beautiful white dove, who then persuades him to dress her wound. The pair become close friends and when the czar sets him impossible and dangerous tasks, he completes them successfully with the help of the magical dove. This well-told, exciting tale is enhanced by dramatic, full-page paintings.

3.80 Kimmel, Eric A. **Rimonah of the Flashing Sword: A North African Tale.** Illustrated by Omar Rayyan. Holiday House, 1995. ISBN 0-8234-1093-5. 32p. 5–9.

Elements from other ancient tales and contemporary ideas about women's roles are incorporated into this adapted tale of a North African Snow White. The artwork by Omar Rayyan really is romantic fantasy. The illustrations are reminiscent of the paintings by the Orientalists of the nineteenth century, particularly those by John Frederick Lewis. Each page is a work of art, with both the text and the illustrations drenched in desert colors.

3.81 Kimmel, Eric A., reteller. **The Three Princes: A Tale from the Middle East.** Illustrated by Leonard Everett Fisher. Holiday House, 1994. ISBN 0-8234-1115-X. 32p. 5–8.

"Once there was and once there was not . . ." begins this Middle Eastern tale of three princes who seek rare wonders in order to win the hand of a wise and beautiful princess. The story is resolved in a satisfying manner when the princes save the princess's life, using the objects they find. Lush navy-blue, purple, and rose colors abound in the gorgeous illustrations. Eric Kimmel's retelling of this story resonates with authenticity and evocative language.

3.82 Kimmel, Eric A., adapter. **Three Sacks of Truth: A Story from France.** Illustrated by Robert Rayevsky. Holiday House, 1993. ISBN 0-8234-0921-X. 32p. 5–8.

Petit Jean is to the French folktale what Jack is to the English. Both are the clever ones who always win out over the selfish and the greedy. Here Petit Jean fulfills three impossible tasks and the king is forced to give him his daughter in marriage.

3.83 Kimmel, Eric A., adapter. **The Witch's Face: A Mexican Tale.** Illustrated by Fabricio Vanden Broeck. Holiday House, 1993. ISBN 0-8234-1038-2. 32p. 5–8.

Don Aurelio falls in love with a beautiful young woman, whom he later discovers is a witch. In order for her to become mortal and return his love, the woman must exchange her beautiful face for an ugly one. When she does this, Don Aurelio's feelings for her change. Entertaining as a simple scary tale, *The Witch's Face* also offers insights into the nature of love. Before he begins his own captivating retelling, Eric Kimmel provides careful documentation of the story's source, upholding his reputation as a fine storyteller and a respected collector of folktales. Mexican artist Fabricio Vanden Broeck's illustrations enhance the authenticity of Kimmel's text.

3.84   Knutson, Barbara. **Sungura and the Leopard.** Illustrated by Barbara Knutson. Little, Brown, 1993. ISBN 0-316-50010-0. 32p. 5–8.

This lighthearted and amusing trickster tale from Tanzania tells how Sungura, the small but clever hare, outwits fiercer and much larger Leopard. Each believes that his ancestors have been helping him build a house, but Hare and Leopard discover that they have, in fact, been building the same house. They agree to share the new living quarters until Leopard gets hungry and decides that Hare and his family would make a tasty meal. Barbara Knutson's lively illustrations enrich her re-telling, as does her author's note, in which she shares some of her knowledge of African folktales.

3.85   Kwon, Holly H., reteller. **The Moles and the Mireuk: A Korean Folktale.** Illustrated by Woodleigh Hubbard. Houghton Mifflin, 1993. ISBN 0-395-64347-3. 32p. 5–8.

Through the retelling of this traditional folktale, Holly Kwon shares a part of her Korean heritage with us. It is the whimsical story of a mole's adventures in search of the best husband for his perfect daughter and the lesson he learns about the elements of the universe and their powers. The illustrations, bright and full of brilliant contrasts, complement the large-print, easy-to-read text with vivid colors and lines. An excellent read-aloud book for primary classrooms.

3.86   Lang, Andrew, editor. **The Rainbow Fairy Book.** Illustrated by Michael Hague. Morrow, 1993. ISBN 0-688-10878-4. 288p. 6–8.

Illustrator Michael Hague selected thirty-one of the best-known tales from Andrew Lang's Fairy Books. The choices make up a basic collection of folktales for reading aloud. The format is a glossy deluxe production similar to a coffee-table book.

3.87 Lattimore, Deborah Nourse, reteller. **Arabian Nights: Three Tales.** HarperCollins, 1995. ISBN 0-06-024585-9. 63p. 8–12.

Three tales from *The Arabian Nights*—"Aladdin," "Queen of the Serpents," and "Ubar, the Lost City of Brass"—are all reduced in length but not in the depth of the telling. The mysterious setting is captured by the illustrations, with their luxuriant patterns and the jewel tones of an open treasure chest.

3.88 Lawson, Julie. **The Dragon's Pearl.** Illustrated by Paul Morin. Clarion, 1993. ISBN 0-395-63623-X. 32p. 6–10.

When drought comes to Xiao Sheng's river area of China, he goes off to search for grass. On the highest hill far away, he finds a wonderful patch, cuts it, and sells it in his village so that he and his mother can eat. Returning the next day, he discovers that the grass has grown again and he finds a pearl under the surface. He carefully puts the pearl in a near-empty rice jar but the next day the rice has doubled. He and his mother share their prosperity with their neighbors but one night two men try to rob them. Morin's illustrations, based on field research in China, dramatically capture the expressive faces of the Chinese people and the shimmering vistas of the landscape. As is characteristic of his work, Morin includes samples of crops, soil, fabric, money, and, of course, a pearl to heighten the artistic depth of his work.

3.89 Lewis, J. Patrick. **The Frog Princess.** Illustrated by Gennady Spirin. Dial, 1994. ISBN 0-8037-1624-9. 32p. 8–10.

In this lovingly retold variant of a Russian folktale, it is the princess, not the prince, who has been turned into a frog and must be rescued. In this tale the rescuer is the youngest son of the czar. Acclaimed Russian illustrator Gennady Spirin brilliantly brings this tale to life with an attention to detail that provides the perfect context and tone for this richly complex tale. The combination of tale and illustration is dazzling.

3.90 Litzinger, Rosanne. **The Old Woman and Her Pig: An Old English Tale.** Illustrated by Rosanne Litzinger. Harcourt Brace, 1993. ISBN 0-15-257802-1. 32p. 5–8.

How is the old woman going to get her stubborn new pig over the stile? She needs help, but help is hard to find, leading to a rousing cumulative tale that invites participation. Illustrations are lively and surprising, with the pig turning up in unexpected places.

3.91   Luenn, Nancy (translated by Alma Flor Ada). **Nessa's Story/El Cuento de Nessa.** Illustrated by Neil Waldman. Atheneum, 1994. ISBN 0-689-31782-4 (English); 0-689-31919-3 (Spanish). 32p. 5–9.

Longing to find a story of her very own to tell, Nessa discovers a mysterious egg from which hatches a silaq, a legendary Inuit beast that may be distantly related to the woolly mammoth. Although the silaq quickly burrows into the earth and disappears, Nessa now has her story and has begun her journey to independence. Neil Waldman's pastel watercolors effectively capture the spirit of the North and its inherent mystery. Editions are available in English and Spanish.

3.92   Maddern, Eric. **The Fire Children: A West African Creation Tale.** Illustrated by Frané Lessac. Dial, 1993. ISBN 0-8037-1477-7. 28p. 5–8.

This West African creation myth explains the origin of the moon and stars, the earth, and the people of many colors who inhabit it. Nyame, the Sky God, hangs in the sky as a basket filled with soil, trees, flowers, insects, and birds. This becomes the earth. Two of his spirit people leave the sky to explore this new land and, lonely for company, decide to create children by molding them from clay and baking them over a fire. Their creations vary in color depending on the length of time they have been baked. Frané Lessac's illustrations enhance Eric Maddern's already colorful text. She found inspiration for them in African masks and in designs on West African houses and pottery.

3.93   Maddern, Eric. **Rainbow Bird: An Aboriginal Folktale from Northern Australia.** Illustrated by Adrienne Kennaway. Little, Brown, 1993. ISBN 0-316-54314-4. 26p. 5–8.

This retelling of the Northern Australian aboriginal explanation for the origin of fire invites comparison with pourquoi tales of other cultures on the same theme. In this story, Crocodile, who owns fire and breathes it from his huge throat, greedily keeps it for himself until Birdwoman cleverly tricks him into sharing it with other living creatures. Adrienne Kennaway's vibrant watercolors enliven Eric Maddern's written text, giving the book special appeal.

3.94   Manitonquat. **The Children of the Morning Light: Wampanoag Tales.** Illustrated by Mary F. Arquette. Macmillan, 1994. ISBN 0-02-765905-4. 72p. 9–11.

This book is a collection of traditional tales from the Wampanoag of southeastern Massachusetts, written down by an elder of the tribe. The collection includes creation stories, but those that tell of the rivalry between the twins born of Sky Woman and West Wind are most memorable. The language has the engaging quality of a storyteller and the full-page colored illustrations are realistic and dignified.

3.95   Marks, Alan. **The Thief's Daughter.** Illustrated by Alan Marks. Farrar, Straus, 1994. ISBN 0-374-37481-3. 46p. 6–10.

Magpie, "the thief's daughter," instinctively believes in the goodness and honesty of her father, a poor farmer who loves to tell stories and whom people call "a bad lot." When Magpie finds a golden key one day, she discovers the mystery of her father's past and the tragic yet heartwarming tale of the events surrounding her birth. Through her belief in goodness and her own honesty, she is able to right the wrongs of the past. The subtle color and black-and-white sketches beautifully illustrate this enchanting traditional tale.

3.96   Mayhew, James, reteller. **Koshka's Tales: Stories from Russia.** Illustrated by James Mayhew. Kingfisher, 1993. ISBN 1-85697-943-1. 80p. 9–11.

Four of the best-known Russian tales, including "The Snow Maiden" and "The Baba Yaga," are retold here by a narrator cat. These tales are stories within a story of two wicked stepsisters and a czar of Russia.

3.97   Mayo, Margaret, reteller. **Magical Tales from Many Lands.** Illustrated by Jane Ray. Dutton, 1993. ISBN 0-525-45017-3. 128p. 9–11.

Because Margaret Mayo's retellings are so faithful to her carefully documented sources, this collection is an excellent reference for a study in comparative folklore. Mayo includes stories from fourteen cultures. From the lively, rhythmic, and amusing Zulu tale of Unanana, who rescues her children from the belly of a one-tusked elephant, to the gentle, haunting Native American legend "Featherwoman and Morningstar," Mayo allows the voice of the story and the culture it represents to speak louder than her own. The authenticity of the written text extends to Jane Ray's detailed illustrations.

3.98   Medearis, Angela Shelf, adapter. **The Singing Man: Adapted from a West African Folktale.** Illustrated by Terea Shaffer. Holiday House, 1994. ISBN 0-8234-1103-6. 36p. 9–11.

In this retelling of a Nigerian folktale, the story of a praise singer named Banzar is recounted. Cast out from his family and village for wanting to be a musician, Banzar meets an old blind man who teaches him the power of keeping history alive through singing. Colorful oil paintings bordered by traditional textile designs reveal a sense of Nigerian culture. There is a fair amount of text in this story, which would work well in discussing folktales and different cultures.

3.99 Mills, Lauren, reteller. **Tatterhood and the Hobgoblins: A Norwegian Folktale.** Illustrated by Lauren Mills. Little, Brown, 1993. ISBN 0-316-57406-6. 32p. 5–8.

This is a retelling of a series of Norwegian folktales revolving around the wondrous adventures of the totally unconventional Tatterhood, from her magical birth to her rescue of her beautiful twin sister and their subsequent adventures. The story ends when her Prince Charming accepts her tattered appearance, recognizing that she has the power to be as beautiful as her sister any time she chooses. Mills's full-page watercolor portraits, with their attention to detail, bring Tatterhood's world to life in all of its magical splendor in this delightful account of one of Norway's most popular heroines.

3.100 Mohr, Nicholasa, and Antonio Martorell. **The Song of El Coqui and Other Tales of Puerto Rico/La Cancion del Coqui.** Illustrated by Antonio Martorell. Viking, 1995. ISBN 0-670-85837-4 (English); 0-670-86296-7 (Spanish). 41p. 5–8.

This beautifully illustrated book recounts three folktales explaining the arrival of the three founding peoples of Puerto Rico: the indigenous Tainos, the Africans, and the Spaniards. Each group is allegorically represented by an animal tale: the Song of el Coqui (the frog), the stowaway hen, and the cimarron mule, respectively. The book is available in both English and Spanish, and would offer great learning potential in bilingual education settings.

3.101 Mollel, Tololwa M. **The King and the Tortoise.** Illustrated by Kathy Blankley. Clarion, 1993. ISBN 0-395-64480-1. 32p. 5–7.

A king who thought of himself as the most clever person in the world challenged all the creatures in his kingdom to make him a cloak of smoke. Many tried and failed. The tortoise ventured forth at last to try. He asked for a week and then when everyone was assembled asked for thread to weave it. When it was brought, he said it would not do—such a cloak had to be made with the thread of fire. Everyone was dumbstruck, especially the king, but he soon realized with pleasure that he had met his match. Tanzanian-born Mollel's retelling is alive with fast-paced action and good humor. The lively pace is reflected in the broad gestures and expression of the illustrations. Designs on either side of each spread suggest African cultural designs and reflect the mood of the action.

3.102 Namioka, Lensey. **The Loyal Cat.** Illustrated by Aki Sogabe. Harcourt Brace, 1995. ISBN 0-15-200092-5. 40p. 5–8.

This delightful tale conjures up a world of undisturbed scholarly and meditative peace, embodied by a monk named Tetsuzan, juxtaposed against a world of desire and miraculous will expressed by his cat, Huku. Tetsuzan and Huku live in a poor temple that attracts little support from the people. Soon all the other priests leave the temple, as do the mice, leaving no food for Huku. Huku uses his secret magic powers to attract attention by raising a coffin during the funeral procession of an old lord. Only when Tetsuzan is sent for and asked to pray does Huku lower the coffin. The reward of three gold pieces helps Tetsuzan to repair the temple and the priests and mice return. The temple is then renamed the cat temple. The text and illustrations evoke a Japan of long ago, where magic cats and saintly priests manifest quite naturally.

3.103 O'Brien, Anne Sibley, adapter. **The Princess and the Beggar: A Korean Folktale.** Illustrated by Anne Sibley O'Brien. Scholastic, 1993. ISBN 0-590-46092-7. 32p. 6–9.

This Korean folktale has been adapted and translated into English by the author/illustrator, who first heard the story as a child growing up in South Korea. A young princess of marrying age, who wants to pursue a more meaningful life than that of the superficial world of the court, refuses her father's choice of a husband and is banished for her disobedience. She begins a new life as the wife of a beggar and in the relationship gains an understanding of herself and of what is truly meaningful in life. The brightly colored illustrations convey the essence of this traditional folktale and the atmosphere of dynastic Korea.

3.104 Onyefulu, Obi, reteller. **Chinye: A West African Folk Tale.** Illustrated by Evie Safarewicz. Viking, 1994. ISBN 0-670-85115-9. 26p. 5–8.

This West African folktale tells the story of Chinye, a Cinderella-like figure forced to work for her stepmother and stepsister. One night, while fetching water, Chinye is accosted by an antelope, a hyena, and a mysterious woman who tells her about a magic gourd. Chinye follows the advice of the old woman and finds her fortune.

3.105 Passes, David. **Dragons: Truth, Myth, and Legend.** Illustrated by Wayne Anderson. Golden, 1993. ISBN 0-307-17500-6. 45p. 9–11.

Fantastic dragons from around the world are lavishly depicted and their stories told. Marduk and Fiamat, Beowulf and the Fire Dragon, St. George and the Dragon, Cadimus and the Golden Dragon, and Prince Gurd and the Dragon Fafnir are only some of the tales in this collection that kindle the imagination. The stories are excellent for reading aloud and in grades 3 to 8 the dragon theme could be explored. The index, table of contents, and brief introductory statements for each story are helpful.

3.106 Perrault, Charles. **The Complete Fairy Tales of Charles Perrault.** Illustrated by Sally Holmes. Clarion, 1993. ISBN 0-395-57002-6. 156p. 9–11.

These stories—"Cinderella," "The Sleeping Beauty," and other classic tales— come complete with Perrault's morals, which are often omitted in modern collections. The translators provide interesting notes on the stories and stay textually close to the original French.

3.107 Pohrt, Tom, reteller. **Coyote Goes Walking.** Illustrated by Tom Pohrt. Farrar, Straus, 1995. ISBN 0-374-31628-7. 32p. 5–10.

This is a collection of four short coyote stories told with brevity and humor. The illustrations capture the beauty and dignity of the animals as well as the humor of the stories. This text can be used in classrooms to explore different themes linked to mythology, culture, and our relationships to the natural world.

3.108 Rodanas, Kristina. **The Eagle's Song: A Tale from the Pacific Northwest.** Illustrated by Kristina Rodonas. Little, Brown, 1995. ISBN 0-316-75375-0. unpaged. 7–9.

The author, an elementary school art teacher from Cape Cod, adapts this tale from a Pacific Coast First Nations legend. The story recounts the tale of an eagle who helped the people become a community by teaching one boy to drum and dance. Full of movement and texture, the illustrations reflect the theme of the tale by depicting nature in rhythmic motion.

3.109 Rosen, Michael, reteller. **How Giraffe Got Such a Long Neck . . . and Why Rhino Is So Grumpy.** Illustrated by John Clementson. Dial, 1993. ISBN 0-8037-1621-4. 32p. 5–8.

This simply told explanatory story is set in East Africa, the land of the giraffe and the rhinoceros. The outstanding feature of this book is its brilliant collage illustrations.

3.110 Ross, Gayle, reteller. **How Rabbit Tricked Otter and Other Cherokee Trickster Stories.** Illustrated by Murv Jacob. Harper-Collins, 1994. ISBN 0-06-021285-3. 79p. 9–11.

This collection of Cherokee trickster stories demonstrates the commonality of such stories in other cultures. The advantage here is that it is a collection: Children can grasp the pattern and homogeneity of such tales. This attractively produced volume, illustrated with Cherokee designs, gives insight into the animal world.

3.111 Rounds, Glen. **The Three Billy Goats Gruff.** Illustrated by Glen Rounds. Holiday House, 1993. ISBN 0-8234-1015-3. 32p. 5–8.

Glen Rounds offers a lively retelling of the popular Norse tale of the three billy goats outwitting the fierce troll who threatens to devour each one in turn as it attempts to cross the bridge. This version is particularly suitable for readers' theater activities, with print size guiding the reader in oral interpretation. The encounter between the largest billy goat and the troll, for example, is recorded in huge print, demanding that the lines be read loudly and with great force. Young artists will enjoy experimenting with the pastel crayon techniques Rounds uses in his illustrations.

3.112 San Souci, Robert D. **The Faithful Friend.** Illustrated by Brian Pinkney. Simon & Schuster, 1995. ISBN 0-02-786131-7. 40p. 5–8.

Two young men, raised as close as brothers, are threatened by the magic of zombies and an evil curse as they rescue a woman from her uncle. A tale of friendship and loyalty, *The Faithful Friend* has its roots in the folktale traditions of Europe, Africa, and the Americas. This version is set in Martinique, and the lush plantations and Caribbean island life are effectively conveyed in the illustrations. The strong hints of evil that lurk throughout the story are incorporated into Pinkney's scratchboard and oil drawings.

3.113   Sanderson, Ruth, reteller. **Papa Gatto: An Italian Fairy Tale.** Illustrated by Ruth Sanderson. Little, Brown, 1995. ISBN 0-316-77073-6. 32p. 5–10.

This Italian folktale tells of a cat who is advisor to the prince. "Always trustworthy and kind to his fellow townspeople," the cat came to be known as Papa Gatto. Papa Gatto seeks a woman to care for his motherless kittens, and so begins this tale of kind and unkind daughters. The kind one, with her hard work and kind heart, wins her just reward in the end. The rich illustrations, with their delightful cats, evoke the style and culture of the fabulously wealthy merchant princes of the Italian Renaissance.

3.114   Sanfield, Steve. **Strudel, Strudel, Strudel.** Illustrated by Emily Lisker. Orchard, 1995. ISBN 0-531-06879-X. 32p. 4–8.

Author Steve Sanfield owes his inspiration for this original story to traditional tales from Jewish folklore. *Strudel, Strudel, Strudel* tells of a wise but zany teacher and his wife, whose passion for apple strudel results in some crazy consequences, including the passing of three absurd new laws in the village. The warm and engaging humor that characterizes Sanfield's text extends to Lisker's folk-art style oil paintings.

3.115   Sawyer, Ruth. **The Remarkable Christmas of the Cobbler's Sons.** Illustrated by Barbara Cooney. Viking, 1994. ISBN 0-670-84922-7. 32p. 5–8.

This is a new edition of the Austrian folktale first published as "Schnitzle, Schnotzle, and Schnootzle" in Ruth Sawyer's *The Long Christmas* (1941). It is the story of a poor cobbler's family whose potentially bleak Christmas is made merry by a visit from Laurin, King of the Goblins. The goblin king is so impressed by the children's kindness in sharing their own meager comforts that he rewards them with generous gifts. Sawyer would have been delighted with Barbara Cooney's illustrations, which so beautifully match her own remarkable text.

3.116   Scheidl, Gerda Marie. **Loretta and the Little Fairy.** Illustrated by Christa Unzner-Fischer. North-South, 1993. ISBN 1-55858-185-5. 64p. 6–8.

The Little Fairy has been sent to live with humans until she "grows up." Loretta, one of the humans, has a mean streak but tries to find important growing-up experiences for the little fairy such as learning to bake and going to school. However, the solution to the Little Fairy's quest has more to do with Karen, a shy neighbor girl whom Loretta treats meanly. Charming, contemporary German-flavored illustrations appear on every page. This book is translated from German.

3.117 Schroeder, Alan. **The Stone Lion.** Illustrated by Todd L. W. Doney. Scribners, 1994. ISBN 0-684-19578-X. 32p. 5–8.

This picture storybook is based on a folktale plot familiar in all countries, that of the good brother and the wicked brother. The story is well told and successfully conveys the value of honesty and of respect for the environment. The oil paintings in tones of gold and blue highlight the grandeur of the Tibetan mountains.

3.118 Shepard, Aaron, reteller. **The Gifts of Wali Dad: A Tale of India and Pakistan.** Illustrated by Daniel San Souci. Atheneum, 1995. ISBN 0-684- 19445-7. 32p. 5–8.

This is a heartwarming and humorous tale of a poor man with the heart of a king who finds that gifts can be a mixed blessing. Not a word is out of place in Aaron Shepard's superb retelling. San Souci, award-winning illustrator, has created pictures that capture the enchanting characters and exotic setting without overpowering the story.

3.119 Strangis, Joel. **Grandfather's Rock.** Illustrated by Ruth Gamper. Houghton Mifflin, 1993. ISBN 0-395-65367-3. 31p. 5–7.

This traditional tale of the extended family is realistic but humorous. Four children convince their father not to send their grandfather, whom they love dearly, to a home for the elderly. The illustrations are moderately impressionistic with considerable detail and a feel for the Italian countryside.

3.120 Temple, Frances. **Tiger Soup.** Illustrated by Frances Temple. Orchard, 1994. ISBN 0-531-06859-5. 32p. 5–8.

Accounts of trickster Anansi's attempts to outwit creatures larger and stronger than himself offer universal appeal. This tale of the spider's sly effort to rob Tiger of the delicious soup he has prepared is no exception. The retelling is particularly charming because it captures the rhythm and music inherent in the spoken language of the people of Jamaica, where the story originates. Temple complements her text with lively collages created from brilliantly colored tissue paper. Included inside the book jacket is a script of the story complete with suggestions for musical accompaniment.

3.121   Thurber, James. **The Great Quillow.** Illustrated by Steven Kellogg. Harcourt Brace, 1994. ISBN 0-15-232544-1. 56p. 6–8.

The giant Hunder pillages villages until the toymaker Quillow cleverly tricks him into drowning himself in the sea. This story is well crafted, an admirable successor to Jack, the giant killer. Steven Kellogg's illustrations create a whimsical world, teeming along the margins of the text. This is a modern fairy tale with the quality of a classic.

3.122   Trivizas, Eugene. **The Three Little Wolves and the Big Bad Pig.** Illustrated by Helen Oxenbury. Macmillan, 1993. ISBN 0-689-50569-8. 32p. 5–9.

Storytellers continue to find inspiration in the old tales by poking fun at them, rewriting them, or revising them. Here, the sweet little wolves build modern houses and the bad pig wrecks them with modern destruction methods. It all works quite well and ends happily. Oxenbury's illustrations are among her best. Children will enjoy comparing this story with the original.

3.123   Uchida, Yoshiko, reteller. **The Magic Purse.** Illustrated by Keiko Narahashi. Macmillan, 1993. ISBN 0-689-50559-0. 32p. 5–8.

This traditional Japanese romantic folktale is retold with dignity and simplicity. A poor young farmer sets out on a journey to the Iseh shrine. On the way he agrees to accomplish a dangerous task for a strange young girl he meets at the dreaded Black Swamp, and she gives him a magic purse in gratitude. The farmer then sets out to deliver a letter from the girl to her parents at the legendary and fearsome Red Swamp. The watercolor illustrations are in a traditional Japanese style, but vary effectively with the flow of the story.

3.124   Van Laan, Nancy. **The Tiny, Tiny Boy and the Big, Big Cow.** Illustrated by Marjorie Priceman. Knopf, 1993. ISBN 0-679-82078-7. 32p. 5–7.

This is a lesser-known cumulative tale of the same genre as "The Little Old Woman and Her Pig." In this story, a little boy tries all sorts of tricks to make a cow stand still so that he can milk her. Nancy Van Laan describes her work as an adaptation of the Scottish folktale "The Wee, Wee Mannie and the Big, Big Coo" found in Joseph Jacob's *More English Fairytales* (1894). The rich rhymes and rhythms of Van Laan's version should quickly establish it as a familiar favorite with young children.

3.125 Villoldo, Alberto. **Skeleton Woman.** Illustrated by Yoshi. Simon & Schuster, 1995. ISBN 0-689-80279-X. 32p. 5–8.

When a tsunami arrives with no warning and devastates an Aleut village, the beloved Annuk is buried in the sea floor. Years later, a fisherman catches her bones and brings her home to his igloo. He places her in the warmth next to him, where she is miraculously restored to life by his attentions. Thereafter, they live their days out peacefully on the seashore. Just as Annuk's loving spirit animates her skeleton, this dramatic and enchanting story brings the Aleutian Islands to life.

3.126 Walker, Paul Robert. **Giants! Stories from Around the World.** Illustrated by James Bernardin. Harcourt Brace, 1995. ISBN 0-15-200883-7. 73p. 8–12.

This well-researched collection of folktales about giants is presented with interesting theories and facts about the origins of the belief in giants and a brief history of the folktales themselves. Each tale has a full-page illustration in gouache and pencil crayon that is sure to be a hit with monster lovers. Smaller drawings sprinkled throughout the book reveal the human interest of the stories. This book would be a good model for intermediate students doing research projects on monsters or supernatural beings.

3.127 Wang, Rosalind C., reteller. **The Treasure Chest.** Illustrated by Will Hillenbrand. Holiday House, 1995. ISBN 1-8234-1114-1. 32p. 5–8.

In the best of the fairy tale tradition, a poor young man, with the help of his beautiful and wise betrothed, overcomes a corrupt ruler with magical aid earned by an act of unselfish kindness. This tale from China is not as well known as it deserves to be. The illustrations echo the style of Sung Dynasty paintings. They suit the story and satisfy the eye. In addition to its cultural contribution, this book could be used as an impetus for a discussion of the value of kindness.

3.128 Wolff, Patricia Rae. **The Toll-Bridge Troll.** Illustrated by Kimberly Bulcken Root. Harcourt Brace, 1995. ISBN 0-15-277665-6. 24p. 5–7.

On Trigg's first day of school, his mother warns him of the troll living beneath the bridge. Unable to meet the troll's demand for a penny per crossing, Trigg suggests a riddle in lieu of payment.

The poor troll cannot match Trigg's wit and decides on another course of action. Pen-and-ink illustrations capture the lightheartedness of a troll who cannot make it as a scary and disgusting creature. Children will delight in the riddles and the unusual troll.

3.129 Yep, Laurence, reteller. **The Shell Woman and the King: A Chinese Folktale.** Illustrated by Yang Ming-Yi. Dial, 1993. ISBN 0-8037-1395-9. 32p. 6–9.

In classic folktale tradition, a mysterious and talented wife outwits a tyrant by using her magical gift of transformation to complete three seemingly impossible tasks. This retelling of a centuries-old Chinese story invites comparison with numerous folktales of other cultures. Laurence Yep creates dramatic interest in the adventure, and Yang Ming-Yi's watercolor illustrations add to the authenticity and beauty of this engaging picture book.

3.130 Yolen, Jane. **Here There Be Dragons.** Illustrated by David Wilgus. Harcourt Brace, 1993. ISBN 0-15-209888-7. 149p. 9–11.

This collection of stories and poems is steeped in Jane Yolen's deep knowledge of and connection with the folk beliefs and traditions of the past. Here these traditions relate to dragons, the mythical beasts that in Western culture have come to represent our fear of and struggle with the unknown. The eight stories and five poems present dragons from many perspectives. Yolen gives us ferocious, fighting dragons that must be slain along with dragons that inspire sympathy and protectiveness. She prefaces each story with an inspiring personal comment regarding its inception. Every item in this collection is superbly written.

3.131 Young, Ed. **Donkey Trouble.** Illustrated by Ed Young. Atheneum, 1995. ISBN 0-689-31854-5. 32p. 5–8.

Spare but beautiful, simple but rich language and illustrations work together to create this treasure. This well-known tale of an old man and his grandson taking their donkey to market remains accessible to old and young alike. Ed Young, who has won many awards for his highly original illustrations, has produced a stunning book. The collage technique will inspire art projects and the message of the story—that people must follow their own hearts—is one that everyone can benefit from.

Myths and Legends

3.132   Aliki. **The Gods and Goddesses of Olympus.** Illustrated by Aliki. HarperCollins, 1994. ISBN 0-06-023530-6. 48p. 6–9.

After retelling the beginning of the Greek pantheon of the gods succinctly, Aliki provides a brief description of the history and character of each major Olympian. With its accessible text and appealing illustrations, this book is a useful introduction to Greek mythology for elementary school children.

3.133   Bernhard, Emery, reteller. **The Tree That Rains: The Flood Myth of the Huichol Indians of Mexico.** Illustrated by Durga Bernhard. Holiday House, 1994. ISBN 0-8234-1108-7. 32p. 6–9.

The text and unique artwork in this retelling of the flood myth of the Huichol Indians of the Sierra Madre in western Mexico reflect knowledge gained from the Bernhards' study of the culture of the indigenous peoples of Mexico and Central America. It is the story of Nakawe, Great-grandmother Earth, who causes great flooding on the earth to punish its inhabitants, who have been negligent in honoring their gods. Nakawe allows Watakame, a farmer, to survive, instructing him to build a boat, packing it with corn, beans, and squash seeds. Once the flood subsides, Watakame, with Nakawe's help, plants the grains and seeds, and so renews the earth's bounty. In an interesting author's note, Emery Bernhard reports that Huichol shamans recite this myth every year at the Harvest Festival of the New Corn and Squash in thankfulness to the divine mother of the earth and to the rain goddesses.

3.134   Bierhorst, John. **The Woman Who Fell from the Sky.** Illustrated by Robert Andrew Parker. Morrow, 1993. ISBN 0-688-10680-3. 32p. 5–8.

The Iroquois creation tale is retold looking back, "before the world was new," in sky country with sky people. This is the story of a woman whose husband pushes her from the sky. She gives birth to two children, gentle Sapling and hard Flint; their births explain such phenomena as the harshness of cold winters and the two pathways of the Milky Way. This complex version has been adapted from various texts and covers many different aspects of creation.

3.135   Bruchac, Joseph, reteller. **The Great Ball Game: A Muskogee Story.** Illustrated by Susan L. Roth. Dial, 1994. ISBN 0-8037-1540-4. 32p. 5–8.

The animals and birds settle a dispute by playing a ball game. But where does bat fit in? Is he animal or bird? This is a simply told Native American legend. The collage illustrations have tremendous vitality and show that the game is a form of lacrosse.

3.136   Bruchac, Joseph, and Gayle Ross. **The Story of the Milky Way: A Cherokee Tale.** Illustrated by Virginia A. Stroud. Dial, 1995. ISBN 0-8037- 1738-5. 32p. 5–10.

This tale explains how a young boy and an old wise woman work together to rid the tribe of a magical dog that is eating their food. The trail the dog leaves creates the Milky Way. The language is spare and carries the content of the legend with ease. The colors of the charming illustrations are especially appealing. The informative notes by the illustrator and the two storytellers, all Cherokee, make this book useful for social studies. Joseph Bruchac is a highly regarded collector of Native American folklore.

3.137   Ehlert, Lois. **Mole's Hill: A Woodland Tale.** Illustrated by Lois Ehlert. Harcourt Brace, 1994. ISBN 0-15-255116-6. 34p. 5–7.

When Fox tells Mole she must move to make way for a new path, Mole finds an ingenious way to save her home. This story evolved from a fragment of the Seneca legend "When Friends Fall Out." The language is simple but satisfying. Ehlert's striking collages are inspired by the decorative style and technique of the Woodland Indians. This is an enjoyable tale of creative problem-solving and is ideal for teaching cooperation in the classroom.

3.138   Galouchko, Annouchka Gravel. **Sho and the Demons of the Deep.** Illustrated by Annouchka Gravel Galouchko. Annick, 1995. ISBN 1- 55037-398-6. 32p. 5–8.

Annouchka Gravel Galouchko, in her first attempt as an author after a successful career as a children's illustrator, presents her version of this popular Japanese tale relating the origin of kites. The text is a translation by Stephen Daigle of the original French text, *Sho et les dragons d'eau.* Although the tale is respectfully dedicated to "Hokusai," her "guide and inspiration," it is not clear whether the tale is drawn from a Japanese source or is totally original. Clearly, however, the illustrations in gouache are heavily influenced by Japanese artistic traditions, providing a richly detailed and regal backdrop for this magical tale. It is about a girl's courage in saving her people from the demons of the deep, demons created when the villagers thoughtlessly cast their nightmares into the sea.

3.139 Goble, Paul. **Adopted by the Eagles: A Plains Indian Story of Friendship and Treachery.** Illustrated by Paul Goble. Bradbury, 1994. ISBN 0-02-736575-1. 32p. 5–8.

This story about friendship and betrayal is based in the Lakota Indian tradition, revolving around two friends, White Hawk and Tall Bear, and their venture into enemy country to hunt for horses. Despite their sacred bond, their friendship suffers from jealousy and Tall Bear, who is abandoned by his friend, is adopted by eagles on top of a mountain cliff. Can he survive in the wilderness among the Eagle Nation? The story's strong message about the kinship between humans and nature is underlined by the rich India ink and watercolor illustrations by this award-winning artist.

3.140 Goble, Paul, reteller. **Iktomi and the Buzzard: A Plains Indian Story.** Illustrated by Paul Goble. Orchard, 1994. ISBN 0-531-06812-9. unpaged. 5–8.

In Goble's fifth story of the Great Plains trickster figure, the sly and sometimes stupid Iktomi plots a way to get across a river without getting wet. In this instance, Iktomi has taken the form of a human who can shrink to a size small enough for Buzzard to carry through the air. Poetic language and a blend of visual and textual humor characterize this book. Goble uses inviting italic script and varying font sizes. Bright watercolor illustrations in Goble's characteristic flat style add to the sense of playfulness in this morality tale. References and notes to the reader provide a good source of additional information about Iktomi stories and themes.

3.141 Goble, Paul. **The Lost Children: The Boys Who Were Neglected.** Illustrated by Paul Goble. Bradbury, 1993. ISBN 0-02-736555-7. 32p. 5–8.

Children who are neglected and abused can be called "lost." This Blackfoot legend tells of how a group of neglected children became the stars we call the Pleiades. Traditional Blackfoot designs in bright, bold colors complement the simple text. Explanatory notes are provided.

3.142 Greene, Ellin. **The Legend of the Cranberry: A Paleo-Indian Tale.** Illustrated by Brad Sneed. Simon & Schuster, 1993. ISBN 0-671-75975- 2. 33p. 5–8.

This fascinating legend from the time when mastodons still roamed North America is beautifully illustrated by Brad Sneed.

The story tells of how the Paleo-Indians used the mastodons as beasts of burden. The huge beasts become violent and untrustworthy. Finally the Great Spirit tells the people they must destroy the Yah-qua-whee, the mastodons. The author's note at the end of the tale identifies the source of the legend and describes what scientists know and what they surmise about the Paleo-Indians and how they captured and killed the mastodons.

3.143 Greene, Jacqueline Dembar. **Manabozho's Gifts: Three Chippewa Tales.** Illustrated by Jennifer Hewitson. Houghton Mifflin, 1994. ISBN 0-395-69251-2. 40p. 7–10.

These three simply told legends of the great trickster hero of many of the eastern Native American groups are immediately ready for telling or reading aloud. The illustrations are simply and dramatically presented.

3.144 Hausman, Gerald, reteller. **How Chipmunk Got Tiny Feet: Native American Animal Origin Stories.** Illustrated by Ashley Wolff. HarperCollins, 1995. ISBN 0-06-022906-3. 47p. 5–8.

This is a collection of seven Native American origin tales. These simple, often humorous tales are ready for telling aloud without further cutting or refining. The full-page colored illustrations are realistic, with just a hint of a cartoon quality.

3.145 Larry, Charles. **Peboan and Seegwun.** Illustrated by Charles Larry. Farrar, Straus, 1993. ISBN 0-374-35773-0. 32p. 5–8.

This simplified retelling and reshaping of the traditional Ojibwa legend, which explains the changing of the seasons, is often difficult to follow, particularly when one tries to relate specific illustrations to the text. Charles Larry's full-page illustrations are nicely and authentically detailed; the portrait of Seegwun, the spirit of winter, is particularly impressive.

3.146 Lasky, Kathryn. **Cloud Eyes.** Illustrated by Barry Moser. Harcourt Brace, 1994. ISBN 0-15-219168-2. 32p. 6–9.

This tale of Cloud Eyes's courage and ingenuity contains a lesson that is both timely and timeless: All creatures must learn to exist together to survive. Barry Moser's pencil illustrations, realistic yet almost mystical in their detailing, provide the perfect complement to Lasky's magical tale. At the end of the legend, the world is left with the sweetness of the honeybee's gold, never again to be lost. The reader is left with the sweetness of a truly memorable legend.

3.147 Lemieux, Michele, reteller. **The Pied Piper of Hamelin.** Illustrated by Michele Lemieux. Morrow, 1993. ISBN 0-688-09848-7tr, 0-688-09849-5lib. 32p. 5–7.

The fascinating story of the piper who could attract rats or children with his music has inspired many retellings. French Canadian Michele Lemieux uses her talents with oil painting and words to create a story that is compelling in its simplicity. A brief historical background of the legend concludes the book, inviting readers to investigate what is known of the facts and fictions that surround the disappearance of the children of Hamelin centuries ago.

3.148 Lester, Julius. **John Henry.** Illustrated by Jerry Pinkney. Dial, 1994. ISBN 0-8037-1607-9. 40p. 6–9.

As a folk legend, John Henry belongs in the company of other larger-than-life heroes such as Paul Bunyan, Davey Crockett, and the Irish giant Finn McCool. However, John Henry leaves us with a more poignant memory because this story records his death, as well as his incredible feats of strength and kindness, with a rainbow draped around his shoulders. The writing, with its rhythm, exaggerated humor, and a few African American colloquialisms, is worthy of this author of *The Tales of Uncle Remus* and *To Be a Slave.* The full-page and double-page watercolors convey the pride and dignity inherent in the tale.

3.149 MacGill-Callahan, Sheila. **When Solomon Was King.** Illustrated by Stephen T. Johnson. Dial, 1995. ISBN 0-8037-1590-0. 32p. 5–10.

While still a very young man, Solomon befriends a wounded lion. Years later, when the great King Solomon has forgotten humility, he meets with the lion again. This beautiful story reminds us that hunting for pleasure is an act of cruelty. The large illustrations depict the beauty of the lion and the natural world. The language is powerful and the message clear without being didactic. This book would be a good discussion-starter for any grade level.

3.150 McCaughrean, Geraldine. **Greek Myths.** Illustrated by Emma Chichester Clark. Macmillan, 1993. ISBN 0-689-50583-3. 96p. 9–11.

Geraldine McCaughrean brings her formidable creative powers to this unique collection of Greek myths. She mixes together the well-known and the more obscure. Persephone is here and King Midas, too, but so are Echo and Arachne. The stories are both playful and true to their sources. Emma Chichester Clark emphasizes the lively humor in her bright watercolor illustrations.

3.151   McDermott, Gerald. **Coyote: A Trickster Tale from the American Southwest.** Illustrated by Gerald McDermott. Harcourt Brace, 1994. ISBN 0-15-220724-4. 32p. 5–8.

Gerald McDermott's fascination with trickster tales is evident in this delightfully retold Zuni legend of Coyote. As often happens with Coyote, his boastfulness and his envy of others lead him into trouble. This time he wants to sing, dance, and fly like the crows and, of course, he brags about his skill in doing so. The simple yet elegant language allows even very young readers to enjoy the text. As always, McDermott's bold and brilliant illustrations, here inspired by Zuni folklore and southwestern design, are captivating.

3.152   McDermott, Gerald. **Raven: A Trickster Tale from the Pacific Northwest.** Illustrated by Gerald McDermott. Harcourt Brace, 1993. ISBN 0-15-265661-8. 32p. 5–8.

Raven, the Trickster, is a familiar character in Pacific Northwest tales of the First Nations. Through the voice of a storyteller, Raven explains how the sun was stolen from the Sky Chief and given to humans. This legend invites comparisons with similar myths from many other cultures. The illustrations, which incorporate artifacts from several First Nations tribes, are vividly presented in a watercolor wash. *Raven* provides opportunities for children to explore the beliefs and the visual and oral expressions of First Nations cultures in an entertaining picture book.

3.153   Meeks, Arone Raymond. **Enora and the Black Crane: An Aboriginal Story.** Illustrated by Arone Raymond Meeks. Scholastic, 1993. ISBN 0-590-46375-6. 32p. 5–9.

This stirring legend from aboriginal Australian folklore captivates its readers with the story of Enora, a young man whose curiosity about the hidden place in the bush where the birds gather defies the respect for nature his family tries to teach him. Enora learns a solemn lesson when he interferes with the beauty of the natural world. The stunning artwork by aboriginal artist Arone Raymond Meeks beautifully underlines this message and lets young readers share in the richness of his cultural heritage. This book is superb for reading aloud or adaptation.

3.154   Ober, Hal. **How Music Came to the World.** Illustrated by Carol Ober. Houghton Mifflin, 1994. ISBN 0-395-67523-5. 32p. 5–7.

This traditional Mexican myth recounts how the gods of wind and sky put aside their differences to bring music to the world. Dramatic pastel illustrations in traditional Mexican motifs add to the richness of the legend. Topics such as cooperation, music, Mexican culture, and world mythology could easily be explored through this story.

3.155 Oppenheim, Shulamith Levey, reteller. **Iblis.** Illustrated by Ed Young. Harcourt Brace, 1994. ISBN 0-15-238016-7. 32p. 7–9.

This retelling of the Islamic creation myth focuses on Iblis, the great Satan, the tempter, rather than on the traditional role Eve plays in the fall of humankind. With the help of an easily swayed peacock and serpent, Iblis is able to enter Paradise and convince Eve to eat the forbidden fruit, evoking the rage of a clearly vengeful God: "Darkness shall be her den, and dust shall be her food." Ed Young's stunning watercolor illustrations provide a frighteningly surrealistic accompaniment to the tale. In fact, the final portraits of the vengeful God's casting of Iblis into hell may be a bit disturbing for some children.

3.156 Oughton, Jerrie. **The Magic Weaver of Rugs: A Tale of the Navajo.** Illustrated by Lisa Desimini. Houghton Mifflin, 1994. ISBN 0-395-66140-4. 32p. 5–8.

This book is a poetic telling of a traditional Navajo legend. Spider Woman hears two women praying for help for their starving families. Moved by their words, Spider Woman teaches them to shear sheep, to cord, wash, and dye wool, and to weave rugs. The women, in turn, teach these skills to their people, thereby making them all prosperous. The simple, colorful illustrations evoke the desert and the Navajo way of life.

3.157 Pilling, Ann. **Realms of Gold: Myths and Legends from Around the World.** Illustrated by Kady MacDonald Denton. Kingfisher, 1993. ISBN 1-85697-913-X. 93p. 9–11.

Myths of eight cultures are recounted, ranging from Native American to West African and including one Norse and three Greek retellings. The illustrations dance in varied steps across every page and country.

3.158 Rappaport, Doreen. **The Long-Haired Girl: A Chinese Legend.** Illustrated by Yang Ming-Yi. Dial, 1995. ISBN 0-8037-1412-2. 32p. 5–8.

This Chinese legend is about a young peasant girl willing to test her strength against the God of Thunder for the survival of her village. It is retold in the straightforward and beloved style of fairy tales. The heroism of the girl is a good contrast to the passive heroines in some of our better-known fairy tales. Yang Ming-Yi, an award-winning artist trained in China, has illustrated the text with beautiful thick-lined woodcuts filled with soft color washes of watercolor and inks.

3.159 Rodanas, Kristina, adapter. **Dance of the Sacred Circle: A Native American Tale.** Illustrated by Kristina Rodanas. Little, Brown, 1994. ISBN 0-316-75358-0. 32p. 5–10.

In this tale based on a Blackfoot legend, a young boy is able to save his tribe from hunger by bringing them a special gift from the Great Chief in the Sky. With the help of the sacred council of all the trees, animals, and birds, the Great Chief creates a creature that will help the tribe to continue the buffalo hunt so necessary for their survival. The boy, an orphan and outsider before, gains the respect of his tribe and earns an important place as keeper of the Great Chief's gift. The earth tones of the page-and-a-half illustrations greatly enhance the mood and content of the story.

3.160 Sabuda, Robert, reteller. **Arthur and the Sword.** Illustrated by Robert Sabuda. Atheneum, 1995. ISBN 0-689-31987-8. 32p. 6–9.

This is a faithful, if simplified, retelling of Malory's account of Arthur drawing the sword Excalibur from the stone and becoming King of England. The illustrations are like brilliant Gothic stained glass windows. They convey a sense of action and show a great variety of facial expression appropriate to the characters. This picture book is a simplified version of a classic that could lead to a yearning for the original tale.

3.161 San Souci, Robert D. **The Snow Wife.** Illustrated by Stephen T. Johnson. Dial, 1993. ISBN 0-8037-1410-6. 32p. 5–8.

In the tradition of *The Crane Wife* (Sumiko Yagawa) and *Dawn* (Molly Bang), a poor young woodcutter marries a beautiful but mysterious wife who must leave him when he breaks his vow of secrecy. In this story he sets out on a difficult journey to win her back, facing three supernatural challenges before he is able to convince the Wind God to restore her to him. The paintings of Stephen T. Johnston enhance the ethereal, ghostly impressions of the tale. Many connections to the literature of other cultures can be made. *The Snow Wife* is also very suitable for use in a discussion of reading and writing strategies.

3.162 Sloat, Teri, reteller. **The Hungry Giant of the Tundra.** Illustrated by Robert Sloat and Teri Sloat. Dutton, 1993. ISBN 0-525-45126-9. 32p. 5–8.

This Yupik tale provides an entertaining lesson on the consequences of ignoring the good advice of your elders. Dusk is falling but the young children are enjoying their outdoor play and fail to heed their parents' anxious calls. Momentarily the sky darkens further with the shadow of the dreaded Akaguagankak, giant of the tundra. He snaps up the children in his enormous hands and boasts of his plans to eat them for dinner. Only with the help of clever crane and chickadee do the children escape. Teri Sloat first heard this story when she worked as a teacher in Bethel, Alaska. Her simple yet vivid writing preserves some of the flavor of its oral roots and illustrator Robert Sloat creates a suitably scary giant.

3.163 Stafford, Kim R. **We Got Here Together.** Illustrated by Debra Frasier. Harcourt Brace, 1994. ISBN 0-15-294891-0. 34p. 5–7.

This remarkable tale, set in the context of a bedtime story told by a father to his young daughter, is "a song of water, rising and falling." It is also the story of a bubble that rises from the ocean to become part of the air and, simultaneously, a raindrop that returns to become part of the ocean. This provides a metaphor for continuity in the natural world and in the world of the father and daughter. Debra Frasier's brilliant illustrations, patterned paper dyed in a traditional Japanese process usually reserved for cloth, provide a richly textured backdrop for Stafford's elegantly simple tale. The result is a brilliant blending of the talents of two extremely gifted artists.

3.164 Stevens, Janet. **Coyote Steals the Blanket: A Ute Tale.** Illustrated by Janet Stevens. Holiday House, 1993. ISBN 0-8234-0996-1. 32p. 5–8.

Trickster Coyote's arrogance does not allow him to accept advice from anyone. This time he ignores hummingbird's warning to not touch some beautiful blankets laid over some boulders in the desert. Coyote steals a blanket, only to discover one of the boulders tumbling after him. Hummingbird saves Coyote's life after he promises to forever obey the spirit of the great desert. Janet Stevens has retold and illustrated this story in a style that will have particular appeal for young children.

3.165   Taylor, Harriet Peck, reteller. **Coyote and the Laughing Butter-flies.** Illustrated by Harriet Peck Taylor. Macmillan, 1995. ISBN 0-02-788846-0. 26p. 5–7.

In this First Nations story from the southwestern United States, Coyote is tricked by some butterflies. The butterflies laugh so hard at their joke that they cannot fly straight—a delightful image. White outlines instead of black lend a luminous quality to the appealing illustrations fashioned from batik on silk.

3.166   Van Laan, Nancy. **Buffalo Dance: A Blackfoot Legend.** Illustrated by Beatriz Vidal. Little, Brown, 1993. ISBN 0-316-89728-0. 32p. 6–8.

This legend of the Blackfoot people explains the origin of the ritual dance that preceded and followed the buffalo hunt. The buffalo were a major source of food, clothing, and shelter for the Blackfoot, who performed the dance to demonstrate their respect and gratitude. Nancy Van Laan's retelling and Beatriz Vidal's illustrations reflect careful research. This story provokes important thoughts about the relationship between human beings and the natural environment.

3.167   Vuong, Lynette Dyer. **Sky Legends of Vietnam.** Illustrated by Vo-Dinh Mai. HarperCollins, 1993. ISBN 0-06-023000-2. 103p. 9–11.

This book is a collection of short stories based on Vietnamese legends and fairy tales: Fairies leave their homes in the sky to enter the lives of humans, a tree has magical healing powers, and lovers become stars. These six tales, derived from several Asian cultures over centuries, invite comparison with folktales from around the world. The book provides a brief section of background information and a pronunciation guide to assist readers with unfamiliar names.

3.168   Waldherr, Kris. **Persephone and the Pomegranate: A Myth from Greece.** Illustrated by Kris Waldherr. Dial, 1993. ISBN 0-8037-1192-1. 32p. 7–10.

The Greek myth of Demeter and Persephone explains the origins of the seasons. Persephone, the daughter of Demeter, goddess of the harvest, has been abducted by Pluto to live with him in the Underworld. Grieved by the loss of her daughter, Demeter allows nothing to grow on earth. Upset that the earth has become barren, Zeus, the chief god, leads Demeter to her daughter. Persephone agrees to spend half of each year with her mother on earth and the other half with Pluto in the Underworld. When Persephone and Demeter are together the earth enjoys spring and summer. Persephone's return to the Underworld signals the beginning of winter. Kris Waldherr is best known as an illustrator and her remarkable paintings in oil and pastels greatly enrich the text.

3.169 Wood, Audrey. **The Rainbow Bridge.** Illustrated by Robert Florczak. Harcourt Brace, 1995. ISBN 0-15-265475-5. unpaged. 5–9.

Audrey Wood admits she has taken artistic liberties in her adaptation of an oral Chumash tale, but her attention to detail and her initial storyteller's note clearly indicate her respect for the people and culture that created the tale. The tale tells of the origin of humankind, created by the goddess Hutash; the subsequent discovery of fire; and, finally, Hutash's creation of a rainbow bridge that allows half of the tribe to relocate on Limuw, or what is now Santa Cruz island. Robert Florczak's illustrations are paintings executed with layers of transparent oil glazes that provide an almost three-dimensional depth. The tale ends with the portrayal of dolphins frolicking in the sea, dolphins created from people who fell from the rainbow bridge. Florczak's final paintings make us feel that we, too, are in the sea, swimming with these wondrous creatures.

3.170 Young, Ed. **Moon Mother.** Illustrated by Ed Young. HarperCollins, 1993. ISBN 0-06-021301-9. 34p. 5–8.

This Native American creation myth is rich with tender and profound images of the life cycle. A spirit man visits the earth and creates animal and human life for companionship. He then leaves the humans to mate with a spirit woman. The people discover that the couple has left behind their child, who eventually becomes the first wife of the chieftain. This legend, which describes this separation of earthly creatures from the spirit people, is also the story of the moon, whose face in the sky is that of the first spirit woman. She leaves her daughter on earth as a gift and a reminder of the link with the spirits. Ed Young's succinct yet lyrical text is amplified by impressionistic pastel paintings that shimmer with mystery.

3.171 Zeman, Ludmila. **The Last Quest of Gilgamesh.** Illustrated by Ludmila Zeman. Tundra, 1995. ISBN 0-88776-328-6. unpaged. 7–10.

This is the final book in the illustrated trilogy of the epic of Gilgamesh, one of the world's oldest stories. The preceding books are *Gilgamesh the King* and *The Revenge of Ishtar.* Initially inscribed onto clay tablets in Mesopotamia, this universal quest story has survived over five thousand years. Gilgamesh continues his search for immortality, facing an array of adversaries, only to be overcome in the end by exhaustion and sleep. A beloved friend returns from the underworld to show him his true immortality: the kingdom he built. The illustrations are intricately composed to resemble Babylonian artifacts, bas-reliefs, and tablets and are true to the myths and beliefs of the ancient time.

Tall Tales

3.172 Davol, Marguerite W. **Papa Alonzo Leatherby: A Collection of Tall Tales from the Best Storyteller in Carroll County.** Simon & Schuster, 1995. ISBN 0-689-80278-1. 70p. 8–11.

This collection of original tall tales is built around the adventures of the Leatherbys, a turn-of-the-century rural New England family. Papa Alonzo, the clan patriarch and the best storyteller in Carroll County tells the tales. These are not typical tall tales in that they do not focus on the exploits of one particular hero. Instead, they recount strange occasions from Papa's memory, such as the summer when the sun got stuck in the sky. The temperature remained so hot that field corn actually started to pop and the hen laid hard-boiled eggs. This absurdly funny collection is particularly entertaining when read aloud.

3.173 Isaacs, Anne. **Swamp Angel.** Illustrated by Paul O. Zelinsky. Dutton, 1994. ISBN 0-525-45271-0. 40p. 6–8.

Swamp Angel may well become more popular than Paul Bunyan and Finn McCool for her larger-than-life feats of rescue and daring. This original tale with a strong flavor of folklore is set in Tennessee and ends with the heroine's magnificent defeat of the biggest bear in the world. The bear's meat feeds the whole state and ends a famine. Charming oval pictures that give an English Victorian look to American frontier life are contrasted with scenes of activity.

3.174 Shepard, Aaron. **The Legend of Lightning Larry.** Illustrated by Toni Goffe. Scribners, 1993. ISBN 0-684-19433-3. 32p. 6–9.

This tall tale is written in the tradition of the legends of other popular American heroes such as Pecos Bill. Lightning Larry is a tough but kind cowboy. His special way with the bad guys and the bolt of lightning he shoots from his special gun tame even the wildest men. Naturally, Larry becomes the hero to the good folks of Brimstone when he single-handedly takes on Evil-Eye and his gang of thieving marauders. Toni Goffe's illustrations add even more humor to this lively and entertaining tale.

3.175 Shepard, Aaron, reteller. **The Legend of Slappy Hooper: An American Tall Tale.** Illustrated by Toni Goffe. Scribners, 1993. ISBN 0-684-19535-6. 32p. 5–8.

Slappy Hooper is the world's greatest sign painter. Problems arise because Slappy's signs are so realistic that the pictures he paints come alive. Legends of this Depression-era American tall-tale hero were first published in B. A. Botkin's *A Treasury of American Folklore* (1944). Aaron Shepard's lively and updated retelling of one of Slappy's adventures shares the absurd and lighthearted humor found in the stories of more familiar tall-tale heroes such as Pecos Bill and Paul Bunyan. Children will enjoy adding to Slappy's adventures with tales of their own invention.

3.176 Thomassie, Tynia. **Feliciana Feydra LeRoux: A Cajun Tall Tale.** Illustrated by Cat Bowman Smith. Little, Brown, 1995. ISBN 0-316-84125-0. 32p. 5–8.

In this Cajun tall tale, told in a lilting dialect, a young girl wants to go alligator hunting but her Grampa Baby won't let her. She goes anyway, of course, and in the end saves Grampa from a hungry alligator. A history of the Cajun people, a glossary, and a pronunciation guide are included at the beginning of the book. The story is delightful and the lively, action-filled illustrations complement it well.

3.177 Tunnell, Michael O. **Chinook!** Illustrated by Barry Root. Tambourine, 1993. ISBN 0-688-10869-5. 32p. 5–7.

A chinook is a warm, dry air mass that descends the eastern slopes of the American and Canadian Rocky Mountains. It occurs mainly in winter and causes a rise in temperature and thus a rapid melting of snow. Here an old-timer tells tall tales of chinooks to two children from the eastern United States. The exaggerated quality of the storytelling is supported by the lively and colorful artwork.

3.178 Walker, Paul Robert. **Big Men, Big Country: A Collection of American Tall Tales.** Illustrated by James Bernardin. Harcourt Brace, 1993. ISBN 0-15-207136-9. 80p. 6–9.

In this glossy and well-illustrated collection of tall tales, well-known figures of American folklore such as Davy Crockett and John Henry rub shoulders with lesser-known folk such as Ol' Gabe and John Darling. Each tale is followed by a note giving the original source of the tale. This book is of value for young readers and a must for storytellers and storytelling collections.

4 Fantasy

Adventure and Magic

4.1   Alexander, Lloyd. **The Arkadians.** Dutton, 1995. ISBN 0-525-45415-2. 272p. 11–13.

Similar in structure and theme to Alexander's other books, this fantasy is based on ancient Greek geography and mythology. In what is best described as a fantasy romp, the large cast of characters includes Lucien, a young man seeking his calling, as well as an oracle and a poet. These are just a few of the group called the Arkadians who, with humor, daring, and magic, follow their quest across a country torn between two warring factions.

4.2   Cech, John. **Django.** Illustrated by Sharon McGinley-Nally. Four Winds, 1994. ISBN 0-02-765705-1. 40p. 5–7.

As a young boy growing up in northern Florida, Django learns to play the fiddle he inherits from his grandfather. He develops a magical gift through his music, attracting the animals who live in the cypress swamps around his home. When the effects of his music begin to interfere with his duties and his family, Django puts the fiddle away. Eventually, however, Django becomes a legend when he is able to save the animals from a fierce storm through his gift of music.

4.3   Cresswell, Helen. **The Watchers: A Mystery at Alton Towers.** Macmillan, 1994. ISBN 0-02-725371-6. 206p. 10–12.

The story begins strongly in reality when two English children run away from a group home to an amusement park, where they must forage for food and shelter and hide from the authorities. The story then changes to a terrifying fantasy when they discover a parallel world cared for by a gentle magician and peopled with homeless children and find themselves engaged in a battle between good and evil. A powerfully written story with an open ending that makes it particularly chilling.

4.4   Enright, Elizabeth. **Zeee.** Illustrated by Susan Gaber. Harcourt Brace, 1993. ISBN 0-15-299958-2. 48p. 6–9.

One of the Contemporary Classic series, this book is centered around a bad-tempered fairy named Zeee who is visible to animals but not people. She chooses a variety of living quarters, which are always destroyed by people. With the help of creatures such as ants, a snake, and a mole, she seeks her revenge. With the help of a young girl named Pandora, Zeee finds a peaceful place to live. The humorous and dramatic story line flows smoothly and entertainingly. Beautiful, deep-hued watercolor illustrations depict Zeee's delightful miniature world.

4.5   Hathorn, Libby. **Grandma's Shoes.** Illustrated by Elivia. Little, Brown, 1994. ISBN 0-316-35135-0. 32p. 5–7.

In this touching story a young girl discovers that when she puts on the shoes of her beloved grandmother, who has died, she is transported to the magical world that memories create. When she finally finds her grandmother in this magical world, she learns that she must return and tell all that her grandmother has told her. Elivia's abstract watercolors beautifully capture the tone of this picture book fantasy, imaginatively chronicling the heroine's healing process and the magical lesson she learns.

4.6   Hunter, Mollie. **Day of the Unicorn.** Illustrated by Donna Diamond. HarperCollins, 1994. ISBN 0-06-021062-1. 61p. 7–10.

In this sequel to *The Knight of the Golden Plain* and *The Three-Day Enchantment,* young Sir Dauntless answers a distress call from Lady Dorabella, only to find himself challenged with a far more difficult task than he had anticipated. A rampaging unicorn must be caught and restored to the tapestry from which it had escaped, but Dorabella is the only one who can do it. Although he wants to rush to her rescue, Sir Dauntless can only lend support and trust in her courage. Young readers will enjoy this updated telling of a magical story in which children are the doers of heroic deeds. Lovely black-and-white illustrations enhance the story.

4.7   Kinsey-Warnock, Natalie. **On a Starry Night.** Illustrated by David McPhail. Orchard, 1994. ISBN 0-531-06820-X. 32p. 5–7.

Natalie Kinsey-Warnock tells the simple tale of a young girl's imaginative response to a starry night, a special experience she shares with her parents on the hill just above their farm. David McPhail's luminous paintings add the sense of wonder that the girl experiences as she soars on the back of Pegasus, totally immersing herself in the magic that only such a night can bring. This is an excellent text to read to children on a starry night.

4.8	Mayne, William. **Hob and the Goblins.** Dorling Kindersley, 1994. ISBN 1-56458-713-4. 140p. 10–12.

Hob, an ancient house spirit, wants a quiet, peaceful life with a normal family that knows how to treat Hobs. Unfortunately, he adopts a family that unconsciously gets into difficulties. The story ends in an amazing swirl of fantasy skillfully orchestrated through Mayne's use of simple but magical language.

4.9	Napoli, Donna Jo. **Jimmy: The Pickpocket of the Palace.** Illustrated by Judith Byron Schachner. Dutton, 1995. ISBN 0-525-45357-1. 166p. 10–12.

In this variation on the tale of the frog prince, the prince's frog son, Jimmy, must save his home pond from destruction. In pursuing the magic ring that will save the pond and its creatures, Jimmy also begins to unravel the mystery behind his father's disappearance. This novel follows *The Prince of the Pond*, the story of Jimmy's father. Jimmy and his father do not recognize each other until the end, but even young readers will discover the relationship early on. Nevertheless, they will be intrigued to read about the frog's life and family that the prince left behind. These elements, together with the delightful illustrations, are the principal charm of the story.

4.10	Sherman, Josepha. **Gleaming Bright.** Walker, 1994. ISBN 0-8027-8296-5. 170p. 10–12.

This book involves a princess's quest to save herself from a distasteful marriage and her father's kingdom from war. With the help of an enchanted stag, who becomes Prince Charming, she succeeds after some startling adventures. This simply told tale of wizards and magic has a folktale quality that will satisfy young readers who enjoy fantasy.

4.11	Stearns, Michael, editor. **A Wizard's Dozen.** Harcourt Brace, 1993. ISBN 0-15-200965-5. 186p. 10–12.

Twelve short stories by writers of fantasy such as Jane Yolen, Betty Levin, and Patricia Wrede are collected for intermediate to older readers and genuine fantasy buffs. Many of the stories have touches of the quality of Walter de la Mare's short fantasy stories. Most of the plots are highly original and even those based on conventional themes have an unusual and intriguing twist.

4.12   Sterman, Betsy, and Samuel Sterman. **Backyard Dragon.** Illustrated by David Wenzel. HarperCollins, 1993. ISBN 0-06-020783-3. 189p. 9–11.

A dragon from the Middle Ages arrives in modern time through a wizard's mistake. A boy and his grandfather, with the help of a few friends, are finally able to return this dragon to his own time and place in Wales. Life in the past and the present are contrasted. This light, humorous fantasy is appealing, with the magic element well worked out.

4.13   Turner, Ann. **Elfsong.** Harcourt Brace, 1995. ISBN 0-15-200826-8. 168p. 9–12.

Maddy loves to spend the summers with her grandfather in the countryside, where she enjoys being close to nature. One summer promises to be even more enchanting when her search for her missing cat, Sabrina, leads to an exploration of a forest world where elves have lived for hundreds of years. Maddy and her grandfather find that, like the elves, they can hear birds speak and animals quarrel. This suspenseful fantasy, the first of a promised trilogy, is a powerful story that says much about our attitudes and responsibility for the natural world.

4.14   Yolen, Jane. **Wizard's Hall.** Listening Library, 1995. ISBN 0-8072-7568-9. cassette. 9–12.

Jane Yolen uses her storytelling ability to advantage as she reads aloud, in its entirety, her 1991 light fantasy novel *Wizard's Hall*. It is the entertaining story of Henry's adventures with magic that begin when his mother sends him off to Wizard's Hall to be educated as a wizard. It is also the story of what he is able to achieve when he follows his mother's advice to always try his best. The story, along with the large and interesting cast of characters who inhabit it, make this fantasy an ideal listening experience. In fact, it is written in a style that, without too much difficulty, could be worked into a stage or screenplay. Jane Yolen's excellent performance provides a useful model for helping teachers and students improve their oral interpretation skills. Others in the Listening Library series are *The Search for Delicious* by Natalie Babbitt, *Jeremy Thatcher, Dragon Hatcher* by Bruce Coville, and *The Fairy Revel* by Lynne Reid Banks. For each novel the reading aloud is done by its author.

Animal Fantasy

4.15   Andres, Katharine. **Fish Story.** Illustrated by Deloss McGraw. Simon & Schuster, 1993. ISBN 0-671-79270-9. 32p. 6–8.

In this story of a magical encounter, Craig, Anne, their children, Henry and Felix, and their cats, George and Gilbert, meet Otto, a fish who is able to grant wishes and eventually becomes a member of their family. Enriched by evocative, brilliant watercolor art, the story mixes elements of fantasy with everyday events in a family's life to tell about the sometimes funny, sometimes difficult choices everybody has to face when making that one special wish.

4.16   Brown, Marc. **Arthur's New Puppy.** Illustrated by Marc Brown. Little, Brown, 1993. ISBN 0-316-11355-7. 32p. 6–8.

In another delightful tale in the Arthur Adventure series, Marc Brown's beloved character learns about the responsibilities that come with owning a very mischievous new puppy and the challenges of trying to train it. Arthur is the only one in his family who patiently believes he can succeed. Will he be able to prove he is right? Young readers will once again enjoy the humorous dialogue and the expert storytelling in this book and series.

4.17   Chadwick, Tim. **Cabbage Moon.** Illustrated by Piers Harper. Orchard, 1994. ISBN 0-531-06827-7. 28p. 5–7.

In this vividly illustrated tale about a young rabbit's exploration of the world around him, the author combines facts about the natural world and the powers of imagination in a whimsical story line involving a rabbit family. Albert, a very curious bunny, loves to ask questions but hates the cabbage his mother wants him to eat. Through an imaginary trip to the "cabbage moon," Albert learns about the phases of the moon, the difference between adults' and children's perceptions of the world, and the benefits of a good appetite.

4.18   Christian, Peggy. **The Bookstore Mouse.** Illustrated by Gary Lippincott. Harcourt Brace, 1995. ISBN 0-15-200203-0. 134p. 10–12.

In order to escape, a mouse enters the pages of one of the books he is using as a defense against the bookstore cat. Therein, he joins a heroic medieval tale based on the use of words. This is an unusual animal fantasy involving very clever word play. However, the book might be most appealing to the more experienced reader because the use of language is far more sophisticated than that in Norton Juster's *The Phantom Tollbooth*.

4.19   Cowley, Joy. **The Mouse Bride.** Illustrated by David Christiana. Scholastic, 1995. ISBN 0-590-47503-7. 32p. 5–7.

This delightful tale is about a mouse who hates being a mouse because she is so small and weak. One day she is inspired to find someone big and strong to marry so that she can have strong children to compensate for her size. After proposing marriage to the sun, a cloud, the wind, and eventually a house, she is directed to the cellar, where she discovers another mouse. The illustrations are exceptional, drawn from the perspective of a little mouse viewing a looming world. In addition to explorations of perception, this is a good text for exploring themes such as marriage, insecurity, and self-acceptance.

4.20   de Beer, Hans (translated by Silvia Aranap). **Little Polar Bear /El osito polar.** Illustrated by Hans de Beer. North-South, 1994. ISBN 1-55858-358-0 (English); 1-55858-390-4 (Spanish). 26p. 5–8.

A young polar bear is separated from his father during a storm and ends up in a tropical country. Here a friendly hippopotamus arranges for him to get back home on the back of an orca whale. This delightful picture book, with irresistibly appealing animals, contrasts the lands of the north and the south. Editions are available in both English and Spanish.

4.21   Esterl, Arnica. **Okino and the Whales.** Illustrated by Marek Zawadzki. Harcourt Brace, 1995. ISBN 0-15-200377-0. 32p. 6–10.

In this fairy tale within a tale, Okino tells her son a story that was passed down to her from her mother. Okino and her son are waiting on the shores of a bay for the whales to return from the polar seas. As the great beasts appear and begin to leap and spout, Okino tells of Iwa, Queen of the Ocean, who holds her daughter prisoner. Okino agrees to weave a coat from her own hair to secure her daughter's release. With the help of a magic regenerative ointment, she finishes the coat and takes her now-full-grown daughter home. The illustrations match the mystery and grandeur of whales. The paintings fill the pages and the text is superimposed on top. The illustrator uses a gate—called Tori in Japan—to mark the transition into and out of fantasy. This book will augment studies of both whales and fantasy fairy tales.

4.22   Froehlich, Margaret Walden. **That Kookoory!** Illustrated by Marla Frazee. Harcourt Brace, 1995. ISBN 0-15-277650-8. unpaged. 5–8.

Kookoory the rooster is so eager to get to Edgerton Fair that he mistakes the moon for the rising sun and sets off at a very early hour. Along his way he wakes his friends, Grampy Spindleshanks, the Baker, Mrs. Parsley, and baby Babsy. Unknown to the happy-go-lucky Kookoory, a hungry weasel has had his eye on the tasty-looking rooster. In a chase to which Kookoory is completely oblivious, reminiscent of Pat Hutchins' *Rosie's Walk*, the weasel gets what he deserves and more. Whimsical and warmly colored pen-and-ink illustrations complement a text that rolls off the tongue.

4.23 Garner, Alan. **Once upon a Time.** Illustrated by Norman Messenger. Dorling Kindersley, 1993. ISBN 1-56458-381-3. 29p. 5–9.

Alan Garner captures in writing the special qualities of three beloved stories from the oral tradition: "The Fox, the Hare, and the Cock," "The Girl and the Geese," and "Battibeth." The rhythms and repetitions of Garner's language demand audience participation, inviting younger readers to co-tell these tales. The story beginnings and endings, such as "Once upon a time, though it wasn't in your time and it wasn't in my time," immediately transport the listener to the magical world of folklore. Norman Messenger's illustrations offer an exquisite complement to the text.

4.24 Grimsdell, Jeremy. **Kalinzu: A Story from Africa.** Illustrated by Jeremy Grimsdell. Kingfisher, 1993. ISBN 1-85697-886-9. 26p. 5–7.

This story about Kalinzu, a young buffalo calf, is enhanced through realistic illustrations by the author, who works as a biologist in South Africa. Kalinzu learns a lesson about survival in the grasslands of East Africa when she gets separated from her mother, Amani, and has to find her way back to the buffalo herd. Unexpected help arrives from one type of animal, a red-billed oxpecker, that Kalinzu used to think of as a nuisance.

4.25 Hoban, Julia. **Buzby to the Rescue.** Illustrated by John Himmelman. HarperCollins, 1993. ISBN 0-06-021025-7. 64p. 5–8.

Buzby, the hotel cat, helps take care of a special guest, the famous movie star Serena Lovejoy. When Miss Lovejoy's royal ruby disappears, Buzby helps find it. Suspense is created in this simple beginning-to-read chapter book, and Charlie and Louie, two new, suspicious-looking guests, are immediately considered suspects. What actually happened to Miss Lovejoy's ruby remains a mystery right to the end. This An I Can Read Book is well worth including as independent reading fare for beginning readers.

4.26   Hoff, Syd. **Captain Cat.** Illustrated by Syd Hoff. HarperCollins, 1993. ISBN 0-06-020527-X. 46p. 5–8.

This independent beginning-to-read chapter book tells the enjoyable story of a cat who joins the army. Captain Cat learns to march and soon befriends a soldier named Pete. In the course of their army duties, Pete and Captain Cat share several experiences. Finally, at lights-out time, everyone is dreaming of their loved ones: Pete dreams about Captain Cat and Captain Cat about Pete. The endearing qualities of Captain Cat are well portrayed in vibrant-colored line drawings. Cat lovers will readily understand why Pete likes Captain Cat and will find this simple animal story a pleasant reading experience.

4.27   Johnston, Tony. **The Iguana Brothers.** Illustrated by Mark Teague. Scholastic, 1995. ISBN 0-590-47468-5. 28p. 5–7.

This amusing tale of two iguanas, Dom and Tom of Mexico, follows their search for food, identity (are they dinosaurs?), and friendship. The droll illustrations are enlivened with the bright colors of Mexican life, including clothing, plants, wildlife, and buildings. The author uses Spanish words throughout the text in such a way that the meaning remains clear.

4.28   Lester, Helen. **Three Cheers for Tacky.** Illustrated by Lynn Munsinger. Houghton Mifflin, 1994. ISBN 0-395-66841-7. 32p. 6–8.

In this delightful sequel to *Tacky the Penguin,* Helen Lester's endearing, bumbling character tries extra hard to make the team for the Penguin Cheering Contest. However, no matter how much he practices, he is less perfect than his well-organized and synchronized teammates. Tacky's amusing antics, described and illustrated with rich detail, will delight young readers, especially when read aloud. This humorous story also will affirm a positive message about difference and individuality.

4.29   Lisle, Janet Taylor. **Forest.** Orchard, 1993. ISBN 0-531-06803-X. 150p. 10–12.

Amber is a thinker, but she also knows how to take action. When she discovers the treetop world of squirrels above her town, she determines to study them. Similarly, Woodbine is a curious squirrel who would like to know more about the people who live below. When the squirrels and the townspeople come to the brink of war over a misunderstanding, Amber and Woodbine work to avert conflict. The third-person narrative alternates between Amber and Woodbine. Young readers will be intrigued to trace the origins of the conflict and to see the possibility for coexistence among creatures of good will.

4.30   Marshall, James. **Rats on the Range and Other Stories.** Illustrated by James Marshall. Dial, 1993. ISBN 0-8037-1385-1. 80p. 5–7.

The author's sense of fun and imagination does not falter in this sequel to *Rats on the Roof.* This book is excellent for beginning readers and for reading aloud. Eight stories with titles such as "When Pig Went to Heaven" and "Buzzard's Will" are filled with James Marshall's delicious sense of humor and metafictional touches.

4.31   McCully, Emily Arnold. **My Real Family.** Illustrated by Emily A. McCully. Harcourt Brace, 1994. ISBN 0-15-277698-2. 32p. 5–7.

After the final performance of the Farm Family Theater, it is Sarah's turn to choose a family activity for the day, a favorite food for dinner, and a bedtime story. However, these much anticipated highlights are spoiled for Sarah by the arrival of Blanche, a family friend whom Sarah's parents decide to adopt. After the pain of being upstaged by this new member of the family and the frightening experience of running away and missing her family, Sarah learns a valuable lesson and happily reunites with her family, only to discover that Blanche's presence makes the special activities even more fun.

4.32   Palatini, Margie. **Piggie Pie!** Illustrated by Howard Fine. Clarion, 1995. ISBN 0-395-71691-8. 32p. 5–8.

Gritch the Witch has a craving for piggie pie, but when she sets out after this delicious treat, she encounters some surprisingly crafty barnyard animals. Children will delight in predicting, chanting, and listening to the hilariously witty and creative language play in this twisting of a traditional fairy tale. The rich patterning of language and the lively dialogue, along with bold and detailed illustrations, make this exciting picture book a savory treat for young readers, particularly if read aloud.

4.33   Paul, Anthony. **The Tiger Who Lost His Stripes.** Illustrated by Michael Foreman. Harcourt Brace, 1995. ISBN 0-15-200992-2. unpaged. 7–10.

This delightful legend of a tiger who discovers that he has "a remarkable case of stripelessness" is wonderfully illustrated by Michael Forman, who combines wit and intelligence. Tiger's search for his stripes makes him aware of the basic selfishness of his jungle world; fortunately, his ingenuity and an intuitive sense of human psychology serve him well and, in the end, he regains his stately stripes and "everything was just as it should be."

4.34   Potter, Beatrix. **The Tailor of Gloucester.** Illustrated by David Jorgensen. Rabbit Ears Books, 1995. ISBN 0-689-80362-1. cassette and book. 5–9.

Interesting, colorful language, detailed, soft pastel illustrations in the accompanying book, and lively music highlight this Beatrix Potter story dramatically read on tape by Meryl Streep. Children who enjoy playing with sounds, or creating characters with their voices, will appreciate the wonderful variety demonstrated by this well-known actress.

4.35   Rascal. **Oregon's Journey.** Illustrated by Louis Joos. BridgeWater, 1993. ISBN 0-8167-3305-8. 36p. 5–8.

A circus clown named Duke, who is also a dwarf, agrees to assist a performing bear to return to the forests of Oregon. This story blends fantasy and reality. There is pathos in the depiction of the bond shared by the clown and the bear, both of whom seek freedom from the exploitive world of the circus. The spare yet powerful text is complemented by the vibrant illustrations in this oversized picture book. The story is poignant and moving but never sentimental.

4.36   Rogers, Jacqueline. **Best Friends Sleep Over.** Illustrated by Jacqueline Rogers. Scholastic, 1993. ISBN 0-590-44793-9. 32p. 5–7.

This wonderful animal fantasy involves a group of the jungle's finest—rhinos, elephants, crocodiles and such—having a slumber party, replete with pillow fights and pizza. The story focuses on Gilbert Gorilla, for this is his first time away from home. It takes all the ingenuity and affection his friends can provide to make this an evening he will never forget. The author's engaging watercolor illustrations, both realistic and imaginative, graphically portray a party that no child will be able to resist.

4.37   Romanelli, Serena, and Hans de Beer. **Little Bobo.** Illustrated by Hans de Beer and Serena Romanelli. North-South, 1995. ISBN 1-55858-490-0. 26p. 5–7.

A young orangutan finds a small violin in the rainforest and learns to play it. There are humorous moments with noise problems (bananas are stuck into ears to drown out discordant notes), but all ends well with a full orchestra in operation. This forest fantasy picture storybook contains brilliant illustrations.

4.38 Seidel, Ross. **The Rats Came Back.** Illustrated by Rudolf Kurz. Annick, 1995. ISBN 1-55037-402-8. unpaged. 5–8.

In this amusing tale, a family of rats come back to Granny's house and give it a spring cleaning in hopes of being rewarded with boysenberry pies. Although the tale is simply told, Kurz's illustrations, reminiscent of Beatrix Potter's books, provide a magic that will surely delight children who read the text, as they scan every cranny of Granny's house for a glimpse of yet another of these delightful rodents.

4.39 Silverman, Erica. **Don't Fidget a Feather!** Illustrated by S. D. Schindler. Macmillan, 1994. ISBN 0-02-782685-6. 32p. 5–7.

Duck and Gander are always in friendly competition and one day they decide to have a freeze-in-place contest. Whoever can stay still without fidgeting a feather will be the champion; whoever moves first will be the loser. They both stay still while enduring a host of distractions, but bees, bunnies, and crows do not cause them to move. But what happens when a fox comes along and decides which one of the two will make the most delicious dinner? This charming and suspenseful, cumulative tale is beautifully illustrated with pastels and lends itself well to reading aloud and to encouraging children to predict.

4.40 Simard, Remy. **My Dog Is an Elephant.** Illustrated by Pierre Pratt. Annick, 1994. ISBN 1-55037-976-3. 30p. 5–6.

Hector meets an unexpected friend at the sandbox one day: an elephant recently escaped from the zoo. Hector offers him refuge in his home, but has trouble concealing his presence from his mother. He tries out various disguises for the elephant, all of which prove flawed in the end. Finally, he dresses the elephant in his father's suit and puts him on a plane to Africa. When Hector returns, he discovers a new friend: a mouse who in the end proves not to be what he appears. This is an excellent book for discussions of identity, appearances, and reality, and has been used with high school students as an introduction to postmodern literature. Its dramatic narrative makes it very appealing to younger children as well.

4.41   Steig, William. **Zeke Pippin.** Illustrated by William Steig. HarperCollins, 1994. ISBN 0-06-205076-1. 32p. 5–9.

In another delightful tale by well-known author/illustrator William Steig, Zeke Pippin, the musical pig, encounters numerous adventures when he runs away from home with his magic harmonica. The instrument he found on the street one day has a special gift: It makes everybody who listens to it fall asleep. After many exciting and often dangerous events on his journey back home to his loving family, Zeke finally finds fame and happiness.

4.42   Waber, Bernard. **Lyle at the Office.** Illustrated by Bernard Waber. Houghton Mifflin, 1994. ISBN 0-395-70563-0. 48p. 5–8.

Lyle the crocodile is a fantasy animal who is as fresh in this book as in the original creation. Lyle and his mother live with the Primm family, and in this book, Mr. Primm refuses to allow Lyle's picture to be used on a cereal box promoted by his own advertising firm, even though Lyle loves the product. This Lyle book contains warm family feelings, humorous incongruities, and lively artwork.

4.43   Wells, Rosemary. **Max and Ruby's Midas: Another Greek Myth.** Illustrated by Rosemary Wells. Dial, 1995. ISBN 0-8037-1783-0. 25p. 5–8.

Anyone familiar with Wells's lovable rabbit, Max, knows that he always triumphs over his sister, Ruby, in the end. For Max, lover of sweets, Ruby's version of the King Midas legend should provide a good lesson. Miserable because he has turned his whole family into ice cream, cake, and Jell-O, Midas is delighted when he manages to get his family back and rejects a hot fudge sundae for dessert. But will Max learn his lesson?

4.44   Westall, Robert. **The Witness.** Illustrated by Sophy Williams. Dutton, 1994. ISBN 0-525-45331-8. 32p. 6–9.

A kidnapped Egyptian temple cat finds herself giving birth to her kittens in the same stable in which Mary gives birth to Jesus in Bethlehem. The Nativity scene is complete with angels, shepherds, and the three magi, along with a touch of animal fantasy. Joseph and Mary leave for Egypt in order to restore the cat to its rightful place. The detailed text with its glowing illustrations will interest older readers.

4.45   Willard, Nancy. **A Starlit Somersault Downhill.** Illustrated by Jerry Pinkney. Little, Brown, 1993. ISBN 0-316-94113-1. 32p. 5–8.

With detailed watercolor images that fill up every page, Jerry Pinkney has created a captivating focus for the poetic story of a brown bear who invites a rabbit into his cave in anticipation of winter. Reluctant to leave the sweet clover and wide spaces for leaping and spinning, the rabbit accepts the friendly gesture at the first signs of frost. Cozy comfort is not always enough, however, and the rabbit has second thoughts about his winter refuge. The simple and rhythmic text captures a playful sense of what it is like to enjoy winter and nature.

4.46   Wynne-Jones, Tim. **Zoom at Sea.** Illustrated by Eric Beddows. HarperCollins, 1993. ISBN 0-06-021448-1. 32p. 5–7.

In this first book of the Zoom trilogy, Zoom, a cat who loves the sea, discovers in the attic an old map drawn by his mysterious Uncle Roy that reads "The Sea and How to Get There." In following its directions, Zoom begins a series of fantastic adventures filled with mystery and magic. The humor in the subtle, understated text is effectively supported by the captivating black-and-white pencil illustrations. Zoom is bound to become a favorite literary character.

4.47   Wynne-Jones, Tim. **Zoom Away.** Illustrated by Eric Beddows. HarperCollins, 1993. ISBN 0-06-022962-4. 32p. 5–7.

In this second book of the Zoom trilogy, Zoom the cat and his human friend Maria set off to find his uncle, who is lost in the Arctic. In this Canadian classic, the author and illustrator transport young readers to a fantasy world imaginatively created through both the text and black-and-white illustrations. Children will enjoy the adventure and humor involving this very appealing feline character and will want to hear and read each book in the trilogy. *Zoom Upstream* (1994) completes the trilogy.

Humorous Fantasy

4.48   Birney, Betty G. **Tyrannosaurus Tex.** Illustrated by John O'Brien. Houghton Mifflin, 1994. ISBN 0-395-67648-7. 32p. 5–8.

This humorous tale places us around a campfire in Texas where cowboys welcome a strange visitor into their midst: an old Texan dinosaur named Tyrannosaurus Tex. When rustlers threaten their cattle, the inventive cowboys scare the thieves off with popcorn. Meanwhile, T-Tex extinguishes a brush fire with a river of water he collected in his gargantuan Stetson hat. The story makes delightful use of local dialects and the pen-and-watercolor illustrations are cartoonlike and appealing.

4.49   Buehner, Caralyn. **A Job for Wittilda.** Illustrated by Mark Buehner. Dial, 1993. ISBN 0-8037-1150-6. 32p. 5–7.

Wittilda the witch needs a job in order to feed all her cats, and following an unsuccessful episode in a beauty parlor, she competes for a job delivering pizza and wins. Along the way she stops to help a kitten. The illustrations are comical and imaginative.

4.50   Dawnay, Romayne. **The Champions of Appledore.** Illustrated by Romayne Dawnay. Macmillan, 1994. ISBN 0-02-789355-3. 144p. 8–11.

An unlikely quartet—the ineffectual Lord of Appledore Manor, his loyal gourmet cook–manservant, an outspoken Scottish mouse, and a resourceful farm boy—join forces to defeat a pack of wolves that is destroying village life. Toward this end, they recruit a timid old dragon, with surprising results. This fantasy romp is a good read, and lightly humorous. It should appeal to fantasy buffs who can really appreciate the playful spoof on more serious fantasy.

4.51   Howe, James (translated by Alma Flor Ada). **There's a Dragon in My Sleeping Bag/Hay un dragon en mi bolsa de dormir.** Illustrated by David S. Rose. Atheneum, 1994. ISBN 0-689-31873-1 (English); 0-689-31954-1 (Spanish). unpaged. 5–7.

This imaginative picture book depicts friendly, brotherly rivalry. The two brothers finally conjure up two animals in their imaginations, and are thus reconciled. This simple concept is simply expressed, with delightfully monstrous illustrations. The book is excellent for beginning readers as well as for the preschool read-to group. Editions are available in both English and Spanish.

4.52   Mahy, Margaret. **The Three-Legged Cat.** Illustrated by Jonathan Allen. Viking, 1993. ISBN 0-670-85015-2. 26p. 5–7.

Tom, the three-legged tabby, longs to see the world but he lives with the shortsighted Mrs. Gimble who simply wants her cat to eat little and stay put. When Danny, Mrs. Gimble's drifter brother, stops by, things do change. Danny departs to see the world and quite by accident he leaves with a fur cat around his head instead of his fur hat. Mrs. Gimble, on the other hand, is left with Danny's "molting, revolting, Russian hat" and finds it great to stroke and cheap to feed. All in all, everyone is happy. Their dreams are realized, but not always as would have been expected. The subject matter and surprise twists in this story make it appealing.

4.53   Meddaugh, Susan. **Martha Calling.** Illustrated by Susan Meddaugh. Houghton Mifflin, 1994. ISBN 0-395-69825-1. 32p. 5–8.

Continuing from the story *Martha Speaks*, Martha the dog's newly found and much enjoyed ability to speak returns after she eats alphabet soup. Martha develops an affinity for talking on the phone and wins a weekend in a hotel. Much to everyone's disappointment, the official notice states "No Dogs Allowed." Martha's family plans to take Martha anyway, which results in some very funny incidents and unexpected changes at the hotel. The illustrations accompanying Susan Meddaugh's hilarious text are also very humorous.

4.54   Rattigan, Jama Kim. **Truman's Aunt Farm.** Illustrated by G. Brian Karas. Houghton Mifflin, 1994. ISBN 0-395-65661-3. 32p. 5–10.

When Truman opens his birthday present from Aunt Fran, he finds an empty box with a card inviting him to mail away for free ants. Much to Truman's surprise, he starts receiving aunts. Hundreds of loving and playful aunts, who love to eat and begin crowding Truman's tiny house, inspire him to find a solution. Illustrations that combine bright color and playful line highlight the humor of Truman's situation and the silliness of the aunts. Truman's story would be well suited to a discussion of homonyms and families.

4.55   Rayner, Mary. **Garth Pig Steals the Show.** Illustrated by Mary Rayner. Dutton, 1993. ISBN 0-525-45023-8. 32p. 5–8.

The Pig family wants to form a band, but they find that they are too small to play the big instruments. The volunteer sousaphone player who joins them is suspiciously hairy and tends to lick her lips a lot with a remarkably long tongue. William sees the danger, but will he be able to rescue his brother Garth from Madame Wolf in time? This age-old animal story fits well into its new guise, providing lots of information about musical instruments along with an entertaining plot and engaging illustrations.

4.56   Rylant, Cynthia. **Mr. Putter and Tabby Pick the Pears.** Illustrated by Arthur Howard. Harcourt Brace, 1995. ISBN 0-15-200246-4. 44p. 6–8.

Mr. Putter wants to pick his pears, but he has cranky legs and his cat, Tabby, is no help at all. In an attempt to knock the pears off the tree with a slingshot, Mr. Putter shoots all his windfall apples into his neighbor's yard. When she shows up the next day with apple pies, jelly, and cider, he comes up with a plan. This lovely, gently illustrated story has a glorious surprise at the end and guarantees chuckles throughout.

4.57   Scieszka, Jon. **2095.** Illustrated by Lane Smith. Viking, 1995. ISBN 0-670-85795-5. 73p. 7–12.

Fred, Sam, and Joe, the Time Warp Trio, are on another adventure through time with the aid of The Book, which transports them into different eras and harrowing situations. 2095 finds them one hundred years in the future, in the 1990s room of the American Museum of Natural History. Chased by a talking vacuum/robot, the trio encounter low-flying people and floating ads. Having lost their only means of returning to the real 1990s, Fred, Sam, and Joe worry that they have irrevocably changed the past when they meet up with their great-granddaughters. Zany black-and-white illustrations add to the humor of their unbelievable adventure.

4.58   Shannon, Margaret. **Elvira.** Illustrated by Margaret Shannon. Ticknor & Fields, 1993. ISBN 0-395-66597-3. 32p. 5–8.

Elvira is a young dragon who dares to be different from all the other dragons, who delight in fighting and eating princesses. Instead, Elvira is a peaceful dragon girl who likes dresses and daisy chains. In this funny tale of Elvira's adventures among princesses and dragons, young dragons and young readers alike learn some lessons about tolerance and acceptance through rich and delightful language that makes this picture book a wonderful read-aloud.

4.59   Shields, Carol Diggory. **I Am Really a Princess.** Illustrated by Paul Meisel. Dutton, 1993. ISBN 0-525-45138-2. 32p. 5–6.

This joyous romp concerns one of the common fantasies of childhood. A little girl is shown in her chaotic princess role with her own loving family. The pictures are packed with detail as well as humor. This "princess" dresses in jeans, likes riding her pony and rescuing princes, and yodels in between digging tunnels and demanding pizza for breakfast.

4.60   Simard, Remy. **The Magic Boot.** Illustrated by Pierre Pratt. Annick, 1995. ISBN 1-55037-410-9. unpaged. 5–8.

Canadian Governor General Award–winning illustrator Pierre Platt provides the bold and colorful acrylics that bring this legend about the origin of Italy to life. It seems it all started when a young boy with extraordinarily large feet was given a pair of magical boots that grew every time they touched water. The rest is history—sort of.

4.61 Yeoman, John. **The Do-It-Yourself House That Jack Built.** Illustrated by Quentin Blake. Atheneum, 1995. ISBN 0-689-80006-1. unpaged. 5–8.

The traditional creatures—rat, cat, dog, cow—all appear in John Yeoman's lively rendition of this classic story. Playful additions add to the book's humor, including a milkmaid who wants to use the power drill and a cat who frets over being haunted by the recently killed rat. Quentin Blake's cartoon-style watercolor illustrations are delightful and definitely add to the humor.

Imagination and Dreams

4.62 Dorros, Arthur (translated by Sandra Marulanda Dorros). **Isla/La Isla.** Illustrated by Elisa Kleven. Dutton, 1995. ISBN 0-525-45149-8 (English); 0-525-45422-5 (Spanish). 44p. 6–8.

A sequel to the author's *Abuela,* here the child and her grandmother fly though stories to the Caribbean island where the grandmother was born. Brilliant collage illustrations display joyous scenes and warm family life. The English text is interspersed with Spanish words and phrases that are comprehensible in context. A glossary is also provided. This makes it a good text for early English and Spanish learners. The book is absorbing for both its words and its images. Editions are available in both English and Spanish.

4.63 Jones, Terry. **The Fly-by-Night.** Illustrated by Michael Foreman. Peter Bendrick, 1994. ISBN 0-87226-379-7. 24p. 5–7.

In this modern fairy tale, a little girl is swept from her bedroom to a magical land of singing stars. Unfortunately, when she is abandoned there, in the darkness of a far-away forest, the dream quickly becomes a nightmare. Through the moon's assistance, however, she is able to return to her bedroom, hoping, despite her experience, for one more such magical moment. The text may be a bit frightening for some readers, but Foreman's reassuring and witty illustrations provide just the right mood for this wondrous experience.

4.64 McEwan, Ian. **The Daydreamer.** Illustrated by Anthony Browne. HarperCollins, 1994. ISBN 0-06-024426-7. 192p. 10–12.

The daydreamer is ten-year-old Peter who grows up to become "an inventor and a writer of stories." Some of his daydreams include a metamorphosis into the body of a cat, a baby, and an adult. These adventures give him some understanding of another existence. The baby chapter is especially amusing and realistic; the text combines with Browne's evocative illustrations to extoll the imagination.

4.65   Modarressi, Mitra. **The Dream Pillow.** Illustrated by Mitra Modarressi. Orchard, 1994. ISBN 0-531-06855-2. 32p. 5–7.

Ivy and Celeste learn to become friends because of a dream pillow Ivy's mother makes for Celeste's birthday. The pillow produces nightmares for both girls until the mother divides it into two. This is a whimsical story about overcoming mistrust and suspicion in order to make a new friend. It could be complemented with a craft project in which children create their own dream pillows and decorate them.

4.66   Nye, Naomi Shihab. **Benito's Dream Bottle.** Illustrated by Yu Cha Pak. Simon & Schuster, 1995. ISBN 0-02-768467-9. 32p. 5–8.

This lyrical account of how Benito was able to help his grandmother to dream again is illustrated with soft, colorful images. These images alternate between dream sources and depictions of everyday life in a small, southern community. Benito decides there must be a dream bottle inside people that is tipped up when they lie down, forcing dreams to pour into their heads; his job is to refill his grandmother's empty dream bottle. In the end, she dreams that "the whole day felt like a party."

4.67   Rowe, John. **Jack the Dog.** Illustrated by John Rowe. Picture Book Studio, 1993. ISBN 0-88708-266-1. 30p. 5–8.

This fantastic tale of Jack the Dog's adventures in Japan ends with a twist. All the strange happenings are part of Jack's dream. The illustrations are beautiful and help the reader interpret some of the cultural details, although some of the text seems oversophisticated in tone.

4.68   Van Allsburg, Chris. **The Sweetest Fig.** Illustrated by Chris Van Allsburg. Houghton Mifflin, 1993. ISBN 0-395-67346-1. 32p. 6–10.

Van Allsburg's unique blending of humor and suspense with an unexpected conclusion will intrigue the reader. Set in Paris, *The Sweetest Fig* follows Monsieur Bibot as he and his dog discover the magic contained in the two figs he receives in payment for services. The mysterious fantasy sequences of the story are supported by the haunting sepia tone illustrations that are his trademark. Children will enjoy finding the dog, which appears in other stories by Van Allsburg.

4.69 Wild, Margaret. **Going Home.** Illustrated by Wayne Harris. Scholastic, 1994. ISBN 0-590-47958-X. 32p. 5–7.

As Hugo looks out his hospital window, he listens to the animal noises that float up from the zoo below. He soon learns to assuage his homesickness by imagining himself with the different animals in their native environments. His imagination serves him well, and he eventually shares the secret of this adventure with the other children in his hospital room when he is finally discharged. The illustrations are pronounced and richly textured.

4.70 Yep, Laurence. **The Butterfly Boy.** Illustrated by Jeanne M. Lee. Farrar, Straus, 1993. ISBN 0-374-31003-3. 32p. 7–9.

A complex book that explores perception of the world through an Eastern philosophical lens, *The Butterfly Boy* is an intellectual reflection rather than a tale. Events happen, but there is more imagery than story. The book considers sophisticated issues and requires some knowledge of philosophy to make it meaningful, so it is difficult to suggest an appropriate reader age. The boldly colored illustrations and format of the book are striking and unusual, composed of scenes within scenes that contrast with each other.

Other Worlds

4.71 Aura, Alejandro. **The Other Side.** Illustrated by Julia Gukova. Annick, 1995. ISBN 1-55037-405-2. unpaged. 5–9.

Shirley Langer and Sally Stokes Sefami translated Alejandro Aura's *El otro lado* (the original Spanish edition of this book). This is a totally eccentric and delightful book that answers the seldom asked question, "What would happen if Lewis Carroll were illustrated by Hyronimu?" The story is about a king who takes his kingdom to the other side, where everything is backwards. The burden of making some sense, or perhaps nonsense, of this tale clearly falls on Julia Gukova, the illustrator, and her surrealistic explosions provide the perfect visual counterpoint to Aura's enigmatic parable. The book ends as the king and his people are caught in an endless progression of changing worlds that, we are told, will continue until the end of time.

4.72 Coville, Bruce. **Into the Land of the Unicorns.** Scholastic, 1994. ISBN 0-590-45955-4. 159p. 9–11.

This Other World fantasy is in the tradition of C. S. Lewis's *Narnia Chronicles* and Frank Baum's *The Wizard of Oz*. At the bidding of her grandmother, Cara leaps into space and into the land of the unicorns, where she discovers that her quest is to help save the unicorns from annihilation by people from earth. Filled with an assortment of original characters and creatures, this first of a series of the Land of Luster will have readers longing for the next book.

4.73 Lindbergh, Anne. **Nick of Time.** Little, Brown, 1994. ISBN 0-316-52629-0. 204p. 10–12.

A group of modern teenagers and a boy from the year 2094 find a way to visit one another. The two time periods are well contrasted, but the young, well-educated narrator becomes somewhat tiresome and as slick as the title. The boy of the future named Nick never arrives in the nick of time. Young readers will enjoy the sly digs taken at adults in this witty time-travel fantasy.

4.74 Nodelman, Perry. **The Same Place but Different.** Simon & Schuster, 1995. ISBN 0-671-89839-6. 181p. 8–12.

Johnny Nesbit never expected to find himself talking to fairies. Yet an afternoon in the park marks the beginning of an adventure in which he travels between his own world and that of the "Strangers" in an effort to rescue his baby sister, who has been replaced by a changeling. The strengths of this novel lie in its intricate plot and its effective intermixing of folklore and modern popular culture. Some readers may not persist to appreciate these strengths because of the narrator, who embodies the qualities of insolence and solipsism stereotypically attributed to adolescents. However, the accessible language, the pace of the plot, and the vividly descriptive writing will make this an appealing book to many readers.

Science Fiction

4.75 Dunlop, Eileen. **Websters' Leap.** Holiday House, 1995. ISBN 0-8234-1193-1. 168p. 10–12.

Jill hates her brother Tad for choosing to live in Scotland with their father. She resents her parents for trading children during the holidays. When she goes to Castle Gryffe, where her father is caretaker, she expects to have a miserable stay. Contrary to her expectation, Jill finds herself pulled into the sixteenth-century past of the castle through a story that Tad started writing on his computer. In the past, Jill must rescue the lady of the castle from a plot laid by her evil brother-in-law. In the course of the adventure, she is gradually reconciled with Tad. Jill's sixteenth-century experiences are suspenseful and supported by realistic detail that will intrigue readers.

4.76　Hooks, William H. **The Girl Who Could Fly.** Illustrated by Kees de Kiefte. Macmillan, 1995. ISBN 0-02-744433-3. 53p. 7–10.

In this easy chapter book, nine-year-old Adam Lee witnesses many out-of-this-world events and performances by Tom, his new neighbor, who is unlike anybody Adam has ever met: Tom happens to be able to do things no one else is able to do, and also happens to be a girl named Tomasina. When Tom becomes the new baseball coach, together they encounter fantastic adventures that forever change Adam's attitudes about girls and the things they can do.

4.77　Hughes, Monica. **The Golden Aquarians.** HarperCollins, 1994. ISBN 0-00-224253-2. 171p. 11–14.

Walt's father becomes obsessed with the challenge of terraforming the watery planet Aqua. By the year 2092, Earth needs more resources, such as crops of oil-plant, so Colonel Angus Elliot and his research team are to transform the hostile planet. Walt is summoned to join his father but finds it hard to relate to him. In his wanderings, he discovers and communicates with amphibian creatures, the Aquarians, who have telepathic abilities. The novel pits son against father in this life-and-death struggle to save the planet, as the Aquarians have predicted that a massive tidal wave will occur in six days. Strong characterization of both father and son reveal a similarity of traits, yet contrasting degrees of sensitivity to both personal and environmental needs. Who has the right to destroy the environment of others? At what cost?

4.78　Kilworth, Garry. **The Electric Kid.** Orchard, 1995. ISBN 0-531-09486-3. 137p. 10–12.

Hotwire and Blindboy inhabit a dystopic future where they live by sifting through the refuse of affluent city dwellers and avoiding criminals who prey on homeless kids. By chance, their gifts of acute hearing and of repairing gadgets bring them to the notice of crooks who want to use Blindboy and Hotwire to advance their empire of crime. The children find themselves caught between the police and the crooks, both of whom they distrust. Ultimately, the children save the city through their resourcefulness and their adherence to their own moral code. Readers will enjoy the imaginative setting of this suspenseful story. The ending is both satisfying and credible in the context of the novel's futuristic setting.

4.79   Lowry, Lois. **The Giver.** Houghton Mifflin, 1993. ISBN 0-395-64566-2. 180p. 10–12.

"We gained control of many things. But we had to let go of others." Jonas lives in a world of sameness in this science fiction novel. Everything is under control. Children reach the same milestones at the same ages until they become Twelves and are assigned their adult jobs. Jonas is selected to receive the memories, the true memories of the pain and joy of life. This well-written, thought-provoking book won the 1993 Newbery Medal.

4.80   MacDonald, Caroline. **Secret Lives.** Simon & Schuster, 1995. ISBN 0-671-51081-9. 135p. 12–15.

Secret Lives is a complex and haunting story of Ian, a fifteen-year-old Australian boy whose school assignment literally comes alive. The beginning of Ian's spring vacation is marked by the arrival of a mysterious and rebellious character named Gideon. Ian begins to lose control of himself and his life when he is left alone at home for a couple of days. Suspense and a sense of danger make this a captivating story. This book could be used in discussions about fiction, possible futures, and creative writing.

4.81   Rubinstein, Gillian. **Galax-Arena.** Simon & Schuster, 1995. ISBN 0-689-80136-X. 172p. 11–12.

Using the science fiction format, Gillian Rubinstein, a highly respected Australian author, has created a world in which people are kidnapped to become slaves in an intergalactic circus. In this way, she draws clear analogies between the lives of slaves and animals, and about the ethics of our societies. She also works in a contact language derived from the languages of the pebs (performers) and a child's toy (Bro Rabbit), which gives voice to their inner fears—the truths they dare not speak. The inhumanity of the Galax-Arena is all the more terrible when we discover that very little is what it appears to be.

4.82   Skurzynski, Gloria. **Cyberstorm.** Macmillan, 1995. ISBN 0-02-782926-X. 137p. 8–12.

In this futuristic adventure story, Darcy is reluctant to move with her parents to the suburbs, but when animal control officers come to the new neighborhood to take her dog away, the move turns into a nightmare. To escape the dogcatchers, Darcy hides in the Rent-A-Memory machine that her elderly neighbor has hired. The machine malfunctions and Darcy and Mrs. Galloway find themselves trapped in a sequence of increasingly realistic memories that they cannot control. Darcy's friend Erik overcomes distance and the intimidation of bullies to offer an ingenious solution to rescue Darcy, who emerges from the machine with a new empathy for Mrs. Galloway. Readers will be interested in the representation of social and material reality in the future.

4.83   Stearns, Michael. **A Starfarer's Dozen: Stories of Things to Come.** Harcourt Brace, 1995. ISBN 0-15-299871-3. 224p. 11–12.

This science fiction collection will appeal mainly to young adult readers, although it includes several stories, such as "Jones and the Stray," that will interest younger readers and introduce them to this genre, which has been underrepresented for their age range in recent years. The stories are by different authors and the protagonists vary in age, gender, and background, but the stories all address the human concerns of family, friends, and social pressure in futuristic settings.

Supernatural Tales

4.84   Burgess, Melvin. **Burning Issy.** Simon & Schuster, 1994. ISBN 0-671-89003-4. 174p. 9–11.

Set in seventeenth-century England, this novel is loosely based on historical events. As the author indicates in his preface, the book is not an attempt to show things as they really were, but the plot and characters are compelling. Issy is strongly attracted to a nature religious group persecuted by the contemporary Christian church. The kindest people she knows belong to this religion, although the church does not distinguish between them and the evil creatures whom she knows as witches. Ultimately, through no fault of her own, Issy is accused of witchcraft. Young readers will feel sympathy for Issy's difficulty in choosing between what she feels and what she is told is right.

4.85   Byars, Betsy. **McMummy.** Viking, 1993. ISBN 0-670-84995-2. 150p. 8–12.

Mozie has been left in charge of a greenhouse belonging to a professor who is cultivating experimental vegetables. When Mozie enters the greenhouse he finds himself drawn toward an enormous podlike plant that emits a humming sound and resembles an Egyptian mummy. Is McMummy (as Mozie calls it) a plant or a creature? Fear of McMummy turns to concern for its safety as Mozie finds himself involved in a series of bizarre and amusing happenings as he attempts to come to its rescue.

4.86   Johnston, Tony. **Very Scary.** Illustrated by Douglas Florian. Harcourt Brace, 1995. ISBN 0-15-2936254. 32p. 5–8.

This Halloween story-poem is for young readers. A pumpkin is saved from a witch's oven by costumed children. Carved as a jack-o'-lantern, the pumpkin finally scares the witch away, as well as everyone else! The images of bright orange pumpkins and a moon against a rich dark blue sky set the tone for the exuberant watercolor paintings. Childlike in their execution, they will appeal to young eyes and inspire young hands. The poem has repetitive lines for the children to chant and noises from creatures and characters to imitate. There are words falling from mouths and lines of text shaped to the carving of the pumpkin. Children can join in and will delight in saying "BOO!"

4.87   Penn, Malka. **The Hanukkah Ghosts.** Holiday House, 1995. ISBN 0-8234-1145-1. 76p. 9–12.

Susan expects to be bored and lonely when she visits her Great Aunt Elizabeth's manor in Yorkshire. On the contrary, she immediately stumbles upon ghosts from the past who win her sympathy. Susan throws her energy into understanding the past and righting the wrongs that she perceives there. As a consequence, she gains a new perspective on the hurt in her own life, discovering that she really does miss her mother, who died when Susan was small. This gentle story appeals to readers through its Yorkshire setting and its power to evoke compassion for its characters.

4.88   Vaughan, Marcia. **Whistling Dixie.** Illustrated by Barry Moser. HarperCollins, 1995. ISBN 0-06-021030-3. 32p. 5–8.

In the Hokey Pokey Swamp, young Dixie Lee is forever turning up with things to show her mama. Despite her mama's reluctance to keep creatures, Dixie Lee manages to take in an alligator, a snake, and an owl. Her grandpappy, however, orders her to get rid of them. He soon changes his mind when he discovers their protective powers from the Bogeyman and the Mist Sisters.

Large watercolor illustrations are placed against full-page washes that outline the trees and misty feeling of the Hokey Pokey Swamp. Children will enjoy the humor and the hint of the supernatural in Dixie Lee's tale—a good read-aloud.

4.89   Wright, Betty Ren. **Ghost Comes Calling.** Scholastic, 1994. ISBN 0-590-47353-0. 83p. 8–12.

Most kids would be thrilled if their parents bought a cabin at the lake, but Chad can only worry. He is concerned about his father spending their savings, and he dreads the ghost that his friend Jennie says haunts the property. As soon as Chad visits the cabin, he finds evidence of the ghost: the sound of a dog howling and an abandoned truck. It is clear to Chad that the ghost of the cabin's previous owner does not want them there but, despite his fears, Chad likes the cabin. Young readers will admire Chad's courage and his innovative plan to resolve the problem of the ghost, consequently resolving a long-ago wrong in the community.

4.90   Yolen, Jane, and Martin H. Greenberg. **The Haunted House.** Illustrated by Doron Ben-Ami. HarperCollins, 1995. ISBN 0-06-024467-4. 88p. 7–10.

In each of these stories by diverse authors, different children discover different ghosts that haunt various rooms in the same house. The stories are well-written and effectively illustrated, providing the occasional chill while addressing themes of family and friendship.

Time Fantasy

4.91   Burgess, Melvin. **An Angel for May.** Simon & Schuster, 1995. ISBN 0-671-89004-2. 154p. 10–12.

Tam is resentful and wounded over the breakup of his family. He acts out at school and at home. One day, at his refuge in a ruined farmhouse, he attempts to chase away a wretched old woman by throwing a stone at her. Before long, the woman and the dog who protects her draw Tam into a mystery that transports him to his own rural English town during World War II. In this time, Tam experiences cruelty, makes friends, and learns another way of life. When he returns to his own time, he takes with him a new quality of compassion, although his unexplained absence makes new trouble for him. Ultimately, his changed outlook brings him to a startling discovery and a resolution of the relationship between the past and his present life.

4.92 Winthrop, Elizabeth. **The Battle for the Castle.** Holiday House, 1993. ISBN 0-8234-1010-2. 211p. 10–12.

In this sequel to *The Castle in the Attic,* two twelve-year-old boys travel back in time, by aid of a talisman, to medieval times. They help save a castle from an infestation of huge rats under the leadership of a chief rat with super powers. The characters and the differences in living between the past and the present are well-delineated. The events in the past teach both boys that there are different types of courage and that one does not have to prove oneself unnecessarily. All in all, the strength of the book lies in its realism; the magic/fantasy is fairly muted. The writing is straightforward, suspense is well-created, and dialogue is handled well. The author succinctly explains the events that led to the first adventure in the first book.

Toys and Dolls

4.93 Conrad, Pam. **The Tub Grandfather.** Illustrated by Richard Egielski. HarperCollins, 1993. ISBN 0-06-022895-4. 32p. 5–8.

Pat Conrad's sequel to the popular *The Tub People* tells the story of the discovery of the long-lost grandfather by the Tub Child. The charming illustrations vividly enhance the story of how this endearing set of toy characters tries to revive the newest member of their little community. Children will enjoy the lively dialogue and narrative of the story, even though the gender stereotyping and sexist language will trouble some adults.

4.94 Joyce, William. **Santa Calls.** Illustrated by William Joyce. HarperCollins, 1993. ISBN 0-06-021133-4. 40p. 5–8.

It is the year 1908, and Art Atchinson Aimesworth, a young boy and inventor par excellence, takes readers on a magical journey to Santa's Toyland. Of all the fantastic adventures he and his little sister Esther come up against, the most dangerous and exciting is an encounter with the Dark Elves, whose attempt to kidnap Esther inspire Art to some daring and mischievous deeds. When he rescues Esther from the elves, Art learns about the true value of giving and friendship; on their return home to Texas, he finally discovers why Santa called.

4.95 Kleven, Elisa. **The Paper Princess.** Illustrated by Elisa Kleven. Dutton, 1994. ISBN 0-525-45231-1. 32p. 5–7.

Elisa Kleven's charming fantasy tells of a little girl who draws a picture of a paper princess, which she cuts out. Soon the princess comes alive, but is quickly blown away by the wind. Her adventures eventually take her back to the little girl who lost her. The girl immediately begins to make paper crowns and paper beds, creating a kingdom for her paper princess to inhabit. Beautifully illustrated with incredibly colorful and detailed collages, *The Paper Princess* is a marvelous celebration of childhood imagination that children will read again and again.

4.96   Waugh, Sylvia. **The Mennyms.** Avon, 1993. ISBN 0-380-72528-2. 230p. 10–12.

The Mennyms are a family of life-sized rag dolls who live in seclusion in a London house. Their lives revolve around family relationships, which change very little because the dolls never age. Their daily concerns of sleeping and devising ways to make money to pay the rent are supplemented by elaborate "pretends" such as cooking, eating, changing diapers, and birthday celebrations. When a new landlord threatens to visit, the Mennyms' static world is thrown into confusion and alarm. Finally, however, it is a new family member who requires a lasting adjustment to the Mennyms' way of life. Following the Mennyms' daily activities may cause the more mature reader to reflect on the human activities and relationships that the dolls are emulating.

Unique Beings

4.97   Hodges, Margaret, reteller. **Gulliver in Lilliput.** Illustrated by Kimberly Bulcken Root. Holiday House, 1995. ISBN 0-8234-1147-8. 32p. 5–8.

The well-known tale of *Gulliver's Travels* is retold for children. Setting sail from Bristol, England in 1699, Lemuel Gulliver travels to the South Seas, where he is the only survivor of a violent storm. He soon finds himself in a strange land of little people, the Lilliputians, who are at war with the neighboring people of Blefuscu. Gulliver attempts to remain neutral between the two factions, whose disagreement stems from a decision to wear high-heeled shoes. Pen-and-ink illustrations skillfully depict the land of the little people and bring a magical quality to Jonathan Swift's tale.

4.98   Jansson, Tove. **Moominpappa's Memoirs.** Farrar, Straus, 1994. ISBN 0-374-45307-1. 162p. 10–12.

This book is a special treasure among the Moomintroll books. Moominpappa shows himself to be the most complex and experienced and therefore the most interesting member of the family. Here he relates the story of his life, from his orphan childhood to a celebration with friends now known to all readers of the series. He thinks he is "rather nice"—and he is. He likes the truth, "except when it is too boring." There is a tall-tale element in Moominpappa's autobiography, yet one believes in it wholeheartedly.

4.99   Peterson, Gail. **Greg Hildebrandt's Book of Three-Dimensional Dragons.** Illustrated by Greg Hildebrandt. Little, Brown, 1994. ISBN 0-316-15240-4. 12p. 7–10.

Large three-dimensional dragons leap out of this oversized pop-up book; each spread includes the name of the dragon and its history and background. The text is a fascinating compilation of facts and fancy and the artwork is stunning.

4.100   Sierra, Judy. **The House That Drac Built.** Illustrated by Will Hillenbrand. Harcourt Brace, 1995. ISBN 0-15-200015-1. 40p. 5–9.

In the house that Drac built, a set of very scary and intricately illustrated monster characters are bound to put young readers in a delightfully frightened mood. However, the rhythmic textual variations of the popular cumulative rhyme, the child characters who have the upper hand over the monsters, and the Halloween theme will make this book a favorite with young readers.

5 Contemporary Realistic Fiction

Adventure

5.1   Conrad, Pam. **Call Me Ahnighito.** Illustrated by Richard Egielski. HarperCollins, 1995. ISBN 0-06-023322-2. 32p. 5–9.

The true story of the meteorite named Ahnighito is told in the first person, from the meteorite's perspective. Ahnighito explains how it felt to be lying in the Greenland cold for hundreds of years while waiting for something to happen, chipped at and abandoned many times, and then rescued by the Peary expedition and taken by ship to New York in 1897. Full-page watercolor illustrations are rendered in muted colors with a softness that captures the feeling of a historical time and the beauty of the Arctic.

5.2   Hill, Susan. **Beware, Beware.** Illustrated by Angela Barrett. Candlewick, 1993. ISBN 1-56402-245-5. 24p. 5–6.

This book uses an enchanting rhymed text to tell the story of a young girl whose curiosity leads her to explore the world beyond her front door. It is a mesmerizing tale, with excellent illustrations, including two cleverly split pages. The book is a good text for exploring the desire for safety, the need for adventure, and the role that the imagination plays in fear.

5.3   Kastner, Jill. **Snake Hunt.** Illustrated by Jill Kastner. Four Winds, 1993. ISBN 0-02-749395-4. 32p. 5–7.

When Granddad recounts the story of wrestling a rattlesnake, killing it, and eating it in a stew, his granddaughter pleads with him to take her snake hunting. The day in the woods turns out to be more about the bonding of a granddaughter with her grandfather than an adventure involving snakes. Children's fascination with snakes will make this book popular, particularly if read aloud.

5.4   Naylor, Phyllis Reynolds. **The Fear Place.** Atheneum, 1994. ISBN 0-689-31866-9. 118p. 9–12.

Doug and his brother Gordon do not get along. A family camping trip turns into a test of their relationship when the boys' parents leave them to attend their uncle's funeral. After a fight, Doug and Gordon go their separate ways in the wilderness, but a crisis brings them back together, making them realize how important they are to each other. Readers who have siblings will recognize both the resentment and the love that the brothers feel for one another. The wild setting inspires awe and respect for nature and its creatures.

5.5 Valgardson, W. D. **Winter Rescue.** Illustrated by Ange Zhang. McElderry, 1995. ISBN 0-689-80094-0. 40p. 7–10.

Thor, who loves watching television, is not happy when he has to help his grandfather, an ice fisherman, instead of watching Saturday morning cartoons. He learns to endure the cold weather and to ice fish, so that by the end of the day, he unexpectedly becomes a hero just like the characters in his favorite cartoons. The story is set in a Manitoba community of Icelandic fishermen, with accompanying illustrations that enhance the reader's understanding of the fishing methods as well as the drama at hand. The strengths of the story lie in the grandfather/grandson relationship and the depiction of the ice-fishing tradition.

5.6 Wood, A. J. **A Night in the Dinosaur Graveyard.** Illustrated by Wayne Anderson. HarperCollins, 1994. ISBN 0-694-00641-6. 22p. 5–8.

This book of ten holograms is framed in the fictional story of a famous fossil hunter who mysteriously died. The mystery brings a professor and his grandchildren to dark caves filled with ghostly holographic dinosaur images. The holograms are sure to elicit interest and are used creatively.

Animal Stories

5.7 Abercrombie, Barbara. **Michael and the Cats.** Illustrated by Mark Graham. Macmillan, 1993. ISBN 0-689-50543-4. 24p. 5–7.

When young Michael goes to visit his aunt and uncle, he immediately falls in love with their two cats. Because Michael is used to a baby brother and has no pets, he tries to befriend the cats by grabbing their fur, feeding them ice cream, and dressing them up in his clothes. Over the course of his week-long visit, Michael learns to observe the cats and to make friends with the animals.

Full-spread illustrations are captivating with their warm hues and cozy depiction of two happy cats.

5.8   Anholt, Laurence. **The New Puppy.** Illustrated by Catherine Anholt. Artists and Writers Guild, 1995. ISBN 0-307-17516-2. 32p. 5–7.

Anna loves dogs. When her father finally agrees to give her a puppy, she learns that caring for puppies is not as easy as it seems. The text is good for early readers, with labeled diagrams that help to visually identify the various concepts and dimensions introduced (long, tall, loud, neat, hairy). This is a must for any child who dreams of getting a dog or for those lucky enough to have one already.

5.9   Arrington, Frances. **Stella's Bull.** Illustrated by Aileen Arrington. Houghton Mifflin, 1994. ISBN 0-395-67345-3. 32p. 5–8.

This is a predictable tale of a young girl who allows her imagination to turn a bull into a monster. When she finally is forced to face her fears, she learns a lesson about both the silly demons that a child can create and her own strength. The text is pleasingly illustrated by the author's sister, Aileen Arrington, with pleasant, full-page pastels.

5.10   Bunting, Eve. **Red Fox Running.** Illustrated by Wendell Minor. Clarion, 1993. ISBN 0-395-58919-3. 32p. 5–8.

This lyrical account of a day in the life of a red fox traces the meandering journey of the fox as he traverses a wintry landscape in search of food. The paintings by Wendell Minor bring the scenery to life, complemented well by the sensuous poetry of the text. Some pages are wordless, containing detailed illustrations of winter wildlife and vegetation. The rich paintings and rhymed text make this an excellent story for reading aloud to children, providing numerous topics for discussion including all the wild animals found lingering on its pages.

5.11   Carlstrom, Nancy White. **Fish and Flamingo.** Illustrated by Lisa Desimini. Little, Brown, 1993. ISBN 0-316-12859-7. 32p. 5–7.

This tale explores the unlikely friendship between a fish and a flamingo as they attempt to share their radically different lives with one another. The fish wants to show his new friend "the light of a star shining on the edge of a wave," while the flamingo longs to show the fish the pink light of sunrise. In their parting visions of one another, these hopes are fulfilled. The illustrations are rich in color and texture, eliciting emotion and imagination.

5.12 Carson, Jo. **The Great Shaking: An Account of the Earthquakes of 1811 and 1812.** Illustrated by Robert Andrew Parker. Orchard, 1994. ISBN 0-531-06809-9. 32p. 5–8.

A bear gives his impressions of what happened during three earthquakes in New Madrid, Missouri in 1811 and 1812. The bear certainly has a way with words, a sense of the human comedy, and a deep, spiritual feeling for Mother Nature as the ground heaves and shakes. An author's note at the end provides a scientific explanation of earthquakes. The full-page, warm-color illustrations are a fine addition to the text.

5.13 Chekhov, Anton. **Kashtanka.** Illustrated by Gennady Spirin. Harcourt Brace, 1995. ISBN 0-15-200539-0. 40p. 8–10.

This is a new translation of a warm tale of a small dog lost on a walk. The dog is found by a circus clown, trained to join the clown's act, then retrieved by his previous owners after the first stage performance. Chekhov conveys how a dog might feel, his memories and dreams, his sadness and joy. The story has a simplicity that matches the heart of the small dog, who can remember his time with the circus only as a long and confused dream. The illustrations have a dreamlike quality, colored in a sepia tone and drawn in a style that evokes faded oil paintings from the nineteenth century. The book is a good introduction to the story-telling skills of Anton Chekhov. Younger readers will be charmed that the story is told from the dog's viewpoint, while older readers can better appreciate the craft of the short story as mastered by Chekhov.

5.14 Cherry, Lynne. **Armadillo from Amarillo.** Illustrated by Lynne Cherry. Harcourt Brace, 1994. ISBN 0-15-200359-2. 34p. 5–8.

This is an ecological parable written in rhyme that follows the journey of Sasparillo Armadillo as he asks, "Where in the world am I?" Each page displays a postcard sent by Sasparillo to his cousin at the Philadelphia Zoo. Sasparillo explores Texas, then climbs on the back of a golden eagle and flies up to a space ship to get a full view of the world. This story can be used to encourage children to explore a space or environmental theme, to collect postcards, or just to ponder, "Where in the world am I?" Cherry's illustrations are ripe with color and attention to detail.

5.15 Christiansen, Candace. **The Ice Horse.** Illustrated by Thomas Locker. Dial, 1993. ISBN 0-8037-1401-7. 32p. 5–9.

This book will fascinate all readers, young and old alike, as it retells the time of the ice harvests on the Hudson River. Young Jack, in the winter of his twelfth year, helps his Uncle Joe to plow the snow off the river ice. All goes well until one day the ice cracks and his uncle's horse, Max, plunges into the frigid waters. How Jack struggles to save Max is thrillingly told. Renowned painter Thomas Locker captures both the stark beauty of the Hudson River valley in winter and the excitement and danger of the ice harvest. His luminescent oil paintings are panoramic vistas of immense charm and grace.

5.16   Coffelt, Nancy. **Dogs in Space.** Illustrated by Nancy Coffelt. Harcourt Brace, 1993. ISBN 0-15-200440-8. unpaged. 4–8.

In this vividly illustrated picture book, we find out what happens when adventurous dogs take us on a journey through the solar system. Young readers can discover basic facts about the planets in this fun-filled canine romp from Mercury to Pluto. On the concluding pages, more detailed information about the different parts of the solar system complements this visually and textually appealing book. An excellent book for integrating science and language across the curriculum.

5.17   Coffelt, Nancy. **Tom's Fish.** Illustrated by Nancy Coffelt. Harcourt Brace, 1994. ISBN 0-15-200587-0. 32p. 5–7.

When Tom gets a goldfish for a birthday present, he is delighted. He names it Jesse, and it is his favorite present. However, Tom cannot figure out one thing about his goldfish: why he swims upside down. Tom tries in vain to get Jesse to swim like a "normal" fish until he realizes that there is nothing wrong with being different and that there is a creative solution to this predicament.

5.18   Crisp, Marty. **Buzzard Breath.** Atheneum, 1995. ISBN 0-689-31964-9. 140p. 8–12.

Will dreams of the perfect dog—purebred with papers—who will love him and impress his peers. But he gets tangled up with Buzzard Breath, an ordinary shepherd whom he rescues from death at the animal shelter. He plans to find a good home for Buzz and to keep saving for his special dog until Buzz is accused of biting a little girl. Once again, the dog is in danger and Will knows he is innocent. The author presents the world of a young boy with an easy blend of humor and feeling. Sibling and peer rivalries and attachments are as believable as the growing love between boy and dog.

5.19   Day, Alexandra. **Carl Goes to Daycare.** Illustrated by Alexandra Day. Farrar, Straus, 1993. ISBN 0-374-31093-9. 32p. 5–6.

That amazing dog Carl is at it again: This time he and Madeleine spend the morning visiting a daycare center, where he takes charge of the group activities while the supervisor is accidentally locked outside. The watercolor illustrations convey the young children's exuberant, creative fun, while the supervisor attempts various methods to get back inside. The story gives a positive impression of daycare as a happy place, and the humor of the situation (dog saves the day) is delightful. Young prereaders can "read" the visual story themselves and note many details that carry messages about safety, responsibility, and cooperation, messages that these daycare children have already learned. This book is another in the Carl series.

5.20   Falk, Barbara Bustetter. **Grusha.** Illustrated by Barbara Bustetter Falk. HarperCollins, 1993. ISBN 0-06-021299-3. 32p. 5–7.

Grusha, a black bear, learns to ride a bike and becomes famous after he is captured for a Russian circus. Peter, his kind trainer, realizes that Grusha longs to return to the forest and sets him free. Vivid illustrations depict the beauty of the forest, the excitement of the circus, and the bear's moods of sadness and happiness.

5.21   Gantos, Jack. **Not So Rotten Ralph.** Illustrated by Nicole Rubel. Houghton Mifflin, 1994. ISBN 0-395-62302-2. 32p. 5–8.

Rotten Ralph, Sarah's feline companion, is in for a shock and the ultimate challenge to his rottenness when Sarah decides to send him to Mr. Fred's Feline Finishing School. Rotten Ralph is a changed cat after his graduation from the school, but Sarah soon discovers that her old cat was much more fun and she does everything to make Ralph become his rotten self again. Children will want to read the other Rotten Ralph books after hearing or reading this one.

5.22   George, Jean Craighead. **There's an Owl in the Shower.** Illustrated by Christine Herman Merrill. HarperCollins, 1995. ISBN 0-06-024891-2. 134 p. 8–10.

A baby owl is rescued by the son of a logger who has lost his job because of his company's logging practices. The author's observations of animal and human life are appealing and the illustrations complement and enhance the story.

5.23 Gregory, Valiska. **Babysitting for Benjamin.** Illustrated by Lynn Munsinger. Little, Brown, 1993. ISBN 0-316-32785-9. 32p. 5–7.

When Frances and Ralph, two mice, agree to babysit Benjamin, a baby rabbit, they are unprepared for the devastation he leaves in the wake of his play. They try various strategies to minimize the chaos, until they finally devise a way to salvage the peace and order of their home: They open the back door and have him play outside. The story is humorous and children will no doubt see something of themselves in its pages. The ink-and-watercolor illustrations are both detailed and comic. The book could serve as a springboard for discussions of babysitters or housekeeping.

5.24 Hamilton, Virginia. **Jaguarundi.** Illustrated by Floyd Cooper. Blue Sky, 1994. ISBN 0-590-47366-2. 34p. 6–8.

In this beast tale with a strong ecological message, Rundi Jaguarundi invites the other rainforest animals to travel north with him to find a safer home. The marvelously realistic animal paintings of rare and endangered South American animals complement the prose. Facts about each of the animals are provided.

5.25 Hoff, Syd. **The Lighthouse Children.** Illustrated by Syd Hoff. HarperCollins, 1994. ISBN 0-06-022958-6. 32p. 5–8.

An old lighthouse keeper and his wife, Rose, leave their seaside home. The days pass and they miss their seagull friends very much. Rose thinks of a way to let the seagulls know where they are, and once again they are reunited with their friends. This is an enjoyable independent read for beginning readers, who will also enjoy Syd Hoff's cartoonlike illustrations.

5.26 Murphy, Jim. **Backyard Bear.** Illustrated by Jeffrey Greene. Scholastic, 1993. ISBN 0-590-44375-5. 32p. 5–7.

This book looks at one night in the life of a black bear. Frightened by a larger, older bear, the bear protagonist makes his way to a human settlement, where people spot him and call the police. The bear hides in a bush until he can safely return home. The story concludes with factual data on black bears and their communities.

5.27 Naylor, Phyllis Reynolds. **The Grand Escape.** Illustrated by Alan Daniel. Atheneum, 1993. ISBN 0-689-31722-0. 148p. 9–11.

Of course two cats named Marco and Polo would dream of exploring the great world beyond the screen door, especially when

Marco has taught himself to read. The two house cats in this book escape and begin their adventure, echoing other heroic figures such as Ulysses and Indiana Jones. In their efforts to become accepted by the Feline Club of Mysteries, the cats endure three life-threatening tests and earn the admiration of the lovely Carlotta before deciding to rethink their interest in living the free life. This chapter book is action-packed and humorous, enhanced by many black-and-white illustrations.

5.28   Provensen, Alice, and Martin Provensen. **An Owl and Three Pussycats.** Illustrated by Alice Provensen and Martin Provensen. Harcourt Brace, 1994. ISBN 0-15-200183-2. 32p. 5–8.

This reissue of Alice and Martin Provensen's stories of Little Owl and Fat Boy, Crook, and Webster, the three cats from Maple Hill Farm, remains an endearing, timeless portrait of life on a farm and the relationships between people, animals, and nature. With its humorous episodes and simple yet appealing watercolor illustrations, it evokes a serene, peaceful atmosphere that will once again capture young readers' interest.

5.29   Ruepp, Krista. **Midnight Rider.** Illustrated by Ulrike Heyne. North-South, 1995. ISBN 1-55858-494-3. 64p. 7–9.

A secret shared by a little girl named Charlie, a horse named Starbright, and a cranky man named Mr. Grimm is at the heart of this beautifully illustrated story. Although Mr. Grimm refuses permission, Charlie takes Starbright for a night ride along the beach. The adventure results in an accident, but seeing Charlie ride softens Mr. Grimm and gives rise to a rumor in the village about a mysterious midnight rider. Children will empathize with Charlie's affection for the horse, and they will enjoy complicity in the secret of the midnight rider.

5.30   Ryder, Joanne (translated by Sandra Marulanda Dorros). **Bears Out There/Osos por ahi.** Illustrated by Jo Ellen McAllister-Stammen. Atheneum, 1995. ISBN 0-689-31780-8 (English); 0-689-31982-7 (Spanish). 32p. 5–8.

A young boy considers the parallels between his life and the lives of bears through his imagination. This is a good text for bridging fiction and nonfiction materials, while the illustrations help engage the imagination. The author includes a final note outlining factual details on the habits, habitats, and populations of North American black bears. Editions are available in both English and Spanish.

5.31   Sayre, April Pulley. **If You Should Hear a Honey Guide.** Illustrated by S. D. Schindler. Houghton Mifflin, 1995. ISBN 0-395-71545-8. 32p. 5–10.

This is the story of how the honey guide, a small bird of East Africa, calls to invite animals and humans to journey through the countryside of East Kenya in order to reach the prize of wild honey. The reader is pulled along with careful advice about how to travel through the African landscape, which is depicted in beautiful illustrations of muted tones in double-page spreads. The relationship between bird and animal is described in poetic prose, making this a suitable read-aloud and an example of an animal and bird partnership.

5.32   Scamell, Ragnhild. **Three Bags Full.** Illustrated by Sally Hobson. Orchard, 1993. ISBN 0-531-05486-1. 26p. 5–7.

Millie is a kind sheep who enjoys helping other animals in need and ends up giving away her own warm wool coat. Fortunately, when Millie is left out in the cold, without the comforts all the other animals are enjoying, Mrs. Farmer saves her from her predicament by knitting her a warm sweater so she can once more brave the snowy weather—but has Millie really learned a lesson in the end? The story is reminiscent of *Amos's Sweater* by Janet Lunn, and children would enjoy comparing the two versions.

5.33   Walsh, Ellen Stoll. **Hop Jump.** Illustrated by Ellen Stoll Walsh. Harcourt Brace, 1993. ISBN 0-15-292871-5. 32p. 5–6.

This delightful picture book for young readers revolves around the frolicking movements of Betsy the frog, who teaches and entices her friends to jump, dance, and hop between floating leaves. The simple yet evocative cut-paper collage art captures the frogs' movements and encourages effortless connections between the pictures and the rich language. Each page contains easy-to-read large print.

5.34   Wilcox, Cathy. **Enzo the Wonderfish.** Illustrated by Cathy Wilcox. Ticknor & Fields, 1994. ISBN 0-395-68382-3. 32p. 5–7.

The youngest girl in a family finally gets her wish and is given a pet of her own, a goldfish named Enzo. She cares for the fish until one day it learns two tricks that imperil its life: jumping and playing dead. The young girl revives her pet after he lands in a cup of tea! Bright, cartoonlike illustrations add to the appeal of this book.

Cultural Groups

5.35   Ada, Alma Flor. **Where the Flame Trees Bloom.** Illustrated by Antonio Martorell. Atheneum, 1994. ISBN 0-689-31900-2. 75p. 11–12.

In a collection of eleven short stories, the author shares with us characters and memories of her childhood in rural Cuba. One story tells of her grandfather, who lost his fortune because he chose to stay by the bedside of his dying wife; another is of her blind and uneducated great-grandmother, who gave so much love to all members of her large family. These stories, excellent for reading aloud, deal with human courage, perseverance, and love and evoke a strong sense of Cuba.

5.36   Adler, David A. **One Yellow Daffodil: A Hanukkah Story.** Illustrated by Lloyd Bloom. Harcourt Brace, 1995. ISBN 0-15-200537-4. unpaged. 6–10.

This moving story of Morris Kaplan, a Holocaust survivor, is also about the rekindling of love, tradition, and the Hanukkah candles in the menorah. The author notes that the fictional character of Morris was inspired by interviews with actual survivors. Two children befriend Morris, who owns a flower shop because a yellow daffodil once gave him hope and courage to survive in Auschwitz. Gradually Morris becomes part of the children's family as he remembers, mourns, and speaks of his past. The realistic illustrations are compelling, particularly one of Morris as a small boy in a concentration camp.

5.37   Akio, Terumasa. **Me and Alves: A Japanese Journey.** Illustrated by Yukio Oido. Annick, 1993. ISBN 1-55037-222-X. 30p. 6–8.

This story chronicles the adventures of Alves, an exchange student from Brazil. The story unfolds from the perspective of his host family in Japan. We share Alves's discoveries as he tours Japan's northern island, Hokkaido; we learn about daily life when he works in the fields, attends village festivals, participates in a sumo wrestling tournament, and attends a local school. Author Terumasa Akio is the founder of an international exchange program. This book is an excellent introduction to mutual respect and understanding between different cultures.

5.38   Baillie, Allan. **Rebel.** Illustrated by Di Wu. Ticknor & Fields, 1994. ISBN 0-395-69250-4. 32p. 5–7.

The rebel is an anonymous schoolchild who throws a shoe at a Burmese warlord in modern times. With the clever assistance of his schoolmates and teachers, the young culprit is not found. Moreover, the general is mocked with laughter. This war incident is worthy of being discussed with the young. Was the child's action courageous or foolhardy? The pastel illustrations move from the quiet (and later humorous) faces of the villagers to the at first violent faces of the soldiers and the general. Adult assistance is recommended for this picture book.

5.39 Berry, James. **The Future-Telling Lady and Other Stories.** HarperCollins, 1993. ISBN 0-06-021434-1. 139p. 10–12.

These six stories, set in Jamaica, are narrated by boys and girls of a range of ages. The dialect and setting allow young readers to investigate another culture, while the children's stories offer insight into daily lives and concerns that are like those of children around the world. The thoughtful stories explore family relations, issues of responsibility and identity, and the supernatural in a manner that is accessible to both younger and older children. Younger children may enjoy listening to these stories, while older readers may be able to read the dialect for themselves.

5.40 Bond, Ruskin. **Binya's Blue Umbrella.** Illustrated by Vera Rosenberry. Boyds Mills, 1995. ISBN 1-56397-135-6. 68p. 8–12.

Binya is ten years old as far as anyone in her village can guess. She lives in the Indian Himalayas and works tending cattle in the fields. One sunny afternoon, she discovers a rare pendant, which she trades for a fine blue umbrella. This umbrella makes her the envy of her village, especially of the tea shop owner, Ram Bharosa, who does his best to get the umbrella from her, and finally succeeds. In the end, both Binya and Ram learn that generosity can be more valuable than what we possess materially. Indian village life is palpable in this simple yet engaging story.

5.41 Bosse, Malcolm. **Deep Dream of the Rain Forest.** Farrar, Straus, 1993. ISBN 0-374-31757-7. 179p. 11–12.

A fifteen-year-old English boy joins his uncle in a government expedition into the jungles of Borneo in the 1920s. He is kidnapped by two young people of the Iban tribe and comes to learn something of their culture, especially their reliance on dreams. This unusual adventure is a well-written coming-of-age story in a far-off setting.

5.42 Case, Dianne. **92 Queens Road.** Farrar, Straus, 1995. ISBN 0-374-35518-5. 164p. 9–12.

Growing up in her Cape Town neighborhood, Kathy comes to know what it means to be colored and to be born out of wedlock. She is surrounded by a caring family that survives and evolves through unemployment, marriage, and death. As Kathy grows older, she finds that her family is profoundly affected by the apartheid system, which forces relocation of colored neighborhoods, divides the family from relatives who are reclassified as white, and restricts their use of public areas and facilities. The unity of the family is threatened by both personal and political factors. Kathy's story is compelling and her family is made up of realistic and vivid characters.

5.43 Dorris, Michael. **Guests.** Hyperion, 1994. ISBN 0-7868-0047-X. 119p. 9–12.

It is not unusual for adolescents to be irritated by and feel disconnected from their families and the world around them. Moss, a Native American boy, is no exception. In a moment of anger, he runs off into the forest, where he hopes to undergo a vision quest and become a man. What he does experience is not what he had anticipated, but through it he gains an understanding of himself and of his place in his family and world. This is an introspective, provocative novel ideal for reading aloud.

5.44 Dorros, Arthur (translated by Sandra Marulanda Dorros). **Radio Man: A Story in English and Spanish.** Illustrated by Arthur Dorros. HarperCollins, 1993. ISBN 0-06-021547-X. 40p. 5–8.

When his family sets off to pick apples in Washington, Diego is sad at having to part from his good friend David. But he is the son of a migrant farm worker and constantly on the move from state to state in search of work, so parting is inevitable. For his family, and particularly for Diego, the radio is a constant companion. It eases the monotony of the work in the fields, relieves the tedium of the long overnight drives, and provides an important link with both friends left behind and the new community the family is about to join. This warm story of friendship and family is told in both English and Spanish and is complemented by naive-style paintings in bold colors.

5.45 Franklin, Kristine L. (translated by Alma Flor Ada). **The Shepherd Boy/El niño pastor.** Illustrated by Jill Kastner. Atheneum, 1994. ISBN 0-689- 31809-X (English); 0-689-31918-5 (Spanish). 32p. 5–7.

Ben, a Navajo boy, must tend his father's fifty sheep as a summer job. The quiet events of the day from sunrise to sunset are told in rhythmic prose. One day a ewe lamb is missing. Ben must return to the high grazing ground, with its walls of painted pictures, to find the stray before night falls and the coyote screams. The paintings catch the essence of the Navajo territory of the American Southwest. The poetic cumulative text and evocative paintings are a perfect combination. Editions are available in English and Spanish.

5.46   Grifalconi, Ann. **The Bravest Flute: A Story of Courage in the Mayan Tradition.** Illustrated by Ann Grifalconi. Little, Brown, 1994. ISBN 0-316- 32878-2. 32p. 5–9.

A young Mayan boy is chosen to lead the traditional New Year's Day parade from his highland village through the mountains to the cathedral in the valley below. He has to prove that he has enough courage and strength to persevere with this task after months of farming the rocky soil. Playing a cheerful song on his flute and carrying the large, heavy drum on his back at the same time proves to be very difficult until a magical gift from the old master flutist's widow transforms his journey into a joyful celebration of cultural and personal survival.

5.47   James, Betsy. **The Mud Family.** Illustrated by Paul Morin. Putnam, 1994. ISBN 0-399-22549-8. 32p. 5–7.

In the southwest of New Mexico, the elders dance the rain dance but no rain comes. A young girl, Sosi, has created her own mud family near the bank of a pool. When her family decides that they will have to leave because of the drought, Sosi creeps away and holds her own rain dance with her mud family. Now it rains gloriously—so much so that she has to be rescued by her father just before a red wall of mud and water rushes down the canyon. Morin's illustrations reflect the dramatic impact of the desert environment on the culture of the people and convey a feeling for the varying coloration of rock and sand. Powerful portraits of the characters, based on life drawings, add a sense of poignancy and urgency. The final sharing of everyone's muddy handprints on a rock provides a climactic unity for the book.

5.48   Kurtz, Jane. **Fire on the Mountain.** Illustrated by E. B. Lewis. Simon & Schuster, 1994. ISBN 0-671-88268-6. 34p. 6–8.

Set in a mountain village in Ethiopia, this story uses the traditional folk motif of the poor and humble overcoming the rich and proud. With the promise of a reward for success and the threat of punishment for failure, Alemayo's rich and boastful master challenges the young servant to endure a bitterly cold night alone in the mountains outside their village. Alemayo accomplishes the demanding task, but the master offers a tricky reason for reneging on his promise. Other household servants manage to outwit the master at his own game and justice is finally done. The subtle earth-toned watercolors are in lovely harmony with a gentle yet powerful telling.

5.49   London, Jonathan. **The Sugaring-Off Party.** Illustrated by Gilles Pelletier. Dutton, 1995. ISBN 0-525-45187-0. 32p. 5–10.

On a cold March night before Paul's first sugaring-off party, his grandmother recounts her first visit to this traditional Quebec party. This party celebrates the coming of spring, when it is time to boil maple sap into sugar and syrup. Colorful oil paintings in the style of native folk art give a sense of the history of the Quebec countryside. Images of the Montreal Canadians' hockey sweater, fiddling, feasting, and the snowy landscape provide an introduction to French Canadian traditions. French phrases are also included.

5.50   McGee, Charmayne. **So Sings the Blue Deer.** Atheneum, 1994. ISBN 0-689-31888-X. 186p. 12–13.

In this ecological story, based on fact, members of the Huichol Indian group make a dangerous journey to Mexico City to receive a band of white-tailed deer that are necessary to restore their livelihood, culture, and religion.

5.51   Snyder, Carol. **God Must Like Cookies, Too.** Illustrated by Beth Glick. Jewish Publication Society, 1993. ISBN 0-8276-0423-8. 32p. 5–7.

The special outing of a Jewish grandmother and her young granddaughter is presented through the point of view of the young girl. As the two attend Oneg Shabbat synagogue services together, the reader is introduced to some of the traditions of Judaism and the sights, sounds, and smells of a Friday night service. The colorful pastel illustrations are engaging, making readers feel as if they, too, were sitting on the wooden chairs of the synagogue. This egalitarian Shabbat service includes the grandmother's turn to read aloud from the Torah.

5.52   Yep, Laurence. **Thief of Hearts.** HarperCollins, 1995. ISBN 0-06-025342-8. 196p. 9–12.

Stacy has never really thought about being a Chinese American. Although Stacy's great-grandmother, Tai-Paw, lives with her and her parents in the suburbs of San Francisco, she has never paid much attention to the stories of her mother growing up in Chinatown. Stacy is forced to question her identity when she is asked to escort Hong Ch'un, a recent Chinese immigrant, to junior high. Hong Ch'un is accused of stealing and for the first time Stacy feels like an outsider. In her attempt to help a new friend, Stacy gains a deeper understanding of her past and of her mother. Readers may be familiar with the story of Stacy's mother in the novel *Child of the Owl.*

Human Relationships

Death or Illness

5.53   Howard, Ellen. **Murphy and Kate.** Illustrated by Mark Graham. Simon & Schuster, 1995. ISBN 0-671-79775-1. 32p. 5–8.

Kate's dog Murphy dies of old age. She recalls in detail their lives together, from the time they were infant and puppy through to their fourteenth year. Kate realizes how he had been her friend through the years and mourns his passing. She is able to continue with her own life, but vows to always remember her faithful friend. This book would help children who have recently lost a pet or family member to understand the mourning process.

5.54   Mills, Claudia. **Dinah Forever.** Farrar, Straus, 1995. ISBN 0-374-31788-7. 134p. 10–12.

In her fourth book about Dinah Seabrooke, Claudia Mills follows Dinah as she enters grade 7 with old friends, a new boyfriend, and abundant confidence that she will be able to meet the challenges of the year. Dinah quickly finds that events do not always unfold as she might wish, and that she cannot carry off relationships and achievements through the force of her will. New ideas are presented to her in school, together with the means of exploring them through poetry. When she confronts her first major personal loss, Dinah must find a way to reconcile herself to what she cannot change. Dinah is a likable, sincere, and impulsive character whom readers, especially girls, will care about and identify with.

5.55   Smith, Jane Denitz. **Mary by Myself.** HarperCollins, 1994. ISBN 0-06-024517-4. 152p. 9–11.

When crib death claims Mary's baby sister, she and her parents begin to drift apart, isolated from one another in their grief. At summer camp, Mary falls under the spell of her tent-mate Laura, a lonely, mysterious girl who sneaks away each night to an abandoned hunter's lodge. Mary begins to join her and finds herself introduced to seances, voodoo rituals, and the planning of cruel tricks to play on the other camp girls. She finally frees herself of Laura's influence and discovers inner resources that help her deal with her sister's death without allowing grief to destroy her family. With its strong characterization and compelling narrative, this well-written novel will sustain readers' interest and empathy.

5.56　　Weeks, Sarah. **Red Ribbon.** Illustrated by Jeffrey Greene. HarperCollins, 1995. ISBN 0-06-025430-0. 32p. 5–8.

This story is told from the perspective of an eight-year-old girl who tries to understand the life and suffering of a neighbor who is dying of AIDS. When her mother gives her a red ribbon for her birthday, she uses the ribbon first to tie back her hair, then to wrap a present for her neighbor. Her mother cuts off a segment of the ribbon for her to wear on her lapel, representing the hope that one day soon the AIDS epidemic will be over. The artwork by Jeffrey Greene is detailed and realistic, using diverse viewpoints. The book is accompanied by a red ribbon, a tape on which the story is sung, and an appendix outlining the significance and practice of wearing a red ribbon.

5.57　　Wild, Margaret. **Toby.** Illustrated by Noela Young. Ticknor & Fields, 1994. ISBN 0-395-67024-1. 32p. 5–7.

As Sara grows older, she becomes more distant from her childhood dog companion, Toby, until he becomes sick and is to be put down. This is an emotional story of the complex feelings children have for both their pets and death. Watercolor illustrations complement the text well, with their engaging portraits of children at play. This is a good springboard for class discussions of family, animals, death, and grief.

5.58　　Zolotow, Charlotte. **The Old Dog.** Illustrated by James Ransome. HarperCollins, 1995. ISBN 0-06-024409-7. 32p. 5–8.

The richly textured, warm illustrations and large-print, simple text draw the reader into this timeless, sad story of a beloved dog's death. Ben finds his old dog dead one morning and slowly learns what her death means and what it is to grieve. The cycle of life continues with a new puppy at the end, but Zolotow's language sustains Ben's grief even as Ransome's pictures show his joy.

Everyday Life

5.59 Beard, Darleen Bailey. **The Pumpkin Man from Piney Creek.** Illustrated by Laura Kelly. Simon & Schuster, 1995. ISBN 0-689-80315-X. 32p. 5–8.

This historical Halloween harvest story features Hattie, a young girl who lives on a pumpkin farm and yearns to carve her favorite pumpkin into a jack-o'-lantern. Eventually, she gets her wish and is given a pumpkin. The watercolor and pencil illustrations are full of the images and details of nineteenth-century rural America. The book concludes with a pumpkin pie recipe.

5.60 Belton, Sandra. **From Miss Ida's Porch.** Illustrated by Floyd Cooper. Four Winds, 1993. ISBN 0-02-708915-0. 40p. 6–8.

This picture storybook celebrates storytelling. On warm summer evenings, African American children hear of their past and some of the memorable events in the lives of the adults who recount their experiences. The storytellers' warm tones in describing discrimination serve to heighten the injustice of the past. The muted, full-page illustrations, especially those depicting children, reflect the power of the storyteller.

5.61 Cooper, Ilene. **Buddy Love: Now on Video.** HarperCollins, 1995. ISBN 0-06-024663-4. 183p. 10–12.

Until his dad wins a video camera, Buddy Love feels that he is not special. With his new interest in videography, he begins to suspect that he is good at something. Buddy discovers the stories and special qualities of his friends and family as they become the subjects of his interviews for a class project. Increased confidence in himself and in his family and friends helps Buddy resist the pressure of his manipulative best friend and to stand up for himself. Young readers will find Buddy and his family a typical yet interesting collection of individuals. Buddy's dilemma in resisting peer pressure is familiar, but the outcome affirms hope.

5.62 Dunrea, Olivier. **The Painter Who Loved Chickens.** Illustrated by Olivier Dunrea. Farrar, Straus, 1995. ISBN 0-374-35729-3. 32p. 5–7.

Forced to support himself in the city by painting pictures of poodles, penguins, and people, the painter who loved chickens is most unhappy. The only thing that makes him happy is painting chickens in his spare time. His tedious life in the city is abruptly transformed when a wealthy art buyer selects a simple painting of an egg. Warm and richly colored paintings alternate with half-pages of witty text. Small, round paintings of different breeds of chickens are labeled and included on the top of each page of text. Anyone interested in art, chickens, and humor will enjoy this book.

5.63 Goodman, Joan Elizabeth. **Songs from Home.** Illustrated by Joan Elizabeth Goodman. Harcourt Brace, 1994. ISBN 0-15-203590-7. 213p. 10–14.

Eleven-year-old Anna and her father are street singers in Rome, singing such popular American songs as "Bye, Bye Blackbird." Anna adores her father, but she dislikes their nomadic life and longs for a real home rather than a barren existence in an ill-kept pensione. She is also tired of keeping her life a secret from her schoolmates, particularly her best friend. Then she learns about her American family and how they want both Anna and her father to return to them. It is a well-written story and has an extra bonus in its descriptions of Rome; Anna's father is an excellent tour guide for children.

5.64 Griffin, Peni R. **The Brick House Burglars.** McElderry, 1994. ISBN 0-689-50579-5. 138p. 9–11.

Living in their poor, urban neighborhood, Mary Jane and her friends, Rainbow, Donnavita, and Heather, make a game out of imagining the inside of a shut-up brick house on their corner. One day a stray mother cat shows the girls a way into the house, which becomes their secret clubhouse. When an arsonist attempts to make the house a target, the girls begin an investigation of possible suspects in order to protect the house and the cats that live in it. The narrative takes the form of a long report by Mary Jane with transcriptions of evidence given by the other girls. The story is an engaging representation of the girls' lives and neighborhood.

5.65 Hartmann, Wendy. **All the Magic in the World.** Illustrated by Niki Daly. Dutton, 1993. ISBN 0-525-45092-0. 24p. 5–7.

Against the background of the South African urban landscape, home to both author and illustrator, this vivid portrayal of children at play emphasizes the value of everyday things as objects of play. Lena, a little girl who sometimes gets teased for being clumsy, meets Joseph, the odd-job man; he teaches Lena and the other children the magic of play and the power of imagination. The vivid, colorful illustrations underline the magical qualities of the story and provide teachers and readers with a culturally relevant portrait of children at play that, at the same time, appeals to children of all backgrounds with its open-ended language patterns and universal message about human relationships. Children will enjoy having this book read to them.

5.66 Hermes, Patricia. **Someone to Count On.** Little, Brown, 1993. ISBN 0-316-35925-4. 184p. 11–12.

Patricia Hermes explores a favorite topic among children: inadequate mothers. Eleven-year-old Samantha (Sam) tells about life out of a suitcase with her single mom, Elizabeth. Their unstable life is shaken up even more when a whim takes them to grandfather's ranch in Colorado, where Elizabeth teasingly suggests that this might be a permanent home. Who can Sam count on? Although she seems to be surrounded with caricature adults, Sam is fully realized, complex, and easy to identify with.

5.67 Hoberman, Mary Ann. **The Cozy Book.** Illustrated by Betty Fraser. Harcourt Brace, 1995. ISBN 0-15-276620-0. 48p. 5–8.

This richly illustrated and rhyming collection includes all kinds of cozy things ranging from tasty things to eat, such as milk and cookies, to cozy places, people, and feelings, and "cozy games that last all morning." The minute details of the illustrations, along with the rich rhyming pattern of the poetry, will appeal to children's imagination and create a safe and warm environment through the universal theme of caring and safety.

5.68 Howker, Janni. **The Topiary Garden.** Illustrated by Anthony Browne. Orchard, 1995. ISBN 0-531-06891-9. 63p. 11–12.

Young teenager Liz resents the sexist comments offered by her father and older brother, and she is particularly upset by her brother's mutilation of her prize-winning sketchbook. She meets an old woman, who tells Liz the story of her life: She ran away from a poor, oppressive home and, disguised as a boy, became a gardener in a topiary garden. This story encompasses several themes. In the old woman's story we learn of the lot of a poor girl, the class distinctions of the past, and the chasm between rich and poor; in the present we read of the macho male bonding of father and son, and a young girl's determination to be herself and nourish her ability as an artist. The story evokes deep emotion through its simple prose. The full-page colored illustrations of a topiary garden are eerie and somewhat threatening. The story first appeared in the author's book of short stories, *Badger on the Barge and Other Stories.*

5.69   Johnson, Angela. **Julius.** Illustrated by Dav Pilkey. Orchard, 1993. ISBN 0-531-05465-9. 32p. 5–7.

Julius, an Alaskan pig, is a gift to Maya from her granddaddy. Maya teaches Julius some manners while including him in her daily activities such as swinging, dancing, and trying on hats. The colorful illustrations use fabric designs as borders and backgrounds. The book explores themes relating to manners, pets, pigs, sharing, and multiculturalism.

5.70   Johnston, Tony. **The Old Lady and the Birds.** Illustrated by Stephanie Garcia. Harcourt Brace, 1994. ISBN 0-15-257769-6. 32p. 5–8.

This is a day in the life of an old Mexican lady who sits in a garden eating and listening to the birds, until she finally falls asleep. Tony Johnston's simple story is illustrated by Stephanie Garcia's incredible montages, tableaus of wood, paste, cloth, and even dried flowers. Although some children may find the clearly lifeless birds a bit disturbing, the overall impact of Garcia's art is both satisfying and evocative.

5.71   Lachner, Dorothea. **Andrew's Angry Words.** Illustrated by Thé Tjong-Khing. North-South, 1995. ISBN 1-55858-435-6. 27p. 5–8.

Andrew didn't mean to yell angry words at his sister, just as she didn't mean to step on his toys. His words set in motion a whole chain of events, with the angry words passing from person to person to creature to distant parts of the world, all the while being chased by Andrew, who is trying to correct his mistake. Fortunately, the words are stopped and Andrew catches up. He is given a gift that he shares with everyone he has unintentionally affected. All is set right again. The illustrations are lighthearted and amusing, keeping the message about thoughtless words light in delivery. This story could be used to help younger students to deal with anger appropriately.

5.72   MacLachlan, Patricia. **What You Know First.** Illustrated by Barry Moser. HarperCollins, 1995. ISBN 0-06-024413-5. 32p. 5–7.

The exquisite, poetic text echoes the thought processes of a young child reluctant to leave her prairie home for a new home on the coast. She assuages her worries by resolving to take mementos from the prairie with her, and to always recollect her life there, recognizing that "what you know first stays with you." The hauntingly realistic illustrations are woodblock engraved prints by Barry Moser, closely resembling old photographic negatives.

This is an excellent text for exploring attachments to homes and neighborhoods, early memories, and migrations and moving.

5.73 Naylor, Phyllis Reynolds. **Alice the Brave.** Atheneum, 1995. ISBN 0-689-80095-9. 130p. 10–13.

When Chrissa's mother sends her to live with her grandmother in the country for a year, thirteen-year-old Chrissa is determined to locate her long-absent father. As time goes on, her need for him begins to fade, but she still believes she must find him to rescue her Gram from danger. Finally, when Chrissa learns the truth about her father, she and her Gram have already overcome their problem. Chrissa has learned to love herself without his approval, and she is ready to face her father as an equal.

5.74 Paterson, Katherine. **A Midnight Clear: Stories for the Christmas Season.** Lodestar, 1995. ISBN 0-525-67529-9. 212p. 9–12.

Each story in this collection addresses the spirit of Christmas in the lives of ordinary people. Rather than providing the focal point in these stories, Christmas is the context in which the author presents everyday occurrences and relationships. The themes of the stories include the relations between the young and the elderly, parents and children, privileged and poor. The narrators vary in age, background, and gender. The collection will enhance any observance of the Christmas season.

5.75 Pinkney, Brian. **JoJo's Flying Side Kick.** Illustrated by Brian Pinkney. Simon & Schuster, 1995. ISBN 0-689-80283-8. 32p. 5–8.

JoJo's Tae Kwon Do instructor decides JoJo is ready to try for her yellow belt. However, JoJo's self-doubts make her nervous. By applying all the bits of advice from family and friends, she manages to overcome her fears. Interesting scratchboard-style art illustrations give the text vigor and add intrigue.

5.76 Rylant, Cynthia. **Henry and Mudge and the Best Day of All.** Illustrated by Suçie Stevenson. Macmillan, 1995. ISBN 0-02-778012-0. 40p. 6–8.

This early readers' text follows a day in the life of Henry and his dog Mudge— not any old day, but Henry's birthday. The book is divided into four chapters about Henry and Mudge rising in the morning, preparing for a party, attending the party, and then resting after the party. The vocabulary is simple, literary, and repeated, making it a useful text for teaching children to read. The illustrations are colorful and cartoonlike.

5.77 Saul, Carol P. **Someplace Else.** Illustrated by Barry Root. Simon & Schuster, 1995. ISBN 0-689-80273-0. 32p. 5–7.

Mrs. Tillby, tired of living on an orchard, decides one day to pack up and try living in another place. She visits her grown children and grandchildren in the city, seashore, mountains, and other places, but never wants to settle. Eventually, she solves her problem by buying a trailer. The notion of older people wanting excitement and adventure is well related, with a repetitive pattern moving toward a satisfying ending. The gouache illustrations bring a warm, golden glow to this happy tale with a "home is best" theme.

5.78 Soto, Gary. **Local News.** Harcourt Brace, 1993. ISBN 0-15-248117-6. 148p. 9–12.

This collection contains stories narrated by Mexican American boys and girls of various ages. The setting and culture are distinguished by the author's intermingling of Spanish with English words. The vocabulary is made accessible with the inclusion of a glossary, but often the context alone is sufficient for an English language reader to determine the meaning. The cultural backdrop offers young readers insight into another way of life, but the stories' themes are universal. These young people are concerned with family relations, friendship, bullying, pets, and school. The author treats these issues with realism and empathy and without simplification.

5.79 Torres, Leyla. **Subway Sparrow/Gorrion del metro.** Illustrated by Leyla Torres. Farrar, Straus, 1993. ISBN 0-374-37285-3 (English); 0-374-32756-4 (Spanish). 32p. 5–7.

This is a very gentle multicultural picture book in which a sparrow is trapped in a New York subway, and two teenagers (one Asian) and two adults (one Spanish-speaking and one Polish), join forces to rescue it. A few sentences in Spanish and Polish are included in the text. Editions are available in both English and Spanish.

5.80 Tripp, Nathaniel. **Thunderstorm.** Illustrated by Juan Wijngaard. Dial, 1994. ISBN 0-8037-1366-5. 47p. 6–10.

Although cast in story format, this description of a thunderstorm is presented scientifically. Ben, a farmer, wakes at dawn to see to the day's tasks. As he and his wife, Emma, work around the farm, the reader is given a glimpse into various animals' lives. Eventually a storm comes; it is described in great detail, with

each change to the landscape evoked through the prose and illustrations. The realistic artwork complements the text well.

5.81 Udry, May. **Is Susan Here?** Illustrated by Karen Gundersheimer.
HarperCollins, 1993. ISBN 0-06-026142-0. 24p. 5–6.

This preschool picture book chronicles a day in the life of Susan
as she dresses up in various animal costumes to fool her parents.
The book is useful for exploring disguises, Halloween, animals,
and identity. A follow-up classroom activity might be to encourage children to disguise themselves as their favorite creatures.

5.82 Wells, Rosemary. **Lucy Comes to Stay.** Illustrated by Mark Graham. Dial, 1994. ISBN 0-8037-1214-6. 32p. 5–8.

Any child who has ever longed for a dog or lived with one will
relate to this heartwarming story of a new puppy. Set in the late
1940s, the story's main character, Mary Elizabeth, helps care for
newborn puppy, Lucy, and learns that a new puppy is unpre-
dictable and humorous. Beautiful illustrations evoke the tender
mood of the story, which is effectively sectioned into mini-chap-
ters with appealing titles. The ending, which depicts child and
dog snuggling in bed "just for tonight," is a perfect and realistic
conclusion.

5.83 Westall, Robert. **Christmas Spirit: Two Stories.** Illustrated by
John Lawrence. Farrar, Straus, 1994. ISBN 0-374-31260-5. 154p.
9–11.

These two Christmas stories are very English in their settings
and their tellings and catch the traditional spirit of Christmas, including scrumptious descriptions of the food. Both stories have
children at the heart of them—a boy in "The Christmas Ghost"
and a girl in "The Christmas Cat." Although these would be
good for reading aloud by the home fireside on Christmas Eve—
the first story is reminiscent of Dylan Thomas's "A Child's
Christmas in Wales"—there is enough suspense in them for
reading at any time of the year. The charming black-and-white
illustrations resemble the work of Edward Ardizzoni.

5.84 Wright, Betty Ren. **Nothing but Trouble.** Illustrated by Jacqueline Rogers. Holiday House, 1995. ISBN 0-8234-1175-3. 119p.
9–11.

Vannie does not want to stay with her aunt Bert, especially after
she learns that her aunt hates Vannie's little poodle, Muffy. However, Vannie's parents need her to stay behind while they look
for work in California. Soon Vannie realizes that Aunt Bert has

problems too. Someone is trying to scare her off the farm. Aunt Bert worries about prowlers, while Vannie is thrown into a panic when Muffy disappears. Vannie solves the mystery of the prowlers, showing bravery that young readers will admire. When Vannie receives news from her parents and Muffy turns up in the care of an elderly neighbor, Vannie must make a difficult decision. Vannie's problems are realistic and so are their resolutions, and her character is resilient and forward-looking.

5.85 Yolen, Jane. **Before the Storm.** Illustrated by Georgia Pugh. Boyds Mills, 1995. ISBN 1-56397-240-9. 32p. 5–8.

This book captures the sluggish, breathless experience of a summer noon just before an electrical storm arrives to provide cool release. Each page describes an aspect and the pictures use strong, glaring colors to suggest bright sunlight. Then, as the children find ways to cool off, the colors also change, growing darker when the storm strikes. The language is simple and direct and would provide a stimulus for reader response and a discussion of lazy summer days.

Family Life

5.86 Ackerman, Karen (translated by Alma Flor Ada). **By the Dawn's Early Light/Al amanecer.** Illustrated by Catherine Stock. Atheneum, 1994. ISBN 0-689-31788-3 (English); 0-689-31917-7 (Spanish). 32p. 5–7.

An African American mother holds down two jobs to support her two children and her mother. The children see her only at dawn. The social realism of the picture book is melded into family love and understanding of the mother's situation. The illustrations show how the mother's efforts help her family. Editions are available in both English and Spanish.

5.87 Bauer, Marion Dane. **A Question of Trust.** Scholastic, 1994. ISBN 0-590-47915-6. 130p. 10–11.

When their mother moves out of the home, life becomes tense for Brad and his young brother, Charley. Brad takes the lead in distancing himself from his mother and in secretly tending to a cat and its two kittens. Brad eventually learns that his mother still loves him and he needs her. This is an affectionate treatment of a dysfunctional family.

5.88 Best, Carl. **Taxi! Taxi!** Illustrated by Dale Gottlieb. Little, Brown, 1994. ISBN 0-316-09259-2. 32p. 5–7.

This brightly colored picture book about a little girl's Sunday outing with her dad, who drives a taxi and does not live with her and her mother, follows Tina and her father on their day together through the city and out to the country. Father and daughter have a special, warm relationship that carries over to many people in Tina's neighborhood. With a cheery tone and a number of Spanish words and phrases, this heartwarming story lets children relate to the different kinds of families in our world.

5.89 Brown, Jane Clark. **George Washington's Ghost.** Illustrated by Jane Clark Brown. Houghton Mifflin, 1994. ISBN 0-395-69452-3. 87p. 7–10.

As the youngest child in a large family, Celinda Noodle often feels left out and underestimated. It was her idea that the family take her late father's puppet show on the road to avoid starvation, yet she is considered too small to work any of the puppets. In her attempts to prove her abilities, Celinda gets herself and her family into difficulties and adventures as they travel the countryside, performing at fairs and markets. When their prize puppet, George Washington, is taken in payment of a debt, Celinda devises a plan to retrieve him in time for the greatest show of their new career. Celinda is an intelligent, plucky, and well-meaning heroine. Children will identify with her struggle to define her place in a large family.

5.90 Brown, Susan M. **You're Dead, David Borelli.** Atheneum, 1995. ISBN 0-689-31959-2. 155p. 10–12.

David, well-dressed and educated at an exclusive school, finds himself in foster care when his father is imprisoned on charges of fraud. David must adjust to a tough, new school, to life in a new home, and to the other foster kids who live there. Readers will empathize with David, who discovers strength and compassion in himself through building new friendships and standing up to intimidation at school. Ultimately, David and his new friends achieve happiness and well-being.

5.91 Bunting, Eve. **Flower Garden.** Illustrated by Kathryn Hewitt. Harcourt Brace, 1994. ISBN 0-15-228776-0. 32p. 5–7.

This rich and affectionate look at inner-city life is simply and elegantly told. The story chronicles the journey of a flower garden from its purchase at a local market to its final destination, an apartment flower box, and its final purpose, a birthday present for a working mother. Hewitt's richly colored oil paintings perfectly capture the warmth and affection that unite this African

American family, beautifully symbolized by a final painting in which we look over the last piece of birthday cake to the family gazing out their window at the sunset illuminating the city and the flower garden they have created.

5.92   Bunting, Eve. **The In-Between Days.** Illustrated by Alexander Pertzoff. HarperCollins, 1994. ISBN 0-06-023609-4. 119p. 8–12.

When Caroline visits Dove Island, she threatens to change the familiar structure of eleven-year-old George's family. Although he realizes that there is an empty place left by the death of his mother years before, he resists the idea of a new person becoming too close to his father. He finds a perfect way to tell her to leave, but when his plan actually works, he must decide whether the result is what he wants. With humor and sensitivity, Eve Bunting captures the doubts and worries that are so natural for a child beginning a relationship with a new step-parent. The book is reminiscent of *Sarah, Plain and Tall* by Patricia MacLachlan in its honest, simple portrait of a child's view of his world.

5.93   Bunting, Eve. **Smoky Night.** Illustrated by David Diaz. Harcourt Brace, 1994. ISBN 0-15-269954-6. 34p. 6–9.

Eve Bunting's justly acclaimed Caldecott Medal winner tells the quietly eloquent tale of a family that learns an invaluable lesson about friendship and race relations from their cat on the smoky night of the Los Angeles riots. David Diaz's starkly etched paintings, executed by using acrylics on watercolor panels, provide a startling recreation of a night of rage, pain, fear, and, ultimately, enlightenment. This is a very useful book for exploring social issues with children, all within the familiar context of domestic life.

5.94   Calmenson, Stephanie. **Hotter Than a Hot Dog.** Illustrated by Elivia. Little, Brown, 1994. ISBN 0-316-12479-6. 32p. 5–7.

It's a very hot summer day in a large city. A little girl and her grandmother are both very, very hot, so Granny decides to take her granddaughter to the beach. They take the train, play at the beach, buy ice cream, and eventually return home to a cool evening breeze. The warm relationship between the girl and her grandmother can be appreciated by young and old alike for its humor, simplicity, and familiarity. Children can recall and share family outings after reading this story.

5.95   Christiansen, C. B. **I See the Moon.** Atheneum, 1994. ISBN 0-689-31928-2. 116p. 11–13.

Children will relate to twelve-year-old Bitte as she looks forward longingly to becoming an aunt and giving the baby all the love and affection she had received from her Aunt Minna, who now has Alzheimer's disease. When she learns that her unmarried sister intends to give the baby up for adoption, Bitte is devastated and resists relinquishing her personal dreams. Gradually, however, her romanticized view of love is replaced with an understanding of herself, the adults around her, and the knowledge that love may also involve unhappiness. The story, filled with emotion but never sentimental, is beautifully written and filled with poetic images.

5.96   Conrad, Pam. **Our House: The Stories of Levittown.** Scholastic, 1995. ISBN 0-590-46523-6. 65p. 8–12.

Levittown, Long Island, arose from a potato farm called Island Trees. When Mr. Levitt bought the farm and began developing it in the 1940s, he laid the beginnings of a town that would continue to grow into the 1990s. The author skillfully weaves a story for each decade that combines history with fiction. She writes about TeeWee Tator, who fell through the attic floor and landed in his mother's cake in 1948, and young Suzanne Stapleton, who records the long teachers' strike in her diary. Each decade is captured in the voices of the children who once called Levittown home.

5.97   Corcoran, Barbara. **Wolf at the Door.** Atheneum, 1993. ISBN 0-689-31870-7. 194p. 9–11.

Weary from years of following her army father around, Lee and her family finally find themselves in a small house on a forest lake in Montana. While her younger sister pursues an acting career with the help of her screen star grandmother, Lee and her mother find themselves becoming increasingly involved in saving and caring for wolves, an activity which brings hostility from the local cattle ranchers. This is a well-crafted family story with dual plot lines that will hold the interest of young readers.

5.98   Creech, Sharon. **Walk Two Moons.** HarperCollins, 1994. ISBN 0-06-023334-6. 280p. 8–12.

In this Newbery Medal winner, thirteen-year-old Salamanca Tree Hiddle tells the story of her friend Phoebe Winterbottom. They suspect that Phoebe's mother has been kidnapped by a young and good-looking lunatic. Salamanca also tells of her own uncertainty about her father's friend Margaret Cadaver. Salamanca slowly unravels her story during a very important drive with her grandparents from Ohio to Idaho. Humor and suspense are woven into a plot that reveals the imagination and emotions of a young girl who is proud of her Native American heritage and confused over the absence of her mother.

5.99   Cuneo, Mary Louise. **Anne Is Elegant.** HarperCollins, 1993. ISBN 0-06-022992-6. 167p. 10–13.

In this quiet, well-crafted novel set in Chicago at Christmas, 1936, Anna's family is being torn apart by grief caused by the death of her infant brother. Her father buries himself in work, leaving Anna to deal with her mother's intense sorrow. Only her imaginative spirit and the friendship of her unconventional Aunt Maria help her deal with her confusion about death. Young readers will particularly enjoy the descriptions of school life, sledding, Christmas festivities, and family gatherings.

5.100   Duffy, Betsy. **Coaster.** Viking, 1994. ISBN 0-670-85480-8. 114p. 10–12.

Twelve-year-old Kevin's chief link with his divorced and absent father is their love of riding roller coasters. They meet once every summer to indulge in their hobby. He is also resentful of his mother's increasing interest in a TV weatherman whose hobby is entertaining sick children. After a narrow escape riding his homemade coaster, Kevin gains insight into what bravery and heroism really are. The use of roller coasting adds an unusual twist and exotic note.

5.101   Ellis, Sarah. **Out of the Blue.** McElderry, 1995. ISBN 0-689-80025-8. 120p. 9–12.

Eleven-year-old Megan Hungerford is sure that something strange is up with her mother and father. First, she finds her mother putting cereal in the fridge and skipping her university classes, and then learns the surprising news that they are breaking the family tradition of going to the cottage in July. Nothing could have prepared Megan for the news that at seventeen her mother gave a baby girl up for adoption. Megan's younger sister, six-year-old Betsy, is excited about the prospect of meeting her half-sister, but Megan is not so sure about her feelings. This well-written story is rich with family love and humor.

5.102   Emberley, Michael. **Welcome Back Sun.** Illustrated by Michael Emberley. Little, Brown, 1993. ISBN 0-316-23647-0. 32p. 5–8.

In a remote Norwegian mountain village, a little girl dreams of the spring and the warmth of the sun during the long season of murketiden, the murky time at the end of the long winter just before spring. Along with other villagers, the girl and her family climb high up the mountain, seeking the first rays of the sun. Based on an old Norwegian legend of a little girl who went out to find the sun for her people after the dreary winter season, this endearing tale of a modern family observing the old custom gently reinforces the pride in the lasting traditions of our cultures and landscapes.

5.103 Fakih, Kimberly O. **High on the Hog.** Farrar, Straus, 1994. ISBN 0-374-33209-6. 166p. 11–12.

Twelve-year-old Trapp stays with her beloved great-grandparents on their Iowa farm for the summer while her parents and siblings make the great move to New York City. During a happy summer she discovers a family secret: Her deceased grandmother was adopted. Realizing the implications for her family, Trapp finally decides to keep the secret from her parents, as it has been kept for years in the farming community.

5.104 Fenner, Carol. **Yolonda's Genius.** Simon & Schuster, 1995. ISBN 0-689-80001-0. 211p. 8–10.

Although Yolonda does not have any close friends, she is unhappy when her mother decides to uproot her and her younger brother, Andrew, from downtown Chicago to a house in Michigan. Big, strong, and sure of herself, Yolonda finds that unknown territory can be daunting. Yolonda keeps her hidden insecurities at bay through her devotion to Andrew's musical genius. His ability to express himself musically and play the blues on his harmonica convince Yolonda that he is a genius worth fighting for. Yolonda's determination to get Andrew "discovered" is hindered when Andrew suddenly loses his musical ability.

5.105 Fraustino, Lisa Rowe. **Grass and Sky.** Orchard, 1994. ISBN 0-531-06823-4. 155p. 10–11.

When an eleven-year-old is told that her family is going to visit the grandfather who has neglected her, Timmi is outraged, especially because she will miss the best part of the baseball season. Timmi is a star pitcher. The two weeks prove interesting and adventurous, but very strange until Timmi learns why her grandfather had never answered her letters. This book presents the problem of alcoholism in a skillful and unusual way, and the scenes of summer country and island living are strong.

5.106   George, Jean Craighead. **Julie.** Illustrated by Wendell Minor. HarperCollins, 1994. ISBN 0-06-023528-4. 229p. 10–14.

Twenty-two years after writing her classic *Julie of the Wolves*, Jean George continues Julie's story from the ending of the first book: "She pointed her boots toward Kapugen." In this sequel, set in an Eskimo village on the bank of the Avalik River in Alaska, Julie is now reconciled with her father, Kapugen, but the wolves who saved her life are still threatened by her father as his first priority is protecting his musk-oxen herd. Although she loves her father, Julie has to adapt to his modern ways and his new American wife while remaining committed to saving her beloved wolves. The relationships are strongly drawn, the sense of place vivid, and the realistic black-and-white illustrations effective in depicting the people and landscape of the Alaskan tundra.

5.107   Gleitzman, Morris. **Blabber Mouth.** Harcourt Brace, 1995. ISBN 0-15-200369-X. 137p. 9–11.

Australian Rowena Batt experiences a "knots in the guts" tension when she arrives at her new school. Unable to speak since birth, Rowena photocopies a letter explaining that she was born missing bits in her throat. Not to be bullied, Rowena manages to begin her first day by shoving a frog into Darryn Peck's mouth and taping it shut. Her eccentric father manages to cause quite a stir with his cowboy boots and hat and habit of talking in country-and-western song lyrics. With humor and strength of character, Rowena experiences the joy and hurt that come with friendships and family.

5.108   Gleitzman, Morris. **Sticky Beak.** Harcourt Brace, 1995. ISBN 0-15-200366-5. 140p. 9–11.

In this sequel to *Blabber Mouth*, Rowena Batt is as shocked as everyone else at the fact that she has just thrown a bowl of Jelly Custard Surprise across a crowded hall during a farewell party for her teacher and new stepmother. Mute from birth, Rowena has developed a fast hand at signing and writing notes, but has difficulty communicating with the babbling cockatoo she has rescued from her bird-abusing classmate, Darryn Peck. The characters of the small Australian town portrayed in this enjoyable book display humor, sensitivity, and strong will.

5.109   Greene, Constance C. **Nora: Maybe a Ghost Story.** Browndeer, 1993. ISBN 0-15-277696-6hc, 0-15-276895-5pb. 202p. 11–13.

Constance Greene's twenty-fifth book deals with a thirteen-year-old facing her mother's death and her father's remarriage. Naturally, all ends happily. The writing is lively and the events are plausible. The book is a satisfactory, realistic preadolescent novel.

5.110 Hafen, Lyman. **Over the Joshua Slope.** Bradbury, 1994. ISBN 0-02-741100-1. 172p. 11–13.

Thirteen-year-old Brian is at odds with his father, who criticizes his haircut, his friends, and his music, and who feels doubtful about "making a man out of him." Naturally the boy comes through. This familiar plot has a great deal of freshness to it in this well-written novel. The terrain of a Nevada cattle range is so well-described that it becomes a participant in the story. Brian's rites of passage into adulthood are realistically described as he drives the cattle over the Joshua Slope. The cattle experts who become his friends and models are as natural as the environment, and the writing style is as crisp and clean as mountain air.

5.111 Haugen, Tormod. **Keeping Secrets.** Illustrated by Donna Diamond. HarperCollins, 1994. ISBN 0-06-020881-3. 127p. 10–12.

This English translation of a Norwegian story is experimental, moving, and memorable. Nina, with her parents at their summer house, struggles to define her own identity and distinguish herself from her parents. When she discovers a runaway boy in a tree in the garden, she makes her first move toward independence by concealing and befriending him. Nina's desire to help the boy leads her to act on behalf of another person for the first time. Ultimately, she confronts her parents as an individual, confident in her own sense of right and wrong. The narrative takes the form of a segmented prose poem. This unusual style, together with the setting, gives the story a spare, dreamlike quality that is enhanced by the fine black-and-white illustrations.

5.112 Heneghan, James. **Torn Away.** Viking, 1994. ISBN 0-670-85180-9. 185p. 11–13.

Thirteen-year-old Declan is caught up in the turmoil in Northern Ireland and is sent to the coast of British Columbia to live with his uncle and aunt. There he finally comes to terms with the cruelties, betrayals, and ambiguities that are part of the terrorist activities in Ireland, and decides to stay with the family he has come to love. The tension in Declan's world never stops. Here is a provocative book that shows adolescents living in social upheaval. This is a fast-paced story with a frank look at a complex situation.

5.113   Henkes, Kevin. **Owen.** Illustrated by Kevin Henkes. Greenwillow, 1993. ISBN 0-688-11449-0. 32p. 5–7.

Preschooler Owen the mouse is attached to his fuzzy, yellow blanket, which goes everywhere with him and gives him comfort and security. Mother and Father Mouse, under the tutelage of neighbor Mrs. Tweezers, try more and more desperate measures to rid Owen of his blanket. Finally, Mother thinks of a solution acceptable to all. The preschool child's attachment to an object is handled with wit and charm. The endearing watercolor images of wily, persevering Owen and his stumped parents evoke the themes of nurture and independence.

5.114   Herzig, Alison Cragin, and Jane Lawrence Mali. **The Wimp of the World.** Viking, 1994. ISBN 0-670-85208-2. 74p. 9–11.

Ten-year-old Bridget is on her way to being a tomboy and desperate to change the wimpy image her three older brothers have of her. She is also distressed by the pending marriage of her beloved great-aunt. Motel life in a Montana community makes an interesting and realistic background to a well-told story.

5.115   High, Linda Oatman. **Hound Heaven.** Holiday House, 1995. ISBN 0-8234-1195-8. 194p. 9–12.

Even though she lives with her Papaw, Silver feels lonely and isolated after the death of her parents and sister. If only she could have a dog she would feel less empty, but her grandfather is set against the idea. Nevertheless, Silver finds a job and works for money to buy a dog, both impressing and perplexing her friends with her determination. Children will identify with Silver's longing and admire her optimism and courage; the mountain setting offers a glimpse into a way of life that will be new to many readers.

5.116   High, Linda Oatman. **Maizie.** Holiday House, 1995. ISBN 0-8234-1161-3. 180p. 10–12.

Maizie lives in the Welsh Mountain area of Pennsylvania, where she looks after her young sister and her father, who is not always sober. She takes on several summer jobs to buy one of her heart's desires: a strawberry roan pony. Maizie is a strawberry blond like her mother, who left her family five years earlier to escape to a new life in a big city. The telling of this story is fresh and crisp; the adult characters are as interesting as Maizie and just as believable. Although the ending is not happy, Maizie is in control and it is clear that she will carry on and find happiness and success.

5.117 Hodge, Merle. **For the Life of Laetitia.** Farrar, Straus, 1993. ISBN 0-374-32447-6. 214p. 10–12.

Upon winning a scholarship, twelve-year-old Lacey reluctantly leaves her Caribbean village to attend the secondary school in the city and live with her father and his new wife and child. Although happy in her new school life, she has to deal with her homesickness, an uncaring father, and an unpleasant home environment. Lacey is particularly distressed that her father constantly undermines her rural upbringing and tries to change her attitudes and allegiances. Young readers will empathize with this strong-willed, courageous girl as she struggles to come to terms with the demands of the two worlds she inhabits.

5.118 Hoffman, Mary. **Boundless Grace.** Illustrated by Caroline Binch. Dial, 1995. ISBN 0-8037-1715-6. 26p. 5–10.

In the sequel to *Amazing Grace,* Grace and her Nana travel to Africa to meet the father she knows only through letters and photographs. Her father has remarried and has a new family. Grace finally gets to experience what she thinks of as a real family: a mother, a father, a brother, and a dog. However, missing her real mother and knowing stories of wicked stepmothers, Grace is reluctant to embrace her father's family. Large watercolors depict the beauty and colors of African culture and capture the realization that it is possible to love two families.

5.119 Howard, Elizabeth Fitzgerald. **Mac and Marie and the Train Toss Surprise.** Illustrated by Gail Gordon Carter. Four Winds, 1993. ISBN 0-02-744640-9. 32p. 5–7.

Elizabeth Fitzgerald Howard's tale, first told to her by her own father, is the simple but magical story of two African American children who are waiting for the favorite relative, Uncle Clem, to throw them a surprise package from the train on which he works in a dining car. For Mac, the young boy on whom the story focuses, the long wait evokes dreams of someday being an engineer on such a train. Finally, the magical package arrives: a conch shell from Florida and Mac's seemingly impossible dream that someday he too will be bringing back surprises from around the world. Gail Gordon Carter's watercolor-and-pencil illustrations provide the right amount of warmth and detail to bring this inspiring story to life.

5.120   Hughes, Shirley. **Stories by Firelight.** Illustrated by Shirley Hughes. Lothrop, 1993. ISBN 0-688-04568-5. 64p. 5–8.

An interesting collection of winter stories and poems is complemented by warm, poignant artwork. The cover and endpapers set the mood for these "Stories by Firelight" in warm tones of the orange and yellow glow of firelight.

5.121   James, Mary. **Frankenlouse.** Scholastic, 1994. ISBN 0-590- 46528-7. 184p. 10–12.

Blister Military Academy is both home and school for Nick, whose father is the commanding officer and a control freak. Nick decides that events in his own and his friends' lives cannot always be subjected to military discipline, and he begins to gather his courage to embark on a future that his father does not approve of. Although the plot is predictable, some may enjoy this glimpse into the life of a military school in which all of the students are from privileged but dysfunctional backgrounds. Young readers will identify with the challenges to friendship and family loyalty that the characters must face.

5.122   Johnston, Julie. **Adam and Eve and Pinch-Me.** Little, Brown, 1994. ISBN 0-316-46990-4. 180p. 10–12.

An articulate fifteen-year-old relates the story of her life in foster homes and the gradual healing power of the country family with whom she decides to stay. By an award-winning Canadian author, this is a powerfully moving story of a frozen child thawing into love. It is especially marked by the presence of caring but unobtrusive adults. The title, the author's own expression, is derived from a piece of "jokelore."

5.123   Katz, Welwyn Wilton. **Out of the Dark.** Groundwood, 1995. ISBN 0-88899-241-6. 185p. 10–12.

After his mother's death, Ben moves with his father and younger brother to Ship's Cove, Newfoundland, his father's boyhood home. Unlike his father and brother, Ben does not feel any connection to the place, and he does not trust the local boys. Increasingly, Ben withdraws into the world of the Vikings, an interest he shared with his mother. The narrative, and Ben's perceptions, shift between his present, his memory of the violent death of his mother, and his alter-ego in an imagined Vinland past. Consumed by a vision and a sense of necessity, Ben builds a model Viking ship, which he sails in a moment of triumph and release at the height of the novel. Both the story and the narrative strategy powerfully engage the reader, who will empathize with Ben's grief and anger and share in his ultimate affirmation of life.

5.124   Lyon, George Ella. **Mama Is a Miner.** Illustrated by Peter Cata-lanotto. Orchard, 1994. ISBN 0-531-06853-6. 32p. 5–8.

This realistic book portrays the life of a single mother who works in the coal mines. Peter Catalanotto's larger-than-life watercolor illustrations effectively contrast the dark and drab world of the mines with the richness of the world above, suggesting the harshness of the mother's life. The simply told tale focuses pri-marily on the youngest daughter's difficulty in accepting her mother's absences. Although Lyon's documentary-like account justly celebrates the efforts of the mother to merge job and fam-ily, one cannot help but be haunted by Catalanotto's final por-trait of the little girl who so clearly understands the dangers inherent in her mother's career, her daily ritual of "digging for home."

5.125   MacLachlan, Patricia. **All the Places to Love.** Illustrated by Mike Wimmer. HarperCollins, 1994. ISBN 0-06-021098-2. 32p. 5–8.

Eli's world is idyllic, from the woods and hills that surround his farm to the parents and grandparents who cherish him. Eli is born into this special place, grows with it, and in time will pass on "all the places to love" to his little sister, Sylvie. The musical language of this book evokes tender and loving themes of family and place. The full-page paintings capture the beauty of the landscape and enhance the themes. This is an excellent book for an adult to share with a young child, especially when a new baby is due.

5.126   MacLachlan, Patricia. **Baby.** Delacorte, 1993. ISBN 0-385-31133-8. 132p. 9–12.

The end of the island's summer season usually means a change to a quieter life for Larkin's family. This year, the end of summer brings a greater change than usual with the unexpected arrival of baby Sophie. Unable to care for her, the baby's mother leaves her in the care of Larkin's family. The baby's presence is painful but welcome to the family members, who have been unable to reconcile themselves to the death of Larkin's baby brother. In the year that Sophie stays with them, Larkin and her family come to love her, although they try not to. When she must leave, they grieve for her and finally come to accept the loss of their own baby. The family emerges stronger than before. The eccentric and good-hearted characters of this emotionally evocative novel will engage the sympathy and imagination of all readers.

5.127 Marino, Jan. **For the Love of Pete: A Novel.** Little, Brown, 1993. ISBN 0-316-54627-5. 197p. 11–12.

Twelve-year-old Phoebe lives an unusual but happy life with her eccentric grandmother and the three members of her Gram's household staff: Bertie, Gram's companion; Bishop, the butler; and Billy, the chauffeur. All of these people are devoted to the young girl, who regards them as family. But Phoebe's world begins to fall apart when her Gram is moved into a nursing home. Bertie, Bishop, and Billy have been instructed to take her in search of the father she has never known, but Phoebe is certain that he does not want her. The journey by car from Georgia to Maine is eventful and sometimes hilarious. Along the way Phoebe learns a great deal about the adults who love her and some surprising information about her father.

5.128 Marino, Jan. **Mona Lisa of Salem Street.** Little, Brown, 1995. ISBN 0-316-54614-3. 155p. 9–12.

Following the death of their parents, Nettie and John Peter spend most of their time with their tired and impatient Grandma Bessie—that is, until she periodically sends them off to other relatives. Having never met their father's parents, Nettie and John Peter are surprised to find that they are being sent off to their wealthy grandfather, Frank DeAngelus, and his Flower Emporium in Boston. With thoughts of grand houses and cultured lifestyle, Nettie, who assumes the name Natasha for her new life, is most surprised to find her grandfather is neither wealthy nor the owner of a Flower Emporium. What follows is a tender and loving story of a grandfather and his grandchildren.

5.129 McFarlane, Sheryl. **Eagle Dreams.** Illustrated by Ron Lightburn. Philomel, 1995. ISBN 0-399-22695-8. 32p. 6–8.

Flying his kite, a young boy finds a bald eagle with a broken wing. Despite protests from his farmer dad, he is determined to care for the bird. Over the winter, the bird gradually heals in the barn, and all wait patiently until the day the eagle is strong enough to swoop forth "with a scream so full of wildness they could only stand in silence." There is a soft, dreamlike quality to the illustrations, suggesting warm memories of the events. The dramatically changing perspectives entice the reader to notice subtle details. The strong symbolism of the kite is evident in the boy's final evening thoughts. This book was originally published in Canada by Orca Book Publishers.

5.130 McKay, Hilary. **Dog Friday.** McElderry, 1995. ISBN 0-689-80383-4. 133p. 9–12.

Robin Brogan's experience with a biting dog leaves him afraid of all dogs. At first his friends sympathize with his fear, but when the Robinson family moves in next door, the neighborhood children come to like their dog, Old Blanket. Robin is taunted by Dan, the neighborhood bully. The wild and creative Robinson children offer to cure Robin of his fear, as they enthusiastically help Robin's mother with her bed-and-breakfast business. The Robinsons' efforts on Robin's behalf have some effect but he is completely cured when he discovers an abandoned dog on the beach. Robin's wait for Dog Friday, kept by the police in case of a claim by owners, is agonizing for him and for his mother, but the Robinson children manage to keep the Brogans busy with their adventures and mishaps. This is a wonderfully funny novel with warmly depicted characters.

5.131 Mead, Alice. **Crossing the Starlight Bridge.** Bradbury, 1994. ISBN 0-02-765950-X. 122p. 9–11.

The main theme of this book involves a child longing for her suddenly vanished father who finally tells her that he is marrying again. The background is an island in Maine, the traditional home of the Penobscot, the People of the Dawn. The portrayal of a sensitive, artistic child who has to make a transition into the white world gives this story a special quality. The story is simply told and decorated with authentic Penobscot designs.

5.132 Mead, Alice. **Junebug.** Farrar, Straus, 1995. ISBN 0-374-33964-3. 102p. 9–12.

Reeve McLain Jr., known to all as Junebug, fears turning ten in two weeks. Around the project housing where he lives, gangs wait to claim him and he can see no escape. Possibilities lie in a reading teacher, an older friend, and Junebug's imagination, where a wish has taken shape, a wish he will launch on slips of paper in fifty bottles on his birthday. This is a compelling story, drawing the reader into the gut-wrenching fear and often hopelessness of life in an inner city, but providing an avenue of hope: the resilience of the human spirit.

5.133   Milstein, Linda. **Amanda's Perfect Hair.** Illustrated by Susan Meddaugh. Tambourine, 1993. ISBN 0-688-11153-X. 32p. 5–7.

Amanda wants to be noticed for herself, not for her extra long, extra thick, extra curly, and extra yellow hair. The sensible solution is to cut it, which is what Amanda eventually does. There is a tall-tale ring to this story that explains how Amanda gives herself an attractive, short haircut. The lively text and pictures match very well. This picture book could be used just for fun or for discussing appearances.

5.134   Mitchell, Barbara. **Down Buttermilk Lane.** Illustrated by John Sandford. Lothrop, 1993. ISBN 0-688-10114-3. 32p. 6–8.

The rich oil paintings and lyrical text of this pleasing story follow an Amish family in Lancaster, Pennsylvania through a day in their lives. They shop at the local store and go to Mammie's for lunch before returning home again. The book reads and looks like a historical account; two T-shirt-clad young men in the bakery are the only sign that the story transpires in the twentieth century.

5.135   Mitchell, Margaree King. **Uncle Jed's Barbershop.** Illustrated by James Ransome. Simon & Schuster, 1993. ISBN 0-671-76969-3. 34p. 6–9.

Uncle Jed's niece, Sarah Jean, tells the story of Jed's barber shop. Jed does not get his shop until close to the end of his life because he gives his savings to Sarah Jean's parents for her emergency operation. Then the bank fails during the Great Depression of the 1930s. This text is simple, the pictures are highly realistic, and one cannot doubt the validity of the story line. As a portrayal of the black experience of the period, this book would be useful as part of a collection about black culture.

5.136   Mitchell, Rita Phillips. **Hue Boy.** Illustrated by Caroline Binch. Dial, 1993. ISBN 0-8037-1448-3. 26p. 5–7.

Set in the Caribbean, this story recounts the efforts of a young boy to grow taller. Hue Boy is teased for being too short, but no one seems able to help him. His mother takes him to visit the local "experts," to no avail. Then his father returns home and Hue Boy learns to walk tall, having grown confident with love. The illustrations bring the Caribbean to life.

5.137   Namioka, Lensey. **Yang the Third and Her Impossible Family.** Illustrated by Kees de Kiefte. Little, Brown, 1995. ISBN 0-316-59726-0. 144p. 9–11.

In this amusing sequel to *Yang the Youngest and His Terrible Ear,* Yang changes her name to Mary so that she will be more likely to be accepted by the girls at school. Life is tough for Yang as her family constantly embarrasses her with what she feels are culturally inappropriate comments. Yang's family is highly musical, with no room for pets, but when a girl at school offers a runt kitten, the solution to being accepted appears. The fun starts as she and her brother try to keep the kitten's existence a secret from the rest of the family. Namioka shares many experiences facing a Chinese American family, giving young readers an insight into some of the frustrating aspects of trying to live in two cultures.

5.138 Naylor, Phyllis Reynolds. **Being Danny's Dog.** Atheneum, 1995. ISBN 0-689-31756-5. 150p. 8–12.

When T.R. moves to Rosemary Acres with his mother and his older brother, Danny, he is prepared for a difficult transition. He will miss the city, his aunt, and his friends, just as he misses his father, who left the family two years earlier. In their new life, T.R. knows that Danny wants to be the man of the family, and T.R. is prepared to help out as the "watchdog" who will keep Danny out of trouble as they meet new friends and adjust to the neighborhood. The brothers begin to make friends and to discover, along with the reader, the diverse circumstances that rearrange families, move people around, and bring them together in communities. Unfortunately, the management of Rosemary Acres is not very friendly to the neighborhood children and T.R. finds himself drawn into trouble. The crisis teaches T.R. the value of family, friendship, and tolerance.

5.139 Pearson, Gayle. **The Fog Doggies and Me.** Atheneum, 1993. ISBN 0-689-31845-6. 119p. 10–12.

Starr and Ivy are best friends, but when Ivy, who is six months older than Starr, turns thirteen and acquires a boyfriend, Starr is jealous. Her unhappiness makes her even more impatient than usual with her nine-year-old sister, who adores her. Starr's mother, who writes for a computer magazine, and her father, an expert in the kitchen, are sympathetic to Starr's troubles.

5.140 Peterson, Jeanne Whitehouse. **My Mama Sings.** Illustrated by Sandra Speidel. HarperCollins, 1994. ISBN 0-06-023854-2. 32p. 5–8.

Mama has singing in her bones; she has the perfect song for every time of year and every occasion. Her son and his friends join in the simple family treats of cocoa, popcorn, and mama's old dance records. Then mama is dismissed from her job and the songs stop until the boy makes up one for his mother. The simple text is filled with musical images. The artwork is a fine combination of realism and impressionism as the artist visually presents a single-parent black family in its joys and sorrows. A happy ending for them is embedded in their songs.

5.141   Porte, Barbara Ann. **When Grandma Almost Fell Off the Mountain and Other Stories.** Illustrated by Maxie Chambliss. Orchard, 1993. ISBN 0-531-05965-0. 32p. 6–8.

In the same tradition as her subsequent book, *When Aunt Lucy Rode a Mule and Other Stories,* Barbara Ann Porte presents a series of family folkloric tales that blend the fine art of storytelling with the transmission of elder wisdom. On a visit to their grandmother, Stella and Zelda are treated to Grandma's lively and funny stories about a family trip to Florida in her own youth. One adventure follows another as the two girls keep asking questions about the people and places in Grandma's stories and thereby become reconnected with events from their family's past and details of life generations ago. A good read-aloud.

5.142   Quinlan, Patricia. **Tiger Flowers.** Illustrated by Janet Wilson. Dial, 1994. ISBN 0-8037-1408-4. 32p. 6–9.

In this brightly illustrated story, Joel, a young boy whose favorite uncle, Michael, died of AIDS, has come to terms with this loss. Through Joel's eyes, young readers are able to appreciate the special gifts Michael brought to the relationship with his nephew. Joel is able to express his feelings of love and hurt and to preserve his memories of Michael through sharing a special gift of "tiger flowers," his uncle's favorite flowers, with his young sister, Tara.

5.143   Rattigan, Jama Kim. **Dumpling Soup.** Illustrated by Lillian Hsu-Flanders. Little, Brown, 1993. ISBN 0-316-73445-4. 32p. 6–8.

This engaging and colorful story of a culturally and racially mixed family depicts the customs surrounding their New Year's celebration in Hawaii. Told through the eyes of a young girl, it incorporates elements of the different languages and cultures present in the family: Korean, Japanese, Chinese, Hawaiian, and haole (Hawaiian for white people). In engaging language and style, Marisa tells about her family's traditions and customs when they get together to celebrate the New Year.

Together, author and illustrator have created a heartwarming picture book that reinforces the positive and enriching aspects of cultural diversity.

5.144   Rodowsky, Colby. **Hannah in Between.** Farrar, Straus, 1994. ISBN 0-374-32837-4. 152p. 11–13.

Turning twelve is definitely an in-between time for Hannah. Family traditions such as renting a summer house, eating Friday night pizza with her parents, and appearing in her grandfather's newspaper column maintain a level of comfort and predictability that Hannah has always enjoyed. That is, until she begins to notice a change in her mother. Headaches, clumsiness, and unpredictability seem to go unnoticed by everyone except Hannah, who is left feeling like she is the only one who suspects her mother is an alcoholic. Through well-developed characters and strong family relationships, some of the difficulties associated with alcoholism are illuminated.

5.145   Russo, Marisabina. **Trade-in Mother.** Illustrated by Marisabina Russo. Greenwillow, 1993. ISBN 0-688-11416-4. 32p. 5–7.

Realistic and expressively painted illustrations help tell the story of a young boy frustrated with his mother's "no's" and directives. All young children who have ever told their parents "I hate you!" when they did not get their way will relate to Max's comment: "You are the worst mother in the world." When Max outlines all the mothers who could replace his own mother, she deals with it in a wise, calm, and loving manner.

5.146   Sachs, Marilyn. **Thirteen Going on Seven.** Dutton, 1993. ISBN 0-525-45096-3. 133p. 9–11.

It is not always easy being one of two. Dee and Dezzy are having a difficult time deciding how they should spend their thirteenth birthday, one of many issues that they no longer agree on. Despite the fact that they are identical twins, they now seem to have little in common. Dee is an A student, the star of the school play, and eager to become a teenager. Dezzy, on the other hand, struggles with a reading disability, lacks confidence, and clings to the world of her childhood. However, after the sudden death of their grandmother, Dezzy reveals unexpected strengths that bring her the admiration of her family and a feeling of her own worth.

5.147   Say, Allen. **Grandfather's Journey.** Illustrated by Allen Say. Houghton Mifflin, 1993. ISBN 0-395-57035-2. 32p. 6–10.

Tracing three generations of his family, Allen Say shares his personal experiences of being attached to two homelands, Japan and the United States, both of which compete for his loyalty. This Caldecott Medal picture book wistfully demonstrates how an adopted land and a country of birth each offer a compelling variation of home. The illustrations, paintings arranged like a family album, offer glimpses of the history of Allen Say and his grandfather as the two of them are drawn back and forth between their homelands.

5.148 Scott, Ann Herbert. **A Brand Is Forever.** Illustrated by Ronald Himler. Houghton Mifflin, 1993. ISBN 0-395-60118-5. 48p. 6–9.

Growing up on a cattle ranch, young Annie has to face the frightening experience of having her own baby calf, Doodle, branded. On branding day, the events that unfold around Annie and her calf are part of a vivid and detailed portrait of western cattle ranches and the family history connected with them, narrated in three short chapters and illustrated with evocative watercolors. Young, independent readers will get a glimpse of the rich customs of branding days and the family traditions connected with life on a cattle ranch.

5.149 Snyder, Carol (translated by Alma Flor Ada). **One Up, One Down/Una arriba, uno abajo.** Illustrated by Maxie Chambliss. Atheneum, 1995. ISBN 0-689-31828-6 (English); 0-689-31994-0 (Spanish). 32p. 5–6.

Katie is an only child until the twins arrive and she becomes a big sister. This leaves her perplexed, as she had not noticed herself becoming bigger. In this happy family story, the parents praise Katie for all her help with the twins. Katie is delighted to discover, when she goes shopping for shoes, that she has grown and needs a larger-size shoe. The title refers to the twins: When one is asleep, the other is awake, and so on. This is an amusing and realistic concept with even more amusing and realistic illustrations. Editions are available in English and Spanish.

5.150 Stolz, Mary. **Coco Grimes.** HarperCollins, 1994. ISBN 0-06-024232-9. 89p. 8–11.

In this fourth book about Thomas and his grandfather, Thomas celebrates a perfect eleventh birthday with an outing to a baseball game and a dinner with family and friends. His new interest in the history of Negro League baseball earns him an invitation to visit an elderly former player who lives near grandfather's friend. Thomas and his grandfather enjoy the visit, but they return home with a renewed sense of appreciation for their quiet life on the Gulf of Mexico. The appeal of the novel lies in its portrait of a warm family life and its description of a shared enthusiasm for baseball that unites the generations. Young readers will also enjoy the fact that Thomas ages from one book to the next and that each book becomes more sophisticated as Thomas and his readers grow older.

5.151   Van Leeuwen, Jean. **Two Girls in Sister Dresses.** Illustrated by Linda Benson. Dial, 1994. ISBN 0-8037-1230-8. 49p. 6–8.

In this short chapter book about two young sisters, Jennifer and Molly, children will enjoy reading about episodes in their lives, such as their adventures during their annual summer vacation at their grandparents' house by the sea and the arrival of their baby brother, Timothy. The author highlights the common joys and problems of sibling and family relationships in descriptive narrative language, enriched by the beautiful black-and-white pencil sketches of illustrator Linda Benson.

5.152   Waggoner, Karen. **Partners.** Illustrated by Cat Bowman Smith. Simon & Schuster, 1995. ISBN 0-671-86466-1. 95p. 7–10.

Jamie buys two mice because he loves them, only to discover that his older brother and partner in the purchase intends to raise them for sale. With the solving of a mathematical problem and the help of a classmate, another partner, he averts disaster. This lively, simply written, attractively produced story is reminiscent of the larger-than-life child problems presented by Beverly Cleary a generation ago in her Henry Huggins series.

5.153   Williams, Karen Lynn. **A Real Christmas This Year.** Clarion, 1995. ISBN 0-395-70117-1. 164p. 9–12.

Megan is in grade 7 and has considerable responsibilities at home helping to look after a disabled young brother. Megan also has problems with school friendships, being attracted to a boy for the first time, and worrying about money, especially in preparing for Christmas, which she wants to be perfect this year. Megan gets her wish, but she knows that she can never make everything right all the time. This is a poignant picture of a low-income family struggling to raise a severely disabled child.

5.154   Woodruff, Elvira. **Magnificent Mummy Maker.** Scholastic, 1994. ISBN 0-590-45742-X. 132p. 9–12.

When Andy's stepmother, stepbrother, and father discuss what colors represent their personalities, Andy privately decides that he is grey. He feels that his stepbrother, "Mr. Gifted," overshadows him in school, at home, and even in his own father's admiration. Andy's grey existence suddenly changes when he makes a special connection with an Egyptian mummy during a school museum visit. With the assistance, he thinks, of the mummy's spirit, Andy begins to excel at school and to gain confidence from his initial successes. This confidence allows Andy to look beyond himself for a new perspective on his family. Young readers will warm to Andy and sympathize with his conflicts in the home and at school. The resolution is realistic rather than magical, yet it is still satisfying.

5.155   Yolen, Jane. **Honkers.** Illustrated by Leslie Baker. Little, Brown, 1993. ISBN 0-316-96893-5. 32p. 5–8.

When five-year-old Betsy's mother is expecting a new baby and has to spend long, boring hours in bed, the young girl is sent to her grandparents' farm. Betsy feels homesick and lonely despite the loving care of her grandparents, until she helps to hatch and raise an abandoned nest of "honkers." Betsy learns about bonding, mothering, and letting go through her relationship with Little Bit, the gosling that becomes attached to her. Jane Yolen's rich language and Leslie Baker's warm watercolor illustrations together have created a treasured book about the universal themes of caring and growing up. An excellent read-aloud.

5.156   Zalben, Jane Breskin. **Pearl Plants a Tree.** Illustrated by Jane Breskin Zalben. Simon & Schuster, 1995. ISBN 0-689-80034-7. unpaged. 5–6.

Charmingly bordered and appealing illustrations enhance this simple, heartwarming text. Pearl plants an apple seed, as her grandfather did when he came from the old country. Grandpa helps Pearl plant her small tree and they picnic beside it, thinking of future generations. The book ends with a summary of tree-planting holidays around the world, including Tu B'Shvat, the Jewish New Year of Trees. Directions on how to grow a tree are also included. The beautiful endpapers are hand-made from the bark of a fig tree.

Friendship

5.157   Bantle, Lee F. **Diving for the Moon.** Macmillan, 1995. ISBN 0-689-80004-5. 163p. 9–12.

Bird has always had Josh for a friend, and their families have always spent summers together. But the summer before grade 7 is different. Bird and Josh must face new schools in the fall and work through the challenges to their friendship as they grow older. This summer Bird also learns that Josh has been infected with HIV through a blood transfusion. Suddenly she has to confront the possibility that her best friend may become sick and die. The story is a moving and complex treatment of issues surrounding friendship, illness, and grieving. Children will empathize with the realistically and humanely drawn characters and the choices they must make.

5.158   Broome, Errol. **Dear Mr. Sprouts.** Knopf, 1993. ISBN 0-679-83714-0. 123p. 9–12.

The cover illustration portrays Anke and Freddie as eleven or twelve, which is about their age when they first begin writing to one another. This book consists of their letters over the span of ten years, although most of the book takes place between their fifteenth and nineteenth years. Anke is a shy but articulate city girl. Freddie lives alone on a farm with his father; not given to writing much, he is incisive. As they grow to know one another through their letters, they become trusted souls who can console, prod, praise, tease, and hurt one another. Reforestation and place names set this novel in contemporary Victoria, Australia, but Anke's stutter and the personal trauma of teenage relationships place this novel firmly in the realm of universal human experience.

5.159   Champion, Joyce. **Emily and Alice Again.** Illustrated by Suçie Stevenson. Harcourt Brace, 1995. ISBN 0-15-200439-4. 32p. 6–8.

These three short stories recount the further adventures of Emily and Alice as they follow their abiding friendship into new terrain: trading a younger sister for pink sunglasses, wearing new hats, or telling tales of imaginary creatures such as the Secret Sisters during a sleepover. Young girls particularly will appreciate this text for its warmth and verisimilitude. The cartoonlike illustrations add to its appeal. This is a good book for students to read on their own or with one another.

5.160   Clark, Emma Chichester. **Across the Blue Mountains.** Illustrated by Emma Chichester Clark. Harcourt Brace, 1993. ISBN 0-15-201220-6. 26p. 5–7.

Miss Bilberry takes her dog, cat, two birds, and possessions to the other side of the blue mountains. In the end, she finds a house, which only the cat recognizes to be the house in which they began. The rich colors and humorous illustrations contribute substantially to the reading experience. There is a good section that breaks down images labeled *fields, forest, rain, sunshine, uphill,* and *downhill.*

5.161 Conly, Jane Leslie. **Crazy Lady!** HarperCollins, 1993. ISBN 0-06-0213574. 180p. 10–12.

Vernon has come to a crossroads in his young life. With his mother recently dead, his brothers and sisters growing and changing, and a new junior high school, he wonders whether he can meet the new challenges that confront him. Then Vernon meets the alcoholic Maxine and her mentally disabled son, Ronald. Through his friendship with them, he discovers new strength in himself and begins to face his own pain and fears. The reader is drawn into Vernon's realistically evoked neighborhood and is compelled to share in the author's compassion for her characters, regardless of their flaws.

5.162 Danziger, Paula. **Amber Brown Is Not a Crayon.** Putnam, 1994. ISBN 0-399-22509-9. 80p. 7–9.

Amber and Justin have been best friends since preschool. They help each other with schoolwork, they have a cooperative technique for eating Oreo cookies, and they have constructed a large ball of used chewing gum. When Justin's father gets a job in another city, Amber is faced with losing her best friend. To make matters worse, Justin refuses to talk about it. Instead of enjoying their remaining time together, Amber and Justin have a big fight. Finally, they begin to talk over their feelings about the move and they resolve to stay friends even though they will be apart. Young readers will appreciate the sadness, but there is optimism in this story, which is told by Amber with an amusing emphasis on the preoccupations and priorities of grade 3.

5.163 Day, Alexandra. **Frank and Ernest on the Road.** Illustrated by Alexandra Day. Scholastic, 1994. ISBN 0-590-45048-4. 41p. 5–7.

The bear and elephant friends, Frank and Ernest, are together again. This time they are forming a partnership as truckers, and this leads them into learning new tasks and a new language. Frank and Ernest find that they are "cradle babies" (shy new truckers and CB operators), but before long they are checking out the "front yard" (the road ahead) for a good "bean store" (roadside restaurant) where they can "put on the food bags" (eat) and have a cup of "roadtar" (coffee). The language is clearly presented in illustrated glossaries at the front and back of the book and in boxes on individual pages. Detailed oil and water-color illustrations showing different types of trucks, in a variety of situations and landscapes, extend the text and invite the reader to share in the friendship and pleasures of the road.

5.164 Doherty, Berlie. **Willa and Old Miss Annie.** Illustrated by Kim Lewis. Candlewick, 1994. ISBN 1-56402-331-1. 92p. 7–10.

Willa, a shy little girl, is afraid that she will have no friends when her family moves to a far-away town. Instead, she finds Old Miss Annie with her twisted, twiglike hands and a voice full of tiny words. She also finds Joshua, who starts as a ghost but turns into a goat. With Old Miss Annie's help, Willa makes other friends as well. Berlie Doherty spins a story filled with love and beauty and ties it together with the joy of friendship.

5.165 Ernst, Lisa Campbell. **The Luckiest Kid on the Planet.** Illustrated by Lisa Campbell Ernst. Bradbury, 1994. ISBN 0-02-733566-6. 34p. 5–7.

With a special name like his, Lucky Morgenstern considers himself to be the luckiest kid on the planet until one day he discovers that his real name is Herbert. All at once his life seems to change completely. Only when Herbert discovers the one thing in his life that makes him especially lucky—his grandfather, who gave him his nickname and who is his best friend—does his luck return once again.

5.166 Feuer, Elizabeth. **Lost Summer.** Farrar, Straus, 1995. ISBN 0-374-31020-3. 185p. 9–12.

In the aftermath of her parents' divorce, Lydia finds herself a first-time camper at the camp where her older sister is a counselor. Reluctantly, she is drawn into the life of the camp and into friendship both with gentle, fearful Karen and with Karen's persecutor, Carla. Lydia gradually discovers that she must choose between these friends. She also learns that her loyalty and affection for her absent father are not reciprocated, and that she and her sister have more in common than she had believed. Lydia is a likable character whose mistakes and problems attract readers' empathy. The camp setting, treated with realistic ambivalence between the ridiculous and the idyllic, will also appeal to young readers.

5.167   Herman, Charlotte. **Max Malone the Magnificent.** Illustrated by Cat Bowman Smith. Holt, 1993. ISBN 0-8050-2282-1. 59p. 7–10.

A show at the local library inspires Max to become a magician. With the support of his mother and friends, and despite interference from his sister, Max develops a repertoire of illusions and gets his first engagement to perform for money. Max's friends at the magic store teach him that he needs more than tricks to entertain an audience, and the reader, like Max, learns something about the art of performance. When the big day arrives, Max has some problems with his routine, but he also learns something about improvisation and entertainment. Young readers will like this story for the magic and for the friendship that develops in its pages.

5.168   Hicyilmaz, Gaye. **Frozen Waterfall.** Farrar, Straus, 1994. ISBN 0-374-32482-4. 325p. 11–13.

A modern Turkish family has to make a new life in Switzerland. For twelve-year-old Selda, the move is traumatic beyond her worst expectations. She has to learn German and go to a new school, and sees her sisters adapt more readily than she does. She becomes involved with illegal immigrants, suspects her older brother of wrongdoing, makes friends with a wealthy Swiss girl her own age, and always writes to a grandmother back in Turkey who cannot read—all within a school year. The title comes from Selda's first knowledge of and delight in a Switzerland winter.

5.169   Hirsch, Karen. **Ellen Anders on Her Own.** Macmillan, 1994. ISBN 0-02-743975-5. 111p. 9–12.

Ellen, Abby, and Jen start grade 6 as best friends, united against the frivolous concerns of the popular girls in their class. Their friendship means a lot to Ellen, who lost her mother near the beginning of the school year. When Abby begins to make friends with the popular girls, Ellen and Jen feel confused, betrayed, and resentful. With the help of her mother's childhood diary, Ellen tries to sort out her feelings and reconcile herself to the changes associated with friendship and growing up. Young readers will sympathize with Ellen's ambivalent feelings. They will also enjoy the ending, which promises a realistic if not perfect reconciliation.

5.170   Johnston, Tony. **The Last Snow of Winter.** Illustrated by Friso Henstra. Tambourine, 1993. ISBN 0-688-10749-4. 32p. 5–7.

With the first snowfall, famous artist Gaston Pompicard decides to turn his creative talents to sculpting children out of snow. During the last snowfall of winter, the children reciprocate by sculpting an image of Gaston and his dog. The story takes place in a little French town, depicted by comic ink-and-watercolor illustrations in all its eccentricities and charm.

5.171 Kovacs, Deborah. **Moonlight on the River.** Illustrated by William Shattuck. Viking, 1993. ISBN 0-670-84463-2. 32p. 6–8.

This poetic story begins as two young brothers silently sneak out of their bedroom to go on an evening sail, journeying down a river on a moonlit night. The calm night quickly changes to a raging storm that tests the nautical abilities of the two erstwhile sailors as well as their trust in each other. They return in the morning with their evening catch, a five-pound fish that their mother discovers when she comes to wake them in the morning. The story ends as the mother fondly remembers similar journeys when she was a child and thanks the river for returning her children safely. William Shattuck's silver-and-white charcoals, reminiscent of the illustrations of Chris van Allsburg, lovingly capture the tone of this timeless adventure.

5.172 McDonald, Megan. **Insects Are My Life.** Illustrated by Paul Brett Johnson. Orchard, 1995. ISBN 0-531-06874-9. 32p. 5–7.

Amanda, who is a bug's best friend, collects dead bugs and steps around spiderwebs. "Insects are my life!" she declares to her long-suffering family. At school her obsession gets her into trouble and causes difficulties with classmates, but she meets another child just as fascinated with a topic: "Reptiles are my life!" cries her new friend. Realistic illustrations help depict a child who is her own person.

5.173 Schotter, Roni. **A Fruit and Vegetable Man.** Illustrated by Jeanette Winter. Little, Brown, 1993. ISBN 0-316-77467-7. 32p. 5–8.

This heartwarming story about the friendship between old Ruby Rubenstein, who owns a fruit and vegetable store, and Sun Ho, a young immigrant boy, touches on the themes of helping, learning, and relating across generations and cultures. Roni Schotter's engaging dialogue and descriptive text, together with Jeanette Winter's bright, detailed watercolors, make this picture book a good read-aloud in any primary classroom.

5.174 Shelton, Rick. **Hoggle's Christmas.** Illustrated by Donald Gates. Dutton, 1993. ISBN 0-525-65129-2. 79p. 8–10.

Isabel, who is six, and Richard, who is ten, befriend Mr. Hoggle, a new high school teacher up the road whose shed and cupboards are full of wonderful things: drums, masks, and "everything you need to build a kite." Hoggle may be magical: Kites fly, the rains stop, and dinosaur fossils loom out of cave walls. When Hoggle moves, he leaves them two African masks and drums and wonderful memories of their friendship. This small novel is rich in prose and characterization and generously illustrated with warm, lifelike black-and-white illustrations.

5.175 Spinelli, Eileen. **Lizzie Logan Wears Purple Sunglasses.** Illustrated by Melanie Hope Greenberg. Simon & Schuster, 1995. ISBN 0-671-74685-5. 122p. 7–10.

When Heather moves into a new neighborhood, she is accosted by an older, outrageously wild girl named Lizzie Logan. Soon the two girls become best friends, joining one another on a series of adventures that include various tête-à-têtes in Willie's gas station bathroom. The typeface is large and the vocabulary is both simplified and hip, making it an attractive book for young readers. The text is supported by cartoonlike black-and-white sketches.

5.176 Taylor, Theodore. **Timothy of the Cay.** Harcourt Brace, 1993. ISBN 0-15-288358-4. 192p. 10–12.

In this prequel/sequel to *The Cay,* the stories of two young men, Timothy and Philip, are told in alternating chapters. Their lives came together when Timothy was an old man and Philip a boy of eleven, which is the story narrated in *The Cay.* In the prequel, Timothy, penniless and black, dreams of becoming a captain of his own boat and sailing in the Caribbean. In the sequel, Philip, privileged and white, longs to regain his sight so that he can return to the Cay and see the world he once inhabited with Timothy. The chapters depict the sufferings Timothy endures on the sailing ships at the hands of cruel people. These accounts and the characterization of Philip's inner strength and courage make this a deeply moving tale.

5.177 Turner, Ann. **One Brave Summer.** HarperCollins, 1995. ISBN 0-06-023732-5. 163p. 8–10.

Katy Williams is angry that her mother has rented a cabin in the mountains for the summer. She has just finished grade 4 at a new school and is not in the mood for an adventure. Katy begins by making a list of things she will not like about the summer. Thinking herself to be cautious, neat, and the opposite of her mother's outgoing nature, Katy is surprised to find herself in the company of the friendly and outgoing Lena May, who is big on adventures and homemade root beer. With humor and insight, Ann Turner reveals the secrets and joys of being best friends.

5.178 Wallace, Bill. **True Friends.** Holiday House, 1994. ISBN 0-8234-1141-9. 169p. 10–12.

Courtney begins grade 6 holding the world by the tail. She is friends with the popular kids, she becomes a cheerleader, and she feels closer to her stepmother than ever before. Then disaster strikes. Courtney's brother is arrested, her stepmother leaves, her father's business fails, and Courtney is accused of theft at school. She feels scrutinized and persecuted by teachers and ostracized by her former friends. Only Judy, a spunky disabled classmate, remains loyal to Courtney, inspiring her with the courage to go on and be a source of strength to her family. The contrasts of fortune in the story are exaggerated, but readers will empathize with the sincerity of the characters.

5.179 Wild, Margaret. **The Slumber Party.** Illustrated by David Cox. Ticknor & Fields, 1993. ISBN 0-395-66598-1. 32p. 6–7.

Jane invites seven friends, including two boys, for a birthday slumber party; the resulting antics, wonderfully captured in the illustrations, are chaotic and believable. Along with the fast-paced fun, the emotional ups-and-downs of friendship are strongly conveyed in this story, set in Australia.

5.180 Wynne-Jones, Tim. **The Maestro.** Douglas & McIntyre, 1995. ISBN 0-88899-242-4. 223p. 11–12.

It all begins with a piano flying over a northern Ontario lake, suspended by wires from a helicopter. When young Burl decides to run away from his abusive father, he flees into the woods, where he faces the exigencies of survival. On the second day of his exile, he is relieved to discover a pyramidlike house on a lake, where he knocks and is met by Baron Gustav von Liederhosen, later to be known as Nathaniel Orlando Gow—the Maestro. The two develop a friendship and the eccentric composer-pianist lets Burl stay in his house after he returns to Toronto. When Burl learns of the Maestro's death, he follows a series of adventures in his attempt to retrieve the final composition of the great pianist.

His father intervenes and Burl eventually finds himself saving the life of his abuser.

5.181   York, Carol Beach. **The Key to the Playhouse.** Illustrated by John Speirs. Scholastic, 1994. ISBN 0-590-46258-X. 70p. 6–9.

Alice Ann and Megan are cousins and friends who spend time each summer visiting their grandmother and enjoying an elaborate playhouse. This summer, new neighbors are living in the small, unpainted house down the road, whose daughter, Cissie, would like nothing more than to be invited into the girls' friendship and playhouse. Alice Ann and Megan snub Cissie because she is shy, fat, and unattractive. They make their playhouse into a fortress against her. When their grandmother asks them to say goodbye to her, the girls visit Cissie's house, observe her poverty, and feel some stirrings of compassion. The playhouse setting will appeal to children, who will also identify with the novel's themes of friendship and exclusion.

Grandparents

5.182   Butler, Geoff. **The Killick: A Newfoundland Story.** Illustrated by Geoff Butler. Tundra, 1995. ISBN 0-88776-336-7. 32p. 9–12.

This is an extremely moving account of the dignity and quiet heroism of a grandfather who sacrifices his life for his grandson. During a sudden squall, he and his grandson are marooned on an icepan. Slipping off, the old war veteran leaves behind a killick, a homemade anchor that clearly symbolizes the life of a man of the sea. The tale is an unobtrusive but powerful comment on contemporary Newfoundland, where war heroes are called barbarians for hunting seals. Ultimately, Maritimer Butler, who illustrated the text with a series of powerfully evocative, full-page paintings, provides a sensitive and memorable portrait of this rich tradition.

5.183   Hickman, Janet. **Jericho.** Greenwillow, 1994. ISBN 0-688-13398-3. 135p. 10–12.

Upper-intermediate readers will relate to Angela's mixed feelings as she and her family spend the summer with her grandparents and great-grandmother. Although she recognizes the difficulties involved in caring for her great-grandmother and sympathizes with her family, she misses her friends and longs for the summer to be over. Through two parallel narratives—Angela in the present and GrandMin in the past—readers gain insight into the young girl's growing maturity and an understanding of the great-

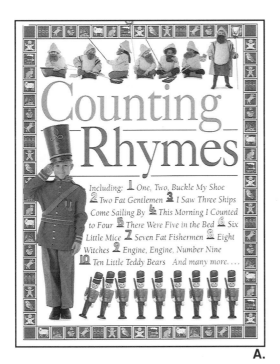

A.

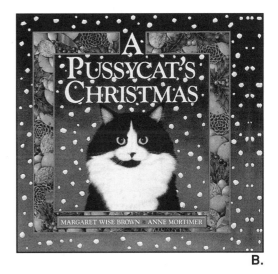

B.

C.

D.

A. *Counting Rhymes* selected by Shona McKellar (see 1.29). **B.** *A Pussycat's Christmas* by Margaret Wise Brown; illustrated by Anne Mortimer (see 1.54). **C.** *Time for Bed* by Mem Fox; illustrated by Jane Dyer (see 1.72). **D.** *African Animals ABC* written and illustrated by Philippa Alys-Browne (see 1.1).

A.

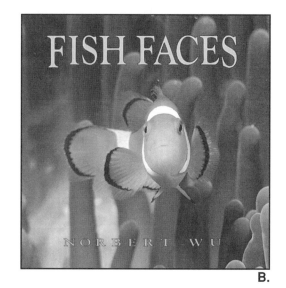

B.

C.

A. *Pablo's Tree* by Pat Mora; illustrated by Cecily Lang (see 1.107). **B.** *Fish Faces* written and photographed by Norbert Wu (see 1.144). **C.** *Two by Two* written and illustrated by Barbara Reid (see 1.117).

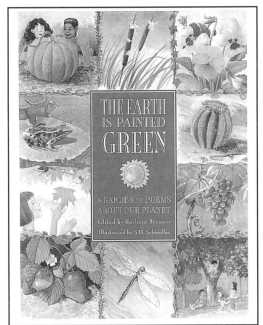

A.

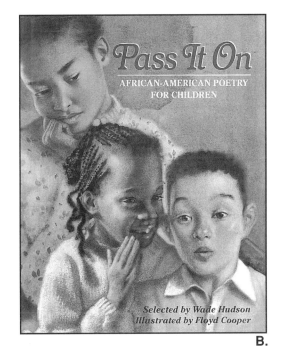

B.

C.

D.

A. *The Earth is Painted Green: A Garden of Poems about Our Planet* edited by Barbara Brenner; illustrated by S. D. Schindler (see 2.5). **B.** *Pass It On: African-American Poetry for Children* selected by Wade Hudson; illustrated by Floyd Cooper (see 2.22). **C.** *My Song is Beautiful: Poems and Pictures in Many Voices* selected by Mary Ann Hoberman (see 2.12). **D.** *Soul Looks Back in Wonder* selected and illustrated by Tom Feelings (see 2.9).

A.

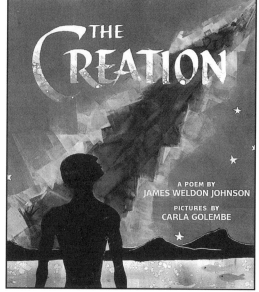

B.

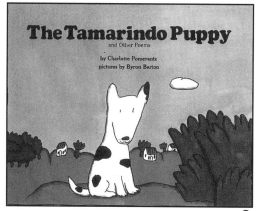

C.

D.

A. *A Moon in Your Lunch Box* by Michael Spooner; illustrated by Ib Ohlsson (see 2.83).
B. *The Creation* by James Weldon Johnson; illustrated by Carla Golembe (see 2.104).
C. *The Tamarindo Puppy and Other Poems* by Charlotte Pomerantz; illustrated by Byron Barton (see 2.73). **D.** *Snuffles and Snouts* selected by Laura Robb; illustrated by Steven Kellogg (see 2.35).

A.

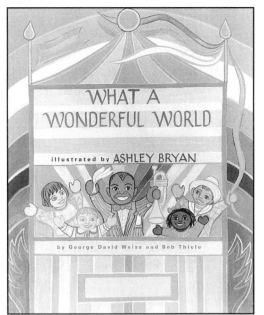

B.

C.

A. *Good Luck Gold and Other Poems* by Janet S. Wong (see 2.88). **B.** *What a Wonderful World* by George David Weiss and Bob Thiele; illustrated by Ashley Bryan (see 2.130). **C.** *Knoxville, Tennessee* by Nikki Giovanni; illustrated by Larry Johnson (see 2.101).

A.

B.

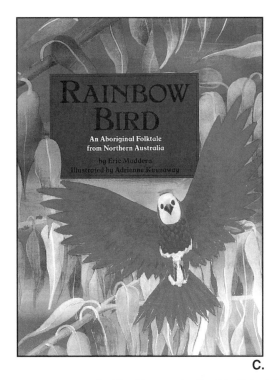

C.

D.

A. *The Dreamer* by Cynthia Rylant; illustrated by Barry Moser (see 3.19). **B.** *The Woman Who Fell from the Sky: The Iroquois Story of Creation* retold by John Bierhorst; illustrated by Robert Andrew Parker (see 3.134). **C.** *Rainbow Bird: An Aboriginal Folktale from Northern Australia* by Eric Maddern; illustrated by Adrienne Kennaway (see 3.93). **D.** *De Colores and Other Latin-American Folk Songs for Children* selected, arranged, and translated by José-Luis Orozco; illustrated by Elisa Kleven (see 3.28).

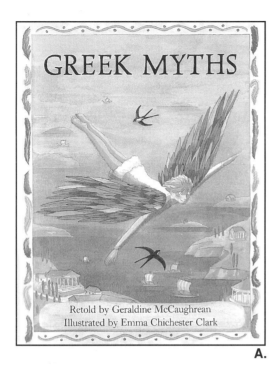

A.

B.

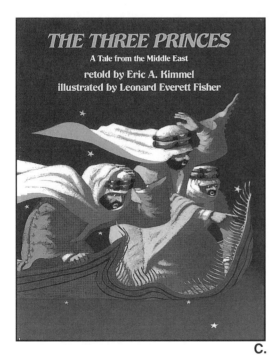

C.

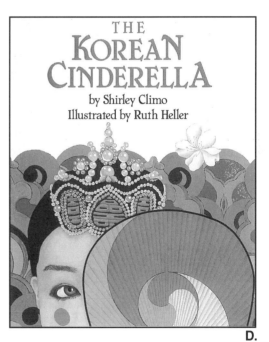

D.

A. *Greek Myths* retold by Geraldine McCaughrean; illustrated by Emma Chichester Clark (see 3.150). **B.** *Swamp Angel* by Anne Isaacs; illustrated by Paul O. Zelinsky (see 3.173). **C.** *The Three Princes: A Tale from the Middle East* retold by Eric A. Kimmel; illustrated by Leonard Everett Fisher (see 3.81). **D.** *The Korean Cinderella* by Shirley Climo; illustrated by Ruth Heller (see 3.44).

A.

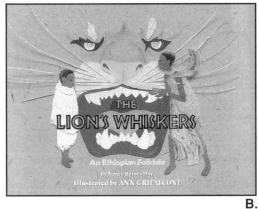

B.

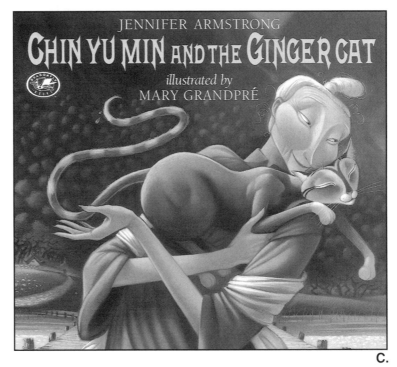

C.

A. *The Goose Girl: A Story from the Brothers Grimm* retold by Eric A. Kimmel; illustrated by Robert Sauber (see 3.78). **B.** *The Lion's Whiskers: An Ethiopian Folktale* by Nancy Raines Day; illustrated by Ann Grifalconi (see 3.47). **C.** *Chin Yu Min and the Ginger Cat* by Jennifer Armstrong; illustrated by Mary GrandPré (see 3.3).

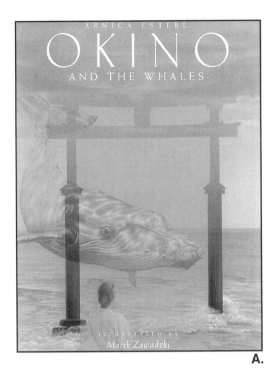

A.

B.

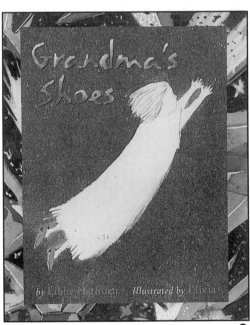

C.

D.

A. *Okino and the Whales* by Arnica Esterl; illustrated by Marek Zawadzki (see 4.21).
B. *Isla/La Isla* by Arthur Dorros; illustrated by Elisa Kleven; translated by Sandra Maru-landa Dorros (see 4.62). **C.** *Grandma's Shoes* by Libby Hathorn; illustrated by Elivia (see 4.5). **D.** *A Starlit Somersault Downhill* by Nancy Willard; illustrated by Jerry Pinkney (see 4.45).

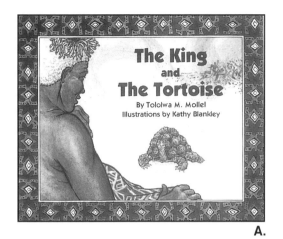

A.

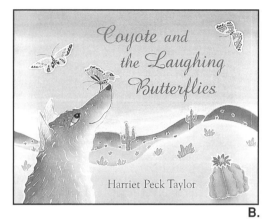

B.

C.

A. *The King and the Tortoise* by Tololwa M. Mollel; illustrated by Kathy Blankley (see 3.101). **B.** *Coyote and the Laughing Butterflies* retold by Harriet Peck Taylor (see 3.165). **C.** *The Gifts of Wali Dad: A Tale of India and Pakistan* retold by Aaron Shepard; illustrated by Daniel San Souci (see 3.118).

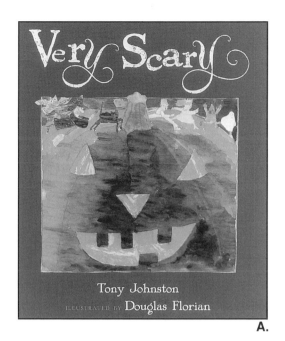

A.

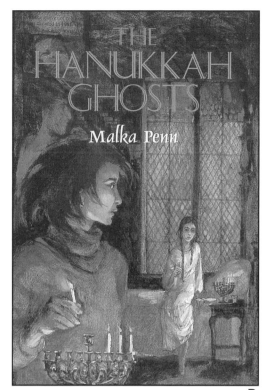

B.

C.

A. *Very Scary* by Tony Johnston; illustrated by Douglas Florian (see 4.86). **B.** *The Hanukkah Ghosts* by Malka Penn (see 4.87). **C.** *Kalinzu: A Story from Africa* written and illustrated by Jeremy Grimsdell (see 4.24).

A.

B.

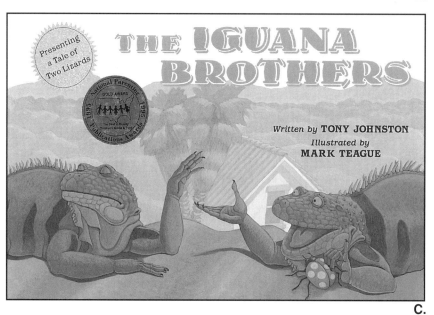

C.

A. *Dumpling Soup* by Jama Kim Rattigan; illustrated by Lillian Hsu-Flanders (see 5.143). **B.** *If You Should Hear a Honey Guide* by April Pulley Sayre; illustrated by S. D. Schindler (see 5.31). **C.** *The Iguana Brothers* by Tony Johnston; illustrated by Mark Teague (see 4.27).

A.

B.

C.

D.

A. *Crazy Lady!* by Jane Leslie Conly (see 5.161). **B.** *The Paper Princess* written and illustrated by Elisa Kleven (see 4.95). **C.** *From Miss Ida's Porch* by Sandra Belton; illustrated by Floyd Cooper (see 5.60). **D.** *Where the Flame Trees Bloom* by Alma Flor Ada; illustrated by Antonio Martorell (see 5.35).

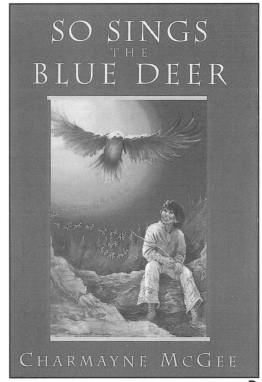

A. *The Future-Telling Lady and Other Stories* by James Berry (see 5.39). B. *So Sings the Blue Deer* by Charmayne McGee (see 5.50). C. *Parents in the Pigpen, Pigs in the Tub* by Amy Ehrlich; illustrated by Steven Kellogg (see 5.203). D. *Red Ribbon* by Sarah Weeks; illustrated by Jeffrey Greene (see 5.56).

A.

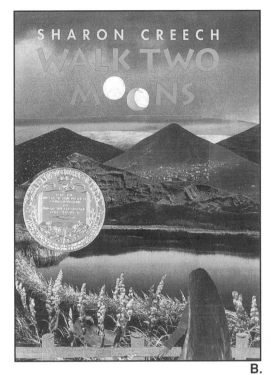

B.

C.

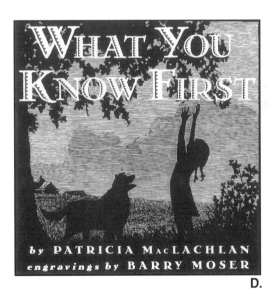

D.

A. *Julie* by Jean Craighead George; illustrated by Wendell Minor (see 5.106). **B.** *Walk Two Moons* by Sharon Creech (see 5.98). **C.** *Welcome Back Sun* written and illustrated by Michael Emberley (see 5.102). **D.** *What You Know First* by Patricia MacLachlan; illustrated by Barry Moser (see 5.72).

A.

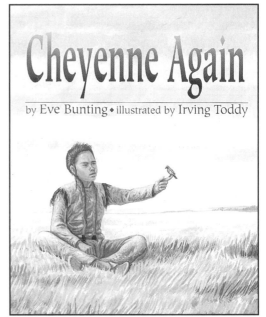

B.

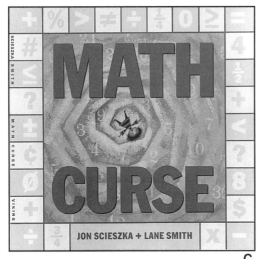

C.

D.

A. *Catherine, Called Birdy* by Karen Cushman (see 6.2). **B.** *Cheyenne Again* by Eve Bunting; illustrated by Irving Toddy (see 6.11). **C.** *Math Curse* by Jon Scieszka; illustrated by Lane Smith (see 5.221). **D.** *Sweet Clara and the Freedom Quilt* by Deborah Hopkinson; illustrated by James Ransome (see 6.20).

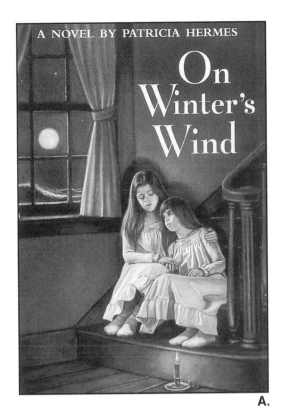

A.

B.

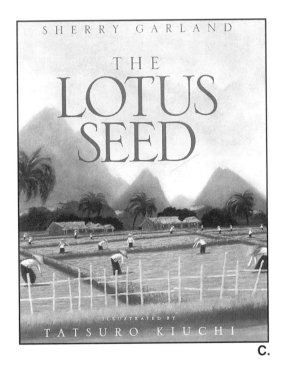

C.

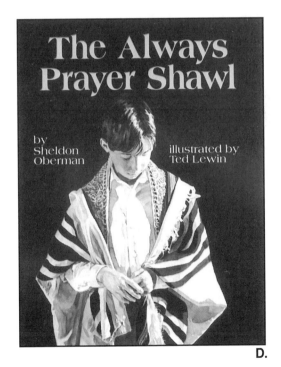

D.

A. *On Winter's Wind* by Patricia Hermes (see 6.19). **B.** *The Fifth of March: A Story of the Boston Massacre* by Ann Rinaldi (see 6.9). **C.** *The Lotus Seed* by Sherry Garland; illustrated by Tatsuro Kiuchi (see 6.58). **D.** *The Always Prayer Shawl* by Sheldon Oberman; illustrated by Ted Lewin (see 6.50).

A.

B.

C.

D.

A. *Dragon's Gate* by Laurence Yep (see 6.39). **B.** *Frida Kahlo* written and illustrated by Robyn Montana Turner (see 7.10). **C.** *Selina and the Bear Paw Quilt* by Barbara Smucker; illustrated by Janet Wilson (see 6.32). **D.** *Waiting for the Evening Star* by Rosemary Wells; illustrated by Susan Jeffers (see 6.53).

A.

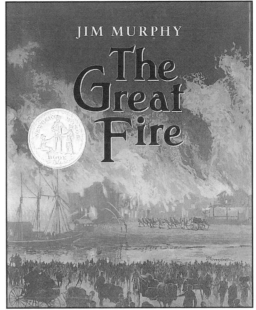

B.

C.

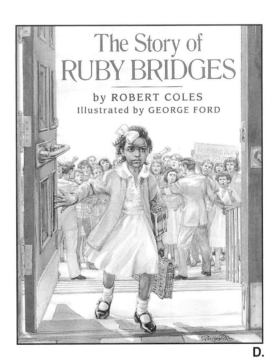

D.

A. *Raoul Wallenberg: The Man Who Stopped Death* by Sharon Linnéa; photographs by Thomas Veres (see 7.16). **B.** *The Great Fire* by Jim Murphy (see 8.55). **C.** *Honest Abe* by Edith Kunhardt; illustrated by Malcah Zeldis (see 7.24). **D.** *The Story of Ruby Bridges* by Robert Coles; illustrated by George Ford (see 8.41).

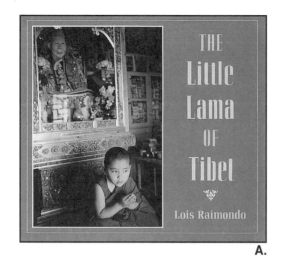

A.

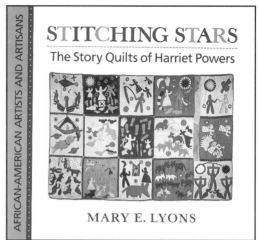

B.

C.

A. *The Little Lama of Tibet* written and photographed by Lois Raimondo (see 7.26).
B. *Stitching Stars: The Story Quilts of Harriet Powers* by Mary E. Lyons (see 7.8).
C. *Pablo Remembers: The Fiesta of the Day of the Dead* written and photographed by George Ancona (see 8.4).

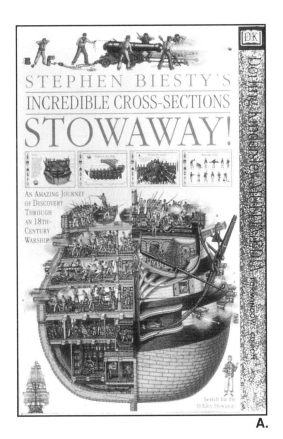

A.

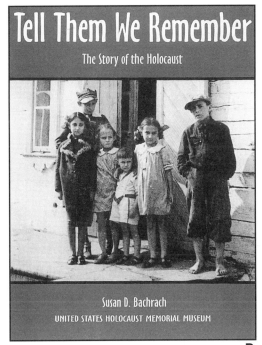

B.

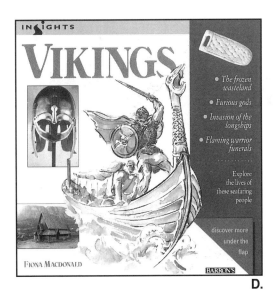

C.

D.

A. *Stephen Biesty's Incredible Cross-Sections: Stowaway!* written and illustrated by Stephen Biesty (see 8.62). **B.** *Tell Them We Remember: The Story of the Holocaust* by Susan D. Bachrach (see 8.60). **C.** *Voices from the Fields: Children of Migrant Farmworkers Tell Their Stories* written and photographed by S. Beth Atkin (see 8.83). **D.** *Vikings* by Fiona Macdonald (see 8.71).

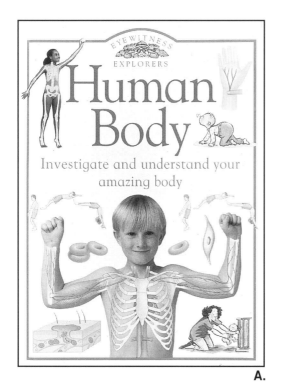

A.

B.

C.

D.

A. *The Human Body* by Steve Parker (see 9.4). **B.** *Monarchs* by Kathryn Lasky; photographs by Christopher G. Knight (see 9.45). **C.** *Tracks in the Wild* written and illustrated by Betsy Bowen (see 9.13). **D.** *Penguin* by Mary Ling; photographs by Neil Fletcher (see 9.32).

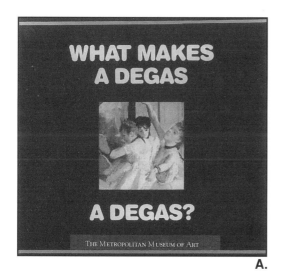

A.

B.

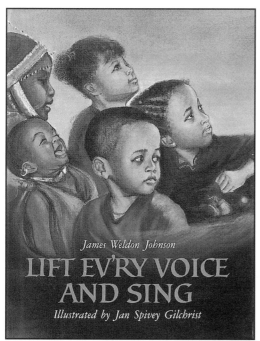

C.

D.

A. *What Makes a Degas a Degas?* by Richard Muhlberger (see 10.12). **B.** *The Quilt-Block History of Pioneer Days: With Projects Kids Can Make* by Mary Cobb; illustrated by Jan Davey Ellis (see 11.4). **C.** *Lift Ev'ry Voice and Sing* by James Weldon Johnson; illustrated by Jan Spivey Gilchrist (see 10.4). **D.** *Artistic Trickery: The Tradition of Trompe L'Oeil Art* by Michael Capek (see 10.8).

A.

B.

C.

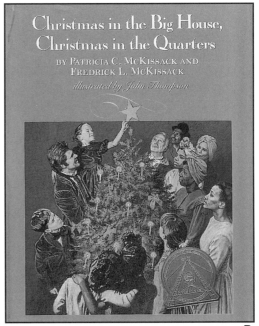

D.

A. *My Nature Craft Book* written and illustrated by Cheryl Owen (see 11.5). **B.** *Happy New Year, Beni* written and illustrated by Jane Breskin Zalben (see 12.17). **C.** *Seven Candles for Kwanzaa* by Andrea Davis Pinkney; illustrated by Brian Pinkney (see 12.23). **D.** *Christmas in the Big House, Christmas in the Quarters* by Patricia C. McKissack and Fredrick L. McKissack; illustrated by John Thompson (see 12.4).

grandmother's life. The stories combine to reveal the family connection across four generations.

5.184 Lasky, Kathryn. **My Island Grandma.** Illustrated by Amy Schwartz. Morrow, 1993. ISBN 0-688-07946-6. 32p. 5–7.

This picture book is a gentle account of one summer that a young girl and her parents spend with her grandmother off the coast of Maine. Swimming, picking berries, watching clouds, and discovering the natural world are part of the loving relationship between Abbey and her grandmother, which is strongly portrayed in both text and illustrations. This is a vigorous and active story with a realistic look at the affinity between the old and the young.

5.185 McCutcheon, Marc. **Grandfather's Christmas Camp.** Illustrated by Kate Kiesler. Clarion, 1995. ISBN 0-395-69626-7. 32p. 5–8.

When Mr. Biggins, Grandfather's three-legged dog, doesn't come home, Lizzie and Grandfather dress warmly and go up the mountain in search of him. They end up spending Christmas Eve on the mountaintop, using their supplies and Grandfather's knowledge of survival outdoors before their search is successful. The strength of this picture book is the superb illustrations, which give the viewer a real sense of sharing the quiet, magical beauty of the mountain wilderness in winter.

5.186 Nye, Naomi Shihab. **Sitti's Secrets.** Illustrated by Nancy Carpenter. Four Winds, 1994. ISBN 0-02-768460-1. 32p. 5–8.

Mona and her father travel to the Middle East to see her grandmother. The story recounts their daily lives together as the relationship between grandmother and granddaughter develops. When she returns home, Mona reflects on her experiences and comes to understand that the miles between them cannot really separate them. Middle Eastern scenery comes alive with exceptional illustrations.

5.187 Thomas, Abigail. **Wake Up, Wilson Street.** Illustrated by William Low. Holt, 1993. ISBN 0-8050-2006-3. 32p. 5–8.

Nana and Little Joe are always the first ones up in their family, and they enjoy watching how Wilson Street slowly wakes up on a Sunday morning. Through the eyes of the young child and his grandmother and their appreciation for the familiar routines around them, we experience the reassuring details of life on their street, such as the paper boy delivering the newspaper, the grocery store opening up, and Mr. Oakley feeding the ducks. The warm, bright oil paintings enhance the serene atmosphere of this peaceful portrait that unfolds around the special relationship between a grandmother and her grandchild.

5.188 Wild, Margaret. **Our Granny.** Illustrated by Julie Vivas. Ticknor & Fields, 1994. ISBN 0-395-67023-3. 32p. 5–8.

A small child shares her point of view about grannies in general and her own granny in particular. " Some grannies wear jeans and sneakers" and others "high heels or comfortable slippers. Our granny wears a funny bathing suit." This celebration of grandmothers has a smooth rhythm and is full of rollicking good humor that is heightened by the exuberant and vibrant watercolor paintings on every page.

School Life

5.189 Asch, Frank. **Hands around Lincoln School.** Scholastic, 1994. ISBN 0-590-44149-3. 217p. 9–12.

Amy usually follows Lindsay's enthusiasms, and Lindsay's Save the Earth Club at school is no exception. Unfortunately, tensions emerge between the club's members and the school's cool clique. When Lindsay is blamed for vandalizing school property, Amy, despite her shyness, takes on the task of investigating the crime. The result is unexpected, testing the girls' friendship as well as Amy's gift for moderation and diplomacy. Young readers will enjoy this story of growth and change in friendship, which includes an element of suspense together with themes of social and environmental concern.

5.190 Finchler, Judy. **Miss Malarkey Doesn't Live in Room 10.** Illustrated by Kevin O'Malley. Walker, 1995. ISBN 0-8027-8386-4. 36p. 5–7.

This is a story of a grade 1 boy who is shocked when his teacher moves into his apartment building; he assumed that teachers lived at school. The colorful and comical illustrations explore the teachers' imagined after-school lives, including scenes of them lining up at water fountains, robed and slippered, to brush their teeth and playing ball in the gymnasium. The boy's imaginative constructions are challenged by the teacher's normal life activities around the apartment building. She throws out the garbage, carries groceries, entertains guests, and even walks barefooted around her apartment. This humorous book could be enjoyed by both younger and older students.

5.191 Larson, Kirby. **Second-Grade Pig Pals.** Illustrated by Nancy Poydar. Holiday House, 1994. ISBN 0-8234-1107-9. 87p. 7–9.

Quinn and Manuela know that they will be good friends on the first day Manuela arrives at school as a new student. After the first day, however, the friendship seems to fade as one misunderstanding follows another. Readers will like Quinn for her sincerity and good intentions, and they will empathize with her difficulties with friends and with finding a suitable contribution to the pig project at school. Quinn's interactions with family members and friends are interesting and realistic. Black-and-white drawings complement the text.

5.192 Munsch, Robert, and Saoussan Askar. **From Far Away.** Illustrated by Michael Marchenko. Annick, 1995. ISBN 1-55037-396-X. unpaged. 5–7.

This story grew out of a series of letters Robert Munsch received from a seven-year-old girl who had recently moved to North America from Beirut, Lebanon. The story is told in the first person, from the perspective of a young girl trying to adapt to a new school and culture after enduring traumatic events in a war-torn country. In particular, the Halloween rites are particularly baffling to the young girl. With time, she finds a place and a voice in the new country she calls home.

5.193 Myers, Laurie. **Earthquake in the Third Grade.** Illustrated by Karen Ritz. Clarion, 1993. ISBN 0-395-65360-6. 63p. 6–8.

A beloved teacher is leaving her grade 3 pupils and three of them think up schemes to keep her. Sensitive to the feelings of young children, the author has captured their humor and resilience in a very pleasing short novel.

5.194 Rodowsky, Colby. **Sydney, Invincible.** Farrar, Straus, 1995. ISBN 0-374-37365-5. 140p. 10–13.

Entering her junior year in a high school where students call their teachers by their first names, Sydney Downie is about to experience how it feels to have your mom as a history teacher, become a big sister for the first time, and become a newspaper editor. The arrival of nonconformist writing teacher Zephyr Kennealy challenges Sydney and her friends to tackle issues of censorship and truth. This sensitive, realistic novel is the sequel to *Sydney, Herself.*

5.195 Skinner, David. **The Wrecker.** Simon & Schuster, 1995. ISBN 0-671-79771-9. 106p. 10–12.

When Michael moves to a new school he is prepared to be an outsider. He is not prepared to be recruited as Theo's ally against a school bully. Theo has an odd gift for creating gizmos out of junk, and he and Michael decide to use this gift to make a machine that will "wreck" the bully. Through his relationship with Theo, Michael's compassion and his desire for friendship are rekindled. Young readers will identify with the boys' school life and with the thorny issue of standing up to a school tyrant.

5.196 Tryon, Leslie. **Albert's Field Trip.** Illustrated by Leslie Tryon. Atheneum, 1993. ISBN 0-689-31821-9. 32p. 5–8.

In her third story about Albert the Duck, Leslie Tryon engages young readers with a blend of fascinating information, a story about an imaginary outing by a class made up of all kinds of animals, and delightful watercolor-and-pencil art. When Albert takes a grade 3 class from Pleasant Valley School on a field trip to an apple orchard, young readers get an opportunity to learn about the daily routine on an apple farm while keeping track of the details of the field trip along with Gary the Skunk.

Humorous Stories

5.197 Breathed, Berkeley. **Red Ranger Came Calling: A Guaranteed True Christmas Story.** Illustrated by Berkeley Breathed. Little, Brown, 1994. ISBN 0-316-10881-2. 48p. 6–8.

A Christmas story with a difference, this delightful book tells the tall tale of a boy named Red whose only desire is to become the Red Ranger. Fortunately, his neighbor is Santa Claus, who helps Red procure a Tweed bicycle for Christmas. The imaginative and rich illustrations by cartoonist Berkeley Breathed add depth to this humorous text.

5.198 Brennan, Herbie. **The Mystery Machine.** McElderry, 1995. ISBN 0-689-50615-5. 91p. 8–11.

Hubert only wants to go to the circus, but his desire sets off a series of bizarre events. Before the story concludes, Hubert loses his soccer ball, attempts a career as a human cannonball, visits outer space, and witnesses the breakup of his parents' marriage over a dirty chimney. With a touch of magic realism, the author treats all of these events as equally probable, and Hubert meets each challenge with equanimity and resourcefulness. Hubert is a sympathetic figure, and his surreal experiences, particularly with adults, will strike young readers as familiar.

5.199 Conford, Ellen. **Get the Picture, Jenny Archer?** Illustrated by Diane Palmisciano. Little, Brown, 1994. ISBN 0-316-15247-1. 64p. 8–10.

At first, Jenny does not consider the present of a used camera very exciting. When she comes across a photo contest, however, she begins taking pictures of "peoples, pets, and places." Jenny's first efforts produce poor results, but as she learns how to use the camera, her pictures improve. Out in the neighborhood, the camera leads Jenny to discover secrets and mysteries she might otherwise have overlooked. Jenny is convinced that one neighbor wants to kill her husband's dog; another has begun to steal cars. Her efforts to set the neighborhood right stir up trouble, and in the end Jenny's photographic evidence reveals something quite unexpected. Readers will be amused by Jenny's unique approach to photographic excellence and by her imaginings.

5.200 Cresswell, Helen. **Posy Bates, Again!** Illustrated by Kate Aldous. Macmillan, 1994. ISBN 0-02-725372-4. 112p. 9–11.

This sequel to *Meet Posy Bates* is a charming and funny story about Posy and the scrapes she gets into, especially when she wants to keep a stray dog. Although young readers will find her solutions to problems perfectly logical, much of the fun is found in realizing that adults will not view her actions in the same way.

5.201 DeFelice, Cynthia. **Mule Eggs.** Illustrated by Mike Shenon. Orchard, 1994. ISBN 0-531-06843-9. 32p. 5–7.

This is a twist on the tale in which the experienced farmer tricks the newcomer from the city. Here, however, the "city slicker" gets his own back—and more. This is an excellent tale for telling and reading aloud.

5.202 Doyle, Brian. **Spud in Winter.** Groundwood, 1995. ISBN 0-88899-224-6. 140p. 10–12.

Spud Sweetgrass notices everything and what he has noticed is that he is probably the only witness who can identify the murder suspect. But there's a problem: The man is his girlfriend Connie Pan's client and Spud is afraid of what might happen to her. Brian Doyle's cast of wonderfully human characters include Dink the Thinker and the ESL students Connie Pan chaperones. They live through the coldest Canadian winter on record in this simultaneously tense and hysterically funny murder mystery. The scene on the Rideau Canal may be the greatest chase scene ever written.

5.203 Ehrlich, Amy. **Parents in the Pigpen, Pigs in the Tub.** Illustrated by Steven Kellogg. Dial, 1993. ISBN 0-8037-0928-5 lib, 0-8037-0933-1. 40p. 6–10.

What can you do when chickens, sheep, and pigs take over the house? Move out to the barn and relax from chores for a while! In this wildly improbable but humorous story, the animals demand equal access to the farm family's human comforts, with all the confusion and trouble imaginable. Kellogg's illustrations add to the carefree atmosphere and give the outrageous situations a playful realism that leaves readers shaking their heads.

5.204 Fine, Anne. **Flour Babies and the Boys of Room 8.** Little, Brown, 1994. ISBN 0-316-28319-3. 178p. 12–13.

A group of school underachievers join a child development class and are given bags of flour to care for as babies. The story contains many moments of fun and surprise. Although the boys seem bright, competent, and verbal, the events are tilted in favor of Simon, the protagonist. His flour baby has eyes, eyelashes, and a dress, whereas those of his classmates are plain flour bags!

5.205 Gershator, Phillis. **Rata-pata-scata-fata: A Caribbean Story.** Illustrated by Holly Meade. Little, Brown, 1994. ISBN 0-316-30470-0. 32p. 4–5.

The magical nonsense rhyme of the title forms the crux of the wishes of a lazy little boy who lives in a Caribbean country. As in many other folktales, such as Jack and the beanstalk, Junjun's wishes come true. Colorful, simple artwork supports a story that begs to be told aloud, perhaps with music.

5.206 Hendrick, Mary Jean. **If Anything Ever Goes Wrong at the Zoo.** Illustrated by Jane Dyer. Harcourt Brace, 1993. ISBN 0-15-238007-8. 32p. 5–7.

Leslie invites zookeepers from her local zoo to bring their animals to her house if they ever need a new home! When heavy rains flood the zoo grounds, many of the keepers select her house and yard to give the animals refuge, bringing the zebras, elephants, monkeys, alligators, and lions. The animals stay only one night, but to Leslie's utter delight. The watercolor illustrations are exceptional, bringing this delightful story to life with considerable appeal.

5.207 Johnson, Doug. **James and the Dinosaurs.** Illustrated by Bill Basso. Atheneum, 1995. ISBN 0-689-31965-7. 32p. 5–8.

James typifies the student who is obsessed with dinosaurs. His teacher, in an attempt to direct some of this energy toward his studies, announces that James will be excused from classwork if he can produce a dinosaur. Cheered with the prospect of never having to be bothered with studies again, he begins his search, which in the end surprises both James and his teacher. Bright cartoon-style illustrations of familiar scenes accompany the text. There is just enough predictable dialogue that children can participate with James in his quest. Children will also relate to the desirable prize of no more classwork!

5.208 Johnson, Paul Brett. **The Cow Who Wouldn't Come Down.** Illustrated by Paul Brett Johnson. Orchard, 1993. ISBN 0-531-05481-0. 32p. 5–7.

Everyone knows that cows can't fly, but Gertrude has a mind of her own. Miss Rosemary tries many ways to lure her down, but succeeds in this task only by sewing a cow-shaped cushion on which Gertrude can land. This is a humorous book that can be used with a domestic animal or farm theme, or that might inspire creative writing tasks.

5.209 King-Smith, Dick. **The Invisible Dog.** Illustrated by Roger Roth. Crown, 1993. ISBN 0-517-59424-2. 73p. 7–10.

Seven-year-old Janie wants a dog more than anything in the world and is delighted when her wish comes true, even though Henry, her Great Dane, is invisible to everyone except her elderly neighbor, Mrs. Gallow. Through a series of coincidences, and perhaps a little magic, Henry becomes a real, flesh-and-blood dog. King-Smith is a wonderful storyteller and his characters, in this and his many other stories for young readers, are engaging and distinct and well worth revisiting.

5.210 Mahy, Margaret. **The Rattlebang Picnic.** Illustrated by Steven Kellogg. Dial, 1994. ISBN 0-8037-1319-3. 32p. 5–8.

In this hilarious romp, seven children, their parents, and their grandmother escape from the lava of a volcano in an old car that loses a wheel. The solution? It is too good to give away except to say that it is refreshing to meet a grandmother who cannot cook. The illustrations are as lively and exaggerated as the story, conveying a New Zealand summer mountain setting.

5.211 Mark, Jan. **Silly Tails.** Illustrated by Tony Ross. Atheneum, 1993. ISBN 0-689-31843-X. 26p. 6–10.

If you have ever wondered why vegetables don't talk, this outrageous story explains how a war developed between the rabbits and the carrots, back in the days of pilgrims and pumpkins. Tony Ross's humorous drawings make this silly metafictive tale even sillier. Some of the text contains perplexing social commentary: "Underground grass roots continue to discuss important matters."

5.212 Martin, Jane Read, and Patricia Marx. **Now Everybody Really Hates Me.** Illustrated by Roz Chast. HarperCollins, 1993. ISBN 0-06-021293- 4. 32p. 5–7.

Patti Jane Pepper is sent to her room for "touching her brother really hard" and other fussing during his birthday party. There she fantasizes about escape and retribution, until she is carried out by her parents, stating, "It appears they really want me to come down for cake and ice cream." The story and illustrations are humorous and imaginative.

5.213 McGilvray, Richard. **Don't Climb out of the Window Tonight.** Illustrated by Alan Snow. Dial, 1993. ISBN 0-8037-1373-8. 26p. 5–7.

Written by a seven-year-old boy, this picture book depicts many of the frightening creatures children imagine live outside at night: alligators, goblins, ghosts, Frankenstein's monster, witches, giants, aliens, dragons, bats, and monsters. The illustrations by Alan Snow are very imaginative. This is an excellent book to explore fears and imagination with children, and could work well with Halloween themes. The book offers an excellent opportunity for encouraging children to write and even publish stories of their own.

5.214 McKenna, Colleen O'Shaughnessy. **Live from the Fifth Grade.** Scholastic, 1994. ISBN 0-590-46684-4. 145p. 9–11.

Roger is the unappreciated clown of his school. Adults and some of his classmates frown on his antics, but he does not let this crush him. However, it is a different matter when one of Roger's pranks sets off events that might result in the firing of his friend, the school caretaker. To right the situation, Roger, his best friend, and his worst enemy find themselves collaborating to solve the mystery behind a theft in the school. Roger's cheerful personality draws the reader into the story. Young readers will also find the description of school life entertaining.

5.215 Parish, Peggy. **Thank You, Amelia Bedelia.** Illustrated by Barbara Siebel Thomas. HarperCollins, 1993. ISBN 0-06-022979-9. 64p. 6–8.

The antics of Amelia Bedelia in this familiar story are enriched by Barbara Siebel Thomas's revised, more colorful illustrations. Daughter of the original illustrator, Thomas reworks the drawings from the 1964 edition and includes several new scenes. All of these illustrations retain the original flavor as Amelia prepares the household for Great Aunt Myra's visit, taking every direction literally with hilarious results.

5.216 Paulsen, Gary. **Harris and Me: A Summer Remembered.** Harcourt Brace, 1993. ISBN 0-15-292877-4. 157p. 10–12.

This is a robust, rollicking comedy with elements of pathos. The vulnerable, eleven-year-old narrator is forced to spend the summer on the farm of his relatives, including his cousins Glennis and Harris. Nine-year-old Harris, curious, inventive, and downright naughty, draws his cousin, at first unsuspecting but soon a willing participant, into a series of suspenseful adventures that young people will relish for their elements of daring, recklessness, and humor. With antics reminiscent of Tom Sawyer and Huckleberry Finn, this is an excellent book for reading aloud.

5.217 Petersen, P. J. **I Hate Company.** Illustrated by Betsy James. Dutton, 1994. ISBN 0-525-45329-6. 87p. 8–10.

Dan is presented with a challenge when his mother's friend, Kay, and her three-year-old son, Jimmy, come to stay while Kay looks for work. Dan must give up his room, protect his belongings, and sacrifice his time to make a place for Kay and Jimmy. To please his mother, Dan is as patient as he can be. However, Jimmy gets into all sorts of typical toddler trouble, which annoys Dan and will amuse readers. Dan tries to move the guests out more speedily by looking for a job for Kay, and the result is unexpected. When Kay and Jimmy finally leave, Dan discovers that he has grown attached to them. Young readers with younger siblings or friends will empathize with Dan in this situation.

5.218 Ray, Mary Lyn. **Alvah and Arvilla.** Illustrated by Barry Root. Harcourt Brace, 1994. ISBN 0-15-202655-X. 32p. 5–8.

For many years, Arvilla has dreamed of seeing the Pacific Ocean. Finally, after over thirty years of being tied to the farm she has with her husband, Alvah, Arvilla finds an ingenious way to make her dream come true and, along with Alvah and all their animals, she sets off to cross the country in their unique vehicle. The vivid watercolor illustrations enrich the many details of this delightful and humorous travel tale.

5.219 Robinson, Barbara. **The Best School Year Ever.** HarperCollins, 1994. ISBN 0-06-023039-8. 117p. 9–11.

Like Robinson's earlier novel, *The Best Christmas Pageant Ever,* this book is a collection of postwar school-life anecdotes narrated by Beth and featuring the Herdmans, especially Imogene. All the children's classmates are back and this year's special project is to think of something nice to say about everyone. The episodes are as humorous as the ones in the first book, and the characters now have more depth. Imogene may actually have a kind streak. This sequel is actually better than the original story and begs to be read aloud.

5.220 Rylant, Cynthia. **Mr. Putter and Tabby Walk the Dog.** Illustrated by Arthur Howard. Harcourt Brace, 1994. ISBN 0-15-256259-1hc, 0-15-200891-8pb. 44p. 6–8.

The adventures of Mr. Putter and his cat, Tabby, with their neighbor's "dream dog," Zeke, will appeal to young readers making the transition from easy picture books to short chapter stories. Humorous illustrations accompany the disasters that happen when Mr. Putter and Tabby volunteer to take care of Zeke, who turns out to be a nightmare. The unusual tricks the cat and his owner resort to in order to "tame" Zeke will please young readers.

5.221 Scieszka, Jon. **Math Curse.** Illustrated by Lane Smith. Viking, 1995. ISBN 0-670-86194-4. 32p. 5–10.

A simple statement from her math teacher, "You know, you can think of almost everything as a math problem," and one student finds herself on an adventure to transform her world through mathematical eyes. She concludes that she must be under a math curse! This humorous book of ridiculous questions will make even the most reluctant math students laugh. Jon Scieszka and Lane Smith have produced a picture book that will appeal to students of all ages. One of the strengths of the book is that it will help children to see, albeit in an extreme way, how math is an integral part of our daily lives. Students will enjoy learning how the student finally eludes the curse.

5.222 Viorst, Judith. **Alexander, Who's Not (Do You Hear Me? I Mean It!) Going to Move.** Illustrated by Robin Preiss Glasser. Atheneum, 1995. ISBN 0-689-31958-4 (English); 0-689-31984-3 (Spanish). 32p. 5–9.

Alexander is back at it again, asserting his independence. This time he insists he will not go when the rest of the family move a thousand miles away. As Alexander explains why he cannot go, he is actually saying his goodbyes and deciding what he will do to adjust to his new location. Robin Preiss Glasser's black ink depictions show Alexander as endearingly obstinate as ever. Whether or not children are on the verge of moving, they will identify with Alexander and his battle with life's changes and challenges. Editions are available in both English and Spanish.

5.223 Wynne-Jones, Tim. **The Book of Changes.** Orchard, 1995. ISBN 0-531-09489-8. 143p. 9–12.

Unlikely heroes enliven this offbeat collection of seven stories. Have you ever tried to sell subscriptions to a TV magazine when you knew you couldn't—even when people were willing to buy? Did you ever suffer the indignity of being picked on by a school bully on your way home, yet were saved by your ability to give a Donald Duck impression? Can real-life ghosts return to possess junior hockey stars? The fast-paced commentary is filled with this award-winning Canadian author's wit, sparkling dialogue, and quirky sense of humor.

Mystery Stories

5.224 Bellairs, John. **The Drum, the Doll, and the Zombie.** Dial, 1994. ISBN 0-8037-1462-9. 155p. 9–12.

When a friend receives a voodoo drum and a request to destroy it, Johnny, Fergie, and Professor Childermass find themselves involved in a supernatural mystery. In this sequel to *The Secret of the Underground Room*, the adventurers encounter sorcery, zombies, and terrifying creatures in their attempts to rescue the victims of the drum. This novel is enjoyable even for those who have not read others in the series. The characters are engaging and the resolution of the mystery is exciting and satisfying, with far-reaching consequences. The appeal of the novel is enhanced by Edward Gorey's artwork.

5.225 Byars, Betsy. **The Dark Stairs.** Viking, 1994. ISBN 0-670-85487-5. 130p. 8–12.

This is the first in a promised series starring Herculeah Jones and her sidekick, Meat. This suspense tale involves a killer, an old rambling house, a police detective, and a private investigator. It reads aloud well and will keep readers on the edge so that they will stay involved to the end. Well-defined characters, believable dialogue, and a suspenseful plot make this a worthwhile literary experience.

5.226   Carris, Joan. **Beware the Ravens, Aunt Morbelia.** Little, Brown, 1995. ISBN 0-316-12961-5. 141p. 10–12.

In this sequel to *Aunt Morbelia and the Screaming Skulls*, Aunt Morbelia takes Todd and his friend Jeff on a holiday to England. England has changed since she left decades before, as has the family estate at Harrowwood. Todd and Jeff discover a mysterious journal at Harrowwood and, as they try to discover its meaning, they find themselves plagued by ghosts and spied on wherever they go. The friendship between the boys and the elderly aunt is a highlight of the novel and the initial suspense of the story works well.

5.227   George, Jean Craighead. **The Fire Bug Connection: An Ecological Mystery.** HarperCollins, 1993. ISBN 0-06-021490-2. 148p. 8–12.

Maggie and Mitch had met before and did not get along. They begin the summer at a Maine research station apprehensively, but soon discover their common interest in living things and ecosystems. Together they learn about the ravens that have moved into the area, about bats, and about a variety of insects, including some specimens from Europe that are dying mysteriously. Solving the mystery of the dying fire bugs reconciles Maggie and Mitch and brings them to a new understanding of the interrelatedness of creatures and their environment. Readers will be attracted to the forest research station setting and interested by the scientific details that emerge in unraveling the natural mysteries.

5.228   Hildick, E. W. **The Case of the Absent Author.** Macmillan, 1995. ISBN 0-02-743821-X. 151p. 8–12.

This mystery novel will be welcomed by fans of the McGurk series. Jack McGurk, Joey Rockaway, and the other members of the McGurk Organization must solve the disappearance of a crime writer and his manuscripts. The trail leads the young detectives to the stories of Edgar Allan Poe and to revisit earlier McGurk cases before this case is closed. Young readers will identify with the detectives and appreciate the ingenuity that allows members of the McGurk Organization to solve mysteries without the help of adults.

5.229 Hildick, E. W. **The Case of the Fantastic Footprints.** Macmillan, 1994. ISBN 0-02-743967-4. 155p. 9–11.

Youthful detectives have been a staple of children's fiction since Erich Kaestner's *Emil and the Detectives* was published in English in 1929. Hildick's McGurk runs a detective agency that is well known and respected in the neighborhood. Here the children are up against a bewildering set of clues that will also keep the reader guessing. An easy-to-read but well-plotted mystery.

5.230 Walker, Paul Robert. **The Sluggers Club: A Sports Mystery.** Harcourt Brace, 1993. ISBN 0-15-276163-2. 153p. 9–12.

Many baseball players are superstitious and the players for the Granada Little League are no exceptions. When B.J.'s friend, Wash, loses his prized bat to a thief, he also loses his ability to hit. As the team's season heads for disaster, B.J., Wash, and Tony form the Slugger's Club to investigate the disappearance of the bat and of other pieces of equipment owned by members of the league. The boys gradually eliminate names from their list of suspects until they are surprised by the answer to the mystery and presented with another challenge in its place. Baseball fans will enjoy the sports detail in this novel, but there is also enough mystery to interest those who like a whodunit.

5.231 Woodruff, Elvira. **Ghosts Don't Get Goose Bumps.** Illustrated by Joel Iskowitz. Holiday House, 1993. ISBN 0-8234-1035-8. 167p. 9–12.

Jenna goes to spend the summer on her cousins' farm with her little brother, Nelson, who is mute. Immediately, she meets a very special friend and an amusing character, the aspiring actress Angel Always. When they hatch a plan to surprise Nelson into speaking, the girls accidentally stumble onto a mystery. An old marble factory near the farm appears to be haunted. The girls involve another visitor, Zeke, in an investigation of the haunted factory, which leads the children into danger. Ultimately, the mystery of the factory is solved, Nelson speaks, and the children succeed in helping the previous owners of the factory. Young readers will enjoy the colorful characters, suspenseful story, and happy outcome.

5.232 Wright, Betty Ren. **The Ghost of Popcorn Hill.** Illustrated by Karen Ritz. Holiday House, 1993. ISBN 0-8234-1009-9. 81p. 6–8.

Martin, Peter, and their parents have moved to Popcorn Hill to live more cheaply because their father has lost his job. One good thing about their new country life is that they can now have a dog. Unfortunately, the dog their father chose is not one that the boys want. To make matters worse, the boys' bedroom is haunted by a very persistent ghost. Children will identify with Martin and Peter's fears, and they will applaud the boys' bravery and ingenuity in addressing their problems.

5.233   Wright, Betty Ren. **The Ghost Witch.** Illustrated by Ellen Eagle. Holiday House, 1993. ISBN 0-8234-1036-6. 103p. 9–11.

Jenny faces a dilemma. Old Mrs. Nagle left her house to Jenny and her mother, but Jenny is afraid to live there because the house is haunted by the ghost of Mrs. Nagle's grandmother, who was a witch. Jenny fears that she will be tormented by the ghost, who delights in scaring children with her apparitions. If she refuses to live in the house, she knows that she will make her mother angry and unhappy. Fortunately for Jenny, the upcoming Halloween celebrations in her neighborhood may offer a solution. Young readers will sympathize with Jenny's problem and her difficulty in making adults understand. The happy ending emphasizes coexistence rather than confrontation. Even so, Jenny must find courage to resolve the situation.

Respect for Nature

5.234   Asch, Frank. **Up River.** Photographs by Ted Levin and Steve Lehmer. Simon & Schuster, 1995. ISBN 0-671-88703-3. 45p. 7–10.

This is based on Frank Asch's thirteen-year-old son's participation in the Otter Creek River Cleanup, held every May near their home in Vermont. The text is long and details the events and environmental concerns of the project from the perspective of Devin and his friend Caleb, both of whom learn about river ecology in the process. Photographs accompany the text.

5.235   Dewey, Ariane. **The Sky.** Illustrated by Ariane Dewey. Green Tiger, 1993. ISBN 0-671-77835-8. 34p. 5–7.

This book is a poetic and scientific look at what goes on in the sky: clouds, kites, butterflies, space shuttles, smog, and fireworks, to name just a few. The chalk-pastel artwork is colorful and dramatic. Because of the small type and its placement on the page, this fascinating book will be difficult to use with a group but is excellent for child-adult interaction.

5.236   Dugan, Barbara. **Leaving Home with a Pickle Jar.** Illustrated by Karen Lee Baker. Greenwillow, 1993. ISBN 0-688-10836-9hc, 0-688-10837-7pb. 32p. 5–7.

This book deals with the familiar theme of a child's life disrupted by moving to a new environment. Here a child, his mother, and his sister travel from an urban neighborhood to a country home with an aunt in Minnesota. This child of a single-parent family takes along a grasshopper in a pickle jar.

5.237   Franklin, Kristine L. (translated by Zubizaretta). **When the Monkeys Came Back/El aullido de los monos.** Illustrated by Robert Roth. Atheneum, 1994. ISBN 0-689-31807-3 (English); 0-689-31950-9 (Spanish). 32p. 6–8.

When a section of wooded land in Central America is cut down, the monkeys disappear. This picture storybook has both an environmental message and a valuable sidelight on the position of women in certain cultures at certain times. Dona Marta and her husband inherit the farm from her father, but she has to ask her husband for a piece of land for her reforestation project. She and her children work for many years restoring the forest until finally, when she is old, the monkeys return. Editions are available in both English and Spanish.

5.238   Garland, Sherry. **The Summer Sands.** Illustrated by Robert J. Lee. Harcourt Brace, 1995. ISBN 0-15-282492-8. 32p. 5–7.

Using the story of one family, this is an account of how Christmas trees are recycled to restore sand dunes that have been destroyed by storms. The wildlife of the fragile seashore and sand dune community, and the action and effects of the wind, are described through the experiences and reactions of the family. Soft watercolors help convey the family's love and concern for the area. This is a good example of how a community can contribute to conservation efforts.

5.239   Havill, Juanita. **Sato and the Elephants.** Illustrated by Jean Tseng and Mou-Sien Tseng. Lothrop, 1993. ISBN 0-688-11155-6. 32p. 5–7.

When Sato expressed the wish to become a master ivory carver like his father, he was still unaware of the plight of African elephants. His feelings change when he discovers a bullet lodged in a piece of ivory that he is working on. The realistic illustrations are clear and interesting. This is a good text for looking at the subject of elephants, ethics, endangered species, and other environmental issues.

5.240 Martin, Jacqueline Briggs. **Washing the Willow Tree Loon.** Illustrated by Nancy Carpenter. Simon & Schuster, 1995. ISBN 0-689-80415-6. 32p. 5–8.

This is an account of how a group of people from various occupations work together for the common love of birds who need rescue, cleaning, and release. In this case, they are oil-matted birds affected by an oil spill. The importance of conservation and the rewards of caring for the afflicted birds are told through the story of one bird in particular, the loon. Rich illustrations from various viewpoints show the progress of the rescue operations, adding reader involvement. This excellent read-aloud would encourage discussion and greater knowledge about rehabilitation efforts for wildlife after oil spills.

5.241 McNulty, Faith. **A Snake in the House.** Illustrated by Ted Rand. Scholastic, 1994. ISBN 0-590-44758-0. 32p. 6–8.

A young boy catches a snake and accidentally lets it escape in the house. When the snake desperately tries to find its way out of the unfamiliar environment, it encounters numerous frightening adventures. Told from both the boy's and the snake's perspectives and illustrated beautifully from a snake-eye view, this engaging picture book gives young readers a gentle yet powerful message about conservation and the importance of respect for nature and its creatures.

5.242 Napoli, Donna Jo. **The Bravest Thing.** Dutton, 1995. ISBN 0-525-45397-0. 135p. 10–12.

Laurel loves pets, and with the support of her tolerant parents she has had many. When she becomes a rabbit owner, however, she runs into difficulty and heartbreak. Her first rabbit dies, and her second, Bun Bun, refuses to be an attentive mother to her litters. Laurel does everything she can to care for the baby rabbits. Through her attentions to her pets and her relationships with family and friends, readers get to know Laurel as a caring and determined person who challenges the realities of life and death as they apply to both humans and animals. The story is filled with detail that will fascinate animal-loving readers.

5.243 Norman, Lilith. **The Paddock: A Story in Praise of the Earth.** Illustrated by Robert Roennfeldt. Knopf, 1993. ISBN 0-679-83887-2. 32p. 6–8.

Ecological changes that occur over millennia are explored in this Australian picture book. The story focuses on a small patch of ground, or paddock, and depicts its formation and subsequent change as dinosaurs, animals, aboriginal people, and foreign settlers inhabited the land. Simple text and large landscape illustrations provide a good introduction to the ongoing changes occurring in nature and hint at the healing ability of the earth. Coupled with an optimistic ending, Robert Roennfeldt's dark and somewhat haunting illustrations provide a sense of the earth's frailty. This book could be used in discussions of Australia, nature, pollution, and conservation.

5.244　Orie, Sandra DeCoteau. **Did You Hear the Wind Sing Your Name? An Oneida Song of Spring.** Illustrated by Christopher Canyon. Walker, 1995. ISBN 0-8027-8350-3. 32p. 5–7.

"Did you smell the sweet scent of the sacred Cedar? Did you see Sun's face in the Buttercup?" These are a few of the questions posed in this exploration of an Oneida spring. Readers are taken on a tour of the sights and smells of a day and evening in spring. The question format of the story provides a wonderful opportunity to read aloud. With vivid colors and subtle texture, the full-spread illustrations provide varying viewpoints of nature. An author's note about the symbolism in Oneida culture provides a good introduction to the book and to the Oneida people.

5.245　Stock, Catherine. **Where Are You Going Manyoni?** Illustrated by Catherine Stock. Morrow, 1993. ISBN 0-688-10352-9. 41p. 6–8.

Catherine Stock's simple story of a little girl's morning walk to school in a sparsely settled area of Zimbabwe, near the Limpopo River, is a vital introduction to the beauty of the African veld. Her richly detailed watercolors meticulously capture the uniqueness of this spectacular area and her appendices annotating both the wildlife pictured in the text and the language of the land provide the reader with a marvelous primer to this tradition. A book clearly meant to be read aloud over and over again.

5.246　Stolz, Mary. **Say Something.** Illustrated by Alexander Koshkin. HarperCollins, 1993. ISBN 0-06-021158-X. 32p. 5–7.

The text of this picture book is a prose poem about nature, suggesting questions and comments that may encourage young children to arrive at their own answers. The illustrations are a satisfying interpretation of the natural world, combining both realism and imagination.

5.247 Yerxa, Leo. **Last Leaf First Snowflake to Fall.** Illustrated by Leo Yerxa. Orchard, 1994. ISBN 0-531-06824-2. 32p. 5–8.

A parent and child take a canoe journey together along the forest waterways, appreciating the last leaves of autumn and the joy of the first snowflakes. The sensual imagery of the narrative is enhanced by the text's poetic quality. Magnificent tissue-paper collages depict the impact of the changing seasons and the overwhelming presence of the landscape. The illustrator's First Nation heritage can be seen in the sensitive compositions, which in themselves make a poetic statement. The delicate effect of the overlapping layers of tissue paper enriches the changing perspectives and light conditions.

5.248 Zolotow, Charlotte. **When the Wind Stops.** Illustrated by Stefano Vitale. HarperCollins, 1995. ISBN 0-06-026972-3. 32p. 5–8.

As a little boy lies down to sleep, he asks his mother why the day has to end. She explains that nothing ends; it only begins somewhere else. As the question and answer format winds through the seasons, the wind, and the waves, the mother reassures her son of new beginnings and the changing of seasons. The simple text is printed against full-page landscape paintings on wood. The texture and grain of the wood emphasize the presence of life and regeneration in every aspect of nature. Young readers can enjoy reading this book themselves or having it read aloud.

Social Issues

5.249 Elzbieta. **Jon-Jon and Annette.** Illustrated by Elzbieta. Holt, 1993. ISBN 0-8050-3299-1. 30p. 5–7.

Jon-Jon and Annette play together every day, until the war comes and separates them. The brook where they once played becomes a thorn bush, and they are forbidden to play together. Jon-Jon's father goes to fight in the war, and Jon-Jon becomes very lonely. He does not understand why he cannot play with his friend. He comes to see war itself as the true enemy. At last the children are reunited when the war ends. This book is an excellent allegory for exploring the negative effects of war and illustrating the capacity of love and human affection to transcend borders and military conflict. A good text for teaching peace.

5.250 Gray, Libba Moore. **Dear Willie Rudd.** Illustrated by Peter M. Fiore. Simon & Schuster, 1993. ISBN 0-671-79774-3. 32p. 7–9.

This is a poetic text with richly textured, realistic illustrations. A middle-aged woman from the South remembers her childhood nanny with fondness, warmth, and some remorse at the inequities shown to this beloved person by the bigoted people and practices of the time. The theme could serve as a useful springboard for discussions of the lack of recognition accorded certain people, and more specifically those who love and raise children, particularly women and people of color.

5.251 Hill, Anthony. **The Burnt Stick.** Illustrated by Mark Sofilas. Houghton Mifflin, 1995. ISBN 0-395-73974-8. 53p. 8–10.

When the government agent comes to take young John Jagamarra away to a residential school, his family hides him by darkening his light skin with a burnt stick. Ultimately, the ruse is discovered and John is removed from his people and his home. The tragedy of the separation is mitigated only by the adult John's strong affirmation of cultural survival. This distressing story unfolds with uncompromising directness, yet without recourse to stereotypes. The characters achieve a realistic complexity that is remarkable in so short a book. Charcoal illustrations enhance the text.

5.252 Levine, Arthur A. **Pearl Moscowitz's Last Stand.** Illustrated by Robert Roth. Tambourine, 1993. ISBN 0-688-10753-2. 32p. 6–9.

Pearl Moscowitz has lived on Gingko Street all her life. Through her eyes, we see the changes to the street—both the positive ones that came with people from different cultural backgrounds, and the negative ones brought on by encroaching industrialization. This vividly narrated and illustrated story of how Pearl stands up for her beliefs and for the preservation of her neighborhood illuminates the values of cultural diversity, history, and community.

5.253 Meyer, Carolyn. **White Lilacs.** Harcourt Brace, 1993. ISBN 0-15-200641-9. 242p. 11–14.

In a small town in Texas in the 1920s, the small African American community faces racism on a daily basis. Intolerance reaches a peak when the white majority takes legal steps to oust the blacks in order to obtain their land for a park and other amenities. The events are narrated through the voice of Rose Lee, a black schoolchild, and the simple narrative tone lends even more poignancy to the inevitability of the crisis. The author tells us in an afterword that the plot is based on actual recorded events.

5.254 Neufeld, John. **Almost a Hero.** Atheneum, 1995. ISBN 0-689-31971-1. 147p. 9–12.

To complete a grade 7 assignment, Ben finds himself volunteering at Sidewalk's End, a daycare center for the children of the homeless. After his first day, he sees "an accident" involving one of the children, launching him and his friends on a heroic adventure to "save" the child. However, they soon discover that the lives of others are not always what they seem. Together, the youths negotiate important social issues such as poverty, homelessness, child abuse, and social responsibility with minimal adult intervention. The writing style would appeal to youths.

Survival Stories

5.255 Cottonwood, Joe. **Quake! A Novel.** Scholastic, 1995. ISBN 0- 590-22232-5. 146p. 9–12.

Franny looks forward to her visit with Jennie, whom she has not seen in four years, but when the girls meet Franny is disappointed with how much Jennie has changed. However, the reunion difficulties are quickly overshadowed by a disastrous earthquake. Cut off from their parents and from help in their remote community, the girls plunge into salvaging property and easing the suffering of injured neighbors. In the aftermath of the disaster, the girls help to rebuild Jennie's family home and neighborhood, even as they begin to renew their friendship after its long lapse. The girls' resourcefulness and quickness to act will appeal to readers, as will the realism with which the author depicts California's 1989 earthquake.

5.256 Hill, Kirkpatrick. **Winter Camp.** Macmillan, 1993. ISBN 0-689-50588-4. 185p. 10–13.

In this sequel to *Toughboy and Sister,* Natasha, the elderly neighbor who has assumed responsibility for the orphans, takes them to her isolated winter camp to teach them how to trap and survive in the Alaska wilderness. Through trial and error, the children learn to adapt to the harsh and primitive conditions. Their new knowledge and strength are put to the test when they must care for themselves and a seriously injured miner while Natasha goes for help. This is a dramatic and touching glimpse of life in the north.

6 Historical Fiction

Prehistoric Times

6.1 Craig, Ruth. **Malu's Wolf.** Orchard, 1995. ISBN 0-531-09484-7. 187p. 8–12.

Set in Stone Age Europe, this novel explores the changes that probably took place when wolves were first domesticated. Malu, the young heroine, and the wolf, Kono, that she adopted as a cub, are involved in a series of dangerous and compelling adventures. As the well-written story unfolds, much information is provided about the daily life, traditions, and values of prehistoric hunters and gatherers.

Medieval Times

6.2 Cushman, Karen. **Catherine, Called Birdy.** Clarion, 1994. ISBN 0-395-68186-3. 170p. 10–12.

"I am commanded to write an account of my days: I am bit by fleas and plagued by family. That is all there is to say." Hardly. Catherine's account of her fourteenth year is refreshingly earthy and vital. Taking after her mother, she ministers to the sick but spares them no sympathy. Her father beats her regularly. Disdaining the life of a girl, she peevishly wonders why "everyone is so certain they are mine" when the remains of many unfinished tapestry works are dug out from the privy. Catherine's unpretentious observations and aspirations are so engaging that this Newbery Honor Book account of everyday life in medieval England is riveting from start to finish. Readers of all ages will be eager to follow the reading of this novel with Karen Cushman's *The Midwife's Apprentice.*

6.3 Garfield, Leon. **The Saracen Maid.** Illustrated by John O'Brien. Simon & Schuster, 1994. ISBN 0-671-86646-X. 26p. 9–11.

This British author, reminiscent of Charles Dickens in his style, is noted for his historical novels set in the eighteenth century such as *Smith* and *Jack Holborn.* In this short, witty story, a merchant's son, Gilbert, is captured by Barbary pirates and held for ransom. Unfortunately he is too absent-minded to remember his father's name or where he lives and seems doomed to remain imprisoned. However, a young Saracen maid helps him escape to London where the two are eventually reunited and marry. Watercolor and ink drawings effectively capture the medieval setting and fanciful tone of the story.

6.4   Tomlinson, Theresa. **The Forestwife.** Orchard, 1995. ISBN 0-531-09450-2. 170p. 9–12.

Forestwife bears similarities to the Robin Hood legend but with a twist. Here the hero is fifteen-year-old Marian, who runs away from her guardian because he is about to force her to marry an elderly widower "with rotten black stumps of teeth and a smell of sour ale and saddle grease." Marian searches out the company of the outcasts who live in the forest. Gradually she assumes an important role in their society as she learns the art of healing. This is a fascinating glimpse into the world of medieval England as seen from a female perspective. This novel could be read with other novels that explore this period, such as *The Ramsay Scallop* by Frances Temple and *Catherine, Called Birdy* by Karen Cushman.

Fifteenth and Sixteenth Centuries

6.5   Greene, Jacqueline Dembar. **One Foot Ashore.** Walker, 1994. ISBN 0-8027-8281-7. 196p. 11–12.

A twelve-year-old Jewish girl and her family are victims of the Portuguese Inquisition. Modern children will find the background unfamiliar, but the fast-paced plot includes stowaways, the taming of a rat, hunts, chases, and a look at the home life of Rembrandt. This plot balances the rich tapestry of the setting and the historical events.

6.6   Llorente, Pilar Molina (translated by Robin Longshaw). **The Apprentice.** Illustrated by Juan Ramon Alonso. Farrar, Straus, 1993. ISBN 0-374-30389-4. 101p. 9–11.

This book is a simply told story of a thirteen-year-old Renaissance boy who longs to be a painter rather than following the family tradition of tailoring. His apprenticeship to a well-known but ill-tempered and aging Florentine artist brings some misery until he discovers a secret in his master's house and acts with sympathy and discretion. As a result, his apprenticeship becomes worthwhile. The details of everyday living in this era become a natural part of the plot. The writing is simple but not condescending and will appeal to able readers.

Seventeenth and Eighteenth Centuries

6.7   Haley, Gail E. **Dream Peddler.** Illustrated by Gail E. Haley. Dutton, 1993. ISBN 0-525-45153-6. 32p. 6–9.

This historical picture book extols the pleasures of reading. John Chapman is the hero of the story. His name conjures up the chapmen (or cheapmen) who traveled around England from the sixteenth to the early nineteenth centuries. John Chapman begins to make books as well as sell them and, in true folktale fashion, becomes wealthy by following his dream. By photocopying the endpapers, children can make their own chapbooks. The dark, vibrant pictures depict country and London life in the eighteenth century. A chapbook is also shown.

6.8   Kinsey-Warnock, Natalie, and Helen Kinsey. **The Bear That Heard Crying.** Illustrated by Ted Rand. Dutton, 1993. ISBN 0-525-65103-9. 32p. 5–8.

Based on an actual event that took place in 1763, this is a suspenseful story of how three-year-old Sarah wanders off into the woods and becomes lost. She is kept warm and safe by a black bear, which she believes to be a dog. After four days of no luck, Sarah is rescued when people follow directions from the dream of a stranger. Ted Rand's use of watercolors with dark green hues creates a deep, threatening wood, and his illustrations of the characters add to the drama of the tale.

6.9   Rinaldi, Ann. **The Fifth of March.** Harcourt Brace, 1993. ISBN 0-15-200343-6. 272p. 11–12.

The year is 1770 and fourteen-year-old Rachael Marsh is an indentured servant in the home of John and Abigail Adams. Rachael respects and likes her employers and is happy living in Boston but is disturbed by the talk of revolution. She is determined not to become involved in politics despite the actions and intentions of some of her friends. This situation changes after she meets Matthew Kilroy, a young and impetuous British soldier. Rachael begins to question the right of the British to rule over the colonies and is soon forced to take a stand.

Nineteenth Century

United States

6.10   Beatty, Patricia. **The Nickel-Plated Beauty.** Morrow, 1993. ISBN
0-688-12360-0. 259p. 10–12.

Even with the rich resources of the Pacific Northwest coast in the
late nineteenth century—oysters, clams, and berries—the seven
Kimball children find it difficult to earn $27 to buy their mother a
new stove. The young narrator's voice is fresh and childlike as
she recounts the lives of her parents, siblings, and adults around
her in her small village. The simple village pleasures, the kind-
nesses and generosities of many adults, and the warm family life
are similar to those in the "Little House" series. This updated
version should be widely read for its diverse and courageous
subject matter. Reissue.

6.11   Bunting, Eve. **Cheyenne Again.** Illustrated by Irving Toddy.
Clarion, 1995. ISBN 0-395-70364-6. 32p. 5–7.

Young Bull, at the age of ten, is taken to a Native American
reservation school. Nothing familiar is left to him: His clothes
are different, his hair is cut, he is taught and must speak English, and he has to sleep in a bed in a dormitory. When it becomes too much for Young Bull, he runs away. But he is caught,
returned to the school, and punished. He eventually learns to
cope by retaining the Cheyenne inside him while outwardly appearing to have changed. Coupled with the deep, rich colors of
the illustrations, the tight prose lends authenticity to the story.
This packs a powerful protest about the injustices Native American children suffered.

6.12   Bunting, Eve. **Dandelions.** Illustrated by Greg Shed. Harcourt
Brace, 1995. ISBN 0-15-200050-X. unpaged. 5–10.

Zoe, her young sister Rebecca, and their parents leave their
grandparents' home in Illinois and travel across the prairie by
ox-drawn wagon to homestead in Nebraska. The father's enthusiasm is in sharp contrast to Zoe's homesickness. On a trip into a
small prairie town, Zoe returns with a gift for her mother that
she hopes will lend a sense of identity to their sod home. The text
is embedded in full spreads of hazy golden-toned illustrations
that convey the lonely beauty of the new land that the early settlers encountered. This is an excellent text for classroom content
studies on pioneer or frontier life, and for at-home reading to
enjoy the depiction of a family's strength and unity.

6.13 Fleischman, Paul. **Bull Run.** Illustrated by David Frampton. HarperCollins, 1993. ISBN 0-06-021446-5. 104p. 10–12.

This highly acclaimed fictional account explores the lives of sixteen people affected by the first battle of the Civil War, the battle of Bull Run. The characters include people of all ages, both southerners and northerners, males and females, blacks and whites, whose experiences paint a more personal account of the Civil War than textbook treatments of the subject. With its rich prose, this book can be read as a novel or as readers' theater.

6.14 Gaeddert, Louann. **Breaking Free.** Atheneum, 1994. ISBN 0-689-31883-9. 136p. 10–12.

Set in upper New York State around the year 1800, this is the story of Richard, a twelve-year-old orphan who is sent to live on his uncle Lyman's farm. Accustomed to living with relatives who value books and music, Richard finds life on the farm difficult, his uncle harsh, and his younger cousin a bully. He particularly hates the fact that there are slaves on the farm. Secretly he teaches a young slave, Georgina, to read. Later he helps Georgina and her father escape to Canada, where they will be reunited with Georgina's mother. After convincing his uncle that he is too clumsy to do farm chores, Richard is allowed to attend school, where he becomes absorbed in learning Greek and rekindles his love of music. The historical setting, the strong characterization, and the underlying theme of personal freedom make this a satisfying novel.

6.15 Gaeddert, Louann. **Hope.** Atheneum, 1995. ISBN 0-689-80128-9. 165p. 8–12.

After the death of their mother, Hope and her little brother, John, are sent to live in a Shaker community. Hope finds the Shaker world dull and restrictive, with so many rules to follow. She finds particularly harsh the fact that men and women must live completely apart because this separates her from her brother. John, on the other hand, finds comfort in the security of the community and readily adapts to the rules and customs. Hope longs for the time when her father, who is panning for gold in California, will send for them to join him and is unaware that John does not share her dreams. In an afterword the author provides readers with insight into the actual writing of a historical novel. This is a good novel to accompany the many picture books that are available on Shaker furniture, cooking, crafts, and way of life.

6.16   Goble, Paul. **Death of the Iron Horse.** Illustrated by Paul Goble. Aladdin, 1993. ISBN 0-689-71686-9. 28p. 7–9.

This true story is recounted through evocative words and pictures. On August 7, 1867, a train—an iron horse—was derailed by Native Americans. This text can be used to explore the impact of colonization of the American West on First Nations people. It also introduces the particular role technologies such as the railroad played in that process.

6.17   Gregory, Kristiana. **Jimmy Spoon and the Pony Express.** Scholastic, 1994. ISBN 0-590-46577-5. 125p. 10–12.

Riding the Pony Express was a glamorous career for a young man in 1860. In this sequel to *The Legend of Jimmy Spoon,* Jimmy grabs the opportunity to ride for the Express. In his isolated outpost, Jimmy works hard and considers his future. He loves his family in Salt Lake City and feels an attraction to a girl back home, but he also feels a desire to return to his adopted Shoshoni family and to Nahannee, to whom he has been promised in marriage. Ultimately Jimmy must make a decision, but he attempts to reconcile his two lives. It is possible to read the novel alone and to enjoy it for the adventures involved in delivering the mail, but readers of the first novel will have an advantage in their prior knowledge of some pivotal characters. Interest is added when the narrative introduces historical figures such as Samuel Clemens, Jack Slade, and Bill Cody.

6.18   Haddix, Margaret Peterson. **Running Out of Time.** Simon & Schuster, 1995. ISBN 0-689-80084-3. 184p. 10–12.

In the rest of the United States the year is 1996, but in Clifton, Indiana, the younger children know it is the year 1840. Now the children are being struck with diphtheria and no modern medicine is available because the village appears to be under a very strange siege. Eleven-year-old Jessie escapes the village to tell what is going on and to get medical help. This page-turning story combines elements of historical fiction, science fiction, and mystery. It also poses questions about scientific experiments carried out in the name of progress for future generations.

6.19   Hermes, Patricia. **On Winter's Wind.** Little, Brown, 1995. ISBN 0-316-35978-5. 163p. 9–12.

No word has been heard from her sea captain father since he set sail three years earlier. Eleven-year-old Genevieve, unlike her younger sister Leila, is losing hope that he will ever return and her mother has withdrawn into despair. To save her family from destitution, Genevieve finds work at a local store run by a Quaker family and discovers that the Quakers help runaway slaves escape to Canada. Her discovery results in a great temptation: She would receive one hundred dollars for turning in a runaway slave but would be betraying the trust of the Quakers who have helped her. This poignant story of a young girl's resourcefulness and inner strength provides a glimpse into the social turmoil and difficult decisions faced by many Americans during the years preceding the Civil War.

6.20 Hopkinson, Deborah. **Sweet Clara and the Freedom Quilt.** Illustrated by James Ransome. Knopf, 1993. ISBN 0-679-82311-5. 33p. 6–8.

This story is based on a true, little-known chapter in African American history. At age twelve, Sweet Clara is forced to move to a new plantation away from her mother. Her surrogate mother, Aunt Rachel, teaches her to sew. One day Sweet Clara comes up with the idea of designing a quilt with a map pattern to guide her out of slavery into freedom. She succeeds in doing so, bringing her mother, sister, and her friend Jack along. She leaves the quilt behind on the plantation so others can follow. A useful text for launching discussions on slavery, freedom, and cooperation.

6.21 Johnson, Dolores. **Now Let Me Fly: The Story of a Slave Family.** Illustrated by Dolores Johnson. Macmillan, 1993. ISBN 0-02-747699-5. 32p. 5–9.

In Africa, young Minna is captured and taken as a slave on a ship to America. On the voyage, she is befriended by Amadi, a boy her own age. Upon arrival, they are bought by master Clemmons to work on his cotton plantation. Later, Amadi and Minna marry and have four children of their own. What little happiness they have is slowly destroyed as Amadi is sold and sent away and most of their children are sold or forced to flee. Minna is left to dream of flying away to freedom. Although fictitious, the story is based on the actual accounts of slaves, written from the perspective of one family. The text is accompanied by richly colored oil paintings depicting the ordeals of the slave family. This would also be a suitable short read-aloud to introduce the topic of slavery to a young child.

6.22 Kalman, Esther. **Tchaikovsky Discovers America.** Illustrated by Laura Fernandez and Rick Jacobson. Orchard, 1995. ISBN 0-531-06894-3. 32p. 5–8.

Intricately weaving fiction with historical fact, this story describes a visit Russian composer Peter Ilyich Tchaikovsky made to the United States in 1891, two years before his death. The story is based on the factual details of Tchaikovsky's diary. However, this account is told from the perspective of an eleven-year-old girl, Jenny Petroff, writing in her own diary. The text discusses the homesickness of travelers and immigrants, with details added for local color and historical accuracy. As the composer of *Swan Lake* and *The Nutcracker,* the shy Tchaikovsky is an attractive musical legend for aspiring dancers and musicians. The text is illustrated with richly textured oil paintings.

6.23   Karr, Kathleen. **Gideon and the Mummy Professor.** Farrar, Straus, 1993. ISBN 0-374-32563-4. 137p. 10–12.

In 1855, twelve-year-old Gideon looks after his showman/lecturer father as they travel down the Mississippi with an Egyptian mummy. The events explode into a plot worthy of Conan Doyle, ending with voodoo, the demise of the villain of the story, and Gideon's surprising decision about his future life. This is a larger-than-life historical adventure in the tradition of Mark Twain's work.

6.24   Krupinski, Loretta. **Bluewater Journal: The Voyage of the Sea Tiger.** Illustrated by Loretta Krupinski. HarperCollins, 1995. ISBN 0-06-023436-9. 32 p. 7–10.

Benjamin Solcum and his family set sail on the *Sea Tiger,* a clipper ship, in a race from Boston to Hawaii against another clipper ship. Through his diary, Benjamin shares his experiences at sea, reporting of exotic Rio de Janeiro, the excitement and danger of the high seas, and the cold perils of rounding the Horn. He also conveys the monotony and boredom of shipboard life and his fears about the other clipper ship as he anxiously tries to see it in the distance. The writing has the sound of a young voice with enough formality to convey a sense of a different era. This could be used in the classroom to give children an insight into the life of early explorers through the eyes of a young boy. The colorful, full-page paintings that accompany each diary entry reflect the content and mood of the journey.

6.25   Littlesugar, Amy. **Josiah True and the Art Maker.** Illustrated by Barbara Garrison. Simon & Schuster, 1995. ISBN 0-671-88354-2. 25p. 5–7.

Patience Cage travels from home to home, community to community, painting portraits. Much to Josiah's delight, she comes and stays at his home to paint his family's portrait. Josiah is fascinated by Patience's craft and his future career is presaged with a gift of his very own brush when Patience departs. This book gives insight into how family albums and, later, the tradition of the family photograph began. The style of the illustrations adds to the charm of the story, confirming its setting in a bygone era. This book would be useful as an example of collage for art instruction; it also shows students how the work of one person often inspires others.

6.26   Love, D. Anne. **Dakota Spring.** Illustrated by Ronald Himler. Holiday House, 1995. ISBN 0-8234-1189-3. 90p. 7–10.

When their widowed father is injured in an accident, Caroline and her nine-year-old brother take on the responsibility of running their Dakota farm. Feeling the task is too much for the young children, their father asks their maternal grandmother, a city woman, to come to the farm to help. At first Mrs. Ravenell is stern and remote, but she gradually softens and responds to the children's need for her affection and acceptance. Set in the year 1800, this novel conveys a clear sense of time and place. The relatively simple text and short chapters make this an excellent novel for the younger reader.

6.27   MacBride, Roger Lea. **Little House on Rocky Ridge.** Illustrated by David Gilleece. HarperCollins, 1993. ISBN 0-06-020842-2. 353p. 8–11.

This book is a continuation of the Little House on the Prairie series by an adopted member of the Wilder family. Here we follow seven-year-old Rose Wilder as she journeys with her father and mother from Dakota to a new and easier life in Missouri. Although the first few chapters have something of the feel of Wilder's writing, the book lacks the vitality of this well-loved author. However, fans of the earlier books will enjoy this book and continue to gain insights into another era.

6.28   Myers, Walter Dean. **Glory Field.** Scholastic, 1994. ISBN 0-590-45897-3. 375p. 10–12.

In 1753, eleven-year-old Muhammad Bilal is chained aboard a ship and brought from Africa to America as a slave. In 1864, during the Civil War, his great-great-granddaughter Lizzy steals away to freedom, but her family's problems are far from over. During the Depression, Luvenia tries to find a way to go to university in Chicago. In the 1960s, Tommy is torn between an invitation to attend a white university on a basketball scholarship and the desire to do something to forward the cause of civil rights. Finally, a reunion draws the family back together and back home. Through the stories of five members of the Lewis family over nine generations, the book spans two-and-a-half centuries of American history.

6.29   Rosen, Michael J. **A School for Pompey Walker.** Illustrated by Aminah Brenda Lynn Robinson. Harcourt Brace, 1995. ISBN 0-15-200114-X. 48p. 7–12.

At the dedication of a school named in his honor, Pompey narrates his life story to a group of children. Jeremiah, a white man, buys Pompey and sets him free. They then collaborate to make money to build a school for African American children, devising a plan whereby Jeremiah sells Pompey, who then escapes, and they pocket the money. After repeating this routine thirty-nine times, they build the school, which they name Sweet Freedom. The entertaining story originated from a brief newspaper account based on an Ohio man's experiences. Pompey speaks eloquently in a style akin to an Aesop's fable or an American tall tale. Aminah Brenda Lynn Robinson uses colored pencils and dyes to create bright illustrations that come alive with strong, exaggerated lines.

6.30   Ruby, Lois. **Steal Away Home.** Macmillan, 1994. ISBN 0-02-777883-5. 192p. 9–12.

In her family's newly purchased, old Kansas house, Dana discovers what many young people dream of: a secret place and a mystery. Behind layers of ugly wallpaper and a partition, Dana finds skeletal remains together with a hundred-year-old diary. Using the journal, an autopsy report, speculation, and research into local history, Dana, her family, and her friends attempt to reconstruct life and death in the house, which was an underground railway station on the eve of the Civil War. The narrative alternates among Dana's present, the 1865 journal of Quaker Millicent Weaver, and the perceptions of Millicent's son, James. The novel is remarkable for its full, realistic treatment of each setting and each set of characters.

6.31   Sanders, Scott Russell. **Here Comes the Mystery Man.** Illustrated by Helen Cogancherry. Bradbury, 1993. ISBN 0-02-778145-3. 32p. 6–8.

In the early 1800s in a small pioneer community, excitement is building as news spreads about the impending arrival of the pedlar. His semiannual appearance is welcomed, not just for his wares but for the news he brings about the rest of the world and descriptions of sights many have never seen. The anticipation and the effect of such a visit are told from the perspective of the Goodwin family. The parents and their four young children greet the pedlar when he arrives at their door to eat, talk, and spend the night. When the pedlar departs in the morning, memories of the taste of the maple sugar he gave them lingers along with his tales about compasses, whales, and steamboats. The clear, warm colors of fall match the joyful mood of the community, which is depicted in a believable manner. The insight into how the tedium of daily life was relieved in pioneer settlements also makes this book a useful resource for content area studies.

6.32 Smucker, Barbara. **Selina and the Bear Paw Quilt.** Illustrated by Janet Wilson. Lester, 1995. ISBN 1-895555-70-1. unpaged. 6–9.

A young Mennonite girl living in Pennsylvania in 1860 finds that her life is about to take a dramatic shift. As the Civil War gets closer and reports continue about the burning of pacifist homes, her family realizes they must flee to Canada. Selina has always been close to her grandmother and now she takes particular interest in her quilting, especially the new bear's paw design. Fabric pieces from special family clothes are used. Deciding that she is too old to travel and start life anew, Grandmother sends her treasured quilt with Selina to Canada so that she will remember her family's history. The warmth of the story and the tenderness of the family relationships are lovingly caught in the gold-tinged earth tones of the illustrations. Each one is framed with a section of quilt design.

6.33 Stone, Bruce. **Autumn of the Royal Tar.** HarperCollins, 1995. ISBN 0-06-021492-9. 160p. 10–12.

Twelve-year-old Nora, daughter of a sea captain, is the feisty protagonist of this novel, set off the coast of Maine. From the outset of the story, the reader is aware of a tension between Nora and her mother as they work together, preparing the salted cod for the drying rack. One night during a fierce storm Nora awakens to see a ship burning on the ocean. There are few survivors from the *Autumn of the Royal Tar,* which was carrying passengers and circus animals. Two survivors, a young boy with a badly burned leg and an elephant, play a significant role in Nora's life. This well-written historical novel has interesting plot lines, strong characterization, and a richly described setting.

6.34 Turner, Glennette Tilley. **Running for Our Lives.** Illustrated by Samuel Byrd. Holiday House, 1994. ISBN 0-8234-1121-4. 198p. 9–12.

On the eve of the American Civil War, Luther's family escapes from the plantation where they were slaves and heads north to Canada and freedom. Sharing their journey, the reader also shares the fear of capture, the pain and uncertainty of separation, the gratitude for humane treatment and assistance, and the joy of freedom and reunion in Canada. The story is told from Luther's point of view and in his dialect, and the reader quickly empathizes with him. A narrative frame of prologue and epilogue impresses the reader with the importance of such stories in family histories. An author's note clarifies points of historical accuracy and artistic license.

6.35 Van Leeuwen, Jean. **Bound for Oregon.** Dial, 1994. ISBN 0- 8037-1527-7. 167p. 9–11.

Nine-year-old Mary Ellen tells the story of her family's life and adventures as they travel by covered wagon from Arkansas to Oregon in 1852. The reader gains a fascinating glimpse of life on the Oregon trail: the hardships, fears, joys, and sadness experienced by those who sought a better life in the West. In an afterword, the author provides information about her research and the "original account of Mary Ellen Todd's Oregon Trail Journey," on which her story is based.

6.36 Whelan, Gloria. **Once On This Island.** HarperCollins, 1995. ISBN 0-06-026248-6. 186p. 11–12.

Michilimackinac in the War of 1812 is the setting for this sensitive novel about family loyalty, patriotism, and growing up. When the British army takes the fort at the beginning of the war, Mary O'Shea sees her community divided between supporters of the British and of the United States. Her own father joins the American forces, leaving Mary with her older brother and sister to take care of the farm and to cope with the British occupation. Through hardship and friendship, Mary comes to realize that the war is more complex than she had ever imagined. Friends and enemies can be found on either side. Mary's courage and resourcefulness, together with the details of her life on the farm, make this an appealing read.

6.37 Wisler, G. Clifton. **Jericho's Journey.** Lodestar, 1993. ISBN 0-525-67428-4. 138p. 10–12.

"Gone to Texas, 1852." These are the last words written in the family Bible just before twelve-year-old Jericho and his family load their possessions into a covered wagon and leave their home in Tennessee, bound for Texas. Jericho's head is filled with dreams of adventure, kindled in his imagination by the exploits of Davy Crockett, Sam Houston, and his Uncle Dan, who arrived in Texas just after the battle at the Alamo. The adventures he experiences are not quite what he had expected, nor is he prepared for the realities of the trip: endless chores, rain and mud, swamps, and bitter cold. With the help of his much-admired older brother, Jake, Jericho survives these hardships and arrives in Texas ready to begin a new life. This story is based on information taken from an actual journal of a similar westward trek.

6.38   Wright, Courtni C. **Journey to Freedom: A Story of the Underground Railroad.** Illustrated by Gershom Griffith. Holiday, 1994. ISBN 0-8234-1096-X. 32p. 6–9.

This picture book story of the escape of black slaves to freedom in Canada has a built-in dramatic energy as well as an emotional impact. This suspenseful survival tale is a historically based account of a family's frightening twenty days as, led by Harriet Tubman, they make their way on the Underground Railway from Kentucky to Canada.

6.39   Yep, Laurence. **Dragon's Gate.** HarperCollins, 1993. ISBN 0-06-022971-3. 272p. 11–12.

Otter's search for his heroic uncle becomes a search for courage within himself as he faces the reality of life in "The Land of the Golden Mountains." The grim working conditions and disillusionment of Chinese workers constructing the railroad in the mid-nineteenth century are the background to this adventure. The author provides a short postscript that explains the authenticity of characters and situations in the story. This is a prequel to *Dragon Wings.*

World

6.40   Howard, Elizabeth Fitzgerald. **Papa Tells Chita a Story.** Illustrated by Floyd Cooper. Simon & Schuster, 1995. ISBN 0-02-744623-9. 32p. 5–7.

This exaggerated tale is told by an African American father to his daughter. It details a heroic adventure he had as a youth assigned to deliver an important military letter in the Spanish-American War in Cuba in 1898. After outsmarting an alligator and sleeping in an eagle's nest, the hero achieves his goal. This picture book effectively conveys the adoration of a daughter for her father in an imaginative and engaging text with dreamlike illustrations.

6.41 Nichol, Barbara. **Beethoven Lives Upstairs.** Illustrated by Scott Cameron. Orchard, 1994. ISBN 0-531-06828-5. 48p. 9–11.

The year is 1822 when ten-year-old Christoph begins the first of a series of letters to his uncle. Christoph's father has recently died, and his mother has rented the upstairs flat of their home in Vienna to Ludwig van Beethoven. At first the noisy, eccentric behavior of Beethoven is a source of great irritation to Christoph, but gradually he feels compassion for the lonely, tormented composer and appreciation for his musical genius. Through this fictional correspondence, the author informs the young reader of events in the composer's life and provides an understanding of a historical period.

Twentieth Century

United States: Early in the Century

6.42 Antle, Nancy. **Hard Times: A Story of the Great Depression.** Illustrated by James Watling. Viking, 1993. ISBN 0-670-84665-1. 54p. 8–12.

Hard Times is part of the Once Upon America series, which presents fictional stories of children living in diverse historical periods. In this novel, set in Oklahoma during the Great Depression, Charlie and his family find it increasingly difficult to make ends meet. When his father loses his job, the entire family must move in with Charlie's grandparents. The writing is historically accurate without being didactic. Young readers will be interested to discover how children lived during the Depression, and they may be inspired by the strong family bond that helps Charlie and his family to endure hard times.

6.43 Blos, Joan W. **Brooklyn Doesn't Rhyme.** Illustrated by Paul Birling. Scribners, 1994. ISBN 0-684-19694-8. 86p. 10–12.

At first, when Rosey's grade 6 teacher assigns her the task of keeping a journal about herself and her family, she feels that she has nothing to say. However, as she delves into her family's past and looks more closely at family relationships, she creates a series of vignettes that capture the life of her immigrant family and friends living in Brooklyn at the beginning of the century. The language is accessible and the voice and perspective remain true to that of a child, making the book valuable both for reading aloud and as a springboard for journal writing and class discussion.

6.44 Geras, Adele. **Golden Windows and Other Stories of Jerusalem.** HarperCollins, 1993. ISBN 0-06-022941-1. 148p. 8–12.

These five stories range in time from 1910 to 1954, demonstrating the fine storytelling and rich imagery we have come to expect from the author of the Egerton Hall trilogy. These fine stories cross cultural and time barriers to reveal the constants in childhood. Nine-year-old Pnina is captivated by the magical look of the street with golden windows. Forty-four years later, her grand-niece Malka discovers that you cannot buy friendship when cruel Aviva ruins a precious gift scarf. Two of the stories are linked with the 1948 Arab-Israeli conflict. Adele Geras knows children's dreams, fears, and longings and knows that these do not simply disappear when we grow up.

6.45 Hall, Donald. **Lucy's Summer.** Illustrated by Michael McCurdy. Browndeer, 1995. ISBN 0-15-276873-4. 40p. 5–8.

This story provides a rare glimpse into the summer of 1910 in a New Hampshire farming community. Lucy and her younger sister, Caroline, follow their mother as she establishes a millinery shop in their home to make and sell hats to neighborhood women and traveling gypsies. As the story progresses, they also preserve and can vegetables and fruit for the winter. Michael McCurdy's scratchboard illustrations evoke the nostalgic quality of the historical period and place. The story is based on actual anecdotes recounted to the author by his mother.

6.46 Lawlor, Laurie. **Gold in the Hills.** Walker, 1995. ISBN 0-8027-8371-6. 160p. 8–12.

Hattie and her brother, Pheme, are staying with their cousin Tirzah and her children until their father comes back from prospecting for gold. They are unhappy with Tirzah, but the children befriend a gruff old neighbor, Old Judge, who teaches them to fish and hunt. As the summer draws on, Tirzah doubts Hattie's father will come back. She plots to sell the children into service. Their rescue depends on their own resourcefulness and on Old Judge. Hattie and Pheme are not angelic, but through their sincere good will they change the lives of those around them. The frontier setting of the novel provides an exciting backdrop for the actions of interesting and appealing characters such as the impulsive Hattie and the irascible Old Judge.

6.47   Lucas, Barbara M. **Snowed In.** Illustrated by Catherine Stock. Bradbury, 1993. ISBN 0-02-761465-4. 32p. 5–7.

Set in a 1915 Wyoming landscape, this family story depicts the seasonal changes from winter to spring that settlers in the American West experienced. Luke and Grace, along with their mother and father, are snowed in on their farm during the winter. We find out about their preparations for this seasonal event, their activities, and the details of their life on the farm. The rich watercolor illustrations give present-day children an evocative portrait of the differences between their own lifestyle and that of farm children during this period. A good read-aloud.

6.48   MacLachlan, Patricia. **Skylark.** HarperCollins, 1994. ISBN 0-06-023328-1. 87p. 8–10.

This book is a sequel to *Sarah, Plain and Tall,* winner of the Newbery Medal. Because of a prairie drought, Sarah, Anna, and Caleb leave their farm to visit Sarah's aunts in Maine. The lush East Coast environment and the ocean at first fascinate the two children, but then they long for their father and their real home. As in the first book, Anna recounts the events through her journal in simple, concrete language, leaving readers, both young and old, to read between the lines as suits their understanding and sensitivity. It is rare that a sequel equals the original, and even rarer, as in this case, that it outdoes it. This glimpse of the American past and family love and support is truly memorable.

6.49   McGugan, Jim. **Josepha: A Prairie Boy's Story.** Illustrated by Murray Kimber. Red Deer, 1994. ISBN 0-88995-101-3. unpaged. 9–11.

This powerful account of immigrants on the prairies at the turn of the century details the friendship of a young pioneer boy with Josepha, an older boy who cannot speak English. Even though Josepha is over fourteen years old, he is made to sit in the primary row until he learns the language. Bitter frustration and anger, hidden by the silence of his inability to speak English, are reflected in his determination to leave the situation. Readers will be caught up in an oral reading of the text, highlighted by the strength of the writer's sense of rhythm, terse repetition, and word sounds suggestive of action. The illustrations swoop across the pages, capturing the immense and sparse prairie scene.

6.50   Oberman, Sheldon. **The Always Prayer Shawl.** Illustrated by Ted Lewin. Boyds Mills, 1994. ISBN 1-878093-22-3. 34p. 6–9.

Adam is a young boy in Russia. When his family decides to leave the hardships behind to face a new future, Adam's grandfather gives him his prayer shawl to carry on the boat to the new country. He works hard and when the fringes wear out, he sews on new ones. Eventually, Adam has his own children and they in turn have theirs, and it is time to give the prayer shawl to his grandson. Lewin's illustrations provide an insight into the love between generations, especially of grandfathers for their grandsons. The use of black-and-white watercolors to indicate past events gives young readers an indication of the passing of time. The warm, realistic interpretations of the boy, his grandfather, and the shawl illustrate the book's theme: Time goes on and so does the shawl.

6.51   Rayner, Mary. **Echoing Green.** Illustrated by Michael Foreman. Puffin, 1994. ISBN 0-14-136006-9. 78p. 9–12.

Young Kath is sent to spend half-term break with her stiff Aunt Kitty and ill but companionable Uncle Stan. The family discussions about the dedication of a new war memorial transport Kathy to the days of World War I and enlistment. She begins to understand the lingering resentment and bitterness felt by those who lost loved ones during the war. Michael Foreman's gentle illustrations capture the simple, honest mood of the story.

6.52   Taylor, Mildred D. **The Well: David's Story.** Dial, 1995. ISBN 0-8037-1803-9. 92p. 9–11.

During a Mississippi drought in the early 1900s, David and Hammer Logan find themselves forced to share their well, the only one to survive a drought in the community, with the racist white teenagers who continue to torment them. In an environment where fighting with a white boy could mean death by hanging, Hammer Logan defies his mother's strict upbringing. In defense of his younger brother, ten-year-old David, Hammer knocks out Charlie Simms and leaves him for dead. Once again this author presents an instance in the history of American race relations with sensitivity, complexity, and realism. Children will empathize with the brothers' attempts to reconcile their sense of justice with an oppressive social reality. Readers may recognize young David as the father of Cassie, Stacey, Christopher-John, and Little Man in *Roll of Thunder, Hear My Cry* and *Let the Circle Be Unbroken*.

6.53   Wells, Rosemary. **Waiting for the Evening Star.** Illustrated by Susan Jeffers. Dial, 1993. ISBN 0-8037-1399-1. 32p. 6–8.

This book is about a Vermont farm family who follow the seasons before and during World War I. The younger boy can imagine nothing finer than his home. The older boy hears the whistle of the train and believes it signals the first step on a great adventure. He joins the army and leaves by train. His younger brother wishes on the evening star. The story is a powerful evocation of how life changes, with humankind's eternal wish to venture further afield. The illustrations present realistic indoor and outdoor scenes, full of detail and human emotion.

United States: World War II and Later

6.54   Cutler, Jane. **My Wartime Summers.** Farrar, Straus, 1994. ISBN 0-374-35111-2. 153p. 10–12.

The war in the title is World War II and the time is the entry of the United States into the conflict. Eleven-year-old Ellen progresses through grade 5 to high school while her uncle is fighting in Europe. The horror of the war to Ellen and her family at home is realized through Uncle Bob's letters. When he returns from the war, Ellen sees that he has slumped into depression. Ellen's life also changes as she grows older and more perceptive. The story focuses on Ellen's home and school life, but the brutality of war and its destructive effects on the individual soldier are also touched upon.

6.55   Hall, Donald. **The Farm Summer 1942.** Illustrated by Barry Moser. Dial, 1994. ISBN 0-8037-1502-1. 32p. 6–8.

Donald Hall's nostalgic portrait of the past chronicles a summer in the life of a young boy who moves to his grandparents' farm in New Hampshire during the peak of World War II. Meanwhile, his mother works in the war effort and his father serves on a destroyer in the Pacific. Peter's initial unhappiness in his new surroundings is quickly replaced with a genuine love for both the farm and his quietly dignified grandparents. Barry Moser's realistic watercolors complement this simple tale eloquently, providing a detailed and affectionate glimpse of a time and place seldom examined in contemporary picture books.

6.56   Pinkney, Gloria Jean. **The Sunday Outing.** Illustrated by Jerry Pinkney. Dial, 1994. ISBN 0-8037-1199-9. 32p. 5–7.

The soft, fluid pencil and watercolor illustrations by award-winning illustrator Jerry Pinkney heighten the dreamlike quality of this gentle story, which is based on the author's recollections of her own childhood and is the prequel to her earlier picture book

Back Home. Each Sunday Ernestine and her great-aunt Odessa go to the North Philadelphia Station to watch the trains, especially those going south to North Carolina, which stop by the farm where she was born. She dreams of making the trip to visit her birthplace and relatives and tries to help her parents save money for her train ticket. This story is a loving portrait of an African American family working together to make Ernestine's dream come true.

World: World War I and Later

6.57 Disher, Garry. **The Bamboo Flute.** Ticknor & Fields, 1993. ISBN 0-395-66595-7. 82p. 9–12.

Set in rural Australia during the 1932 depression-era, this eloquently written short novel traces the emotional bond that develops between a lonely twelve-year-old farm boy and his rancher father. Although he has been warned to stay away from the roaming tramps, Paul is drawn to Eric the Red by the rich music the drifter creates with his flute. He teaches Paul, who has a natural musical talent, to make a flute out of bamboo. His growing ability with the flute earns Paul the respect of his peers and gives him the necessary confidence to talk with his worry-ridden father, and together, they bring music back into their family's life.

World: World War II and Later

6.58 Garland, Sherry. **The Lotus Seed.** Illustrated by Tatsuro Kiuchi. Harcourt Brace, 1993. ISBN 0-15-249465-0. 32p. 5–8.

This beautiful, spare blend of poetic prose and art spans four generations and two continents. In Vietnam, the narrator's grandmother plucks a lotus seed to remember her fallen emperor by. Through marriage, childrearing, war, and escape to America, she keeps the seed with her always. For many years she works hard and her children grow. Then one day the narrator's little brother takes the seed and plants it in the mud. The grandmother's treasure is gone, or so she believes, until the seed grows into a beautiful pink lotus whose seeds she distributes to each of her grandchildren.

6.59 Manson, Ainslie. **Just Like New.** Illustrated by Karen Reczuch. Groundwood, 1995. ISBN 0-88899-228-9. 32p. 6–10.

What can you give to a girl in England who doesn't have any toys for Christmas because of the war and the bombing? Sally is in a quandary when her Sunday School teacher tells them that next Sunday is White Gift Sunday and each child should bring a gift that is not bought but just like new. She finally decides it must be one of her three dolls, and she chooses Ann Marie. Sally worries about the doll's journey until spring, when a letter arrives from Deborah, who loves Ann Marie as much as Sally did. Reczuch's poignant illustrations, done with graphite pencil and watercolors, give insight into the time period of World War II. The black-and-white scenes of wartime Britain contrast with the golden glow of fall colors that illustrate the warmth and security of Sally's life in Canada.

6.60   Schnur, Steven. **The Shadow Children.** Illustrated by Herbert Tauss. Morrow, 1994. ISBN 0-688-13281-2. 88p. 10–12.

This thought-provoking novel, set in France after World War II, will heighten students' awareness of the difficult decisions faced by people in wartime and the tragedies and guilt that result. While visiting his grandfather on his farm, an eleven-year-old boy sees children begging and hiding in the woods. He is distressed that none of the villagers acknowledge the children's ghostly presence. A series of mysterious events result in his grandfather's revelation of a secret that he and the other villagers have suppressed: the surrendering of Jewish children to the Nazis during the war.

6.61   Wild, Margaret. **A Time for Toys.** Illustrated by Julie Vivas. Kids Can, 1995. ISBN 1-55074-023-7. 32p. 7–10.

It was not a time for toys—it was a time for survival in a concentration camp. Miriam can remember having toys and having enough to eat, but young David and Sarah have no such memories. With the end of World War II approaching, the prisoners, anticipating liberation, make toys for the children as a special surprise. They beg, gather, and hoard scraps of material, buttons, and thread with which to sew while the guards sleep. They make an owl and an elephant for David and Sarah for the day when they are set free. The pastel colors in the accompanying illustrations soften the horror of the rags, shaven heads, and stark living conditions. The plight of the victims is sensitively conveyed and woven with a thread of hope. This story was inspired by a collection of stuffed toys made by the Polish women in Belsen.

6.62   Yep, Laurence. **Hiroshima.** Scholastic, 1995. ISBN 0-590-20832-2. 56p. 10–12.

Through brief, vivid glimpses, the story of the bombing of Hiroshima is told from a variety of perspectives: from the air, as three American bombers approach the city and perform their mission, and from the ground, as two Japanese schoolchildren go about their daily routines until the nuclear bomb changes their world. The story is powerful and could serve as a companion piece to *Sedako* by Ed Young and *Sedako and the Thousand Paper Cranes* by Eleanor Coerr. In this novella, Laurence Yep provides enough information about the war, the bombing, and its aftermath to fascinate and instruct young readers without horrifying them.

7 Biography

Athletes

7.1   Littlefield, Bill. **Champions: Stories of Ten Remarkable Athletes.** Illustrated by Bernie Fuchs. Little, Brown, 1993. ISBN 0-316-52805-6. 132p. 8–12.

In short chapters, the lives of ten stars in such sports as baseball, dogsled racing, basketball, and soccer are vividly told. The determination and hard work they needed to succeed are detailed. These men and women, who overcame adversity of all kinds to become champions, will be an inspiration to all young athletes. The paintings by Bernie Fuchs, popular with *Sports Illustrated* fans, add to the excitement of this book.

Creative Artists

7.2   Bjork, Christina. **The Other Alice: The Story of Alice Liddell and Alice in Wonderland.** Illustrated by Inga-Karin Eriksson. R & S Books, 1993. ISBN 91-29-62242-5. 93p. 9–11.

This book offers a potpourri of information about the original Alice (Alice Liddell), her family, her friends, and the creator of *Alice's Adventures in Wonderland*, Charles Lutwidge Dodgson, better known as Lewis Carroll. The illustrations are a mixture of authentic photographs, static drawings in color, and more natural drawings in black and white. Although much has been written about Liddell and Carroll, this presentation might attract some children to read the world's most quoted children's book and make the world of Alice familiar to the modern child.

7.3   Brust, Beth Wagner. **The Amazing Paper Cuttings of Hans Christian Andersen.** Illustrated by Hans Christian Andersen. Ticknor & Fields, 1994. ISBN 0-395-66787-9. 80p. 9–11.

This elegant little biography, with many brilliant black-and-white reproductions of the intricate papercuttings of Hans Christian Andersen, is written in an accurate and simply told manner that will appeal to young readers. Andersen made many of these papercuttings for young children as he was telling stories, often showing the influence of his foreign travels. The introduction, which tells of his storytelling technique, as well as the bibliography, source notes, and index, make this a valuable reference for teachers, librarians, and storytellers.

7.4   Cech, John. **Jacques-Henri Lartigue: Boy with a Camera.** Four Winds, 1994. ISBN 0-02-718136-7. 32p. 8–12.

As well as celebrating Jacques-Henri Lartigue's artistic brilliance, this biography of the early life of the renowned French photographer provides a pictorial view of French society during the first two decades of the twentieth century, a time known as *la belle epoque*. It was an era of enthusiasm for the new and inventive. Lartigue's photographs of family members engaging in adventurous activities such as flying and race car driving, or in the parks of Paris, capture the excitement of that time. The accompanying text gives insight into Lartigue's work that will instruct and inspire young photographers.

7.5   Cummings, Pat, compiler. **Talking with Artists: Volume Two.** Simon & Schuster, 1995. ISBN 0-689-80310-9. 96p. 9–12.

Pat Cummings's long-awaited sequel to her award-winning *Talking with Artists* does not include the same dazzling array of artists that graced the first collection, but its first-person accounts of the lives and artistic careers of thirteen contemporary artists are a gold mine of information. This book is suitable for aspiring artists or any child who wants to know more about a favorite artist. Richly illustrated with examples from each artist's past and present work, this collection asks questions that children truly would ask: Do you have any pets? What is a normal day like? Cummings includes an appendix on the artists' secret techniques. Thoroughly entertaining, Cummings's second *Talking with Artists* book is a must for anyone interested in illustrators of children's literature.

7.6   Heslewood, Juliet. **Introducing Picasso.** Little, Brown, 1993. ISBN 0-316-35917-3. 32p. 10–12.

This well-designed introduction to the life and work of Pablo Picasso combines details of his personal life with major world events and ideas from the art world of the twentieth century. It includes reproductions of Picasso's works, early photographs from his life, and reprints of some of the artwork by colleagues who greatly influenced Picasso's development. The layout of the candid, informative text is balanced with the reprints. Readers will want to go through the book several times to gather information, read the captions supporting the reprints, and study the paintings.

7.7   Lyons, Mary E. **Starting Home: The Story of Horace Pippin, Painter.** Illustrated by Horace Pippen. Scribners, 1993. ISBN 0-684-19534-8. 42p. 8–12.

Horace Pippin's art is reminiscent of Picasso or Matisse. This book's rich colors and moving scenes from American history make it a valuable book for either fine arts or social studies. Pippin's subjects include rural Pennsylvania, World War I, and biblical stories. The text is well-written and easy to read. The color reproductions and sketches provide a representative sample of his work. Another book in this fine series is *Deep Blues: Bill Traylor, Self-Taught Artist.*

7.8   Lyons, Mary E. **Stitching Stars: The Story Quilts of Harriet Powers.** Scribners, 1993. ISBN 0-684-19576-3. 42p. 8–12.

At age forty-nine, Harriet Powers began to work on a quilt to chronicle her spiritual life. This story quilt was followed by another. The design of the quilts demonstrates African influences and the content of the quilts reveals religious influences. Striking color photographs of the quilts, along with close-ups of individual squares, highlight the text.

7.9   Stanley, Diane, and Peter Vennema. **Charles Dickens: The Man Who Had Great Expectations.** Illustrated by Diane Stanley. Morrow, 1993. ISBN 0-688-09110-5. 48p. 9–11.

This thoroughly researched and incisively written biography captures the reader immediately with an intimate story from Dickens's early childhood and proceeds through the major events in the life of this inspired writer. Dickens is warmly portrayed as someone sensitive to life around him and determined to bring pleasure into everyone's life. The illustrations accurately detail life in nineteenth-century England and balance the reading experience. This book could be read aloud, discussed in connection with the lives of writers, or used as part of any biography unit.

7.10   Turner, Robyn Montana. **Frida Kahlo.** Illustrated by Robyn Montana Turner. Little, Brown, 1993. ISBN 0-316-85651-7. 32p. 10–12.

The life and art of Mexican artist Frida Kahlo are portrayed in this picture-book biography. Full-color reproductions of some of her paintings are balanced with black-and-white photographs of Frida's family and her relationship with Mexican muralist Diego Rivera. Students interested in art history, women's history, and Mexican history and culture will be interested in the well-written text that illuminates the personal and cultural forces that shaped Frida Kahlo's expressive and often disturbing paintings. Others in the series are *Faith Ringgold* and *Dorothea Lange*.

7.11   Wolf, Sylvia. **Focus: Five Women Photographers.** Photographs by Margaret Bourke-White et al. Whitman, 1994. ISBN 0-8075-2531-6. 64p. 10–14.

Through an examination of the lives and work of five extraordinary women, Wolf shows how the art of photography differs with the vision and expression of each artist. Fascinating glimpses are provided into the times and lives of Julia Margaret Cameron, whose magnificent portraits broke the nineteenth-century tradition, and Margaret Bourke-White, inspired news photographer for *Life* magazine who documented the news and made art of what she saw. The modern period is represented by photographers Flor Garduno, Sandy Skoglund, and Lorna Simpson. This is a book for the student who has a special interest in photography and for the teacher who wishes to foster in students an appreciation of photography as art. A selected bibliography is provided.

Explorers

7.12   Marrin, Albert. **Sea King: Sir Francis Drake and His Times.** Atheneum, 1995. ISBN 0-689-31887-1. 168p. 9–12.

Although this book comes with impressive documentation, it is not a dull retelling of history. Details such as the knighting of this pirate hero are presented in interesting, well-written text. Master mariner, navigator, and commander, Drake's legend survived through World War II, when the ghostly throbbing of his drum was believed to call him back from the grave to save England once more. The slave trade, the Spanish Inquisition, and the dreadful life of sailors of the time are all vividly portrayed in this book that will appeal to students, particularly those interested in explorers.

7.13   Stanley, Diane. **The True Adventure of Daniel Hall.** Illustrated by Diane Stanley. Dial, 1995. ISBN 0-8037-1469-6. 40p. 6–11.

Daniel Hall left New England for a life of adventure on a whaling ship. Before he returned to his home and family, he had traveled all over the world, experiencing the hard work of whaling and spending a harsh winter in Siberia. Young readers will be attracted to this true story of a boy's life in the nineteenth century, which is enlivened by maps and color illustrations.

Heroes

7.14 Adler, David A. **A Picture Book of Sojourner Truth.** Illustrated by Gershom Griffith. Holiday House, 1995. ISBN 0-8234-1072-2. 32p. 7–9.

This is a compelling biography of a woman born into slavery but presented to President Lincoln and President Grant. David Adler portrays Sojourner as an outspoken champion of equality for both women and African Americans. Beginning with a moving account of her childhood as a slave, the book traces her struggles for freedom, her self-naming, and her life as an itinerant preacher. Her tireless advocacy and support of newly freed slaves led to her formal address on their behalf to Congress and President Grant, requesting western land grants. The illustrations are watercolor renditions of Sojourner Truth at significant points in her life. The books in this Picture Book Biography series can be used for easy reading or to read aloud. This particular biography would be an appropriate text for studies of the American Civil War, slavery, and the lives of remarkable people.

7.15 Hurwitz, Johanna. **Anne Frank: Life in Hiding.** Illustrated by Vera Rosenberry. Beech Tree, 1993. ISBN 0-688-12405-4. 52p. 9–11.

This biography of Anne Frank is written in clear, accessible language. The book includes background material about Anne's life before and after she wrote her diary. This would be an excellent text to read in conjunction with the actual diary. The biography deals with questions of courage, human rights, racism, and the atrocities of war.

7.16 Linnéa, Sharon. **Raoul Wallenberg: The Man Who Stopped Death.** Photographs by Thomas Veres. Jewish Publication Society, 1993. ISBN 0-8276-0448-3. 151p. 10–14.

This spellbinding account of the life, work, and mysterious disappearance of Swedish architect Raoul Wallenberg reads like a novel. One feels his disappointments and triumphs working in Budapest during the latter part of World War II to save Jewish people from death at the hands of the Nazis. Interspersed within the chapters are authentic photographs taken by Thomas Veres at the scene. Sharon Linnéa's sensitive and honest portrayal of evil and destruction is balanced by the very human depiction of an ordinary man who refused to sit idle. The book ends with historical bits of rumor regarding Wallenberg's fate. This biography presents history embedded in the lives of real people in difficult situations.

7.17 Marzollo, Jean. **My First Book of Biographies: Great Men and Women Every Child Should Know.** Illustrated by Irene Trivas. Scholastic, 1994. ISBN 0-590-45014-X. 79p. 6–10.

This is an excellent biographical reference book for home, school, or library. It includes thirty-seven biographies of remarkable people from Christopher Columbus to Yo-Yo Ma. The biographies introduce people from a variety of cultural backgrounds, with a good balance between men and women. Each biography covers two pages; one page is a simplified biographical text and the other is a full-page watercolor illustration of the subject.

7.18 van der Rol, Ruud, and Rian Verhoeven. **Anne Frank: Beyond the Diary: A Photographic Remembrance.** Viking, 1993. ISBN 0-670-84932-4. 113p. 11–14.

Anna Quindlen introduces this photographic remembrance of Anne Frank's life before she and her family went into hiding. Quindlen writes that she reread Anne Frank's diary as a "companion work to the photographs in this book." The photographs by the authors are grouped and then explained with detailed captions, beginning with Anne's birth in Frankfurt in 1929. Maps are included to pinpoint places where Anne lived or where the Nazis occupied territory. Explanatory text is interspersed with photographs. Photographs of documents such as pages from the actual diary give an authentic flavor to this historical photobiography. The book ends with compelling photos of the extermination camps and information on the Anne Frank house.

Humanitarians

7.19 Greenfield, Eloise. **Rosa Parks.** Illustrated by Gil Ashby. Harper Trophy, 1995. ISBN 0-06-442025-6. 41p. 7–11.

This reissue of an outstanding text for young readers features new, evocative pencil-sketched illustrations that render this dramatic biography even more engaging than the original. The language is simple and easy to read, recounting a captivating story in honor of the fortieth anniversary of Rosa Parks's courageous fight against racial discrimination on public buses. The story is an excellent text for young readers. The historical and biographical details offer important content and role models for students.

7.20   Roberts, Jack L. **Booker T. Washington: Educator and Leader.** Millbrook, 1995. ISBN 1-56294-487-8. 32p. 8–12.

This biography of Booker T. Washington begins with his life as a slave in Virginia. It continues with the post–Civil War emancipation and Washington's struggles to educate himself and his people. The text is complemented by good archival photographs.

7.21   Robles, Harold. **Albert Schweitzer: An Adventurer for Humanity.** Millbrook, 1994. ISBN 1-56294-352-9. 64p. 9–12.

Albert Schweitzer, humanitarian, musician, theologian, philosopher, medical doctor, and winner of the 1954 Nobel Peace Prize, is introduced in this excellent biography. Good archival photographs complement the text as we journey through his remarkable life, including his childhood, his European studies, his medical work in Africa, and his later work for world peace. The text could provide an effective springboard for discussions of ethics.

Political Leaders

7.22   Cooper, Michael L. **From Slave to Civil War Hero: The Life and Times of Robert Smalls.** Lodestar, 1994. ISBN 0-525-67489-6. 74p. 9–11.

One of the Rainbow Biography series, this introduction to the life of Robert Smalls, an African American who rose from slavery to become an influential political leader, also provides an informative account of slavery and the Civil War period. Black-and-white photographs, maps, and illustrations add interest to the text.

7.23   Harness, Cheryl. **Young John Quincy.** Illustrated by Cheryl Harness. Bradbury, 1994. ISBN 0-02-742644-0. 42p. 6–8.

Although this book incorporates many factual details of John Quincy Adams's life, the narrative text and visual details are most effective in portraying the life of a young boy during the year 1776, leading up to the Declaration of Independence and the founding of the United States. Young readers will find this glimpse into history appealing.

7.24 Kunhardt, Edith. **Honest Abe.** Illustrated by Malcah Zeldis. Greenwillow, 1993. ISBN 0-688-11189-0. 32p. 5–8.

Malcah Zeldis's bright and colorful folk art paintings illustrate this simplified biography of Abraham Lincoln. The accessible text details the major events in Lincoln's life, highlighting the Gettysburg Address of 1863, the text of which concludes the book. Lincoln's honest nature, love of people, and great gift for public speaking are portrayed in a direct, easy-to-read style. This book would be useful for young readers as a read-aloud or as independent reading.

7.25 Marzollo, Jean. **Happy Birthday, Martin Luther King.** Illustrated by J. Brian Pinkney. Scholastic, 1993. ISBN 0-590-44065-9. 32p. 5–8.

This biography of Martin Luther King, designed for younger children, explores his life's work in a simple text with full-spread illustrations. It also chronicles the racist policies and practices against which King organized his inspirational resistance movement. This is an excellent book for classroom or library use, appropriate for themes about great people, racism, and United States history.

Religious Leaders

7.26 Raimondo, Lois. **Little Lama of Tibet.** Photographs by Lois Raimondo. Scholastic, 1994. ISBN 0-590-46167-2. 40p. 5–8.

This delightful book portrays the life of Ling Rinpoche, a six-year-old Tibetan boy recognized as the reincarnation of a high lama. The photographs chronicle his daily activities, including special ceremonies and trips. There is a preface by the Dalai Lama and a section with historical information on Tibet. This book could be used with themes of multiculturalism, religious studies, endangered cultures, and refugees. The book ends with Ling Rinpoche's advice to American children and their parents.

Scientists and Inventors

7.27 Fisher, Leonard Everett. **Marie Curie.** Illustrated by Leonard Everett Fisher. Macmillan, 1994. ISBN 0-02-735375-3. 32p. 9–11.

The life of this remarkable scientist is told in picture storybook format. The text is simple and the black-and-white illustrations resemble old-fashioned daguerreotypes. This biography is valuable for both its information and its accessible format.

7.28   Towle, Wendy. **The Real McCoy: The Life of an African-American Inventor.** Illustrated by Wil Clay. Scholastic, 1993. ISBN 0-590-43596-5. 32p. 6–9.

This is the first major biography for children on the life of Elijah McCoy, an African American engineer and inventor. His name is associated with the origin of the expression "the real McCoy" because many people imitated his inventions, but his were recognized as the best. The author traces McCoy's life from his birth to fugitive slaves through his adult life as a successful, respected inventor and businessperson. The artwork is rich with authentic detail and warm, intense colors. This valuable introduction to an African American pioneer in engineering is a fine addition to biography collections.

8 Social Studies

Careers

8.1 Kalman, Maira. **Chicken Soup, Boots.** Illustrated by Maira Kalman. Viking, 1993. ISBN 0-670-85201-5. 34p. 6–9.

This delightfully zany book is about a choice of careers. A whole range of occupations is offered, including many that are rarely discussed with children. The illustrations are as outrageous as the text, and together they provide a humorous treat. The title is a short-order cook's term for chicken soup to go.

Communication

8.2 Gibbons, Gail. **Puff . . . Flash . . . Bang . . . A Book about Signals.** Illustrated by Gail Gibbons. Morrow, 1993. ISBN 0-688-07377-8. 32p. 5–8.

"People use signals to say things to each other without using spoken or written words." With this simple explanation, Gibbons introduces young readers to the many types of signals found in everyday life. She uses examples that are easily recognizable such as pointing or waving. Several historical examples of signals are also given: beacon fires, drums, and smoke signals. Other signals such as flares, flags, horns, cannons, guns, lights, and lighthouses are explained and illustrated in Gibbons's familiar graphic style. This would be a useful book for studies of how we communicate.

8.3 McIlwain, John. **The Dorling Kindersley Children's Illustrated Dictionary.** Dorling Kindersley, 1994. ISBN 1-56458-625-1. 256p. 7–10.

This dictionary includes about five thousand words, defined in a clear and concise manner and, in most cases, illustrated with a color photograph or diagram. There are also twenty-six full-page, expanded entries on such topics as the alphabet, costumes, and the universe. Five appendices are included: abbreviations, a spelling guide, word-building, facts and figures, and countries of the world. This resource book is useful for new readers, writers, spellers, and young ESL students.

Cultural Groups

8.4   Ancona, George. **Pablo Remembers: The Fiesta of the Day of the Dead.** Photographs by George Ancona. Lothrop, 1993. ISBN 0-688-11249-8. 48p. 8–10.

This account of how Pablo, a young Mexican boy, and his community spend the three-day fiesta honoring their dead relatives blends interesting details about this special holiday, el Dia de los Muertos, with Spanish words in the text and captions (a glossary is provided). The stunning photographs of the celebrations provide an authentic look at this cultural feast.

8.5   Ancona, George. **Piñata Maker/El Piñatero.** Photographs by George Ancona. Harcourt Brace, 1994. ISBN 0-15-261875-9 (English); 0-15-200060-7 (Spanish). 40p. 5–8.

This Spanish/English photoessay describes how Don Ricardo, a craftsman from southern Mexico, makes piñatas for all the birthdays and special fiestas held in his village. The book begins by introducing this skilled craftsman and continues by clearly outlining the step-by-step process of making a piñata. The color photographs help the reader follow the process and add details on life in this Mexican village. The reader can sense the dedication of someone making something of beauty and share in the fun of watching the children of the village break open the piñata just made by Don Ricardo. This would be a useful text for studies on life in Mexico or for making crafts from different cultures.

8.6   Ancona, George. **Powwow.** Photographs by George Ancona. Harcourt Brace, 1993. ISBN 0-15-263268-9. 48p. 9–11.

This is a vivid, energetic look at the summer Crow Fair, the largest powwow held in the United States. Native people from Canada and United States attend this celebration of friendship and the traditions of the powwow. The color photographs detail the kaleidoscope of color and movement as men, women, and children dance to the pounding beat of the drums.

8.7   Bial, Raymond. **Shaker Home.** Photographs by Raymond Bial. Houghton Mifflin, 1994. ISBN 0-395-64047-4. 37p. 10–12.

This book is a direct, simple, and loving account of Shaker homes, cottage industries, artifacts, and religious beliefs. The book is recommended highly for regional collections. It is also recommended for adult collections in architecture, furniture, auctions, and religion.

8.8   Crum, Robert. **Eagle Drum: On the Powwow Trail with a Young Grass Dancer.** Photographs by Robert Crum. Four Winds, 1994. ISBN 0-02-725515-8. 48p. 9–11.

The well-written text and full-color illustrations guide the reader through the preparation and presentation of a ceremonial grass dance by a nine-year-old boy of the Pend Oreille tribe. Details of the history, traditions, and stories of these Native Americans also provide insight into the custom of the powwow and why it continues to flourish today.

8.9   Dolphin, Laurie. **Neve Shalom/Wahat al-Salam: Oasis of Peace.** Photographs by Ben Dolphin. Scholastic, 1993. ISBN 0-590-45799-3. 48p. 9–12.

This book is a sensitive portrayal of how two young boys from two neighboring cultures meet in a special school dedicated to harmonious living. Realistic photographs and a straightforward narrative supply interesting information as we follow the boys' meeting at Neve Shalom, a school in a cooperative village where Jews and Arabs coexist peacefully. As the boys learn about one another's language and culture, they become friends, and the reader is introduced to some of the teaching strategies that have earned this school four Nobel Peace Prize nominations. The story is treated very apolitically and fairly, without taking sides or offering judgmental pronouncements.

8.10   Filipovic, Zlata (translated by Janine Di Giovanni). **Zlata's Diary: A Child's Life in Sarajevo.** Viking, 1994. ISBN 0-670-85724-6. 200p. 9–15.

"I'm not writing to you about me anymore. I'm writing to you about war, death, injuries, shells, sadness and sorrow," writes eleven-year-old Zlata of her changing life in Sarajevo. In her diary, self-centered childishness begins to give way to the despair of war as she and her parents endure shelling, shooting, and lack of electricity, water, and food. We see how a young girl's normal childhood filled with piano lessons, TV, and Monopoly is disrupted by war. Zlata writes about the loss of small comforts, the death of friends and relatives, and constant fear. Zlata calls her diary Mimmy (like Anne Frank's diary, Kitty) and fills the pages with compelling word images that tug at the heart, such as a packed suitcase waiting. The diary is a naturally written, in-process account of life in wartime conditions for "a schoolgirl without a school, a child without a childhood." The diary offers a fascinating glimpse of another culture and the book tells how the diary became popularized by journalists.

8.11   Hoyt-Goldsmith, Diane. **Cherokee Summer.** Photographs by Lawrence Migdale. Holiday House, 1993. ISBN 0-8234-0995-3. 32p. 8–10.

This photoessay documents the summertime life of ten-year-old Bridget, a Cherokee girl from Oklahoma. She shares her personal history and the history of her people. The reader learns about her life today and how her family struggles to keep their heritage alive. The book includes some Cherokee language. The many traditional work or play activities that are part of the rich cultural heritage of the Cherokee nation are highlighted. The book includes a detailed glossary and general index.

8.12   Leigh, Nila K. **Learning to Swim in Swaziland: A Child's-Eye View of a Southern African Country.** Illustrated by Nila K. Leigh. Scholastic, 1993. ISBN 0-590-45938-4. 48p. 5–9.

This documentation of life in Swaziland is richly illustrated with pictures and photos, all the more remarkable considering that the author is a grade 4 student who lived in Swaziland for a year. She explores the customs and culture from a child's perspective, including rich details and imaginative, playful asides. The book concludes, "You should not be afraid of what you have never done. You can do all kinds of things you never dreamed you could do. Just like swimming. Just like writing a book. Just like living in Africa."

8.13   Lyon, George Ella. **Dreamplace.** Illustrated by Peter Catalanotto. Orchard, 1993. ISBN 0-531-05466-7. 32p. 6–8.

A modern child visits the cliff dwellings of the Pueblos of the twelfth century and recreates their lifestyle in dreamlike prose. Another glimpse of the Pueblo's history is given through the watercolors based on the landscape of New Mexico.

8.14   Malan, John. **Indiana Jones Explores the Incas.** Arcade, 1993. ISBN 1-55970-199-4. 47p. 6–12.

Indiana Jones is the ostensible narrator of this investigation of the ancient culture of the Incas. Even without this device, young readers will be intrigued by the aspects of Inca life represented in the book. Descriptions of daily life, agriculture, infrastructure, medicine, religion, and the empire's decline are accompanied by photographs, maps, and diagrams. The narrative makes frequent reference to archaeological evidence. A glossary, index, and a few suggestions for further reading increase the accessibility and value of this book.

8.15   Margolies, Barbara A. **Olbalbal: A Day in Maasailand.** Photographs by Barbara A. Margolies. Four Winds, 1994. ISBN 0-02-762284-3. 32p. 5–8.

This beautiful photoessay introduces young readers to the life and culture of the seminomadic people of Maasailand in East Africa. By presenting the details of a day in the life of the people in a Maasai village, the well-written text and color photographs reveal the important role of women, food, religious beliefs, and rites of passage in their society.

8.16   McLerran, Alice. **The Ghost Dance.** Illustrated by Paul Morin. Stoddart, 1995. ISBN 0-7737-2898-8. 32p. 5–7.

This story recounts the history of the First Nations peoples as the white settlers invade their lands. The poetic text traces the political and spiritual causes for the violent resistance of the native peoples to the invasion of white settlers and white culture. When resistance fails, the people place their hope to counteract the destructive forces of colonization with dream, dance, and songs, and the promise that all nations might work together peacefully. The textured illustrations use native regalia to dramatic effect.

8.17   Onyefulu, Ifeoma. **Emeka's Gift: An African Counting Story.** Photographs by Ifeoma Onyefulu. Cobblehill, 1995. ISBN 0-525-65205-1. 19p. 5–8.

A young Nigerian boy sets out to visit his grandmother in a nearby village. As he passes through the market, he thinks about presents he could take to her and the various things mentioned become the countable objects, such as four new brooms, seven musical instruments (ishaka), and eight water pots. The text and excellent color photographs of people and objects give a glimpse of some traditions and customs of the Igala tribe of southern Nigeria.

8.18   Ray, Mary Lyn. **Shaker Boy.** Illustrated by Jeanette Winter. Harcourt Brace, 1994. ISBN 0-15-276921-8. 48p. 5–8.

Mary Lyn Ray has long been a student of Shaker life. In this book she shares some of her knowledge of the history, customs, and beliefs of this unique community in a way that would interest even very young children. She does this through the story of Caleb, a young boy who comes to live with the Shakers in the nineteenth century. Ray's writing and the style of Jeanette Winter's illustrations reflect the simple, spare, high-quality craft for which the Shakers themselves are known. The text also includes the words and music to several Shaker songs.

8.19   Reynolds, Jan. **Amazon Basin: Vanishing Cultures.** Photographs by Jan Reynolds. Harcourt Brace, 1993. ISBN 0-15-202832-3pb, 0-15-202831-5hc. 32p. 5–8.

Through the eyes of a young boy named Tuwenowa, Jan Reynolds details the daily life and customs of the Yanomama, an indigenous people who live in the tropical rainforests of the Amazon River Basin. A simple narrative explains the routines of food gathering and preparation, work, and play. The narrative culminates with a community gathering to mourn the death of a family member and to celebrate life. Reynold's appealing, informative photojournalistic style will enhance classroom activities related to the life of indigenous people. Other titles in her series on vanishing cultures include *Frozen Land* (1993), *Down Under* (1992), *Far North* (1992), *Himalaya* (1991), and *Sahara* (1991).

8.20   Reynolds, Jan. **Mongolia: Vanishing Cultures.** Photographs by Jan Reynolds. Harcourt Brace, 1994. ISBN 0-15-255312-6. 30p. 8–12.

This engaging text, complemented by outstanding photographs, chronicles the lives of two children and their Mongolian family as they conduct their daily chores and resettle their camp. The lives of these nomadic people revolve around horses and other animals, and the book explores how their culture engenders a sense of connection to the natural world. A concluding section contains useful data on the history, geography, and wildlife of the region.

8.21   Siy, Alexandra. **The Efe: People of the Ituri Rain Forest.** Dillon, 1993. ISBN 0-87518-551-7. 72p. 9–12.

This is an enchanting portrait of the Efe, a group of African Pygmy rainforest-dwellers. The book introduces aspects of the lives of these people through their own myths and legends. The book is an accessible introduction to anthropology for older children and youths, with bright and engaging pictures. A concluding activities section provides creative ideas for extending this knowledge into children's activities.

8.22   Siy, Alexandra. **The Penan: People of the Borneo Jungle.** Dillon, 1993. ISBN 0-87518-552-5. 72p. 9–12.

Beginning with the words and legends of the Penan, this book explores many aspects of life among these forest-dwelling people. In addition to the culture, history, natural history, geography, and climate of the area, the text considers the contributions of the Penan and the Borneo rainforest to the global community. Rich photographs complement the text.

8.23   Sneve, Virginia Driving Hawk. **The Hopis: A First Americans Book.** Illustrated by Ronald Himler. Holiday House, 1995. ISBN 0-8234-1194-X. 32p. 7–10.

"If the land is abused, the sacredness of Hopi life will disappear." In this book evocative of the Hopi culture, the success of the Hopi, despite attack from many sources, is clearly shown by the illustrations as well as the text. Descriptions of a snake dance, secret societies, kachinas, and food such as piñon nuts help the reader compare this society to others. *The Navajos, The Iroquois,* and *The Sioux* are other books in this fine series.

8.24   Sneve, Virginia Driving Hawk. **The Seminoles: A First Americans Book.** Illustrated by Ronald Himler. Holiday House, 1994. ISBN 0-8234-1112-5. 32p. 9–12.

With such sections as "Creation Story," "Life in the Everglades," "Green Corn Dance," and "The Seminoles Today," this book draws a rich and often tragic portrait of this Native American people through short episodes enhanced by evocative watercolor illustrations. Details of the history, past and present lifestyle, beliefs, and customs of the Seminoles are interwoven with quotations and poetry by members of this proud people who earned the name of "the people who never surrendered."

Food, Clothing, and Shelter

8.25   Greenlaw, M. Jean. **Ranch Dressing: The Story of Western Wear.** Lodestar, 1993. ISBN 0-525-67432-2. 78p. 12–14.

This book offers a brief introduction to the history of Western clothing. Any self-respecting cowboy has six hats. The felt is made from beaver, rabbit, and nutria fur. A standard hat is marked 4X. The more beaver in it, the higher the number, all the way to 100X. Cowboys often spent two months' wages on boots. These and other facts, and the history, manufacture, and use of everything from hats to jeans to whips to bolo ties capture the spirit of the Old West.

8.26   Hausherr, Rosmarie. **What Food Is This?** Photographs by Rosmarie Hausherr. Scholastic, 1994. ISBN 0-590-46583-X. 40p. 3–10.

This book looks at different foods and their sources. It includes one page with a photograph and a simple question, and an accompanying page with a more technical and historical explanation. This provides an excellent introduction to human foods, food forms and families, and food groups. The photographs are deliciously tempting and the text clear and easy for children to read.

8.27   Paulsen, Gary (translated by Gloria De Aragon Andujar). **The Tortilla Factory/Tortilleria.** Illustrated by Ruth Wright Paulsen. Harcourt Brace, 1995. ISBN 0-15-292876-6 (English); 0-15-200237-5 (Spanish). 32p. 4–6.

The author of several powerful realistic novels of survival, such as *The River* and *Hatchet,* uses just a few lines in a picture book format to describe the making of a tortilla and to link it to the colors of the human family. Although the text is simple, the illustrations are sophisticated works of art and may have greater appeal for children a bit older. Editions are available in English and Spanish.

8.28   Rounds, Glen. **Sod Houses of the Great Plains.** Illustrated by Glen Rounds. Holiday House, 1995. ISBN 0-8234-1162-1. 32p. 5–8.

Quirky pastel line drawings and a simple text introduce young readers to the sod houses once built on the Great Plains. Earth tones and highly stylized figures are used to evoke the vastness and solitude of life for settlers. Children will enjoy reading about the process of collecting and laying sod, as well as discovering some of the problems that plagued people living with nothing but a roof of dirt and grass over their heads.

8.29   Thomson, Peggy. **Siggy's Spaghetti Works.** Illustrated by Gloria Kamen. Morrow, 1993. ISBN 0-688-11373-7. 32p. 6–8.

"It's a great day for spaghetti" as Siggy conducts a tour of his Spaghetti Works for a group of schoolchildren. He shows them, from start to finish, how spaghetti and all its related pasta forms are produced in a large factory. The main text is supported by lively diagrams, historical anecdotes, balloon captions, and humorous bits of information. The picture book format and animated illustrations make this a pleasurable read as well as an accurate source of information. This is a useful book to support themes on food and nutrition or to read aloud.

8.30 Wilkes, Sybella. **One Day We Had to Run.** Millbrook, 1995. ISBN 1-56294-557-2. 64p. 8–12.

This collection introduces refugee issues in a unique fashion by presenting the words and paintings of refugee children from the Sudan, Somalia, and Ethiopia. Photographs, maps, and background information are interspersed with the children's messages in an attractive manner that allows for easy reading. Effective use is made of subheadings and captions. The book includes ideas for curriculum use and additional resources.

8.31 Wilkinson, Philip. **Amazing Buildings.** Illustrated by Paolo Donati and Studio Illibill. Dorling Kindersley, 1993. ISBN 1-56458-234-5. 48p. 9–12.

This book brings a whole new perspective to how we look at buildings. A general introduction describes types of structures, building materials, and techniques that have been used for hundreds of years, and is followed by an exploration of twenty-one famous ancient and modern buildings from around the world. Each building was selected for its originality and its unique story, including the Palace of Minos, legendary home of the Minotaur, and the Taj Mahal, a memorial to the wife of an Indian mogul. Magnificent full-spread, colored drawings feature cut-away sections and roofs that lift off to reveal seldom-viewed interior structures. The lavish illustrations are surrounded by readable text and captions that provide information about the buildings, the construction, and the designer. An index is included.

Geography

8.32 Boyle, Bill. **My First Atlas.** Illustrated by David Hopkins. Dorling Kindersley, 1994. ISBN 1-56458-624-3. 45p. 5–8.

An excellent introduction to maps and atlases, this large reference work uses colorful maps and photographs to identify the countries and continents of the world. Full spreads combine picture maps, photographs, and interesting factual information;

each spread features a different region, such as Northern Europe and Australasia. Distinctive mountains and famous places are a few of the features highlighted on each map. Open-ended questions are posed to encourage use and knowledge of maps and atlases. Popular questions such as "What is the longest river?" are answered in a short section near the end. Endpapers provide a colorful display of world flags.

8.33   **Cartopedia: The Ultimate World Reference Atlas.** Dorling Kindersley, 1995. ISBN 0-7894-0045-6. CD-ROM. 8–12.

Cartopedia is an interactive atlas. Within the program, the reader can choose to explore the Physical World, the A–Z Listing of Countries, the Atlas Index, or the World in View. All these explorations bring the reader in touch with articles and maps of many countries of the world. From this information, readers can click on images or words highlighted in red to activate relevant animation, sounds (such as national anthems), and textual details. The strength of this CD-ROM is its ability to quickly, easily, and visually compare the attributes of one country (such as population) with another. A wonderful resource for teaching atlas research methods, it can be purchased in Mac or PC format.

8.34   Harrison, Ted. **O Canada.** Illustrated by Ted Harrison. Ticknor & Fields, 1993. ISBN 0-395-66075-0. 28p. 7–12.

Here Canadian artist Ted Harrison offers twelve beautiful paintings with accompanying texts to depict the ten provinces and two territories of Canada. The geography, history, people, and culture of each area come alive in the pages, an effect created in large part by the striking, bold, full-color illustrations. The artwork is influenced by native Canadian artistic traditions.

8.35   Jakobsen, Kathy. **My New York.** Illustrated by Kathy Jakobsen. Little, Brown, 1993. ISBN 0-316-45653-5. 32p. 6–8.

This book combines a simple text and vibrant paintings focusing on a tour of New York City through the eyes of a young girl. The text is a letter she has written to a friend whose family will soon be moving to New York. We see her favorite parts of the city, such as the Central Park Zoo, the Sixth Avenue Flea Market, toy stores, and the Plaza Hotel. The wonderfully detailed paintings are full of the exuberant life of this great city. Two large fold-out pages highlight the Empire State Building and the construction of a new skyscraper. These pages give the reader a sense of the height of these buildings, as if one were standing there. This book would be suitable for reading aloud or independent reading.

8.36 Morris, Neil. **Student's Activity Atlas.** Gareth Stevens, 1993. ISBN 0-8368-1041-4. 48p. 8–10.

Elementary students will enjoy learning about the world around them in this well-designed first atlas. The book begins by providing brief, clear explanations of scale bars, longitude, and latitude. The book also suggests several activities for practicing map-reading skills. There are full-color, up-to-date maps with scale bars and symbols representing each of eighteen regions of the world. Each region is illuminated with a full spread that includes a map, a fact box, an activity box, and a description. Color photographs depicting distinctive land features, wildlife, and culture are also included. Simple language makes this book accessible to children.

8.37 **My First Amazing World Explorer.** Dorling Kindersley, 1995. ISBN 0-7894-0294-7. CD-ROM. 5–8.

This is an excellent introduction for young readers to the world of maps and atlases. Students can explore the world on a global scale or zero in on specific countries and explore the local geography. National anthems, textual explanations, sounds, clear graphics, and animation help to bring this world atlas to life. Readers are encouraged to develop map-making and map-reading skills through games. They are also encouraged to learn about global landmarks, flora, and fauna by collecting stickers for their sticker books and to use their passports to explore a wide variety of countries. Users can also send postcards from anywhere in the world, and can take a guided tour of any place in the world that interests them. This disk is shipped in a cross-platform format, allowing both PCs and Macs to use the same disk.

History

United States

8.38 Appelbaum, Diana. **Giants in the Land.** Illustrated by Michael McMurdy. Houghton Mifflin, 1993. ISBN 0-395-64720-7. 32p. 5–8.

This large picture book describes the history of early logging practices in New England, including the harvesting of giant white pines used as the masts for ships in the British Royal Navy.

Appelbaum vividly details the size and might of these trees. He also describes the ingenious ways that people cut these trees and transported them to the rivers, where they were sold to British officials. Award-winning illustrator Michael McMurdy captures the majesty of these giant trees in bold black-and-white etched drawings. This book would be an excellent introduction to life in colonial New England and could lead to further inquiry about the industries of this time period.

8.39   Brenner, Barbara. **If You Were There in 1776.** Bradbury, 1994. ISBN 0-02-712322-7. 136p. 9–11.

The Declaration of Independence and the "one people" for whom it was written are presented in accessible text. This very readable description of the lives of the children who lived at that time, along with stories of the circumstances that led to the writing of this historic document, will enliven the study of this landmark period in American history. Interesting excerpts from diaries and letters combine with well-chosen historical illustrations to bring 1776 to life for young readers.

8.40   Chalk, Gary. **Yankee Doodle: A Revolutionary Tail.** Illustrated by Gary Chalk. Dorling Kindersley, 1993. ISBN 1-56458-202-7. 32p. 6–9.

Without trivializing the story of the American Revolution, the rhyming text set to the tune of "Yankee Doodle" presents major events surrounding the war. The animal characters, riding hobbyhorses and sporting popguns, are appealingly illustrated with careful attention to costume detail of the period. The book is a successful blend of fact, fiction, and humor.

8.41   Coles, Robert. **The Story of Ruby Bridges.** Illustrated by George Ford. Scholastic, 1995. ISBN 0-590-57281-4. 32p. 6–8.

In 1960 Ruby Bridges broke the color bar by attending an all-white elementary school in New Orleans. Although she studied alone in a boycotted classroom, for months she was the focus of intense protest as she walked to school under the protection of federal marshals. In this book, her story is told with an emphasis on the tolerance that grew from her perseverance. Children will be intrigued by this story of a real little girl's courage in the face of injustice.

8.42   Fraser, Mary Ann. **Ten Mile Day and the Building of the Transcontinental Railroad.** Illustrated by Mary Ann Fraser. Holt, 1993. ISBN 0-8050-1902-2. 35p. 8–12.

This book tells the story of Ten Mile Day, April 28, 1869, when over five thousand workers completed part of the last miles of the first transcontinental railroad in one day. The story unfolds with clarity, authority, and great detail without losing the excitement of a great adventure. Tribute is paid to the hard work of Chinese and Irish American workers, as well as to the spirit of the great visionaries who saw the railroad as the way to unite the country. Illustrations were carefully researched and evoke the emotion of that historic day. Four separate boxes of text give background information on the railroad story. An afterword, glossary, and reading list are included. This would be an excellent text to begin a history unit on the railroad.

8.43   Freedman, Russell. **Kids at Work: Lewis Hine and the Crusade against Child Labor.** Photographs by Lewis Hine. Clarion, 1994. ISBN 0-395-58703-4. 104p. 10–12.

The haunting, powerful black-and-white photographs by Lewis Hine will draw children into the early twentieth century, when child labor was rampant in the United States. Hine, a teacher and photographer, became an investigative reporter for the National Child Labor Committee. His accounts and photographs contributed to laws that were enacted to prevent the exploitation of children by American business. This is an important book to share with children so they can relate to and share a sense of compassion for youngsters their age who suffered hardships and had no hope of improvement in their lives. A useful companion reference is *Cheap Raw Material: How Our Youngest Workers are Exploited and Abused* by Milton Meltzer.

8.44   Hamilton, Virginia. **Many Thousand Gone: African Americans from Slavery to Freedom.** Illustrated by Leo Dillon and Diane Dillon. Knopf, 1993. ISBN 0-394-82873-9. 151p. 9–12.

Three dozen true stories, carefully researched, draw the reader through the history of African Americans from slavery to freedom. In 1710, Ukawsaw Gronniosaw left his home in what is now Nigeria to see new things. A merchant betrayed him and he was sold into slavery, ending up in New York. But Ukawsaw escaped to England, where he married and then wrote his autobiography. A century later, a woman named Eliza ran from Kentucky carrying her baby. She crossed the Ohio River to freedom by jumping from one ice floe to the next. Leo and Diane Dillon's black-and-white illustrations are as rich and evocative as the text they accompany.

8.45   Harness, Cheryl. **The Amazing Impossible Erie Canal.** Illustrated by Cheryl Harness. Macmillan, 1995. ISBN 0-02-742641-6. 32p. 5–10.

This is the history of the Erie Canal, beginning with details of how it was built. The book continues with an account of its completion on October 26, 1825, and its inauguration, the ceremonial mixing of the waters of Lake Erie and the Atlantic Ocean on November 4, 1825. Maps interspersed throughout the book trace the progress of the canal's construction. Diagrams depict the locks' functioning and cross-sections of the packet boat. The colorful illustrations bring the place, people, boats, and celebrations to life.

8.46   Haskins, Jim. **Get on Board: The Story of the Underground Railroad.** Scholastic, 1993. ISBN 0-590-45418-8hc, 0-590-45419-6pb. 152p. 11–12.

This book is a collection of biographies, archival photographs, social and political histories, and factual information. The material covers many aspects of the underground railroad as it evolved in the years before the end of the Civil War. The book includes a chapter on Harriet Tubman and John Brown. Although this book is a fairly dense text for children under twelve years old, the short chapters could be used for reference purposes by students working with a teacher.

8.47   Klausner, Janet. **Sequoyah's Gift: A Portrait of the Cherokee Leader.** HarperCollins, 1993. ISBN 0-06-021235-7. 111p. 9–11.

The fascinating story of the only person in five thousand years of recorded history to invent a complete writing system without being literate himself is compellingly told. Sequoyah served as a role model for the Cherokee of his time. Despite betrayal, turmoil, war, the forced emigration to Oklahoma, and a personal bout with alcoholism, he persisted in his vision of the value of the "talking leaves" for his people. His development of the Cherokee syllabary made possible documented eyewitness accounts and a substantial body of publishing. But it is the man himself—a disabled artist, blacksmith, silversmith, inventor, farmer, and statesman—who serves as an inspiration and a role model for the young of today.

8.48   Kroll, Steven. **By the Dawn's Early Light: The Story of the "Star-Spangled Banner."** Illustrated by Dan Andreasen. Scholastic, 1994. ISBN 0-590-45054-9. 40p. 5–8.

With simple text and paintings evocative of the era, this picture book will be a valuable addition to library and classroom collections. After a brief outline of the War of 1812, the events that led to the writing of "The Star Spangled Banner" are carefully portrayed. Children will be interested in Key's courage in pursuing the entire British fleet in a small boat. A photograph of the original text, lyrics and music, historical maps, an etching of the writer, and a bibliography and index will help children with research projects.

8.49 Kroll, Steven. **Lewis and Clark: Explorers of the American West.** Illustrated by Richard Williams. Holiday House, 1994. ISBN 0-8234-1034-X. 30p. 8–12.

In the early 1800s Captain Meriwether Lewis was asked by President Thomas Jefferson to lead an expedition from the Mississippi River to the Pacific Ocean. Lewis chose William Clark to accompany him. Beautiful oil paintings provide a powerful visual history of the territory, explorers, and native people. A map showing the routes traveled, a list summarizing important dates, and an index will assist students engaged in research projects

8.50 Lasky, Kathryn, and Meribah Knight. **Searching for Laura Ingalls: A Reader's Journey.** Photographs by Christopher G. Knight. Macmillan, 1993. ISBN 0-02-751666-0. 48p. 9–11.

This documentation of a journey taken by a Laura Ingalls Wilder fan to discover the roots of the Little House series is accompanied by excellent color photography. The historical setting and the life of Wilder parallel the diary entries of the young present-day traveler.

8.51 Lawlor, Veronica, selector. **I Was Dreaming to Come to America: Memories from the Ellis Island Oral History Project.** Illustrated by Veronica Lawlor. Viking, 1995. ISBN 0-670-86164-2. 40p. 9–11.

Over twelve million immigrants passed through Ellis Island between 1892 and 1954. This is the story of some of them as recorded in the Ellis Island Oral History Project. Celia Adler made the trip from Russia alone when she was only twelve years old. "My little basket, that's all I had with me. There was hardly any things. My mother gave me the sorrah (a kind of sandwich), and I had one change of clothes." Another child told of getting oatmeal for breakfast and did not know what it was, so she put it on the window sill and let the birds eat it. The moving stories are beautifully complemented by brilliant collages. A valuable companion book is *Ellis Island: Doorway to Freedom* by Steven Kroll, illustrated by Karen Ritz.

8.52   Lawrence, Jacob. **The Great Migration: An American Story.** Illustrated by Jacob Lawrence. HarperCollins, 1993. ISBN 0-06-443428-1. 48p. 6–10.

Originally published by the Museum of Modern Art, New York, this pictorial history chronicles the great migration of African Americans from the South to the North between 1916 and 1919. Jacob Lawrence painted the sixty panels in 1940 and 1941 at the age of twenty-two to twenty-three years. The paintings are rich, highly textured, and evocative accounts of the migrants' lives, exploring their decisions to leave, their journeys and hardships, and their joys and disappointments on arriving at their destinations. Although the value of the book lies largely in its striking art, there is a simple accompanying text and a moving poem by Walter Dean Myers. This is an excellent book for exploring both art and social history.

8.53   Levinson, Nancy Smiler. **Turn of the Century: Our Nation One Hundred Years Ago.** Lodestar, 1994. ISBN 0-525-67433-0. 127p. 10–12.

The United States of the 1890s was a dynamic and interesting place. This book seeks to convey the excitement of the era through a series of chapters that examine the economy, society, and politics. Black-and-white photographs, maps, and political cartoons furnish readers with a visual context for the textual information. The book's organization and appearance suggest that its primary use will be curricular, and an index to text and illustrations make this a useful reference work for the historical period.

8.54   McCurdy, Michael, editor. **Escape from Slavery: The Boyhood of Frederick Douglass in His Own Words.** Knopf, 1994. ISBN 0-679-84651-4. 63p. 11–13.

Through the words of Frederick Douglass, the reader experiences the bitter harshness of his boyhood as a slave: the suffering he endures from hunger and cold, the lack of a bed or covering, the deep pain he felt when separated from his mother and siblings, and the cruel and unreasonable punishment inflicted on him. But Douglass has a dream that one day he and all black people will live in freedom. This account is the beginning of the fulfillment of that dream. This shortened, edited, and illustrated version of the first volume of Douglass's autobiography is accessible to young readers. The power of the words is heightened by the wood engravings. Explanatory chapter introductions provide smooth links between events.

8.55   Murphy, Jim. **The Great Fire.** Scholastic, 1995. ISBN 0-590-47267-4. 144p. 10–12.

In 1871 a fire swept through Chicago, destroying property and leaving one hundred thousand people homeless. This compelling account of the disaster draws on the memories of survivors together with documentary history of the city. Extensive use is made of maps, photographs, and illustrations. An index makes this a useful reference book and the narrative, emphasizing the social and personal consequences of the fire, is compelling to read.

8.56   Sandler, Martin W. **Pioneers: A Library of Congress Book.** HarperCollins, 1994. ISBN 0-06-023023-1. 93p. 9–11.

This book shows what it was like for a family to make the journey to the unknown West and the difficulties of clearing land, building houses, and facing danger. Vintage photographs, posters, maps, and quotes from pioneer diaries from the Library of Congress collection illustrate the text. One picture of a sod house shows pots of flowers in one window and two birdcages hanging in front of another. These details will help any student in a study of pioneer times. Other titles is this series are *Cowboys, Presidents,* and *Immigrants.*

8.57   Spedden, Daisy Corning Stone. **Polar the Titanic Bear.** Illustrated by Laurie McGraw. Little, Brown, 1994. ISBN 0-316-80625-0. 64p. 7–11.

This story of life in the privileged classes of early twentieth century America is told by Polar, a stuffed bear who accompanied his young master on travels between the United States and Europe, including the voyage of the ill-fated Titanic. This appealing book is bound to be a great favorite with young readers.

World

8.58   Adler, David A. **Child of the Warsaw Ghetto.** Illustrated by Karen Ritz. Holiday House, 1995. ISBN 0-8234-1160-5. 32p. 8–12.

The story of the Warsaw Ghetto is both a great tragedy and an incident of fierce Jewish resistance of the Holocaust. In this sophisticated picture book, the experiences of Froim Baum introduce young readers to life before, during, and after the ghetto, and to the brutality of this period in history. The narrative alternates between episodes in Froim's life and parallel historical events, so that the reader appreciates the impact of large-scale upheaval on the daily lives of individuals. The presentation of historical information is accurate and relatively detailed, with additional information available in an author's note. The color illustrations are historically and emotionally evocative, many of them resembling actual photographs from the period.

8.59   Adler, David A. **Hilde and Eli: Children of the Holocaust.** Illustrated by Karen Ritz. Holiday House, 1994. ISBN 0-8234-1091-9. 32p. 8–11.

This book portrays Hitler's Germany through the lives of two Jewish children, Hilde and Eli. The reader learns of the children's interests and family life, even as persecution and violence escalate in Europe. Ultimately, the reader follows Hilde and Eli to their deaths in Nazi-occupied Eastern Europe. Based on the lives of two real children, the story is historically accurate.

8.60   Bachrach, Susan D. **Tell Them We Remember: The Story of the Holocaust.** Little, Brown, 1994. ISBN 0-316-69264-6. 112p. 10–13.

This excellent book about the Holocaust could also be used to support novel studies dealing with this historical event. This selection is also a fine choice for students seeking specific information. The book provides excellent background knowledge as well as information defining events, issues, terms, and points of view. The tone of the book is realistic but not overly grim, making the topic manageable for children. The book introduces twenty young people, describing their lives before, during, and after the war as their stories unfold from 1933 to 1945. An excellent chronology, glossary, and suggestions for further reading are included at the end of the text. A thorough index and table of contents make the text especially useful.

8.61   Besson, Jean-Louis. **October '45: Childhood Memories of the War.** Illustrated by Jean-Louis Besson. Harcourt Brace, 1995. ISBN 0-15-200955-8. 96p. 11–13.

This French author was twelve years old when World War II ended. Here he recounts his childhood impressions of the events in a journal format. The language is starkly simple—there are no comments until a significant last sentence. The illustrations enhance this interesting look at one person's view of the war.

8.62   Biesty, Stephen. **Stephen Biesty's Incredible Cross-Sections: Stowaway!** Illustrated by Stephen Biesty. Dorling Kindersley, 1995. ISBN 1-56458-903-X. CD-ROM. 8–12.

Based on the book of the same title, this CD-ROM is a highly detailed and animated look into the construction of an eighteenth-century war ship and the lifestyles of the people who sailed such ships. Readers can use the mouse to point and click on icons to explore cross-sections of the ship, meet the crew, or chase down a stowaway. During exploration, the reader can listen to the crew, hear the ship groan and creak, observe a battle, watch the sailors at work, and read interesting explanations about life on the war ship. Students can choose to explore the ship according to their interests and hope to catch the stowaway before they return to port. This CD-ROM book could be used to supplement a unit on the explorers. It can be purchased in Mac or PC format.

8.63   Brenner, Barbara. **The United Nations 50th Anniversary Book.** Atheneum, 1995. ISBN 0-689-31912-6. 90p. 8–12.

This commemorative book is also a reference work, organized according to the diverse functions of the United Nations. A detailed table of contents and index enhance access to the content, which includes directory information, brief factual data, excerpted UN documents, and many photographs. This book will be most useful as a curriculum resource or as part of a library reference collection.

8.64   Carrick, Carol. **Whaling Days.** Illustrated by David Frampton. Clarion, 1993. ISBN 0-395-50948-3. 40p. 5–8.

Carrick traces the history of the whaling industry from its beginnings among twelfth-century Europeans and native peoples of North America. The sophisticated, efficient methods of twentieth-century whaling are also included. Various hunting practices, methods of killing, and the harvesting of baleen, blubber, and oil are explained in a tightly written text. The woodcut illustrations add a sense of history to the text, dramatically portraying the power and beauty of the whales. The efforts of conservation groups are emphasized with a call for continued action to extend the ban on whaling. This book is an excellent addition to classroom and school libraries.

8.65   Chicoine, Stephen, and Brent Ashabranner. **Lithuania: The Nation That Would Be Free.** Photographs by Stephen Chicoine. Dutton, 1995. ISBN 0-525-65151-9. 60p. 10–12.

Extensive photographs and a comprehensive text bring the historical and contemporary trials and triumphs of Lithuania to life. The book begins with a chapter on the Lithuanian declaration of independence from the Soviet Union in March 1990, and then describes the bloody encounters of January 1991, in which fourteen demonstrators died. Subsequent chapters deal with Lithuania's earlier history, the Jews of Lithuania, the environmental movement, basketball in Lithuania, and Lithuania's connections with the United States. This is a well-organized book that will inspire children, students, and adults alike with the rich history and culture of this small but enduring Baltic state.

8.66   Gibbons, Gail. **Pirates: Robbers of the High Seas.** Illustrated by Gail Gibbons. Little, Brown, 1993. ISBN 0-316-30975-3. 32p. 5–8.

With balance and accuracy, Gibbons describes the history of pirates and piracy. The pirates' actions are candidly explained with no attempts to glamorize their lifestyle. Information on how they carried out their robberies, where they operated, and what they did with the things they stole is detailed and illustrated. Brief sketches are given on eight famous pirates and four well-known treasure mysteries. This appealing subject for young readers is handled in an informative and entertaining way.

8.67   Granfield, Linda. **In Flanders Fields: The Story of the Poem by John McCrae.** Illustrated by Janet Wilson. Lester, 1995. ISBN 1-895555-65-5. unpaged. 8–12.

Written in 1915, two years before the United States entered World War I, John McCrae's poem "In Flanders Fields" still has a powerful message for young people. It is well-known in Canada and often recited at school or civil Remembrance Day ceremonies; its central image, the poppy, has become the symbol of remembrance. This book recreates the story of the war and astutely summarizes its beginnings. Granfield vividly conveys the daily boredom of soldiers who are always aware of what might come in the next few moments. Poignant moments of war are also caught in the broad vistas of expressionistic oil paintings, a technique selected to represent the artistic style of the time. These illustrations received the prestigious 1995 Governor General's Award for Illustrations (Canada).

8.68   Howarth, Sarah. **The Middle Ages.** Viking, 1993. ISBN 0-670-85098-5. 48p. 8–12.

This title in the See Through History series has four cutaway, overlay pages so that the reader can peek into an abbey, a castle, a watermill, and a street scene. The book is a comprehensive introduction to European life in the Middle Ages. The text is organized under general topic sections, with subheadings guiding the reader. Information is easy to access through a contents page, glossary, timeline, and index. Maps, photos of historic places, pictures from old books and records, artifacts, and artists' illustrations support the text, providing a rich visual experience and a glimpse into the Middle Ages. The topics presented include social customs, habits, pastimes, rules and regulations, social hierarchy, food, work, education, and religion.

8.69 Kodama, Tatsuharu. **Shin's Tricycle.** Illustrated by Noriyuki Ando. Walker, 1995. ISBN 0-8027-8376-7. 33p. 9–11.

This is a true story about a boy named Shin as told by his father, Nobuo Tetsutani. On August 6, 1945, Shin and his best friend, Kim, are joyously riding Shin's new red tricycle in the yard when a blinding flash interrupts them, followed by darkness. Nobuo and his wife bury Shin and their two daughters and Shin's friend, Kim. Forty years later, Nobuo digs up the bones for a proper burial. Finding the tricycle there, rusted but intact, Shin decides to donate it to the Peace Museum as a reminder that the world should be a peaceful place where children can laugh and play unharmed. The paintings are highly evocative, conveying the horror and tragedy of that day. This poignant story would be an excellent text to mark the anniversary of the bombing of Hiroshima or Remembrance Day. Older children could use the story to discuss the effects of war on the lives of children.

8.70 Langley, Andrew. **Industrial Revolution.** Viking, 1994. ISBN 0-670-85835-8. 47p. 8–11.

This is a beautifully presented book, balancing visuals with textual information for those who want to know more about the Industrial Revolution. Although the book has an excellent table of contents, a small glossary, a table of key dates, and a thorough index, it will be most accessible for students who already have an awareness of this period of history.

8.71 Macdonald, Fiona. **Vikings.** Barron's, 1993. ISBN 0-8120-6375-9. 57p. 8–12.

This is a useful reference book on all facets of Viking life, including their language, international trade, and religion. Viking history is discussed primarily in the context of the period of their marine conquests, but the book includes some description of their later conversion to Christianity. A time chart is provided.

Throughout the book, color photos, diagrams, and some fold-out painted scenes from the Vikings' daily lives illustrate the text.

8.72 Martell, Hazel Mary. **Over 900 Years Ago: With the Vikings.** Illustrated by Roger Payne. Macmillan, 1993. ISBN 0-02-726325-8. 32p. 8–10.

This book would be a worthwhile addition to a collection of resources on Viking history. Illustrations and photographs of artifacts are balanced with artistic recreations of daily life and informative text. Information not readily available in other sources, such as the use of currency, is clearly presented.

8.73 Meltzer, Milton. **Gold: The True Story of Why People Search for It, Mine It, Trade It, Steal It, Mint It, Hoard It, Shape It, Wear It, Fight and Kill for It.** HarperCollins, 1993. ISBN 0-06-022983-7. 168p. 9–12.

Students will be intrigued by the insights into history, science, economics, biography, geography, and art that are gained from the study of one topic: gold. The past and present are connected by stories about the role of gold in the ancient world, African empires, the California and Klondike gold rushes, and contemporary technology. This well-researched, interestingly written text is supported by photographs, personal narratives, and an annotated bibliography.

8.74 Pearson, Anne. **Vikings.** Viking, 1994. ISBN 0-670-85834-X. 48p. 8–10.

This book is an excellent representation of all aspects of Viking life. Information difficult to find in other sources is clearly presented here. The four peel-away transparencies add realism and promote understanding for young researchers. Information is accurate and the book pays attention to detail. One caption debunks the stereotypical representation of a Viking warrior: "Viking warriors never wore helmets with horns on them!" This is a fine resource for social studies in the intermediate grades.

8.75 Platt, Richard. **Castle.** Illustrated by Stephen Biesty. Dorling Kindersley, 1994. ISBN 1-56458-467-4. 32p. 9–12.

This book presents minutely detailed illustrations of life in a fourteenth-century castle. All aspects of daily activity are represented, including building, the economy, defense, society, and entertainment. Fascinating explanatory text accompanies the illustrations, making each page an engaging glimpse into a lively historical world. The book includes both glossary and index, enhancing its value as a reference work as well as an enjoyable read. Other works in the Stephen Biesty's Cross-Sections series include *Stephen Biesty's Incredible Cross-Sections* and *Stephen Biesty's Cross-Sections Man-of-War.*

8.76   Sabuda, Robert. **Tutankhamen's Gift.** Illustrated by Robert Sabuda. Atheneum, 1994. ISBN 0-689-31818-9. 32p. 8–9.

The life of the well-known Egyptian boy king, Tutankhamen, is presented through bold pictures outlined in black against a background of painted, handmade Egyptian papyrus. An afterword provides historical details. This is an excellent, sophisticated book.

8.77   Williams, Brian. **Forts and Castles.** Viking, 1995. ISBN 0-670-85898-6. 48p. 8–12.

This is a good resource book on the architecture and history of castles and forts around the world. The diagrams and photographs bring each structure alive with the people and activities that once filled their corridors. The use of overlays demonstrates the exterior design while revealing the interior furnishings and life within. The book includes a glossary, timeline, and index and is in the See Through History series.

8.78   Wood, Tim. **The Renaissance.** Viking, 1993. ISBN 0-670-85149-3. 48p. 8–12.

This title in the See Through History series has four see-through pages where the reader can peek into a palace, a print shop, St. Peter's in Rome, and the Santa Maria. The text is organized under general topic sections, with subheadings guiding the reader. Information is easy to access through the inclusion of a contents page, glossary, timeline, and index. Maps, photos of historic places, pictures from old books and records, artifacts, and illustrations support the text, providing a rich visual experience. Some of the topics presented include art, architecture, science, commerce and shipping, technological advances, religion, and wars. This book is a comprehensive introduction to European life during the Renaissance.

8.79   Zhang, Song Nan. **Little Tiger in the Chinese Night: An Autobiography in Art.** Illustrated by Song Nan Zhang. Tundra, 1993. ISBN 0-88776-320-0. 48p. 10–14.

Through words and paintings, Zhang, now a Canadian immigrant, tells the story of his life. This story begins when he was a child and his family hid in the mountains while the Japanese occupied Shanghai. Zhang recounts a life marked by changing regimes, policies, and conditions from the end of World War II to the massacre at Tiananmen Square. With Zhang and his fellow art students, we experience the physical and psychological hardships of the years of the Great Leap Forward, the Cultural Revolution, and the opening of China to the world. Zhang, who witnessed the massacre on TV in Montreal, began the process of getting his family out of China to begin a new life in Canada. Historical background in chronological form and maps are provided at the end of the book.

Religion

8.80   Edwards, Michelle. **Blessed Are You: Traditional Everyday Hebrew Prayers.** Illustrated by Michelle Edwards. Lothrop, 1993. ISBN 0-688-10759-1. 32p. 5–8.

This beautifully illustrated book presents each traditional Hebrew prayer in Hebrew, with an English pronunciation, along with a simple translation of the meaning. Three children are depicted in the picture that accompanies each prayer, and the varied scenes of everyday life tell a story related to the prayers. This book should be shared to promote discussion of the religious blessings and the events connected to them. The thirteen prayers (and thirteen is a lucky number in Judaism) include some more obscure blessings.

8.81   Hastings, Selina. **The Children's Illustrated Bible.** Illustrated by Eric Thomas. Dorling Kindersley, 1994. ISBN 1-56458-472-0. 320p. 8–12.

A rich variety of paintings and photographs, combined with skillful retelling of the traditional stories, makes this a wonderful resource for children and teachers. Interesting sidebars provide information such as the type of first aid given by the Good Samaritan and the kinds of dyes used to produce Joseph's coat of many colors.

8.82   Waddell, Martin. **Stories from the Bible: Old Testament Stories.** Illustrated by Geoffrey Patterson. Ticknor & Fields, 1993. ISBN 0-395-66902-2. 69p. 6–12.

In language that is clear, down-to-earth, and contemporary, Martin Waddell retells seventeen stories from the Hebrew Bible, rendering them understandable and appealing. The stories are ordered so that one connects to the next; for example, the story of Joseph in Egypt precedes the story of Moses, with interconnecting text.

Social Issues

8.83 Atkin, S. Beth. **Voices from the Fields: Children of Migrant Farmworkers Tell Their Stories.** Photographs by Beth S. Atkin. Little, Brown, 1993. ISBN 0-316-05633-2. 96p. 9–11.

Crowded into small, crude shacks, working long hours for little pay, constantly moving from one place to another, subject to illness and prejudice, nine migrant children tell their stories in their own words, with moving simplicity. Most remarkable is their persistent hope for a better life.

8.84 Carter, Jimmy. **Talking Peace: A Vision for the Next Generation.** Dutton, 1995. ISBN 0-525-45517-5. 206p. 11–13.

In this revised edition, comprehensive and up-to-date, former U.S. President Jimmy Carter addresses young people on important issues concerning world peace, democracy, and human rights. Referring to recent historical events throughout the world, he draws the reader into the complexities of conflict, racism, war, peace, and the rights of children. The text is suitable for advanced readers with an interest in politics and social issues. All royalties go to the Carter Center, a philanthropic organization founded by the former president and his wife.

8.85 Hoose, Phillip. **It's Our World, Too: Stories of Young People Who Are Making a Difference.** Little, Brown, 1993. ISBN 0-316-37241-2. 166p. 11–14.

These stories of many young people who are making a difference are a refreshing breath of hope. Some have worked to eliminate racism or discrimination. Justin Lebo started at age ten to rebuild bicycles for less fortunate youngsters and in four years had given almost two hundred bicycles away. Another youngster helped set up a food service for the poor. The second half of the book shows young people how to start their own projects and explains some of the tools to use to facilitate change.

8.86 Meltzer, Milton. **Cheap Raw Material.** Viking, 1994. ISBN 0-670-83128-X. 165p. 11–14.

This history of child labor—from ancient times to the present—examines the reasons why children work, the ways in which they have been and continue to be exploited, and what has been done to protect them. Documents included in the text provide eyewitness accounts and the actual words spoken by children, telling of the appalling conditions to which they have been subjected. We also learn about the people who have worked to protect children and who still strive to prevent young people from having to work in intolerable conditions. Black-and-white photographs highlight the text. With teacher assistance, this book would be of great interest to students.

8.87   Wolf, Bernard. **Homeless.** Photographs by Bernard Wolf. Orchard, 1995. ISBN 0-531-06886-2. 48p. 5–10.

This rare photographic and textual essay explores the life of a homeless boy and his family in New York City as they struggle to find a home. Though honest and authentic in its portrayal of their suffering, the book also offers some optimism through the many people who rally to help and the family's own efforts to better their circumstances. The comprehensive photographs are of exceptional quality. This is an excellent tool for cultivating empathy in children while focusing on the lives of children often neglected by mainstream media and literature.

Social Life and Customs

8.88   Bial, Raymond. **Frontier Home.** Photographs by Raymond Bial. Houghton Mifflin, 1993. ISBN 0-395-64046-6. 40p. 9–11.

The spirit of the pioneers who built a new life in a new land is accurately captured in this detailed story of daily life of early homesteaders. Following their arduous journey, these settlers cleared the land, planted crops, and built homes. The book describes how they made most of the items they needed for survival and wasted very little. The well-researched text is supported by an extensive list of sources and suggested readings. Quotes from actual diaries of several men and women who settled the American West are sprinkled throughout the text. This book would be an excellent source for students studying this period in American history.

8.89   Charley, Catherine. **Tombs and Treasures.** Illustrated by Catherine Charley. Viking, 1995. ISBN 0-670-85899-4. 47p. 8–12.

This introductory reference work on Egyptian tombs and artifacts is a valuable book for curriculum or pleasure reading. The text is accompanied by maps, photographs, and color illustrations, some of which include overlays to reveal layers of detail beneath. The text is readable, making extensive use of subheadings and integrating quotations from students and observers of Egyptian antiquity throughout history. Readers participate in the discovery of the mysteries of ancient Egypt. Access to the book is enhanced by a table of contents, index, and glossary. This serious and useful book also succeeds in capturing the reader's imagination.

8.90 Colman, Penny. **Toilets, Bathtubs, Sinks, and Sewers: A History of the Bathroom.** Atheneum, 1994. ISBN 0-689-31894-4. 69p. 9–11.

In this clear, direct presentation of the history of the bathroom, the author traces sanitation practices from ten thousand years ago on the Orkney Islands of Scotland to the present. Children will be fascinated to learn that some ancient societies placed great importance on cleanliness and developed effective facilities that, in some instances, disappeared as society evolved. Based on careful research, this well-illustrated book will enhance the study of different societies and time periods.

8.91 Giblin, James Cross. **Be Seated: A Book about Chairs.** HarperCollins, 1993. ISBN 0-06-021537-2. 136p. 9–14.

James Cross Giblin provides a fascinating account of the history of chairs from the earliest times to the present. The author describes the technological or style changes that have occurred and also considers the symbolic and artistic importance of this common item of furniture. Through an examination of the function of chairs, the people who used them, and the customs surrounding them, he unfolds a rich tapestry of the social history of many cultures. The wealth of detail provides insights into the lives of people of different backgrounds and times, including the ancient Greeks, the medieval monks, the African Ashanti, and the American Shakers. The expository text is illustrated with many black-and-white pictures.

8.92 King, Elizabeth. **Chile Fever: A Celebration of Peppers.** Photographs by Elizabeth King. Dutton, 1995. ISBN 0-525-45255-9. 32p. 9–11.

From the instant the cover is opened and the endpapers revealed, readers will feast their eyes on a colorful range of chile peppers. Hatch, New Mexico, is the chile capital of the world and the source for Elizabeth King's interesting photographs. The life cycle of the chile is followed, from seed to rooftop drying. The use and importance of chiles is discussed from historical to contemporary times. Students will be interested in uncovering the secret of what makes chiles so hot. A pronunciation guide and list of chile heat scores make this a particularly good resource for studying the chile industry.

8.93   Lester, Alison. **My Farm.** Illustrated by Alison Lester. Houghton Mifflin, 1994. ISBN 0-395-68193-6. 33p. 5–8.

Alison Lester's endearing childhood memories of growing up on a farm in Australia are bound to capture young readers' interest with such tales as herding cattle, delivering a calf, winning ribbons at the local fair, and, best of all, finding a surprise Christmas present under the apple tree. A glossary of Australian terms accompanies the text and the bright, detailed illustrations suit the warm, light-hearted, and humorous tone of this story about a year of growing up on a farm.

8.94   Sandler, Martin W. **Cowboys: A Library of Congress Book.** HarperCollins, 1994. ISBN 0-06-023318-4. 91p. 9–11.

The life of the American cowboy is the material from which legends and heroes are made. This pictorial album of historical photographs, paintings, and engravings, combined with text and quotations, presents a realistic portrait of the life of the American cowboy. Materials are arranged by topic: life on the range, the roundup, the trail drive, cowboys and outlaws, famous cowboys, and cowboys today. The cowboy's life of hardship, danger, and loneliness is contrasted with the growth of the cowboy myth, shown through color posters, book jackets, and sheet music. This could be used with Granfield's *Cowboys* and Marrin's *Cowboys.*

8.95   Schroeder, Alan. **Carolina Shout!** Illustrated by Bernie Fuchs. Dial, 1995. ISBN 0-8037-1678-8. 32p. 5–9.

Her sister does not hear it, but Delia hears music everywhere she goes in the city. This story celebrates the songs and shouts of American street vendors before World War II. Delia introduces readers to characters such as the oyster man, the charcoal man, the waffle man, and the hopscotchers who fill the air of her neighborhood with their songs. The text is accompanied by striking illustrations that are vibrant and nostalgic.

8.96   Scott, Ann Herbert. **Cowboy Country.** Illustrated by Ted Lewin. Clarion, 1993. ISBN 0-395-57561-3. 42p. 5–10.

An old-time cowboy, or buckaroo, shares his knowledge of the days of his craft "before barbed wire and pickup trucks" with a young boy on an overnight trip into the heart of cowboy country. In conversational style, he recounts the rich details of the olden days and contrasts them with life on a modern ranch. The detailed colorful illustrations evoke the beauty and uniqueness of this lifestyle centering around horses, riders, cattle, and the surrounding landscape.

8.97 Thomas, Roy Edwin. **Come Go with Me: Old-Time Stories from the Southern Mountains.** Illustrated by Laszlo Kubinyi. Farrar, Straus, 1994. ISBN 0-374-37089-3. 188p. 9–12.

These stories are recollections by people who grew up in the Appalachian, Ozark, and Ouachita mountains in the late nineteenth and early twentieth centuries. The anecdotes and details of everyday life will interest children who want to know how people used to live. The stories have been transcribed as they were told so that they retain both the regional dialect and the personal feel of storytelling. The collection might be used as an oral history component in a social studies course.

8.98 Waters, Kate. **Samuel Eaton's Day: A Day in the Life of a Pilgrim Boy.** Photographs by Russ Kendall. Scholastic, 1993. ISBN 0-590-46311-X. 40p. 6–9.

Through the retelling of a day in the life of young Samuel Eaton, young readers get a glimpse into seventeenth-century New England and the early English settlers' lifestyle; the story is centered around Samuel's family and their involvement with the rye harvest. The photographs of authentic Pilgrim customs and clothing add authenticity and factual detail to the text. This is a vivid and interesting history lesson for young readers.

Transportation

8.99 Crisman, Ruth. **Racing the Iditarod Trail.** Dillon, 1993. ISBN 0-87518-523-1. 72p. 10–14.

This is the definitive book for young readers on the Iditarod dogsled race held in Alaska every March. The origin of the race is rooted in a historic race to bring medicine to the people of Nome in 1925. Background information is provided on raising and training the dogs and building a team to ensure success in the race. Several chapters take the reader through the grueling, exhausting race. These chapters detail the vast distance, the difficulty of the weather, the terrain, and the indomitable spirit of the many volunteers who make the race possible. The book includes a map of the race route, lists of previous winners, distance charts, a thorough index, and an excellent bibliography.

8.100   Marston, Hope Irvin. **Big Rigs.** Dutton, 1993. ISBN 0-525-65123-3. 48p. 5–8.

Color photographs of many types of tractor trailers highlight this updated edition of a popular book. Information is presented in straightforward, simple text that also includes a glossary of CB radio talk. Young readers will enjoy the close-up look at these huge trucks. They will also learn about the different types and body parts of tractor trailers as well as the emblems and grills that distinguish the various manufacturers. This book could be valuable during studies of transportation.

8.101   Platt, Richard. **Stephen Biesty's Cross-Sections: Man-of-War.** Illustrated by Stephen Biesty. Dorling Kindersley, 1993. ISBN 1-56458-321-X. 27p. 9–12.

The year is approximately 1800 and this book takes the reader on a tour through a man-of-war belonging to the Royal Navy of Great Britain. The ship is divided into ten cross-sections and each is examined in minute detail to show every aspect of the construction of this sailing ship and the way of life of those who sailed on it. The intricate illustrations and the detailed text depict the water-filled bilges, stinking and rat-infested, in contrast to the admiral's dining room with its wood paneling and fine furnishings. Many details of life on the ship are outlined, such as ridding the biscuits of maggots and the art of getting into a hammock. This oversize book with its full-spread illustrations is a visual delight. The textual information arranged around the illustrations brings the ship and its men to life. The man-of-war is based on the plans for Admiral Nelson's flagship, *HMS Victory.*

8.102   Wilson, Anthony. **Dorling Kindersley Visual Timeline of Transportation.** Dorling Kindersley, 1995. ISBN 1-56458-880-7. 45p. 10–12.

In this book, a browser's delight and excellent reference, the author charts the development of transportation on land, on water, and in the air from 10,000 B.C.E. to the present and provides glimpses into the future. Highlights of technical, social, and historical developments provide additional information about each form of transportation. Concise blocks of text are surrounded by full-color photographs and illustrations.

9 Science: Pure and Applied

Activities and Experiments

9.1 Chapman, Gillian, and Pam Robson. **Exploring Time.** Photographs by Rupert Horrox. Millbrook, 1995. ISBN 1-56294-560-2. 32p. 5–10.

This is a very useful resource for classroom teachers and parents looking for an educational activity book for children. The text moves from the simplest concept of a child's daily schedule to a consideration of lifetimes, family trees, geological time, solar time, lunar time, time zones, and space time, among other topics. Each topic is accompanied by project ideas. The instructions are clear and the brightly colored photographs make the book visually appealing.

9.2 Gibson, Gary. **Hearing Sounds.** Illustrated by Tony Kenyon. Photographs by Roger Vlitos. Copper Beech, 1995. ISBN 1-56294-614-5. 32p. 6–8.

This book explores making, hearing, and understanding sounds through twelve easy projects children can do on their own. The text includes instructions for producing some musical and other sound instruments. Children can also learn various laws and principles of physics. Each task is described with cartoons, diagrams, and clear, creative text. The book is useful for developing vocal, music, and early physics skills and knowledge.

9.3 Gibson, Gary. **Making Things Float and Sink.** Illustrated by Tony Kenyon. Photographs by Roger Vlitos. Copper Beech, 1995. ISBN 1-56294-617-X. 32p. 7–9.

Children can explore floating objects in this book of science experiments that includes twelve hands-on projects. Some of the tasks require adult assistance, but most activities could be completed independently by children. The text is a good mixture of theory and practice, complemented by the detailed illustrations.

Other books in the Science for Fun series are *Light and Color* and *Playing with Magnets.*

Anatomy

9.4   Parker, Steve. **The Human Body.** Dorling Kindersley, 1994. ISBN 1-56458-322-8. 59p. 8–12.

Young readers discover the mysteries of their bodies in this authoritative and stimulating book. Detailed, full-color photographs, illustrations, and diagrams explore the vital body organs, the five senses, the care and protection of the body, reproduction, the brain, nerves, the skeleton, and hormones. The emphasis is on finding out about your own body with accurate information and fun activities. A simple table of contents and a two-page index make the information accessible. The small format makes the book appealing and easy to read. It is part of the Eyewitness Explorers series. This book would be useful for parents and teachers teaching children about their bodies and everyday health issues.

Animals

9.5   Bischhoff-Miersch, Andrea, and Michael Bischhoff-Miersch. **Do You Know the Difference?** Illustrated by Christine Faltermayr. North-South, 1994. ISBN 1-55858-371-8. 26p. 5–8.

The similarities and differences between pairs of animals, including rhinoceros and hippopotamus, jaguar and leopard, crocodile and alligator, and shark and dolphin are presented along with carefully chosen facts that will interest young readers. The double-page comparisons combine excellent, lifelike illustrations with smaller illustrations and captions highlighting a particular topic of interest.

9.6   Few, Roger. **Macmillan Children's Guide to Endangered Animals.** Macmillan, 1993. ISBN 0-02-734545-9. 96p. 8–12.

This reference book explores the current threats to wildlife around the world and the measures being take to save animals. Chapters are dedicated to endangered species from each continent, including oceanic islands. Beautiful color diagrams and descriptions introduce each species, and some animals are featured in a more elaborate, double-page format.

9.7   Lauber, Patricia. **Fur, Feathers, and Flippers: How Animals Live Where They Do.** Scholastic, 1994. ISBN 0-590-45071-9. 48p. 9–11.

With striking color photographs and clear, interesting text, this book introduces five distinctly different habitats and animals that live in them. The seas of Antarctica, the grasslands of Africa, forests of New England, the desert of the Southwest, and the tundra of the far north are the specific regions presented. The unique ways in which various animals are suited to their environments are described in text and pictures. A final chapter deals with the adverse effects of human settlement on these areas.

9.8 Machotka, Hana. **Outstanding Outsides.** Photographs by Hana Machotka. Morrow, 1993. ISBN 0-688-11752-X. 32p. 5–6.

Fur, feathers, scales, and shells are just some of the animal body coverings explored in this guess-and-learn book from writer/photographer Machotka. A close-up photo invites the reader to guess the animal. The next page shows the entire animal and gives a simple explanation of its body covering. The format is inviting and informative for the young reader. This book is suitable for science activities related to animals.

9.9 Rauzon, Mark J. **Skin, Scales, Feathers, and Fur.** Lothrop, 1993. ISBN 0-688-10232-8. 24p. 5–8.

This introduction to different kinds of animal hides is written in easy, accessible language and uses beautiful color photographs to support the underlying message that it is up to humans to protect the natural protective cover of animals, be it scales, skin, fur, or feathers.

9.10 Taylor, David. **Nature's Creatures of the Dark.** Dial, 1993. ISBN 0-8037-1631-1. unpaged. 6–10.

This beautiful pop-up book glows in the dark. Each spread introduces a pop-up night creature and is filled with information. A small folded flap on the right presents the name of the creature and interesting facts about it, then unfolds to more pictures. Some of the pop-out pictures contain delicate extensions that must be handled with care.

9.11 Wood, A. J. **Egg! A Dozen Eggs. What Will They Be?** Illustrated by Stella Stilwell. Little, Brown, 1993. ISBN 0-316-81616-7. 28p. 5–8.

Readers must unfold each page to discover what animal hatches out of twelve different eggs in this imaginative book. One page of text offers clues as to which animal it could be and invites the reader to open the fold. The text also indicates that other information about the animal can be found under the fold. The illustrations are accurate, informative, and colorful. The interactive nature of the book invites repeated readings. This book would be useful for science studies on animals born from eggs and for discussion on different ways of making books.

Animal Behavior

9.12   Arnosky, Jim. **I See Animals Hiding.** Illustrated by Jim Arnosky. Scholastic, 1995. ISBN 0-590-48143-6. unpaged. 5–7.

This visual exploration of animal adaptation uses watercolor illustrations to depict animals camouflaged to blend in with the habitats in which they live. The text is an informative presentation of adaptation and survival, and the pictures provide opportunities to develop visual discrimination skills. Some examples are the gray winter coats of deer hiding among the leafless and gray woods of a winter landscape, arctic foxes and owls invisible in their white coats against the snow, and the striped bittern looking like a half-dozen cattails buried in a clump of other cattails.

9.13   Bowen, Betsy. **Tracks in the Wild.** Illustrated by Betsy Bowen. Little, Brown, 1993. ISBN 0-316-10377-2. 32p. 6–10.

Enhanced by beautiful woodcut prints and quotes about nature by well-known Native American leaders, the informative text provides young naturalists with an understanding of wild animals, each with its distinctive track, habitat, and means of survival. Children who enjoy learning the names of dinosaurs will be interested in the Latin names provided for each of the animals, including the black bear, moose, and red fox.

9.14   Brandenburg, Jim. **To the Top of the World: Adventures with Arctic Wolves.** Photographs by Jim Brandenburg. Walker, 1993. ISBN 0-8027-8219-1. 44p. 8–12.

Author/photographer Jim Brandenburg gives a compelling account of his experience in living close to a wolf pack on a remote Ellesmere Island. The simple text and superb color photographs depict the pack members, their characteristics, and the hierarchy that defines the position of each wolf in the pack. The myth of the wolf as villain is dispelled and we are left with an appreciation of the wolf's remarkable adaptation to its harsh environment. The photograph of a lone wolf seated on an iceberg, illuminated by a single shaft of light, is an awe-inspiring sight. Not surprisingly, the author regards this photograph as one of his greatest photographic achievements.

9.15 Brent, Isabelle. **An Alphabet of Animals.** Illustrated by Isabelle Brent. Little, Brown, 1993. ISBN 0-316-10852-9. 56p. 9–11.

This book features an exotic animal for each letter of the alphabet, followed by an exquisite illustration of the creature. Both the text and illustrations are bordered with gold-illuminated designs. The animals are rare or unusual in most cases, so the text is full of fascinating facts. Although the book's small size makes it unsuitable for use with large groups, this book is worth cherishing for its beauty and interesting information.

9.16 Facklam, Margery. **What Does the Crow Know? The Mysteries of Animal Intelligence.** Illustrated by Pamela Johnson. Sierra, 1994. ISBN 0-87156-544-7. 48p. 8–14.

An excellent introduction to animal intelligence, this book will help stimulate appreciation and respect for the animal world in any reader. The book includes entertaining anecdotes from scientific studies with horses, cats, gorillas, parrots, crows, elephants, whales, chimpanzees, dogs, monkeys, dolphins, and sea otters. This text would provide an excellent introduction to evolutionary theory or the nature of learning in all species.

9.17 Ganeri, Anita. **Animals in Disguise.** Illustrated by Halli Verrinder. Simon & Schuster, 1995. ISBN 0-689-80264-1. 24p. 5–9.

The various ways in which ten animals use camouflage to protect themselves and to surprise their prey are presented through brief, interesting text and detailed illustrations, five with well-designed, see-through overlay pages. This book will be enjoyed by both the beginner and the more knowledgeable child.

9.18 George, Jean Craighead. **Animals Who Have Won Our Hearts.** Illustrated by Christine Herman Merrill. HarperCollins, 1994. ISBN 0-06-021543-7. 56p. 9–11.

These ten true stories describe interesting animals who have led heroic or unusual lives. Koko the gorilla learned to use sign language. The Pacing White Mustang was legendary for his speed. Smokey Bear, a badly burned bear cub, became the inspiration for a successful campaign to publicize forest fire prevention. The simply written text is interspersed with color illustrations. Children who love animals will love these stories.

9.19 Hirschi, Ron. **Dance with Me.** Photographs by Thomas D. Mangelsen. Cobblehill, 1995. ISBN 0-525-65204-3. 30p. 5–10.

The concept of movement in nature as dance springs to life in the language and photography of this appealing book. Images of a nightingale hovering over a flower, a prairie chicken strutting and leaping in a mating dance, and butterflies filling the air with gentle motion please the eye. The ways in which jackrabbits, polar bears, eagles, and whales can be seen to dance adds a level of excitement. This book could be an engaging introduction to the exploration of movement in a physical education class, or could provide motivation for writing about nature in a new way.

9.20 Hirschi, Ron. **A Time for Babies.** Photographs by Thomas D. Mangelsen. Dutton, 1993. ISBN 0-525-65095-4. 31p. 5–7.

This photoessay for the beginning reader focuses on the critical time when animal young are born. The simple, interesting text portrays the time of year when animal babies are born, the role of parents, and the unique characteristics of several birds and mammals. The captioned color photographs complement the text and enhance the overall reading experience. This book could be used for science discussions about animals and their young. It could be read aloud or independently. Also in the series are *A Time for Playing* and *A Time for Singing.*

9.21 Hirschi, Ron. **A Time for Sleeping.** Photographs by Thomas D. Mangelsen. Dutton, 1993. ISBN 0-525-65128-4. 31p. 5–7.

This simple, evocative text and the excellent color photographs inform the reader about the sleeping habits of several animals. The book explores where the animals sleep, how they find safe places to sleep, and their unique habits. This book lends itself to reading aloud and to stimulating discussion about sleep. The book will evoke strong, positive feelings toward animals.

9.22 Morris, Desmond. **The World of Animals.** Illustrated by Peter Barrett. Viking, 1993. ISBN 0-670-85184-1. 128p. 8–12.

With the young reader in mind, Morris examines two dozen animals in their natural habitat and provides new insights into their lives. Through a blending of fact and anecdotal account, he reveals how the animals eat, sleep, mate, care for their young, and attempt to survive in a world that threatens their survival. The detailed, full-page illustrations of each animal, combined with smaller illustrations depicting a particular physical trait or behavior, make this a book children can enjoy on their own or share with an adult.

9.23 Patent, Dorothy Hinshaw. **Hugger to the Rescue.** Photographs by William Munoz. Dutton, 1994. ISBN 0-525-65161-6. 32p. 5–8.

This book shows how Newfoundland dogs are trained to find and rescue victims in avalanches and earthquakes and in the water. The natural lifesaving instincts of these creatures make them amenable to training. The text and photographs chronicle the training procedure, including some humorous shots of the dog in "uniform," hanging from a rope, and playing at home. This is a good book for dog lovers and those interested in unusual occupations.

9.24 Schmidt, Jeremy. **In the Village of the Elephants.** Photographs by Ted Wood. Walker, 1994. ISBN 0-8027-8226-4. 32p. 9–11.

The challenges faced by a young Indian boy training to become an elephant driver, a mahout, are presented through interesting, accessible text and color photographs. Young children will be intrigued to learn of the many ways in which elephants are an integral part of the life and culture of the Kurambas people of southern India.

9.25 Whayne, Susanne Sanatoro. **Night Creatures.** Illustrated by Steven Schindler. Simon & Schuster, 1993. ISBN 0-671-73395-8. 45p. 6–10.

Animals from various habitats who are active at night are introduced in this evocative book. The book begins with a short introduction to the concepts of diurnal and nocturnal activity. It continues with detailed information on dozens of animals categorized as sky, country, northern forest, cool forest, rainforest, desert, and ocean creatures. The sensitive, detailed paintings add mystery, wonder, and a sense of discovery to the fascinating subject of nocturnal animals.

9.26 Woelflein, Luise. **Forest Animals.** Illustrated by Barbara Gibson. Scholastic, 1993. ISBN 0-590-46005-6. 10p. 5–8.

This nonfictional pop-up book presents facts about forest animals such as koalas and mandrills in a guessing-game format. Each page opens to reveal the pop-up animal described in the text. Two other interesting animals, the poison frog and crested porcupine, are illustrated and featured in smaller print along with the pop-up. The book is filled with useful information about animals in an appealing format. The same author/illustrator team produced *Desert Animals.*

Birds

9.27   Arnold, Caroline. **On the Brink of Extinction: The California Condor.** Photographs by Michael Wallace. Harcourt Brace, 1993. ISBN 0-15-257990-7. 48p. 8–12.

This readable book recounts the efforts of conservationists to save the California condor from extinction. Arnold and Wallace's informative photoessay chronicles how scientists captured the last free-flying condors and bred them in captivity. The book is filled with great detail, interesting facts, and breathtaking photographs of this magnificent bird. The story reaches a climax with the successful release of the condors to the wild.

9.28   Bernhard, Emery. **Eagles: Lions of the Sky.** Illustrated by Durga Bernhard. Holiday House, 1994. ISBN 0-8234-1105-2. 32p. 6–8.

This informative nonfiction book explores behavior patterns and myths concerning the eagle. The text introduces various species and discusses their role in Native American cultures. In addition, it outlines details about the flight process, sight, wing construction, hunting practices, and mating habits of eagles. A concluding glossary sets out relevant terms. Other fine books by this author/illustrator team are *Reindeer, Ladybug,* and *Dragonfly.*

9.29   Casey, Denise. **Big Birds.** Photographs by Jackie Gilmore. Dutton, 1993. ISBN 0-525-65121-7. 44p. 5–8.

This early introduction to ornithology includes large color photographs and simple descriptions of large birds from around the world, both flying and nonflying varieties. The basic physics of flying are explored, as well as the unique characteristics of each species.

9.30   Craighead, Charles. **The Eagle and the River.** Photographs by Tom Mangelsen. Macmillan, 1994. ISBN 0-02-762265-7. 32p. 9–11.

Spectacular color photographs, with close-up shots of birds and animals, recount a winter day along the Snake River in Wyoming. Although the descriptive and visual images effectively present the countryside, river, and wildlife, the main focus is on the great American eagle and its daily struggle for survival.

9.31   Demuth, Patricia Brennan. **Cradles in the Trees: The Story of Bird Nests.** Illustrated by Suzanne Barnes. Macmillan, 1994. ISBN 0-02-728466-2. 32p. 5–7.

In interesting text accessible to the emerging reader, this author/illustrator team provides a fascinating look at a variety of bird nests. Details of the locations, materials, and construction of nests are presented in a manner that will captivate young children.

9.32 Ling, Mary. **Penguin.** Photographs by Neil Fletcher. Dorling Kindersley, 1993. ISBN 1-56458-312-0. 21p. 5–7.

Excellent border illustrations, repeated in the endpapers, reflect the full-spread depictions of the stages of penguin growth from hatching to adulthood, when the cycle begins anew with the birth of new chicks. The conclusion shows an excellent summary. As in the rest of this series, the photography and one-sentence text make this a superb selection for early research and discovery by young children.

9.33 Markle, Sandra. **Outside and Inside Birds.** Bradbury, 1994. ISBN 0-02-762312-2. 40p. 9–11.

Another in the Outside and Inside series by the author, this book takes a close look at birds. Questions woven into the clear, accessible text encourage children to examine different aspects of bird behavior such as how they fly, what they eat, and how they care for their young. Anatomical features of birds are also presented, as are particular characteristics of specific birds. A pronunciation key and glossary are also included. The excellent color photographs show both the external features and the internal organs of bird bodies.

9.34 McMillan, Bruce. **Beach for the Birds.** Illustrated by Bruce McMillan. Houghton Mifflin, 1993. ISBN 0-395-64050-4. 32p. 10–12.

This authoritative photoessay describes the life of the least tern, an endangered species found on coastal beaches in Maine. Information on their feeding and breeding habits, the raising of chicks, and the role of each parent is supported by detailed color photographs that work exceptionally well with the text. Themes such as the delicate balance of life and the tern's natural place in its coastal habitat are carefully woven into the text. The central theme—that by learning more about this bird, we can ensure its survival—makes this book an excellent choice for students interested in environmental issues.

9.35 McMillan, Bruce. **Penguins at Home: Gentoos of Antarctica.** Photographs by Bruce McMillan. Houghton Mifflin, 1993. ISBN 0-395-66560-4. 32p. 6–11.

Bold topic headings on each page are supported by dramatic color photographs and a paragraph of interesting factual text elaborating on the topic and the picture. Children will learn of the ways in which gentoo penguins are perfectly adapted to the harsh environment of the Antarctic Peninsula. The author's enthusiasm for these unusual, gentle, and appealing birds adds to the appeal of this book.

9.36 Patent, Dorothy Hinshaw. **Looking at Penguins.** Photographs by Graham Robertson. Holiday House, 1993. ISBN 0-8234-1037-4. 40p. 7–9.

The physical characteristics of penguins, their hunting and feeding habits, and their breeding rituals are described clearly. Various species, including the little blue fairy penguin, the harlequin, and the crested rockhopper are shown. Details such as the courting habits of the emperor penguins, who court for about eight weeks of Antarctic winter and stay on the ice the entire time without eating, will appeal to any student. Conservation is stressed.

9.37 Taylor, Barbara. **The Bird Atlas.** Illustrated by Richard Orr. Dorling Kindersley, 1993. ISBN 1-56458-327-9. 64p. 9–12.

Moving from continent to continent, the author describes the most interesting and important birds found in regions such as deserts, forests and woodlands, savannah, and specific mountain ranges. This attractive pictorial atlas introduces young readers to more than 270 birds, giving key facts about each bird's characteristics and behavior. Supporting the well-written text are stunning illustrations and maps that pinpoint each bird's habitat. A concluding chapter provides information on endangered species and what can be done to preserve them. Confirmed birdwatchers and those new to the topic will be captivated by this book, a browser's delight.

Insects and Spiders

9.38 Bernhard, Emery. **Dragonfly.** Illustrated by Durga Bernhard. Holiday House, 1993. ISBN 0-8234-1033-1. 32p. 5–8.

This excellent nonfiction book introduces young readers to the fascinating world of dragonflies. The writer describes the physical characteristics, feeding habits, life cycle, and natural environment of the dragonfly. The book combines a simple scientific text with accurate, appealing pictures. The glossary and carefully labeled diagrams present a great deal of information for the young researcher. This book would be helpful during science units on insects and as an independent reading choice for budding entomologists.

9.39 Demuth, Patricia Brennan. **Those Amazing Ants.** Illustrated by S. D. Schindler. Macmillan, 1994. ISBN 0-02-728467-0. 32p. 5–8.

In easy-to-read, highly informative text and with clear, detailed illustrations, the fascinating world of ants is engagingly presented. Young readers will be intrigued and often surprised by what they learn about these insects.

9.40 Facklam, Margery. **The Big Bug Book.** Illustrated by Paul Facklam. Little, Brown, 1994. ISBN 0-316-27389-9. 32p. 9–12.

The author begins with an explanation of why insects are limited in size. Thirteen of the world's largest insects are then examined and each is featured on a spread with accessible explanatory text and accompanying illustrations. To convey their actual size, each insect is shown with a common household item: a Goliath beetle crawls across a plate of cookies, an Owlet moth flies in front of shirts in a closet, and a Hercules beetle is shown with an apple. The characteristics and habits of the insects are described and illustrated with realistic, full-color, airbrushed paintings that will fascinate children.

9.41 Gaffney, Michael. **Secret Forests: A Collection of Hidden Creepy Crawly Bugs and Insects.** Illustrated by Michael Gaffney. Artists and Writers Guild, 1994. ISBN 0-307-17505-7. 32 p. 8–11.

This entertaining and informative book prepares children for entomological and forest field work. Groups of insects associated with particular types of forests, trees, or subsystems within forests are introduced on a two-page taxonomy. This is followed by another two pages of wordless illustrations in which the classified insects are embedded in their natural forest habitats. The illustrations invite students to test their recognition and recall of the insects they have learned. This format is very useful for helping children to develop their perceptual and attention skills while studying insect taxonomy.

9.42 Gibbons, Gail. **Spiders.** Illustrated by Gail Gibbons. Holiday House, 1993. ISBN 0-8234-1006-4. 32p. 6–8.

Gibbons presents detailed information on spiders through this book's successful format and appealing style. The simple explanations of the physical characteristics, behaviors, habitats, and different kinds of spiders are enhanced by the clear, bright illustrations. This book is an intriguing introduction to the fascinating world of spiders.

9.43   Hariton, Anca. **Butterfly Story.** Illustrated by Anca Hariton. Dutton, 1995. ISBN 0-525-45212-5. 32p. 5–9.

This would be a fine choice along with other butterfly books in a collection. The clear illustrations and straightforward text make the book very readable, even for young children. Full-page illustrations depict other insects, birds, and animals in the butterflies' habitats.

9.44   Johnson, Sylvia A. **A Beekeeper's Year.** Photographs by Nick Von Ohlen. Little, Brown, 1994. ISBN 0-316-46745-6. 32p. 9–11.

This interesting and informative photoessay describes the seasonal work of a hobby beekeeper, John Wetzler. He says his main job "is to assist bees in doing what comes naturally." The reader learns how beekeepers go about their work, what tools they use, and how honey is produced and harvested. The format of this clear and descriptive text includes subject headings, highlighted key words, and a glossary of beekeeping terms. The book evokes the pleasure of beekeeping as a hobby and the satisfaction of supplying the local farmers' market with fresh honey. This book could form the cornerstone of a unit of study on bees and beekeeping. It would also be of general interest to intermediate level students.

9.45   Lasky, Kathryn. **Monarchs.** Photographs by Christopher G. Knight. Harcourt Brace, 1993. ISBN 0-15-255296-0. 63p. 9–11.

The text conveys much valuable information about the migration and metamorphosis of the beautiful monarch butterfly. It includes useful ideas for the study of conservation. The photography is excellent and supports the text well. This selection would appeal to students interested in conservation.

9.46   Markle, Sandra. **Outside and Inside Spiders.** Bradbury, 1994. ISBN 0-02-762314-9. 40p. 9–11.

In this introductory book about spiders, Sandra Markle provides young readers with a valuable guide to this fascinating topic. Through simple, direct language, young readers learn fascinating details about spiders' webs, eggs, and more. Throughout the text, as well as on a "Looking Back" page, children are invited to answer questions related to the stunning photographs that accompany the text. Enhanced by the pronunciation guide, glossary, and index, this book gives children many reasons to appreciate these complex creatures. Others in the series are *Outside and Inside You* and *Outside and Inside Trees.*

9.47 Micucci, Charles. **The Life and Times of the Honeybee.** Illustrated by Charles Micucci. Ticknor & Fields, 1995. ISBN 0-395-65968-X. 32p. 6–9.

A comprehensive discussion of the honeybee is presented in two-page chapters with clearly labeled diagrams and watercolor illustrations. Topics such as beekeeping, how bees make honey, their life cycle, and the history of this useful insect are described in lively, accessible text. Children will find the factual information and illustrations fascinating and at times amusing.

Mammals

9.48 Bash, Barbara. **Shadows of Night: The Hidden World of the Little Brown Bat.** Illustrated by Barbara Bash. Sierra, 1993. ISBN 0-87156-562-5. 32p. 6–8.

Bash has written a lucid, informative introduction to the mysterious world of the little brown bat. The life cycle of this intriguing mammal is explained in an easy text for young readers. Bash's watercolors add detail to the information and provide atmosphere for the reading. Three "More about Bats" pages provide additional information. This would be very helpful in projects on mammals and for children's general reading.

9.49 Bonners, Susan. **Hunter in the Snow: The Lynx.** Illustrated by Susan Bonners. Little, Brown, 1994. ISBN 0-316-10201-6. 32p. 6–10.

Clear, engaging text complemented by stunning pastel illustrations detail the environment and behavior of the lynx, a threatened member of the cat family. Children will be fascinated by the information and charmed by the pictures of this elusive predator.

9.50 Brandenburg, Jim. **An American Safari: Adventures on the North American Plain.** Photographs by Jim Brandenburg. Walker, 1995. ISBN 0-8027-8319-8. 44p. 9–12.

Brandenburg's stunning photoessay conveys both the beauty and the destruction of this ecologically sensitive prairie environment. The author focuses on the wildlife of present-day Minnesota and South Dakota and describes the interdependence of animals and the detrimental effect human activity has had on some species. The author recounts the experiences that turned him from hunting to photographing wildlife. This book urges young readers to embrace the dream of preserving what remains of the American prairie.

9.51 Esbensen, Barbara Juster. **Playful Slider: The North American River Otter.** Illustrated by Mary Barrett Brown. Little, Brown, 1993. ISBN 0-316-24977-7. 32p. 6–10.

Following the success of their collaboration in *Great Northern Diver: The Loon,* Esbensen and Brown have created another poetic, inviting book, this time about the North American river otter. Within a narrative framework, the informative text details the river otter's behavior and characteristics. Full-color artwork that is accurate and engaging enhances this text. One year in the life cycle of a river otter is described, beginning and ending with its frolicking adventures in the snow. These playful mammals seem to be filled with an endless sense of fun. This book could be read aloud or independently.

9.52 Gilks, Helen. **Bears.** Illustrated by Andrew Bale. Ticknor & Fields, 1993. ISBN 0-395-66899-9. 31p. 8–11.

Children fascinated by bears will be intrigued to learn about eight species of bear, each represented by full-color illustrations and interesting factual text. This is an excellent introduction to similarities and differences among bears such as the polar bear, sloth bear, giant panda, and American black bear. Details of their physical characteristics, behavior, and habits and of the complex relationship between bears and humans are discussed.

9.53 Grace, Eric S. **Apes.** Sierra, 1995. ISBN 0-87156-365-7. 62p. 8–12.

This fascinating look at chimpanzees, gorillas, and orangutans touches on such topics as the evolution of hands that can grasp objects and the importance of stereoscopic vision. Separate chapters provide detailed information about the characteristics and behavior of each of these species of primates. Both text and photographs will inspire young readers to care about and become involved in the attempts to save these remarkable animals. Other valuable books in the Sierra Club Wildlife Library series are *Snakes* and *Seals.*

9.54 Grace, Eric S. **Elephants.** Sierra, 1993. ISBN 0-87156-538-2. 64p. 8–12.

Clear, descriptive text, captioned diagrams, and spectacular color photographs introduce the elephant in its natural habitat. Eric Grace relates his personal encounters with elephants and then examines the elephant's prehistoric ancestors and the characteristics of the present-day elephants in Africa and Asia. With information based on several research studies carried out in the bush country of East Africa, we follow a herd through a typical day. We are present at the birth of a baby elephant and share in its first clumsy and amusing efforts at learning how to use its trunk. Fascinating details are included about elephant anatomy and family life, the never-ending search for food and water, and how the elephant is becoming an endangered species. Special feature pages highlight some strange but true stories such as that of Ahmed, the elephant with the world's largest tusks. An index is included.

9.55   Hansard, Peter. **A Field Full of Horses.** Illustrated by Kenneth Lilly. Candlewick, 1994. ISBN 1-56402-302-8. 26p. 5–8.

Interesting facts about horses are delivered through the narrator's sensory commentary during a walk and through the captions that accompany the pictures. This book appeals to children's love for and interest in horses.

9.56   Hirschi, Ron. **When the Wolves Return.** Photographs by Ron Hirschi. Cobblehill, 1995. ISBN 0-525-65144-6. 32p. 9–11.

This text provides valuable information supported by excellent photography. The interdependence of animals and their importance in the life cycle are presented in a story format. Various American conservation agencies and aspects of the law are quoted in the book.

9.57   Hoshino, Michio. **The Grizzly Bear Family Book.** Photographs by Michio Hoshino. North-South, 1994. ISBN 1-55858-350-5. 50p. 8–11.

In a first-person narrative with stunning photographs, the author provides a compelling account of the life cycle and habitat of the grizzly bear. The young reader will be captivated by this sensitive portrayal of the bear and of the beauty and richness of the Alaskan landscape.

9.58   Irvine, Georganne. **Blanca and Arusha: Tales of Two Big Cats.** Simon & Schuster, 1995. ISBN 0-671-87191-9. 45p. 8–11.

One of the Zoo World series, this engaging book tells the story of two endangered big cats: a white tiger named Blanca and a cheetah named Arusha. Both cats end up at the San Diego Zoo, where their stories begin. The text and remarkable photographs explore Blanca's training program and the life-long friendship between Arusha and a golden retriever named Anna. The photographic documentation is particularly rich and interesting, but the stories are compelling by themselves. A concluding section outlines the various species and characteristics of big cats, including lions, leopards, jaguars, cheetahs, and tigers.

9.59   Januck, Andrea, and Larry Points. **Assateague: Island of the Wild Ponies.** Macmillan, 1993. ISBN 0-02-774695-X. 32p. 5–8.

Spring returns to Assateague Island, home of the wild ponies made famous in the Misty books. The life cycle of these ponies is clearly described as they roam the various habitats of the long barrier island. The color photographs enrich the text, showing the wild beauty of the island and the daily habits of the ponies. Other animals and plants that live on the island are also described. This photoessay would be of special interest to devoted fans of horse books, but would also be useful during studies of unique habitats or general environmental activities.

9.60   Knight, Linsay. **Sierra Club Book of Small Mammals.** Sierra, 1993. ISBN 0-87156-525-0. 68p. 9–11.

Students doing research on mammals will find this a treasure trove. Many of the unusual mammals of the five hundred threatened species throughout the world are covered. The aye-aye, black-footed ferret, loris, maned wolf, pangolin, soledon, star-nosed mole, tamandua, and yapok are just a few of the mammals given brief descriptions, often with an accompanying photograph. Because not every detail of reproduction, habitat, and diet is given, the young reader will be motivated to do further research. Did you know that the pangolin is the only mammal with a covering of horny scales? Or that the platypus can inject venom with his spur? Or that the maned wolf looks like a red dog on stilts? These fascinating details will lead to further inquiry.

9.61   Lemmon, Tess. **Apes.** Illustrated by John Butler. Ticknor & Fields, 1993. ISBN 0-395-66901-4. 31p. 9–11.

The similarities and differences among four kinds of apes—gorillas, chimpanzees, orangutans, and gibbons—are presented through full-color illustrations and well-written, accessible text. Children will enjoy learning more about these fascinating species and how people worldwide are working to ensure their survival.

9.62 Lindblad, Lisa. **The Serengeti Migration: Africa's Animals on the Move.** Photographs by Sven-Olof Lindblad. Hyperion, 1994. ISBN 1-56282-669-7. 40p. 9–11.

This book takes the reader on a photographic safari across the African plains, witnessing the annual migration of the vast herds of wildebeest and zebra through Tanzania's Serengeti National Park. The simple, clear text and brilliant, close-up color photographs capture the sounds and sights of this extraordinary event. They also detail the part this migration plays in the cycle of Serengeti wildlife. The captions interpret the photos, identify animals, and provide information about the landscape and climate. A glossary is included as well as an author's note on the Masai people, who still share the Serengeti with the animals.

9.63 Maestro, Betsy. **Bats: Night Flyers.** Illustrated by Giulio Maestro. Scholastic, 1994. ISBN 0-590-46150-8. 32p. 6–8.

A wealth of detail is presented about this intelligent and unusual nocturnal animal. Information as to the types of bats, where they live, and their habits and behaviors is provided in accessible text and appealing illustrations. Many of the myths surrounding these creatures are dispelled and the importance of protecting their habitat is emphasized.

9.64 Meltzer, Milton. **Hold Your Horses! A Feedbag Full of Fact and Fable.** HarperCollins, 1995. ISBN 0-06-024477-1. 133p. 8–12.

Milton Meltzer discusses the role of horses in history, characteristics of particular breeds, horse care, and biographies of some famous animals. His focus, however, is on the domestication of the horse and the influence it has had on the lives of people over the centuries. The black-and-white reproductions and photographs complement the carefully researched, intriguing information.

9.65 Miller, Debbie S. **A Caribou Journey.** Illustrated by Jon Van Zyle. Little, Brown, 1994. ISBN 0-316-57380-9. 32p. 5–9.

The hardships and dangers of the annual caribou are heightened by focusing on a female caribou, her yearling, and her newborn as they struggle for survival in the harsh environment of the Arctic tundra. The drama of this centuries-old migration is captured by evocative acrylic paintings.

9.66   Patent, Dorothy Hinshaw. **Why Mammals Have Fur.** Photographs by William Munoz. Cobblehill, 1995. ISBN 0-525-65141-1. 26p. 6–10.

Through beautiful color photographs and a thorough text, children can enjoy learning all about fur and different kinds of mammals. What is fur? How does fur help animals camouflage? Why do some animals have long hair? These are a few of the questions answered in this clearly organized resource book. Children are also introduced to the ways in which humans use animal fur. An index is included. *Eagles of America* is another fine book by this author/illustrator team.

9.67   Ryden, Hope. **Out of the Wild: The Story of Domesticated Animals.** Photographs by Hope Ryden. Lodestar, 1995. ISBN 0-525-67485-3. 56p. 8–12.

This book traces the history and evolution of various domesticated animals and documents how their lives have diverged from those of their counterparts in the wild. Photographs of fifteen domestic animals are shown along with photographs of their cousins in the wild. The text outlines the characteristics that contributed to each animal's domestication.

9.68   Simon, Seymour. **Wolves.** HarperCollins, 1993. ISBN 0-06-022531-9. 32p. 5–8.

Does the wolf deserve the bad reputation it has been given in fiction? The author poses this question and then examines the facts. The relationship of the wolf to the dog is shown. Information is given about the wolf's anatomy, family and pack life, and hunting behavior. Gradually the myths surrounding the wolf are dispelled as the author reveals how well the wolf adapts to its harsh environment. The informal text is readily accessible to the young reader. Stunning color photographs convey the beauty of the landscape and the magnificence of these animals.

9.69   **The Visual Dictionary of the Horse.** Dorling Kindersley, 1994. ISBN 1-56458-504-2. 64p. 9–12.

Another in the Eyewitness Visual Dictionaries series, this highly illustrated text introduces the reader to every detail of the horse. Chapters deal with the external and internal features of its anatomy, development and growth, and the horse family. It also covers different breeds of horses and all aspects of equestrian activities such as grooming, bits and bridles, jumping, and racing. This will be a very popular book with young horse lovers.

Marine Life

9.70   Aliki. **My Visit to the Aquarium.** Illustrated by Aliki. Harper-Collins, 1993. ISBN 0-06-021458-9. 34p. 5–8.

In this colorful book, young readers are introduced to a wide variety of aquatic creatures and habitats they might find at an aquarium. The vivid, detailed illustrations and labels make this book a valuable and intriguing source of information on life science topics ranging from marine mammals and other ocean creatures to animals that live along the seashore and in rivers, tropical rainforests, and coral reefs. Narrated from a child's perspective, the text is stimulating and easily accessible.

9.71   Burnie, David. **Seashore.** Dorling Kindersley, 1994. ISBN 1-56458-323-6. 61p. 5–7.

This pocket-size book offers the young explorer a beginner's guide to life along the seashore. It includes information on a wide variety of plants and animals that inhabit the beaches, cliffs, and shallow waters of various seashores. The book includes well-captioned and clearly labeled color reproductions, accurate illustrations, and a basic table of contents and index. Young readers are encouraged to engage in naturalistic observations such as bird-watching and beach detection using a notebook to sketch or record. Several simple projects demonstrate scientific principles or suggest activities for displaying found materials. This book is part of a series of twelve titles aimed at young readers interested in exploring the world around them. Other titles include *Birds, Trees, Mammals,* and *The Human Body.*

9.72   Kraus, Scott, and Kenneth Mallory. **Search for the Right Whale.** Crown, 1993. ISBN 0-517-57844-1. 36p. 9–11.

Two authoritative writers describe long-term scientific studies on the North Atlantic right whale. These studies add to our understanding of right whales and their survival. Separate sections of text contain numerous facts about right whales and maps of their locations. The excellent photographs and diagrams are well-captioned, providing another layer of information. A central theme is the importance of learning more about these mammals in order to help them survive. This outstanding book will intrigue children, motivating them to learn more about the efforts of scientists to reverse the tide of extinction.

9.73   Martin, James. **Tentacles: The Amazing World of Octopus, Squid, and Their Relatives.** Illustrated by Gaylord Welker. Crown, 1993. ISBN 0-517-59149-9. 32p. 6–10.

This is an interesting and well-designed book on cephalopods, members of the mollusk family. A general introduction to cephalopods is followed by detailed sections on the defense mechanisms, reproduction, and other characteristics of the nautilus, octopus, squid, and cuttlefish. Color photographs add excitement and wonder to the overall presentation. Several diagrams and simple captions provide extra information. The glossary and index help access the information. This book would be useful for general reader interest or as part of marine life studies.

9.74   Patent, Dorothy Hinshaw. **Killer Whales.** Photographs by John K. B. Ford. Holiday House, 1993. ISBN 0-8234-0999-6. 31p. 6–8.

This informative and up-to-date introduction to the orca is written in a straightforward style with no attempt to romanticize this powerful, beautiful animal. The photoessay style will capture readers' curiosity and motivate them to learn more. The photographs are well-captioned. A simple index offers access to the text. This book will support curriculum topics on ocean life, mammals, and ecology.

9.75   Pringle, Laurence. **Coral Reefs: Earth's Undersea Treasures.** Simon & Schuster, 1995. ISBN 0-689-80286-2. 45p. 9–12.

Coral, one of the earth's most fascinating and complex creatures, is shown in its many shapes, sizes, and colors through striking color photographs. In clear and accessible text, the author describes the structure, behavior, and wonders of coral reef systems. The relationship between coral and other marine animals is explored and the increasing threats to this ecosystem by pollution and human activities are thoughtfully examined. Teachers will find this a valuable book for science study.

9.76   Shahan, Sherry. **Barnacles Eat with Their Feet: Delicious Facts about the Tide Pool Food Chain.** Photographs by Sherry Shahan. Millbrook, 1995. ISBN 1-56294-922-5. 31p. 5–8.

Close inspection of a tide pool reveals many well-hidden and tiny sea creatures that may be eating with their feet or tentacles. Color photographs are used to highlight some of the most interesting creatures that can be found in tide pools. With little more than a paragraph on each plant or crustacean, students will be able to get an overview of the eating habits and living arrangements of creatures living in tide pools. An index and glossary are included.

9.77 Simon, Seymour. **Sharks.** HarperCollins, 1995. ISBN 0-06-023029-0. 32p. 7–10.

Known to exist 200 million years before the first dinosaurs, sharks continue to fascinate and excite children, who are always eager to learn more about this fearsome sea creature. In this striking photoessay, Simon describes many aspects of the shark including the senses, body structure, differences among species, and behavior. Although the photographs present the shark as fierce and terrifying, the author attempts to discredit the sensationalism and myths surrounding the shark.

9.78 Sobol, Richard, and Jonah Sobol. **Seal Journey.** Photographs by Richard Sobol. Dutton, 1993. ISBN 0-525-65126-8. 32p. 5–9.

This excellent photoessay recounts a trip taken by Richard Sobol and his eight-year-old son, Jonah, to the ice fields of the Gulf of St. Lawrence during the spring, when harp seals have their pups. Here the seals' birth and the early weeks of their lives are detailed in an informative, informal style. The color photographs focusing on the harsh environment complement the candid text. This book would be useful to read aloud, to study the harp seal, or to supplement ecology and conservation studies.

9.79 Swanson, Diane. **Safari Beneath the Sea: The Wonder World of the North Pacific Coast.** Sierra, 1994. ISBN 0-87156-415-7. 58p. 9–13.

This book on the marine life of the North Pacific is rich with fascinating details on plants, fish, mammals, and other sea creatures. In five chapters with interest-catching titles such as "Spineless Superstars" and "Mind-Boggling Mammals," intermediate students will find plenty of information in the text, boxes with special and unusual information, and beautiful large photographs with bold captions. This visually varied and appealing publication, winner of the Orbis Pictus award, is bound to enrich children's knowledge about life in this area of the marine world.

9.80 Zoehfeld, Kathleen Weidner. **What Lives in a Shell?** Illustrated by Helen K. Davie. HarperCollins, 1994. ISBN 0-06-022998-5. 32p. 5–8.

An engaging and colorfully illustrated early science concept book, this look at the fascinating world of shells as animal homes caters to young children's natural curiosity about nature. The simple yet meaningful text gives information and stimulates young readers' interest with simple questions, inviting them to think about and draw on their own experiences.

Reptiles and Amphibians

9.81   Arnosky, Jim. **All about Alligators.** Illustrated by Jim Arnosky. Scholastic, 1994. ISBN 0-590-46788-3. 26p. 5–8.

With clear, simple language and pleasing watercolor illustrations, the author provides young readers with a fascinating array of facts about alligators. This is an excellent book for young, beginning readers.

9.82   Bernhard, Emery. **Salamanders.** Illustrated by Durga Bernhard. Holiday House, 1995. ISBN 0-8234-1148-6. 32p. 5–8.

The habitat and life cycle of some of the main varieties of salamanders are explained in easy-to-read text and colorful illustrations. As amphibians, most salamanders spend time in and out of the water. Children will be interested in the differences among salamanders, what they eat, and where they can be found. The large illustrations are done in a flat and stylized manner and effectively place the salamanders in the context of their environment, giving the reader a sense of their size, appearance, and ability to camouflage. A glossary is included.

9.83   Gibbons, Gail. **Frogs.** Illustrated by Gail Gibbons. Holiday House, 1993. ISBN 0-8234-1052-8. 32p. 5–8.

This colorful science book on frogs is packed with information for young readers. It begins with a detailed description of their birth, their life as tadpoles, and their growth into adult frogs. Feeding habits, body parts, sounds, enemies, and hibernation are explained in a simple, candid text supported by Gibbons's illustrations. Two pages of labeled illustrations that distinguish frogs from toads are included. This book would be useful for classroom science projects and for interested young readers.

9.84   Lavies, Bianca. **A Gathering of Garter Snakes.** Photographs by Bianca Lavies. Dutton, 1993. ISBN 0-525-45099-8. 32p. 9–11.

In this skillful blending of text and stunning photographs, the author describes the adaptation of the red-sided garter snake to the harsh northern climate of Manitoba, Canada. Detailed information is provided about the emergence of the snakes from the limestone caves in spring, their mating practices, the birth of the young, and the mystery of their mass migration to the distant marshes. The author's fascination with and respect for these snakes are apparent as she writes of the dangers posed by poachers and of the Canadian government's action to protect the snakes.

9.85   Markle, Sandra. **Outside and Inside Snakes.** Macmillan, 1995. ISBN 0-02-762315-7. 40p. 5–8.

Another in the Outside and Inside series, this book offers a close-up of various snakes. Details of how snakes grow, what they eat, and how they move are only a few examples of the wide range of information that children will find interesting. Readers will discover why snakes stick out their tongues and why they eat only once every few weeks. Large color photographs of snakes in various settings and activities are successfully used to illustrate the text and capture the reader's attention. A pronunciation guide and combined glossary and index increase this book's value as a resource in the classroom.

9.86   Snedden, Robert. **What Is an Amphibian?** Illustrated by Adrian Lascom. Sierra, 1994. ISBN 0-87156-469-6. 32p. 9–11.

Excellent photographs, illustrations, and text are filled with interesting details of the physical characteristics and life cycles of frogs, toads, newts, and salamanders. *What Is a Mammal?*, *What Is a Bird?*, and *What Is an Insect?* are other worthwhile books by this author/illustrator team.

Astronomy

9.87   Branley, Franklin M. **Venus: Magellan Explores Our Twin Planet.** HarperCollins, 1994. ISBN 0-06-020298-X. 56p. 9–11.

The planet Venus comes to life in this chronicle of Magellan, the first shuttle-transported planet probe, as it makes its way into the orbit of Venus. The book explores the existing and discovered knowledge of the planet's motion, evolution, surface, structure, magnetism, and climate. Spectacular graphics and photographs accompany the text.

9.88   Gibbons, Gail. **The Planets.** Illustrated by Gail Gibbons. Holiday House, 1993. ISBN 0-8234-1040-4. 32p. 5–8.

Parents and teachers looking for accurate information on the planets for young readers will find this book invaluable. Gibbons begins with a general explanation of what planets are and how they arranged in our solar system. The concepts of orbit, rotation, daytime, and nighttime are also discussed. Two pages are devoted to each planet, including information on size, distance from the sun, and conditions on the planet. The illustrations are accurate, detailed, and interesting. This book offers young readers a great deal of information in an accessible format.

9.89   Krupp, Edwin C. **The Moon and You.** Illustrated by Robin Rector Krupp. Macmillan, 1993. ISBN 0-02-751142-1. 48p. 6–10.

This accurate and up-to-date book contains a wealth of information on the moon. Factual information is presented in an interesting, realistic way. The text includes fascinating details on how the moon is portrayed in the mythology of various cultures. The black-and-white pencil drawings add to the feeling that the moon is a dark, dusty place. The book tells of the involvement of the space program in the exploration of the moon, including some of the new information learned from those lunar missions. This book will be of great interest to space buffs and could be used in science units on astronomy.

9.90   Verdet, Jean-Pierre. **Earth, Sky, and Beyond: A Journey through Space.** Illustrated by Pierre Bon. Lodestar, 1995. ISBN 0-525-67513-2. 43p. 9–11.

This book begins on the earth and reaches into the sky through the treetops. The flight of birds leads us into a remarkable journey through various perspectives of earth, sky, and space. We end up in the far reaches of the universe, where we can appreciate the vastness of space. The illustrations and design are exceptional, capable of stimulating the interest of even the most indifferent reader.

Biology

9.91   Burnie, David. **Dictionary of Nature.** Dorling Kindersley, 1994. ISBN 1-56458-473-9. 192p. 9–12.

This dictionary contains two thousand key words from the natural world and is arranged thematically in chapters. The book begins with clear details on how to use the book, how we study nature, and how it affects our daily lives. Then the reader is guided through the complex and fascinating world of the life sciences with concise descriptions and clear explanations of many biological concepts. Crisp photographs and colorful illustrations fill every page. The information is presented in logical sequence, with each chapter building on the previous one. Biographical sketches of over 150 pioneers of biology are included. The ten-page index makes the wealth of information easily accessible.

9.92 Burnie, David. **Life: Explore the Microscopic World of Cells, Find Out How Living Things Survive, and Investigate the Origins of Life.** Dorling Kindersley, 1994. ISBN 1-56458-477-1. 64p. 9–12.

Including such topics such as fundamental molecules and the components of cells, genetics, reproduction, and the origin of life, this book is an excellent scientific resource book for adults and children alike. The detailed photographs and illustrations are supported by simple, accessible text. Each page deals with a different subject and includes historical and biographical information on discoveries, anatomical information, charts, life cycles, photographs, and representations of up-to-date methods for measuring physiological and biochemical phenomena.

Conservation and Ecology

9.93 Anderson, Joan. **Earth Keepers.** Photographs by George Ancona. Harcourt Brace, 1993. ISBN 0-15-242199-8. 96p. 9–11.

This environmental photoessay explores three earth keepers who have made a significant impact in their communities, the first by organizing youth volunteers to clean up the Hudson River, the second by reclaiming a garbage-laden vacant lot as a community garden, and the third by monitoring and protecting the black bears of Minnesota. The black-and-white photographs work well with the clear, concise text. This is a book for all ages.

9.94 Bash, Barbara. **Ancient Ones: The World of the Old-Growth Douglas Fir.** Illustrated by Barbara Bash. Sierra, 1994. ISBN 0-87156-561-7. 32p. 5–8.

The world of the old-growth forest of the Pacific Northwest, with particular emphasis on the Douglas fir and the teeming life it supports, is strikingly presented through illustration and text. This unique ecosystem, with its intricate web of life, dramatically unfolds and provides young readers with an appreciation of its importance.

9.95   Dunphy, Madeleine. **Here Is the Tropical Rain Forest.** Illustrated by Michael Rothman. Hyperion, 1994. ISBN 1-56282-637-9. 32p. 5–8.

The cumulative text and lush illustrations make this a prize book for children, adults, and all those learning to read. Every page features a new creature who is added to the text. The final page displays all the animals together. This is an excellent book for discussing the interdependence of life and the tropical rainforest in particular.

9.96   Durell, Ann, Jean Craighead George, and Katherine Paterson, editors. **The Big Book for Our Planet.** Dutton, 1993. ISBN 0-525-45119-6. 136p. 9–12.

In the introduction to this book, the editors direct the reader to take "time to think about our planet." Through stories, poems, and nonfiction pieces by notable authors and illustrators, the reader's attention is drawn to some of the environmental problems that threaten our planet. Contributors include Natalie Babbitt, H. M. Hoover, Pam Conrad, Paul O. Zelinsky, and Chris Van Allsburg. Ways are suggested in which "we can work with our planet and not against it." This thought-provoking book conveys an important message in many engaging ways.

9.97   Dvorak, David. **Sea of Grass: The Tallgrass Prairie.** Photographs by David Dvorak. Macmillan, 1994. ISBN 0-02-733245-4. 32p. 5–8.

This is a lyrical evocation in words and photographs of a rare and endangered ecosystem. Seasonal changes, flowers, animals, and grasses are depicted in striking color. This is a useful book for geographical studies as well as for units on conservation.

9.98   George, Jean Craighead. **Everglades.** Illustrated by Wendell Minor. HarperCollins, 1995. ISBN 0-06-021229-2. 32p. 6–9.

Jean Craighead George's simple but eloquent story chronicles a boat ride that five children take through the environmentally sensitive Everglades. Their guide is a storyteller who meticulously details the evolution of this unique place. Wendell Minor's brilliantly realistic paintings make this book come alive, not just as a story, but as an environmental lesson. At the conclusion, readers are inspired to join the five children in putting what they have learned into practice.

9.99   Gilliland, Judith Heide. **River.** Illustrated by Joyce Powzyk. Clarion, 1993. ISBN 0-395-55963-4. 32p. 5–9.

Poetic text and evocative paintings combine to make this an engrossing book for all ages. The book describes the Amazon river from its birth as a trickle in the mountains to its growth as a mighty river that spans four thousand miles. The book captures the intriguing mysteries of the rainforests surrounding the Amazon: the cycle of rain, the multitude of plants and animals, and the sounds and colors. This book could be read aloud and could launch many activities that focus on building respect for the natural world.

9.100   Jordan, Tanis. **Jungle Days Jungle Nights.** Illustrated by Martin Jordan. Kingfisher, 1993. ISBN 1-85697-885-0. 36p. 8–12.

This informative, richly illustrated book is filled with fascinating details about unusual plants and animals of the Amazon rainforest. The text details the unique habits of leafcutter ants, pacos, poison arrow frogs, caimans, and other exotic animals. The large paintings bring us close to the beauty of life in the deep and mysterious jungle. This book would be excellent for reading aloud during class sessions that nurture respect for nature.

9.101   Lauber, Patricia. **Who Eats What? Food Chains and Food Webs.** Illustrated by Holly Keller. HarperCollins, 1995. ISBN 0-06-022981-0. 32p. 5–9.

Through simple watercolor illustrations and straightforward text, children can gain an understanding of what a food chain is, how it works, and why it is important for the health of all animals and people. In discussing food chains on land and in the sea, children will learn about the interconnectedness of animals and plants and develop a better understanding of how important clean air and water are to everyone and everything on earth.

9.102   Lavies, Bianca. **Compost Critters.** Photographs by Bianca Lavies. Dutton, 1993. ISBN 0-525-44763-6. 32p. 9–11.

This book introduces the reader to the specialized community of tiny insects, fungi, and microscopic bacteria that transform compost material into nutrient-rich humus. Although many of the creatures shown are thought of as creepy or disgusting, this book helps the reader learn that these compost critters perform a valuable role in maintaining the ecological balance of the food chain. These natural recyclers process the raw materials on which all life depends and return them to the air and soil to be used again. This book would be very useful in science units on the food chain and other basic ecology concepts.

9.103   Lavies, Bianca. **Mangrove Wilderness: Nature's Nursery.** Photographs by Bianca Lavies. Dutton, 1994. ISBN 0-525-45186-2. 32p. 9–11.

This impressive photoessay explores "the vast web of animal life that is supported by a remarkable tree—the red mangrove." The author/photographer takes the reader on an intimate and fascinating journey into this complex and interdependent community. The lucid text, complemented by stunning natural photography, explains the life cycle of the unusual mangrove tree, one of the few trees able to grow in salt water. The food chain in this ecosystem is also explored and many examples of simple and complex organisms are given. Teachers of natural science will find this book useful in reinforcing children's understanding of the interrelatedness of all life.

9.104   Poncet, Sally. **Antarctic Encounter: Destination South Georgia.** Simon & Schuster, 1995. ISBN 0-02-774905-3. 48p. 7–10.

"Most people have a special place that they love above all others," says author Sally Poncet in introducing readers to her family's favorite destination: the remote island of South Georgia. The fact that their special place is close to the Antarctic, and can be reached only by boat, makes it more exciting for this family of five. While their scientist parents count birds and collect other data, the three boys explore the island, learning about the wildlife and visiting with the few people who live there. Superb photographs and a lively text make this book an exciting adventure and an interesting ecological study.

9.105   Pringle, Laurence. **Fire in the Forest: A Cycle of Growth and Renewal.** Illustrated by Bob Marstall. Atheneum, 1995. ISBN 0-689-80394-X. 32p. 9–11.

Laurence Pringle describes the complex cycle of forest ecology and the vital role of fire in that cycle. He studies the large Yellowstone Park fires of 1988, using observations from park employees and a biologist working in the area. Bob Marstall's paintings animate the text with full spreads of pine forests, chronicling the forest life before, during, and after the event. Important stages and events that are predicted for the 220 years after the fire are also depicted. Small paintings showing the plants, insects, and other wildlife of the area are interspersed throughout the text. This excellent book helps older children appreciate the interdependence of forests, plants, and wildlife and the part fire plays in the natural cycles of the forest.

Earth Science

9.106 Brandenburg, Jim. **Sand and Fog: Adventures in Southern Africa.** Photographs by Jim Brandenburg. Walker, 1994. ISBN 0-8027-8232-9. 44p. 9–12.

How does life exist in the Namib Desert? Jim Brandenburg explores this question in his photoessay of this remarkable region in southern Africa. Here the rain does not fall for years at a time, but every fifth night or so a thick fog rolls over the dunes and leaves a heavy dew. This dew permits a great variety of animals to adapt to their environment. The author recounts how he pursued the "unicornlike" oryx through a moonscape setting of shifting sand to obtain the remarkable photograph on the cover of the book. The simple text describes the lighting techniques used to evoke atmosphere and mood in the mystical and haunting color photographs.

9.107 Gibbons, Gail. **Caves and Caverns.** Illustrated by Gail Gibbons. Harcourt Brace, 1993. ISBN 0-15-226820-0. 32p. 6–12.

Gibbons applies her familiar style to the subject of caves and caverns, taking the reader on an exciting exploration of this mysterious underground world. Her clear text and labeled illustrations provide information on how caves are formed, the different kinds of caves, the formation of stalactites and stalagmites, and some of the plants and animals living in caves. Spelunking is explained and advice is given on how to have an exciting, safe cave adventure. Teachers will find this title helpful in studies in the earth sciences.

9.108 Locker, Thomas, and Candace Christiansen. **Sky Tree.** Illustrated by Thomas Locker. HarperCollins, 1995. ISBN 0-06-024883-1. 40p. 7–11.

Using the image of a tree on a hill in the foreground of various skyscapes, Thomas Locker chronicles the shifts in color and form associated with changes in seasons and weather patterns. Each image is accompanied by a question to encourage readers to focus on the natural details depicted in the paintings, and these questions are answered or addressed in a concluding section. The illustrations are stunning oil paintings, making the book useful both as both a fine arts and a science text.

9.109 Matthews, Downs. **Arctic Summer.** Photographs by Dan Guravich. Simon & Schuster, 1993. ISBN 0-671-79539-2. 33p. 9–11.

The simple, lively text and color photographs of this photoessay capture the beauty and splendor of the brief Arctic summer. With such a short season, "every moment must be lived at top speed." The reader learns of the special adaptations and habits of the flora and fauna of the Arctic tundra through the birth of new animals and the rebirth of plants dormant over the long winter. This book captures the way the Arctic "springs to joyous life."

9.110   Rauzon, Mark J., and Cynthia Overbeck Bix. **Water, Water Everywhere.** Sierra, 1994. ISBN 0-87156-598-6. 32p. 5–8.

This photoessay for young readers beautifully describes the role water plays as the basic element for supporting life on this planet. The writers evoke the magic, beauty, and power of water and explain the importance of water in our everyday lives. They use rich language to describe how water changes, moves, shapes the terrain, and "brings the gift of life." By focusing on the natural beauty of water and its importance for sustaining life, the authors deliver a subtle yet powerful environmental message. This book could be used as read-aloud to launch a theme on water for primary children or as independent reading for children who enjoy exploring the world around them.

9.111   Rood, Ronald. **Wetlands.** Illustrated by Marlene Hill Donnelly. HarperCollins, 1994. ISBN 0-06-023010-X. 47p. 9–11.

This nature study book provides the young naturalist with a rich and absorbing experience exploring the mysteries of natural wetlands. The text pulls the reader into a wonderful world of beauty that often goes unnoticed. Many plants and animals from the water's edge, the top or the depths of the water, and the living skies are well presented. The illustrations by renowned wildlife artist Marlene Hill Donnelly add detail and mood to this small, intimate, informative book. It could be read aloud or used as an introduction to a study of wetlands or a warm-up or follow-up to a field trip.

9.112   van Rose, Susanna. **The Earth Atlas.** Illustrated by Richard Bonson. Dorling Kindersley, 1994. ISBN 1-56458-626-X. 64p. 9–12.

Color photographs and illustrations present detailed cross-sections that reveal the powerful geological processes that shape oceans, mountains, deserts, coastlines, and valleys. The detailed text is accurate and accessible. Map inserts place each topic within a geographic region.

9.113 van Rose, Susanna. **Earth: Explore the Secrets of the Earth.** Dorling Kindersley, 1994. ISBN 1-56458-476-3. 64p. 9–11.

This book covers the full spectrum of geophysical studies with informative, cursory text and detailed color graphics. It is structured like an encyclopedia, with each spread covering a different topic. Each subject is explored from its most obvious manifestation to the fine details of rock samples and laboratory experiments designed to recreate geophysical phenomena. This is an excellent reference book for home or school, adult or child.

General Science Concepts

9.114 Burton, Robert. **Egg: A Photographic Story of Hatching.** Photographs by Jane Burton and Kim Taylor. Dorling Kindersley, 1994. ISBN 1-56458-460-7. 45p. 6–10.

This fascinating photographic study of eggs and their hatching begins with an introduction to eggs, what they are, who lays them, and how an animal develops inside an egg. The book starts with the familiar chicken's egg but expands into a detailed photographic story of the development and hatching of twenty-seven other animals: swans, penguins, ducks, tortoises, geckoes, goldfish, slugs, and many others. The sharp, close-up photographs are supported with dated captions, clear labeling, and descriptive details. This is a book for browsing but could be very useful in any study of life cycles and animals hatched from eggs.

9.115 Evans, David, and Claudette Williams. **Color and Light.** Photographs by Daniel Pangbourne. Scholastic, 1993. ISBN 0-590-74591-3. 29p. 5–6.

This practical activity book introduces preschoolers to the properties of color and light. Color photographs provide clear visual instruction for completing experiments based on everyday experiences. An introductory note to parents sets the tone for the book, with a strong emphasis on building science concepts around children's natural curiosity. This book is part of a bright, colorful, and fun set of early science books. It would be of interest in early childhood programs and primary classrooms.

9.116 Keeler, Patricia A., and Francis X. McCall, Jr. **Unraveling Fibers.** Illustrated by Patricia A. Keeler and Francis X. McCall, Jr. Atheneum, 1995. ISBN 0-689-31777-8. 36p. 8–12.

Where does cashmere come from? How many silkworms are used to make a silk tie? Color photographs, illustrations, and straightforward text are used to answer these questions and many more. Differences between natural and synthetic fibers are explored. The natural fibers include cotton, wool, and angora and the synthetic fibers include rayon and polyester. Methods of producing and processing twelve different fibers are discussed. The book is well laid-out and includes definitions, an index, and a general overview of the fibers used in the textile industry.

9.117   Kuhn, Dwight. **My First Book of Nature: How Living Things Grow.** Photographs by Dwight Kuhn. Scholastic, 1993. ISBN 0-590-45502-8. 61p. 9–11.

This introductory nature book offers exquisite photographs accompanied by simple text on fungi, plants, and animals. The animal sections include information about worms, insects, fish, reptiles, amphibians, birds, and mammals, including humans. This book would be pleasurable for both children and adults.

9.118   Macaulay, David. **The Way Things Work.** Illustrated by David Macaulay. Dorling Kindersley, 1995. ISBN 1-56458-901-3. CD-ROM. 8–12.

This CD-ROM is a unique and highly motivating exploration into the magical world of inventions, machines, and technology. The full multimedia version of David Macaulay's celebrated book, *The Way Things Work,* is fascinating for readers of all ages. Follow the antics of a woolly mammoth to learn about the principles of science, the history of technology, the inventors themselves, and the variety of machines we use on a daily basis. Readers explore the book with simple mouse clicks, choosing topics that interest them and generate hilarious but highly informative animation, sound, and text. This CD-ROM could be used to complement an exploration into simple machines. It can be purchased in both Mac and PC formats.

9.119   Westray, Kathleen. **A Color Sampler.** Illustrated by Kathleen Westray. Ticknor & Fields, 1993. ISBN 0-395-65940-X. 32p. 6–8.

This is an imaginative exploration of a variety of concepts related to color. The primary, secondary, and intermediate colors are explained and depicted. The book effectively demonstrates how the appearance of colors changes when they are placed on different backgrounds. The book also explores how colors are mixed and the effects of black and white to create tints and hues. Colors are described as soft, warm, vibrant, cool, lighter, and darker in order to show how color affects our daily lives. This book could be applied to science activities on color, art lessons, and children's personal explorations of this interesting subject.

9.120   Westray, Kathleen. **Picture Puzzler.** Illustrated by Katherine Westray. Ticknor & Fields, 1994. ISBN 0-395-70130-9. 32p. 7–11.

Children will delight in trying out and finding out about optical illusions related to lines, shapes, colors, afterimages, trick drawings, and reversible drawings. The gouache illustrations draw on American folk art motifs and are bound to stimulate the reader's eye and mind.

Human Development

9.121   Parker, Steve. **The Body Atlas: A Pictorial Guide to the Human Body.** Illustrated by Giuliano Fornari. Dorling Kindersley, 1993. ISBN 1-56458-224-8. 63p. 10–14.

This striking, large-format pictorial atlas enables the young reader to study and explore the human body region by region, layer by layer, from head to toe. Impressive and accurate full-color illustrations and microphotos provide a detailed, close-up look at the parts of the body and how they interact. Every bone, muscle, and organ is identified. The clearly written text is packed with fascinating information. The illustrations are color-coded throughout; for example, bones are always creamy white, veins are blue, and arteries are red. This outstanding reference book would be a valuable addition to any personal, public, or school library. Classroom teachers developing themes on health or the human body will find this book an excellent teaching aid.

9.122   Sandeman, Anna. **Bones.** Illustrated by Ian Thompson. Copper Beech, 1995. ISBN 1-56294-621-8. 30p. 5–9.

One of the Body Books series, this book explores the science of bones while referring back to the reader's own body and experiences. The chapters include useful discussions of bone structures, joints, muscles, and broken bones. The photographs and diagrams are large, clear, and appealing for children. Other books in the series include *Senses* and *Eating.*

9.123   Sandeman, Anna. **Breathing.** Illustrated by Ian Thompson. Copper Beech, 1995. ISBN 1-56294-620-X. 30p. 5–9.

One of the Body Books series, this interesting exploration of breathing takes us from the animal world into the wonder of our own lungs. The book includes engaging exercises for children to try while learning about breathing, breathing rates, oxygen, the atmosphere, talking, and breathing problems. The text is illustrated with good photographs and diagrams suitable for children.

Mathematics

9.124   Lasky, Kathryn. **The Librarian Who Measured the Earth.** Illustrated by Kevin Hawkes. Little, Brown, 1994. ISBN 0-316-51526-4. 48p. 6–9.

A fine balance between nonfiction and story narrative makes this book a good read-aloud or independent reading choice. The style of the illustrations sets the historical time appropriately, establishing the story of a young, inquisitive boy who grows to adulthood. The story is a great encouragement to budding scientists and mathematicians. The constant personal drive of Erathosthenes carries the story line forward, encouraging children to keep going with hunches or ideas. The well-written text is balanced with excellent illustrations.

9.125   Sharman, Lydia. **The Amazing Book of Shapes.** Photographs by Steven Gorton. Dorling Kindersley, 1994. ISBN 1-56458-514-X. 37p. 6–10.

This is an amazing activity book and teaching resource for teachers, parents, and children. Basic geometric concepts are fully explored as shape and color are used to create pattern and design. The inclusion of practical, historical information makes this publication useful for older children and young adults. Imaginative yet instructive features of the book include a mirror bookmark, a fold-out flap of shape stencils, and pattern grids. Step-by-step instructions and vibrant color photography will encourage children to undertake the suggested projects.

Meteorology

9.126   Casey, Denise. **Weather Everywhere.** Photographs by Jackie Gilmore. Macmillan, 1995. ISBN 0-02-717777-7. 36p. 5–9.

Using interesting photographs and diagrams in conjunction with clear, simple text, this book is an excellent introduction to the various factors that create climate and weather. It begins with an explanation of the causes of latitudinal and seasonal variations in temperature and continues with a consideration of winds, precipitation, and the effect of geography. The book concludes with a useful glossary of terms.

Oceanography

9.127 Ganeri, Anita. **The Oceans Atlas.** Illustrated by Luciano Corbella. Dorling Kindersley, 1994. ISBN 1-56458-475-5. 64p. 9–12.

This is much more than an atlas. The book explores the seas and oceans that cover three-quarters of our world and investigates how these vast expanses of water are a vital resource for food and energy. The reader is taken on an ocean-by-ocean survey that is enhanced by marvelous photographs, three-dimensional computer scans, illustrations, and maps. Some of the book's related topics include exploration, volcanoes, ships and boats, and future predictions. Each section starts with an interesting introduction. The facts are clear, concise, and readable.

Plants

9.128 Creasy, Rosalind. **Blue Potatoes, Orange Tomatoes.** Illustrated by Ruth Heller. Sierra, 1994. ISBN 0-87156-576-5. 40p. 6–11.

In this colorful and imaginative book, young gardeners learn everything they need to know to grow a garden full of fruits and vegetables in a rainbow of surprising colors. The reader learns that many familiar fruits and vegetables grow in a variety of colors. Red corn, orange tomatoes, yellow zucchini, purple beans, and colored radishes are a few of the unusual combinations available. After a brief introduction, the writer gives information on how to order special seeds, prepare the soil, and tend the garden. Detailed information on several colored fruits and vegetables follows. Ruth Heller's illustrations are bright and bold.

9.129 Kite, L. Patricia. **Insect-Eating Plants.** Millbrook, 1995. ISBN 1-56294-562-9. 61p. 7–9.

Children have always been intrigued by the notion of insect-eating plants and this book effectively addresses this fascination by presenting seven of the world's most common carnivorous plants. Sharp color photographs and well-written text reveal how plants such as the cobra plant, the Venus flytrap, and the bladderwort trap their prey. Additional chapters describe how some insects actually benefit by living on carnivorous plants, how one can grow them, and how to find out more about them.

Prehistoric Life

9.130 Cole, Joanna. **The Magic School Bus in the Time of the Dinosaurs.** Illustrated by Bruce Degen. Scholastic, 1994. ISBN 0-590-44688-6. 48p. 5–8.

If you enjoyed such books as *The Magic School Bus at the Waterworks* or *The Magic School Bus Inside the Earth*, you will enjoy this amazing field trip with Ms. Frizzle and her class, traveling to the late Triassic period in search of maiasaura nests. The latest facts about dinosaurs are given in sidebar notes designed like looseleaf pages from a notebook. A Where We Are in Time graphic clearly pinpoints when particular species of dinosaurs lived. The cartoonlike illustrations will entertain readers with their humorous detail.

9.131   Dodson, Peter. **An Alphabet of Dinosaurs.** Illustrated by Wayne D. Barlowe and Michael Meaker. Scholastic, 1995. ISBN 0-590-46486-8. 64p. 5–10.

Twenty-six dinosaurs, from ankylosaurus to zephyrosaurus, are presented in full spreads, one for each letter of the alphabet. Each dinosaur, from the well-known to newly discovered, is shown in a dramatic painting along with a black-and-white sketch of its entire skeleton or skull. In large type accessible to young children, the brief text provides facts that will interest a broad age range. Additional information on the dinosaurs, including a pronunciation guide, is found in the appendix.

9.132   Lindsay, William, and Mark Norell. **Corythosaurus.** Dorling Kindersley, 1993. ISBN 1-56458-225-6. 29p. 9–11.

Corythosaurus is brought back to life in this book, one of a series of books on dinosaurs produced by the American Museum of Natural History. Text and full-color scale models, reconstructions, and photographs detail the discovery and excavation of corythosaurus fossils and examine what the evidence tells us about its appearance and behavior. Dinosaur enthusiasts will greatly appreciate this attractive, oversized book.

9.133   **The Visual Dictionary of Prehistoric Life.** Dorling Kindersley, 1995. ISBN 1-56458-859-9. 64p. 9–11.

This Eyewitness Visual Dictionary provides young readers with the specialized vocabulary related to the anatomy and classification of prehistoric animals and plants. Representations of biological development are divided into sections introduced by text that sets the time frame and evolutionary frame. Each topic is presented on a full spread with text and outstanding full-color, clearly labeled photographs and illustrations.

10 Fine Arts

Performing Arts

Dance

10.1 Anderson, Joan. **Twins on Toes: A Ballet Debut.** Photographs by George Ancona. Lodestar, 1993. ISBN 0-525-67415-2. 32p. 9–11.

This photoessay explores the dedicated and demanding life of students in the School of American Ballet. The pleasures and torments of becoming a classical dancer are told through the experiences of two identical twins working to be accepted as professional dancers. This intimate viewpoint places the reader behind the scenes of the grueling practices and exhilarating performances. The twins' hopes and dreams are warmly told through a personal, candid text. Beautiful color photographs illustrate this story. This book would be of strong interest for young dance students.

10.2 Russell, Darcey. **The Young Dancer.** Dorling Kindersley, 1994. ISBN 1-56458-468-2. 65p. 9–12.

For young students of ballet, this handbook provides a step-by-step introduction to the basic elements of this challenging art form. Organized around the stages in the development of a young dancer's life from class through performance, this book contains clear, informative photographs and concise explanatory text. Information on ballet companies, many useful addresses, and a glossary are also provided. Other books in the series are *The Young Rider* and *The Young Gymnast*.

Music

10.3 Drew, Helen. **My First Music Book.** Dorling Kindersley, 1993. ISBN 1-56458-215-9. 48p. 5–9.

Creating musical instruments such as drums and pipes from things such as plastic flower pots and leftover cardboard tubes is described in this excellent book full of creative ideas. The brightly hued, life-size photographs, along with step-by-step instructions, invite children of all ages to try these projects and form a class or neighborhood band.

10.4   Johnson, James Weldon. **Lift Ev'ry Voice and Sing.** Illustrated by Jan Spivey Gilchrist. Scholastic, 1995. ISBN 0-590-46982-7. 32p. 5–8.

Jan Spivey Gilchrist's magnificent illustrations are the perfect complement to James Weldon Johnson's anthem of struggle and hope for African Americans. The music, composed by Johnson's brother, is included. The artist concludes the book with an inspirational letter to the reader. The superb paintings (colored pencil, gouache, and watercolor) are moving and powerful, capturing the mood of this anthem that "has come to symbolize the history and struggle of African Americans in the United States."

10.5   Oates, Eddie Herschel. **Making Music: 6 Instruments You Can Create.** Illustrated by Michael Koelsch. HarperCollins, 1995. ISBN 0-06-021478-3. 32p. 6–10.

Everyday objects can be used to create instruments that are fun to make and easy to play. A brief introduction defines percussion, wind, and string instruments and identifies the corresponding instruments that are included in the book. For example, the garden-hose trumpet is introduced as a wind instrument and the wrench xylophone is introduced as a percussion instrument. Simple text and colorful illustrations provide instructions that are easy to follow and include hints for making music.

10.6   Oram, Hiawyn, and Carl Davis. **A Creepy Crawly Songbook.** Illustrated by Satoshi Kitamura. Farrar, Straus, 1993. ISBN 0-374-31639-2. 53p. 6–9.

These unique songs range from an irreverent tune about itchy lice to a musical explanation of a praying mantis's nonreligious inclinations. The accompanying illustrations of various insects are delightfully detailed and eye-catching. Each song is followed by the lyrics in verse. The musical scores include lovely waltzes and lullabies and rhythmic polkas and blues. Some of the songs will take practice to learn, but the melodies are original.

10.7   Weeks, Sarah. **Crococile Smile.** Illustrated by Lois Ehlert. HarperCollins, 1994. ISBN 0-06-022867-9. unpaged. 5–7.

These ten songs of the earth are catchy and comical, with undertones of environmental messages. Whether children dance or sing along to the rhythmic music, or pore through the hardcover picture book lush with bright colors, the book and tape are delightful resources for home or classroom.

Visual Arts

10.8 Capek, Michael. **Artistic Trickery: The Tradition of Trompe L'Oeil Art.** Lerner, 1995. ISBN 0-8225-2064-8. 64p. 10–12.

This book chronicles the history of trompe l'oeil ("to trick the eye") art. Windows, doors, shoes, rugs, bulletin boards, a dog in a corner, and people in a stairwell are all created in such vivid realism that the eye is fooled into believing the object is really there. The reproductions included in this book range from a Roman mosaic of a littered floor to a 1992 mural of a door with a man seated in the room beyond.

10.9 Falwell, Cathryn. **The Letter Jesters.** Illustrated by Cathryn Falwell. Ticknor & Fields, 1994. ISBN 0-395-66898-0. 48p. 5–10.

"Hundreds of typefaces, thousands of words—letters are everywhere!" This fanciful yet factual introduction to typography tells young readers about the history and functions of the diverse practical art form of designing and arranging typefaces. The visual appeal of this picture book is greatly enhanced by the many playful antics of jesters and puppy dogs juggling and rearranging words and letters.

10.10 Isaacson, Philip M. **A Short Walk around the Pyramids and through the World of Art.** Knopf, 1993. ISBN 0-679-81523-6. 122p. 9–12.

Illustrated with photographs and color reproductions, the insightful text describes the effects of form, light, and color on art forms and thus on the viewer. Architecture, sculpture, painting, photography, useful objects, towns, and cities are enthusiastically examined by the author. Notes on the featured works are included. This is an outstanding book in both content and presentation.

10.11 Micklethwait, Lucy, selector. **A Child's Book of Art: Great Pictures, First Words.** Dorling Kindersley, 1993. ISBN 1-56458-203-5. 64p. 5–12.

Lucy Micklethwait has compiled a valuable collection of art, arranged by topics children will easily relate to, such as The Family, At Home, and By the Sea. With merely a word or two accompanying each picture to stimulate discussion, the viewer is encouraged to truly look and see. The purpose of this lavish, oversized volume is clearly stated: "By opening our children's eyes to art, we can help them understand the world in which they live and the people with whom they share it." The book is much more than a first-words book. Children can delight in the details, colors, and settings. This book would be useful for primary students and for art appreciation activities on any level. Works of art in order of presentation and brief biographical notes are listed.

10.12 Muhlberger, Richard. **What Makes a Degas a Degas?** Viking, 1993. ISBN 0-670-85205-8. 48p. 10–14.

Each of the books in this Metropolitan Museum of Art series introduces the young reader to a particular artist and his work, leading to an appreciation of the beauty of the paintings and an understanding of how that beauty was created. Information is given about the artist's life, his approach to art, and how his art is related to other artwork of the period. Using a discovery approach, this book guides the reader through twelve of the artist's paintings, looking at composition, color, perspective, and other aspects of technique. The level of language and the balance of text and paintings make this series accessible and appealing to a wide range of readers. Other titles in this series are *What Makes a Rembrandt a Rembrandt?*, *What Makes a Monet a Monet?*, *What Makes a Brueghel a Brueghel?*, *What Makes a Raphael a Raphael?*, and *What Makes a Van Gogh a Van Gogh?*

10.13 Sirett, Dawn. **My First Paint Book.** Photographs by Dave King. Dorling Kindersley, 1994. ISBN 1-56458-466-6. 48p. 6–9.

This life-size guide to painting activities is appealing for young artists. The book outlines equipment that will be needed and suggests important things to remember. The book features several painting techniques such as mono-printing, stenciling, crayon resist, textured painting, and collage, as well as several projects that apply these techniques. Readers can create gift paper, gift bags, totes, jewelry, T-shirts, and picture frames. Each project has clear photographs of equipment, careful step-by-step directions, captioned labels that give hints for success or suggest alternative approaches, and a satisfying look at the finished product. Intermediate-grade students and teachers will enjoy combing this book for ideas and inspiration.

10.14 Sturgis, Alexander. **Introducing Rembrandt.** Little, Brown, 1994. ISBN 0-316-82022-9. 32p. 9–11.

For children beginning to take an interest in art, this story of Rembrandt's life provides excellent information about an artist and his work. The text is well-balanced with a representative sampling of Rembrandt's drawings, paintings, and prints and introduces historical facts of seventeenth-century Holland. Part of the Introducing the Artist series, the book is also a valuable resource for teachers.

10.15 Waters, Elizabeth, and Annie Harris. **Painting: A Young Artist's Guide.** Photographs by David King. Dorling Kindersley, 1993. ISBN 1-56458-348-1. 45p. 10–12.

These authors have created what amounts to a beginner's art course in a book. In this innovative introduction to the world of art, close-up color photographs and clear, practical guidelines are used to introduce different aspects of painting. The paintings of well-known artists of the past and present are complemented by examples of children's art. Practical activities and hands-on projects are presented throughout the book. A large-scale format is used to develop the concepts of color, shape, pattern, and movement. The study of art is supplemented with an emphasis on getting involved and trying the various techniques. Children can explore this book on their own or with the guidance of an adult.

10.16 Welton, Jude. **Drawing: A Young Artist's Guide.** Dorling Kindersley, 1994. ISBN 1-56458-676-6. 45p. 8–13.

This book builds on children's interest in drawing and fosters drawing skills through example and practice. Actual works of art are included. Information about individual artists' style and technique enables young artists to learn about the elements of art. This book encourages experimentation with a wide variety of tools and media in order to explore composition, design, and point of view. The large-format, dramatic presentation makes this a valuable resource for school libraries and private collections.

10.17 Welton, Jude. **Looking at Painting.** Dorling Kindersley, 1994. ISBN 1-56458-494-1. 64p. 9–14.

This excellent introduction to Western paintings and their composition includes some of the greatest paintings since the fifteenth century. The accessible text covers all areas of technique, composition, content, and subject matter. The abundant, richly colored plates illustrate the points covered in the text and make the book a delight for readers of all ages.

11 Crafts and Hobbies

Cooking

11.1   Dahl, Felicity, and Josie Fison, compilers. **Roald Dahl's Revolting Recipes.** Illustrated by Quentin Blake. Viking, 1994. ISBN 0-670-85836-6. 61p. 8–11.

Fans of Roald Dahl will delight in this collection of recipes featured in his many books. There are recipes for every occasion that are sure to tickle the palate of young readers. "Lickable Wallpaper" from *Charlie and the Chocolate Factory* and "Fresh Mudburgers" from *James and the Giant Peach* are just two of the culinary treats amusingly illustrated by Quentin Blake.

11.2   Scobey, Joan. **The Fannie Farmer Junior Cookbook.** Illustrated by Patience Brewster. Little, Brown, 1993. ISBN 0-316-77624-6. 280p. 8–12.

This full-size cookbook provides aspiring cooks with many helpful hints and definitions of ingredients, equipment, and terms. This basic, well-written cookbook offers a variety of recipes for cooks of all ages. Familiar American dishes such as mashed potatoes and chocolate cake are included along with less traditional items such as vegetable lasagna roll-ups and pesto. Decorative line drawings make this an interesting and attractive introductory cookbook.

11.3   Wilkes, Angela. **The Children's Step-by-Step Cookbook.** Photographs by Dave King. Dorling Kindersley, 1994. ISBN 1-56458-474-7. 128p. 9–11.

Large, colorful photographs are used to clarify step-by-step instructions so that readers of any age can learn to prepare and present delicious and attractive treats. Simple recipes such as putting together a hamburger with all of its trimmings will appeal to children. Basic hints for cooking vegetables and preparing sandwich fillings make this a useful and interesting book for young cooks who may have little or no experience in the kitchen.

Handicrafts

11.4   Cobb, Mary. **The Quilt-Block History of Pioneer Days: With Projects Kids Can Make.** Illustrated by Jan Davey Ellis. Millbrook, 1995. ISBN 1-56294-485-1. 64p. 9–11.

This book uses quilts as a focal point for a study of the history of pioneers. The journeys and settlements of the pioneers were represented in the creation of quilt blocks, named for special events as well as everyday activities. The book includes interesting projects that use quilt blocks as their basis of design. Some of the projects discussed are greeting cards, boxes, and a recipe folder. Colorful illustrations depict pioneer life and quilt block designs.

11.5   Owen, Cheryl. **My Nature Craft Book.** Illustrated by Cheryl Owen. Little, Brown, 1993. ISBN 0-316-67715-9. 96p. 9–11.

This collection of craft ideas involves materials found in nature and includes forty-two different projects that range in complexity for different age levels. Simple instructions are given for carving jack-o'-lanterns and painting stones; more detailed projects include decorating miniature straw hats. A clear contents page and index make the book easy to use. Color photographs and illustrations accompany step-by-step instructions.

11.6   Rogers, Mara Reid. **Decorating Easter Eggs.** Photographs by Mark Hill. Little, Brown, 1994. ISBN 0-316-75414-5. 32p. 8–12.

This well-illustrated instruction book is filled with ideas for decorating Easter eggs. The kit contains easy-to-use feathers, dye tablets, sparkled stick-ons, and glitter for decoration. Children will be able to follow the illustrations even if they do not read all the detailed text. The book offers many craft ideas that could lead to children's own creative ventures.

11.7   Wilkes, Angela. **My First Christmas Activity Book.** Photographs by Dave King. Dorling Kindersley, 1994. ISBN 1-56458-674-X. 48p. 9–11.

Large colorful photographs are designed to make instructions interesting and easy to follow for children, but the ideas will interest craft enthusiasts of all ages. Clear instructions for making Christmas decorations such as advent calendars, wreaths, and pomanders are included in this book. Most of the twelve projects tend to be a little more complex than just decorating wrapping paper, but equipment lists and step-by-step instructions are clear. The end of the book offers some gift-wrapping ideas.

Other Projects and Pastimes

11.8   Brown, Dave, and Paul Reeve. **Amazing Magic Tricks.** Dorling Kindersley, 1995. ISBN 1-56458-877-7. 48p. 9–12.

Twenty-one magic tricks and their essential props are described and photographed on large full spreads. A "you will need" list and life-size photographs outline the necessary equipment. Step-by-step instructions are given for making the props and performing the magic tricks. Brightly colored photographs highlight the instructions and make them easy for young children to follow. Children, parents, and teachers will find this book useful for the craft side of making props and performing magic tricks.

11.9   Chapman, Gillian, and Pam Robson. **Making Shaped Books with Patterns.** Photographs by Rupert Horrox. Millbrook, 1995. ISBN 1-56294-560-2. 32p. 5–10.

This useful book explores projects for making shaped books. The text is simple and clear, with color photographs of over seventy easy book designs for children. Nineteen pattern shapes are included that can be traced onto paper and cut out. Decorating ideas are explored as well, making use of a variety of fabric and textured materials in addition to paper. Parents and teachers will find themselves using this resource year after year.

11.10   Fleischman, Paul. **Copier Creations: Using Copy Machines to Make Decals, Silhouettes, Flip Books, Films and Much More!** Illustrated by David Cain. HarperCollins, 1993. ISBN 0-06-021052-4. 122p. 8–11.

Newbery Award–winner Paul Fleischman turns his attention to the world of copy art. This book is a detailed description of how upper elementary students can use the copier to create many useful and fun projects. The author clearly intends the book for older students or adult and child partnerships. He describes all the basic materials needed and strongly cautions readers about copying only materials that are in the public domain. The book begins with simpler projects such as designing letterheads and notecards, and builds to more complex projects such as flip-books, films, and collages. Teachers may find the book useful in designing art projects, and students with easy access to a copier will be keen to try the suggested ideas.

11.11   Kuklin, Susan. **From Head to Toe: How a Doll Is Made.** Photographs by Susan Kuklin. Hyperion, 1994. ISBN 1-56282-667-0. 32p. 5–9.

Colorful photographs and simple text tell the story of the creation of one of the famous Alexander Doll Company characters. Although this doll is probably too expensive for many of the children who read the book, the assembly line process in its making is similar to that of less costly dolls. The many people of different backgrounds who work together give a subtle lesson about diversity. A creative art teacher could use the photograph of doll's eyes as motivation for an art lesson.

11.12   Robins, Deri, Kate Crocker, and Meg Sanders. **Kids Can Do It Book.** Illustrated by Charlotte Stowell. Kingfisher, 1993. ISBN 1-85697-860-5. 80p. 5–9.

Organized in the form of an alphabet book, this book includes a wealth of crafts, experiments, recipes, and games that are easy and cheap to make. Colorful illustrations and simple instructions are provided for activities that children can do on their own or in a group. Symbols are used to classify the activities on the contents pages as making things, playing games, or cooking treats.

11.13   Sullivan, George. **In-Line Skating: A Complete Guide for Beginners.** Photographs by George Sullivan. Dutton, 1993. ISBN 0-525-65124-1. 48p. 8–12.

The popular sport of in-line skating is the subject of this comprehensive instruction guide. The author begins with the development of the sport from the roller skating tradition. He explains everything a beginner needs to know: buying a pair of skates, learning the basic techniques, and learning how to stop. He then outlines the more advanced techniques of swizzling, crossover, and sidesurfing. Safety and responsible use of equipment are strongly emphasized throughout the book. The photographs support the text well by demonstrating concepts explained on that page. This is a high-interest book for many students who enjoy skating.

11.14   Walter, F. Virginia. **Super Toys and Games from Paper.** Illustrated by Teddy Cameron Long. Photographs by Walter Kaiser. Sterling, 1993. ISBN 1-895569-06-0. 104p. 6–12.

For children who are good with scissors and can follow instructions for three-dimensional designs, this collection of paper activities will provide much inspiration. Newspaper, tubes, and paper bags are transformed into papier-maché animals, puppets, games, and airplanes. This book suggests a host of paper projects that can be done with imagination, lots of bright paint, and little expense. Many of the larger projects would be ideal as class projects for art or drama productions.

12 Celebrations: Fiction and Nonfiction

Christmas

12.1   Ganeri, Anita. **The Story of Christmas: A Nativity Tale for Children.** Dorling Kindersley, 1995. ISBN 0-7894-0146-0. 29p. 5–9.

This simple telling of the familiar Christmas story features brightly colored photographs of schoolchildren creating the roles of Mary, Joseph, and the other familiar characters of this story. For teachers, parents, and students planning to stage a Nativity pageant, designing costumes, creating props, and planning stage directions will be a great deal easier after reading this book.

12.2   Graham-Barber, Lynda. **Ho Ho Ho! The Complete Book of Christmas Words.** Illustrated by Betsy Lewin. Bradbury, 1993. ISBN 0-02- 736933-1. 119p. 9–11.

A valuable companion to books dealing with this special celebration, this accessible text introduces young readers to the origins and meanings of familiar words associated with Christmas such as *candle, evergreen tree, jingle bells, candy cane,* and *December.* Details of Christmas customs around the world and other holiday lore are also provided.

12.3   Hennessy, B. G. **The First Night.** Illustrated by Steve Johnson and Lou Fancher. Viking, 1993. ISBN 0-670-83026-7. 24p. 5–8.

In this evocative retelling of the Nativity story, the author and illustrators create a peaceful mood with simple yet rich language and warm watercolors on wood blocks. The story focuses on the baby's birth in the loving company of his parents and the natural setting of the stable and the surrounding landscape.

12.4   McKissack, Patricia C., and Fredrick L. McKissack. **Christmas in the Big House, Christmas in the Quarters.** Illustrated by John Thompson. Scholastic, 1994. ISBN 0-590-43027-0. 68p. 9–11.

This extensively researched and richly illustrated fictional account of Christmas on a Southern plantation before the Civil War portrays the way events around this special time of year unfolded for the white plantation owners and the black slaves. The rich details of different customs, food, songs, and stories set against the historic background of slavery give young readers a compassionate glimpse into the lives of the families who lived in the slaves' cabins and the mansion.

12.5 McPhail, David. **Santa's Book of Names.** Illustrated by David McPhail. Little, Brown, 1993. ISBN 0-316-56335-8. 32p. 5–6.

In this story, Edward cannot read. However, when Santa leaves his *Book of Names* at Edward's house, Edward must use his letter and phonics skills to help Santa. First he signals Santa with the letter *B* stomped into the snow. When Santa loses his spectacles, Edward must sound out the names of the children and their presents. The story could offer encouragement to children who share Edward's situation.

12.6 Price, Moe. **The Reindeer Christmas.** Illustrated by Atsuko Morozumi. Harcourt Brace, 1993. ISBN 0-15-266199-9. 32p. 5–8.

Did you know that Santa did not always have a sleigh pulled by reindeer? In this Christmas story, Elwin and his fellow elves advertise for animals to pull a sleigh they plan to build. All the elephants, crocodiles, huskies, and other animals who apply are unsuitable candidates, but on the day before Christmas, a reindeer asks for help for his friend, who has fallen and broken a leg. Santa's new sleigh is pulled by reindeer for the rescue, and reindeer volunteer to pull Santa's sleigh on Christmas Eve forever after. The story is beautifully illustrated, reads aloud well, and provides ample opportunity for writing and discussion activities.

12.7 Sabuda, Robert. **The Christmas Alphabet.** Illustrated by Robert Sabuda. Orchard, 1994. ISBN 0-531-06857-9. 14p. 5–8.

This pop-up alphabet book features twenty-six intricate and eye-pleasing paper sculptures that unfold like Christmas cards. Each letter appears on a colored card that opens to a cut Christmas shape, labeled *A—angel, B—bell,* and so on. Each paper sculpture is an exquisite work of art, but the pages are delicate.

12.8 Stickland, Henrietta. **The Christmas Bear.** Illustrated by Paul Stickland. Dutton, 1993. ISBN 0-525-45062-9. 26p. 5–7.

A polar bear cub gets a tour of Santa's establishment. Santa shows the Christmas Bear the mail room, the presents, the workshops, and the elves, and gives the bear a special present. Despite his delight, the bear cuddles up back at home with the "best presents of all," his parents. Children will want to pore over the colorful, detailed illustrations.

12.9   Wilson, Sarah. **Christmas Cowboy.** Illustrated by Peter Palagonia. Simon & Schuster, 1993. ISBN 0-671-74780-0. 32p. 5–7.

In this contemporary Christmas fable, an old cowboy wanders into a rough town in a dry, forgotten valley and asks the children, "What would you want if you could have anything that stirs in your heart?" This question is evoked by the fact that there has been "no Christmas here and no miracles for thirty years come last Tuesday." The cowboy departs but returns on Christmas Eve, soaring over the valley in a big, red wagon, bearing gifts of love, laughter, and hope. The story unfolds with beautiful simplicity and demonstrates a warm appreciation for the special spirit of the season. The striking paintings, in dusty browns, successfully capture the unique valley setting.

Halloween

12.10   Martin, Billy, Jr. **Old Devil Wind.** Illustrated by Barry Root. Harcourt Brace, 1993. ISBN 0-15-257768-8. 32p. 5–7.

This cumulative ghost story is perfect for telling, especially at Halloween. "One dark and stormy night Ghost . . . began to WAIL." Stool joins Ghost by thumping, Broom begins swishing, Candle begins flickering, and so on, until Wind finally blows everything and everyone away. This book would be especially useful for choral speaking.

12.11   Stutson, Caroline. **By the Light of the Halloween Moon.** Illustrated by Kevin Hawkes. Lothrop, 1993. ISBN 0-688-12045-8. 32p. 5–8.

The rich rhyming pattern and inventive word play make this Halloween theme picture book a delightful treat for young readers. The evocative watercolor illustrations underline the fun and frolic of this cumulative poetic story that starts out with a toe, a cat, and a witch who tries to snatch the cat who tries to catch the toe. A wonderful read-aloud.

Jewish Celebrations

12.12 Goldin, Barbara Diamond. **Night Lights.** Illustrated by Louise August. Harcourt Brace, 1995. ISBN 0-15-200536-6. 32p. 5–8.

This story introduces the traditions associated with the Jewish holiday Sukkot. Daniel's family builds a small hut (sukkah) without a real roof and decorates the structure with fruit and branches. But this book is also about how Daniel overcomes his fear of the dark when he and sister Naomi sleep overnight in the sukkah without Grandpa. The two of them think about their ancestors, who hurriedly left Egypt and wandered in the desert for forty years, sleeping in temporary shelters like their own sukkah. They find comfort in the same moon and stars that the wanderers in the desert saw at night. Colorful oil and pastel linocuts depict Daniel's nightmarish fears, ghostly ancestors effectively outlined in white and the night sky.

12.13 Kuskin, Karla. **A Great Miracle Happened There: A Chanukah Story.** Illustrated by Robert Andrew Parker. HarperCollins, 1993. ISBN 0-06-023617-5. 32p. 5–8.

This beautiful, poetic story of Hanukkah, told on the first night by the narrator's mother, conveys images filled with warmth: "The two candle flames reflected in my mother's eyes." A story within a story, the traditional tale is recounted to Henry, a non-Jewish friend who is invited to join the celebration. The story is simply told, including some sensitive discussion on killing, miracles, and religious beliefs. Many Hanukkah traditions are embedded in the story.

12.14 Penn, Malka. **The Miracle of the Potato Latkes: A Hanukkah Story.** Illustrated by Giora Carmi. Holiday House, 1994. ISBN 0-8234-1118-4. 32p. 5–10.

The eight days of Hanukkah are enlivened with this warm and happy tale of another long-ago miracle. During a drought in Russia, Tante Golda's potato stock is depleted and, unable to fry her tasty potato latkes (pancakes) for her guests, she cannot hold her yearly Hanukkah party. Golda retains her humor and belief that God will provide. On each successive day of Hanukkah, one more potato appears. Expressive illustrations add flavor to this traditional story.

12.15 Schotter, Roni. **Passover Magic.** Illustrated by Marylin Hafner. Little, Brown, 1995. ISBN 0-316-77468-5. 32p. 5–10.

Charming illustrations and an affectionate story about relatives who arrive for Passover illuminate the traditions of this Jewish holiday. The story naturally folds in events such as cleaning the house in readiness for Passover, preparing the Seder meal, and hunting for the hidden matzo (afikomen). The book ends with a page of explanation about the story of Passover that highlights more traditions. The traditional four questions asked by the youngest at the Seder are also included.

12.16   Weilerstein, Sadie Rose. **K'tonton's Sukkot Adventure.** Illustrated by Joe Boddy. Jewish Publication Society, 1993. ISBN 0-8276-0502-1. 32p. 6–8.

This Jewish Tom Thumb story is set during the Sukkot holiday and features K'tonton, a tiny and adventurous character. As in the traditional tale, K'tonton is born to parents who long for a child, even one no bigger than a thumb. But this tale is decidedly Jewish in flavor. The food on the table includes challah and kugel. During Sukkot K'tonton hides himself in an etrog box, which his father carries to synagogue. The reader learns about some of the traditions associated with Sukkot, such as the lulav, the palm branch that is waved. Grey-scale illustrations add to the Jewish humor that ends the story: Even when K'tonton runs away, he runs to synagogue!

12.17   Zalben, Jane Breskin. **Happy New Year, Beni.** Illustrated by Jane Breskin Zalben. Holt, 1993. ISBN 0-8050-1961-8. 32p. 5–7.

Delightful, detailed pastel illustrations of Beni and Sara, two little bears, immediately command attention in this book about the Jewish New Year, Rosh Hashanah. The story of how their family prepares for and celebrates Rosh Hashanah with their grandparents and other relatives is simply and charmingly told. A fight between two cousins and the family tension it causes provide a clever entry into one New Year tradition: "We get rid of what we did during the year that wasn't so nice and we begin again with a new, clean slate." The children make up and vow to be better, as Grandpa says, "Just be you." The two cousins then play a silly kissing game.

12.18   Ziefert, Harriet. **What Is Passover?** Illustrated by Lillie James. HarperCollins, 1994. ISBN 0-694-00482-0. 16p. 6–8.

This flap book tells the story of Passover as Jake and his mother prepare the food and table setting for the holiday Seder. Passover customs and traditions are introduced through the text and under the flaps. The story is very straightforward but the illustrations and flaps enliven the book. *What Is Hanukkah?* is available in the same format.

Others

12.19 Ancona, George (translated by Osvaldo Blanco). **Fiesta U.S.A./Fiesta U.S.A.** Photographs by George Ancona. Lodestar, 1995. ISBN 0-525-67498-5 (English); 0-525-67522-1 (Spanish). 48p. 6–9.

On All Soul's Day, November 2, Mexican American children eat candy skulls of melted sugar. This and other fascinating facts about four fiestas celebrated by Latinos are shown in brilliant color photographs and text. Some are scary enough for the most avid ghoul fan. The glossary will help even a younger student present an oral report. Available in English and Spanish editions.

12.20 Coil, Suzanne M. **Mardi Gras.** Photographs by Mitchel Osborne. Macmillan, 1994. ISBN 0-02-722805-3. 48p. 6–10.

This delightful extravaganza of color and culture presents the historical and ethnic contributions that make up the annual Mardi Gras celebrations in New Orleans. The book refers to the elaborate myths and traditions that surround this unusual North American festival, including some interesting historical anecdotes as well as contemporary accounts of the celebration. The text describes the contributions of Cajuns, African Americans, and Native Americans to the event, and is supported by rich and detailed photographs. The book is a must for any child lucky enough to attend Mardi Gras.

12.21 Hoyt-Goldsmith, Diane. **Day of the Dead: A Mexican-American Celebration.** Photographs by Lawrence Migdale. Holiday House, 1994. ISBN 0-8234-1094-3. 32p. 9–11.

Azucena and Xumena, fraternal twins, take us for a tour of their family's activities as they prepare for and celebrate the Mexican Day of the Dead on November 1. Color pictures accompany the text, taking the reader through the preparation of food and death masks to the procession, mass, and celebration. A glossary and index make this an even more valuable tool for promoting cross-cultural understanding.

12.22 Krull, Kathleen. **Maria Molina and the Days of the Dead.** Illustrated by Enrique O. Sanchez. Macmillan, 1994. ISBN 0-02-750999-0. 32p. 5–7.

This story about a Mexican family's celebrations on the Days of the Dead combines elements of fiction with the rich factual details of this important Mexican holiday. Through vivid illustrations and text narrated by Maria, we experience the traditions and customs that honor the family members who have died, such as Maria's grandmother and little brother. When Maria's family moves to the United States, a comparison of these customs with the Halloween customs Maria adopts enhances intercultural understanding. The author's notes and a special recipe add to the rich information in this picture book.

12.23 Pinkney, Andrea Davis. **Seven Candles for Kwanzaa.** Illustrated by Brian Pinkney. Dial, 1993. ISBN 0-8037-1293-6. 32p. 5–8.

To honor their African heritage, many African Americans celebrate Kwanzaa, a seven-day harvest festival first introduced in the United States in 1966. Attractive scratchboard illustrations, with border motifs of African designs, detail a family's daily ritual as they light each of the candles in a seven-branched kinara, or candle holder. The simple text, incorporating Swahili words, explains the seven principles of Kwanzaa and the ways in which they may be expressed.

Prizes and Lists

The following awards and recognitions are helpful in locating excellent books. We have included major awards for poetry, fiction, drama, and nonfiction for young readers, given from 1993 to 1996, as well as descriptions of some other useful booklists.

Jane Addams Award

The Jane Addams Award, established in 1953, is given annually to the book for young people that most effectively promotes peace, social justice, world community, or equality of the sexes and of all races. It is given by the Women's International League for Peace and Freedom and the Jane Addams Peace Association.

1993 Temple, Frances. *Taste of Salt: A Story of Modern Haiti.* Orchard Books/Watts.

1994 Levine, Ellen. *Freedom's Children: Young Civil Rights Activists Tell Their Own Stories.* Avon.

1995 Freedman, Russell. *Kids at Work: Lewis Hine and the Crusade against Child Labor.* Clarion Books.

1996 Taylor, Mildred D. *The Well: David's Story.* Dial Books for Young Readers.

Mildred L. Batchelder Award

Given annually (unless no book is deemed worthy) to a United States publisher, the Batchelder Award honors the most outstanding translated book for children. Established in 1968, it is given by the Association for Library Service to Children of the American Library Association.

1993 No award.

1994 Farrar, Straus & Giroux: The Apprentice, by Pilar Molina Llorente. Translated from the Spanish by Robin Longshaw.

1995 Dutton Children's Books: *The Boys from St. Petri*, by Bjarne Reuter. Translated from the Danish by Anthea Bell.

1996 Houghton Mifflin: *The Lady with the Hat*, by Uri Orlev. Translated from the Hebrew by Hillel Halkin.

Booklist's Top of the List

The "Top of the List," initiated in 1991, represents the selections made by the staff of *Booklist* of the very best of their "Editor's Choice" annual lists. The complete lists may be found in *Booklist* each January 15.

1993 **Youth Fiction**

Wolff, Virginia Euwer. *Make Lemonade*. Henry Holt.

Youth Nonfiction

Appelbaum, Diana. *Giants in the Land*. Illustrated by Michael McCurdy. Houghton Mifflin.

Youth Picture Book

Ehrlich, Amy. *Parents in the Pigpen, Pigs in the Tub*. Illustrated by Steven Kellogg. Dial.

1994 **Youth Fiction**

Temple, Frances. *The Ramsay Scallop*. Orchard Books/Richard Jackson.

Youth Nonfiction

Bachrach, Susan D. *Tell Them We Remember: The Story of the Holocaust*. Little, Brown.

Youth Picture Book

Guback, Georgia. *Luka's Quilt*. Illustrated by the author. Greenwillow.

1995 **Youth Fiction**

Morpurgo, Michael. *The War of Jenkins' Ear*. Putnam/Philomel.

Youth Nonfiction

Giblin, James Cross. *When Plague Strikes: The Black Death, Smallpox, AIDS*. HarperCollins.

Youth Picture Book

Scieszka, Jon. *Math Curse*. Illustrated by Lane Smith. Viking.

1996 **Youth Fiction**

Pullman, Philip. *The Golden Compass*. Knopf.

Youth Nonfiction

Fleischman, Sid. *The Abracadabra Kid: A Writer's Life*. Greenwillow Books.

Youth Picture Book

Henkes, Kevin. *Lilly's Purple Plastic Purse*. Greenwillow Books.

Boston Globe–Horn Book Award

Given annually since 1967 by *The Boston Globe* and *The Horn Book Magazine*, these awards are conferred in three categories: outstanding fiction or poetry, outstanding nonfiction, and outstanding picture book.

1993 **Fiction Award**

Berry, James. *Ajeemah and His Son*. HarperCollins.

Fiction Honors

Lowry, Lois. *The Giver*. Houghton Mifflin.

Nonfiction Award

McKissack, Patricia, and Fredrick McKissack. *Sojourner Truth: Ain't I a Woman?* Scholastic.

Nonfiction Honors

Krull, Kathleen. *Lives of the Musicians: Good Times, Bad Times (And What the Neighbors Thought)*. Harcourt Brace.

Picture Book Award

Alexander, Lloyd. *The Fortune-Tellers*. Illustrated by Trina Schart Hyman. Dutton.

Picture Book Honors

McDermott, Gerald. *Raven: A Trickster Tale from the Pacific Northwest*. Illustrated by the author. Harcourt Brace.

Sis, Peter. *Komodo!* Illustrated by the author. Greenwillow.

1994 **Fiction Award**

Williams, Vera B. *Scooter*. Greenwillow.

Fiction Honors

Fine, Anne. *Flour Babies and the Boys of Room 8*. Little, Brown.

Fox, Paula. *Western Wind*. Orchard Books.

Nonfiction Award

Freedman, Russell. *Eleanor Roosevelt: A Life of Discovery*. Clarion Books.

Nonfiction Honor Books

Marrin, Albert. *Unconditional Surrender: U.S. Grant and the Civil War*. Atheneum.

Levy, Constance. *A Tree Place and Other Poems*. Macmillan/Margaret K. McElderry Books.

Picture Book Award

Say, Allen. *Grandfather's Journey*. Illustrated by the author. Houghton Mifflin.

Picture Book Honors

Henkes, Kevin. *Owen*. Illustrated by the author. Greenwillow.

Sis, Peter. *A Small Tall Tale from the Far Far North*. Illustrated by the author. Alfred A. Knopf.

1995 Fiction Award

Wynne-Jones, Tim. *Some of the Kinder Planets*. Orchard Books.

Fiction Honors

Hickman, Janet. *Jericho*. Greenwillow Books.

Nelson, Theresa. *Earthshine: A Novel*. Orchard Books.

Nonfiction Award

Bober, Natalie. *Abigail Adams: Witness to a Revolution*. Simon & Schuster.

Nonfiction Honors

Harris, Robie H. *It's Perfectly Normal: Changing Bodies, Growing Up, Sex and Sexual Health*. Illustrated by Michael Emberley. Candlewick Press.

Murphy, Jim. *The Great Fire*. Scholastic.

Picture Book Award

Lester, Julius. *John Henry*. Illustrated by Jerry Pinckney. Dial.

Picture Book Honors

Isaacs, Anne. *Swamp Angel*. Illustrated by Paul O. Zelinsky. Dutton Children's Books.

1996 Fiction Award

Avi. *Poppy*. Illustrated by Brian Floca. Jackson/Orchard.

Fiction Honors

McGraw, Eloise. *The Moorchild*. McElderry.

White, Ruth. *Belle Prater's Boy*. Farrar, Straus & Giroux.

Nonfiction Award

Warren, Andrea. *Orphan Train Rider: One Boy's True Story*. Houghton Mifflin.

Nonfiction Honors

Bruchac, Joseph. *The Boy Who Lived with the Bears, and Other Iroquois Stories*. Illustrated by Murv Jacob. HarperCollins.

Geisert, Bonnie. *Haystack*. Illustrated by Arthur Geisert. Lorraine/Houghton Mifflin.

Picture Book Award

Hest, Amy. *In the Rain with Baby Duck*. Illustrated by Jill Barton. Candlewick.

Picture Book Honors

Buehner, Caralyn. *Fanny's Dream*. Illustrated by Mark Buehner. Dial.

Perkins, Lynne Rae. *Home Lovely*. Illustrated by the author. Greenwillow.

Randolph Caldecott Medal

Given annually since 1938, the Caldecott Medal honors the illustrator of the most distinguished American picture book published in the United States in the preceding year. This award is conferred by the Association for Library Services to Children of the American Library Association.

1993 **Medal**

McCully, Emily Arnold. *Mirette on the High Wire*. Illustrated by the author. Putnam.

Honor Books

Scieszka, John. *The Stinky Cheese Man and Other Fairly Stupid Tales*. Illustrated by Lane Smith. Viking.

Williams, Sherley Anne. *Working Cotton*. Illustrated by Carole Byard. Harcourt Brace Jovanovich.

Young, Ed. *Seven Blind Mice*. Illustrated by the author. Philomel Books.

1994 **Medal**

Say, Allen. *Grandfather's Journey*. Illustrated by the author. Houghton Mifflin.

Honor Books

Fleming, Denise. *In the Small, Small Pond*. Illustrated by the author. Henry Holt.

Henkes, Kevin. *Owen*. Illustrated by the author. Greenwillow Books.

McDermott, Gerald. *Raven: A Trickster Tale from the Pacific Northwest*. Illustrated by the author. Harcourt Brace.

Raschka, Chris. *Yo! Yes?* Illustrated by the author. Orchard Books.

1995 **Medal**

Bunting, Eve. *Smoky Night*. Illustrated by David Diaz. Harcourt Brace.

Honor Books

Isaacs, Anne. *Swamp Angel*. Illustrated by Paul O. Zelinsky. Dutton.

Lester, Julius. *John Henry*. Illustrated by Jerry Pinkney. Dial.

Rohmann, Eric. *Time Flies*. Illustrated by the author. Crown.

1996 **Medal**

Rathmann, Peggy. *Officer Buckle and Gloria*. Illustrated by the author. Putnam.

Honor Books

Johnson, Stephen T. *Alphabet City*. Illustrated by the author. Viking.

Moss, Lloyd. *Zin! Zin! Zin! A Violin*. Illustrated by Marjorie Priceman. Simon & Schuster.

San Souci, Robert D. *The Faithful Friend*. Illustrated by Brian Pinkney. Simon & Schuster.

Stevens, Janet. *Tops and Bottoms*. Illustrated by the author. Harcourt Brace.

Andrew Carnegie Medal

This medal, first given in 1937 to commemorate the centenary of the birth of Andrew Carnegie, is awarded annually by the British Library Association to an outstanding children's book written in English and first published in the United Kingdom.

1993   Fine, Anne. *Flour Babies*. Hamish Hamilton.

1994   Swindells, Robert. *Stone Cold*. Hamish Hamilton.

1995   Breslin, Theresa. *Whispers in the Graveyard*. Methuen.

1996   Pullman, Philip. *Northern Lights*. Scholastic Ltd.

International Board on Books for Young People Honor List

Established in 1956, this list is published every two years to recognize books published in countries all over the world that represent the best in literature for young readers. Listed below are recent honorees from the United States.

1994   **Text Award**

Paterson, Katherine. *Lyddie*. Dutton Children's Books.

Illustrator Award

Bedard, Michael. *Emily*. Illustrated by Barbara Cooney. Doubleday.

Translation Award

Orlev, Uri. *The Man from the Other Side*. Translated by Hillel Halkin. Houghton Mifflin.

1996   **Text Award**

Cushman, Karen. *Catherine, Called Birdy*. Clarion Books.

Illustrator Award

Johnson, James Weldon. *The Creation*. Illustrated by James E. Ransome. Holiday House.

Translation Award

Jimenez, Juan Ramon. *Platero y Yo (Platero and I)*. Translated by Myra C. Livingston and Joseph F. Dominquez. Clarion.

International Reading Association Children's Book Award

Given annually since 1975, this award honors the first or second book of an author, from any country, who shows unusual promise.

1993 **For Younger Readers**

Wood, Douglas. *Old Turtle*. Illustrated by Cheng-Khee Chee. Pfeiffer-Hamilton.

For Older Readers

Hesse, Karen. *Letters from Rifka*. Henry Holt.

1994 **For Younger Readers**

Hopkinson, Deborah. *Sweet Clara and the Freedom Quilt*. Illustrated by James E. Ransome. Alfred A. Knopf.

For Older Readers

Toll, Nelly. *Behind the Secret Window: A Memoir of a Hidden Childhood during World War Two*. Dial Books.

1995 **For Younger Readers**

Mattaei, Gay, and Jewel Grutman. *The Ledgerbook of Thomas Blue Eagle*. Illustrated by Adam Cvijanovic. Thomasson-Grant.

For Older Readers

Krisher, Trudy. *Spite Fences*. Delacorte Press.

Informational Book

Bowen, Gary. *Stranded at Plimoth Plantation 1626*. HarperCollins.

1996 **For Younger Readers**

Bradby, Marie. *More Than Anything Else*. Illustrated by Chris K. Soentpiet. Orchard Books.

For Older Readers

Alder, Elizabeth. *The King's Shadow*. Farrar, Straus & Giroux.

Informational Book

Quinlan, Susan E. *The Case of the Mummified Pigs, and Other Mysteries in Nature*. Illustrated by Jennifer O. Dewey. Boyds Mills Press.

Coretta Scott King Award

These awards and honor designations have been given annually since 1969 to African American authors and illustrators for books that are outstanding inspirational and educational contributions to literature for children and young people. They are given by the Social Responsibilities Round Table of the American Library Association.

1993 Author Award

McKissack, Patricia C. *The Dark-Thirty: Southern Tales of the Supernatural.*
Illustrated by Brian Pinkney. Alfred A. Knopf.

Illustrator Award

Anderson, David A. *The Origin of Life on Earth: An African Creation Myth.*
Illustrated by Kathleen Atkins Wilson. Sight Productions.

1994 Author Award

Johnson, Angela. *Toning the Sweep.* Orchard Books.

Author Honor Books

Thomas, Joyce Carol. *Brown Honey in Broomwheat Tea.* Illustrated by
Floyd Cooper. HarperCollins Children's Books.

Myers, Walter Dean. *Malcolm X: By Any Means Necessary.* Scholastic.

Illustrator Award

Feelings, Tom. *Soul Looks Back in Wonder.* With contributions by Maya
Angelou, Askia Toure, and Langston Hughes. Illustrated by the author.
Doubleday.

Illustrator Honor Books

Thomas, Joyce Carol. *Brown Honey in Broomwheat Tea.* Illustrated by
Floyd Cooper. HarperCollins Children's Books.

Mitchell, Margaree King. *Uncle Jed's Barbershop.* Illustrated by James E.
Ransome. Simon & Schuster.

1995 Author Award

McKissack, Patricia C., and Fredrick L. McKissack. *Christmas in the Big
House, Christmas in the Quarters.* Scholastic.

Author Honor Books

Woodson, Jacqueline. *I Hadn't Meant to Tell You This.* Delacorte Press.

McKissack, Patricia C., and Fredrick L. McKissack. *Black Diamond: The
Story of the Negro Baseball Leagues.* Scholastic.

Illustrator Award

Johnson, James Weldon. *The Creation.* Illustrated by James E. Ransome.
Holiday House.

Illustrator Honor Books

Medearis, Angela Shelf. *The Singing Man.* Illustrated by Terea Shaffer.
Holiday House.

Grimes, Nikki. *Meet Danitra Brown.* Illustrated by Floyd Cooper.
Lothrop, Lee & Shepard Books.

1996 Author Awards

Hamilton, Virginia. *Her Stories.* Illustrated by Leo and Diane Dillon. Blue
Sky/Scholastic.

Author Honor Books

Curtis, Christopher Paul. *The Watsons Go to Birmingham—1963*. Delacorte.

Williams-Garcia, Rita. *Like Sisters on the Homefront*. Lodestar.

Woodson, Jacqueline. *From the Notebooks of Melanin Sun*. Blue Sky/Scholastic.

Illustrator Award

Feelings, Tom. *The Middle Passage: White Ships Black Cargo*. Illustrated by the author. Dial.

Illustrator Honor Books

Hamilton, Virginia. *Her Stories*. Illustrated by Leo and Diane Dillon. Blue Sky/Scholastic.

San Souci, Robert D. *The Faithful Friend*. Illustrated by Brian Pinkney. Simon & Schuster.

NCTE Orbis Pictus Award for Outstanding Nonfiction for Children

This award commemorates the work of John Comenius, *Orbis Pictus: The World in Pictures*, published in 1657 and historically considered to be the first book actually planned for children. The selection committee chooses one outstanding nonfiction book each year on the basis of accuracy, organization, design, writing style, and usefulness for classroom teaching.

1993 **Award**

Stanley, Jerry. *Children of the Dust Bowl: The True Story of the School at Weedpatch Camp*. Crown Books for Young Readers.

Honor Books

Cummings, Pat. *Talking with Artists*. Macmillan/Bradbury Press.

Cone, Molly. *Come Back, Salmon: How a Group of Dedicated Kids Adopted Pigeon Creek and Brought It Back to Life*. Sierra Club Books.

1994 **Award**

Murphy, Jim. *Across America on an Emigrant Train*. Houghton Mifflin/Clarion Books.

Honor Books

Brandenburg, Jim. *To the Top of the World: Adventures with Arctic Wolves*. Walker.

Brooks, Bruce. *Making Sense: Animal Perception and Communication*. Farrar, Straus & Giroux.

1995   **Award**

Swanson, Diane. *Safari Beneath the Sea: The Wonder World of the North Pacific Coast*. Sierra Club Books.

Honor Books

Dewey, Jennifer Owings. *Wildlife Rescue: The Work of Dr. Kathleen Ramsay*. Boyds Mills Press.

Freedman, Russell. *Kids at Work: Lewis Hine and the Crusade against Child Labor*. Houghton Mifflin/Clarion Books.

McKissack, Patricia C., and Frederick McKissack. *Christmas in the Big House, Christmas in the Quarters*. Edited by John Thompson and Ann Reit. Scholastic.

1996   **Award**

Murphy, Jim. *The Great Fire*. Scholastic.

Honor Books

Pringle, Laurence. *Dolphin Man: Exploring the World of Dolphins*. Atheneum.

Colman, Penny. *Rosie the Riveter: Women Working on the Home Front in World War II*. Crown.

NCTE Award for Excellence in Poetry for Children

Established in 1977, this award is presented every three years to a living American poet for an aggregate body of work for children ages three to thirteen.

1994   Barbara Esbensen. Major works: *Cold Stars and Fireflies: Poems for the Four Seasons* (1984, HarperCollins Children's Books); *Words with Wrinkled Knees* (1987, HarperCollins Children's Books); and *Who Shrank My Grandmother's House? Poems of Discovery* (1992, HarperCollins Children's Books).

John Newbery Medal

The Newbery Medal and honor book designations have been given annually since 1922 to the most distinguished contributions to children's literature published in the United States during the preceding year. The award is given by the Association for Library Service to Children of the American Library Association.

1993   **Medal**

Rylant, Cynthia. *Missing May*. Orchard Books.

Honor Books

Brooks, Bruce. *What Hearts*. HarperCollins.

McKissack, Patricia C. *The Dark-Thirty: Southern Tales of the Supernatural*. Illustrated by Brian Pinkney. Alfred A. Knopf.

Myers, Walter Dean. *Somewhere in the Darkness*. Scholastic.

1994 **Medal**

Lowry, Lois. *The Giver*. Houghton Mifflin.

Honor Books

Conly, Jane Leslie. *Crazy Lady!* HarperCollins Children's Books.

Yep, Laurence. *Dragon's Gate*. HarperCollins Children's Books.

Freedman, Russell. *Eleanor Roosevelt: A Life of Discovery*. Houghton Mifflin/Clarion Books.

1995 **Medal**

Creech, Sharon. *Walk Two Moons*. HarperCollins.

Honor Books

Cushman, Karen. *Catherine, Called Birdy*. Houghton Mifflin/Clarion Books.

Farmer, Nancy. *The Ear, the Eye and the Arm*. Richard Jackson/Orchard Books.

1996 **Medal**

Cushman, Karen. *The Midwife's Apprentice*. Clarion.

Honor Books

Coman, Carolyn. *What Jamie Saw*. Front Street.

Curtis, Christopher Paul. *The Watsons Go to Birmingham—1963*. Delacorte.

Fenner, Carol. *Yolanda's Genius*. McElderry.

Murphy, Jim. *The Great Fire*. Scholastic.

Scott O'Dell Award for Historical Fiction

Established in 1981, the Scott O'Dell Award is given to a distinguished work of historical fiction for children or young adults. The author must be a citizen or resident of the United States, the work must be written in English and published in the United States, and the story must be set in the New World (North, South, or Central America). The award is given annually (if a worthy book has been published) by the Advisory Committee of the Bulletin of the Center for Children's Books.

1993   Dorris, Michael. *Morning Girl*. Hyperion Books.

1994   Fleischman, Paul. *Bull Run*. HarperCollins.

1995   Salisbury, Graham. *Under the Blood-Red Sun*. Delacorte.

1996   Taylor, Theodore. *The Bomb*. Harcourt Brace.

Edgar Allan Poe/Mystery Writers of America Award for Juvenile Mystery

The Mystery Writers of America have given awards for the best juvenile mysteries every year since 1961. Each winner receives an "Edgar," a ceramic bust of Edgar Allan Poe, who was one of the originators of the mystery story.

1993   **Juvenile Mystery**

Bunting, Eve. *Coffin on a Case*. HarperCollins Children's Books.

Young Adult Mystery

Reaver, Chap. *Little Bit Dead*. Delacorte.

1994   **Juvenile Mystery**

Wallace, Barbara B. *Twin in the Tavern*. Macmillan/Atheneum.

Young Adult Mystery

Nixon, Joan L. *Name of the Game Was Murder*. Delacorte.

1995   **Juvenile Mystery**

Roberts, Willo Davis. *The Absolutely True Story . . . How I Visited Yellowstone with the Terrible Rubes*. Macmillan.

Young Adult Mystery

Springer, Nancy. *Toughing It*. Harcourt Brace.

1996   **Juvenile Mystery**

Springer, Nancy. *Looking for Jamie Bridger*. Dial.

Young Adult Mystery

MacGregor, Rob. *Prophecy Rock*. Simon & Schuster.

Booklists

In addition to recognition awarded to a handful of selected titles, several organizations issue annual lists of recommended books. While such lists are too lengthy to include in this volume, we include descriptions of the booklists that would be of interest to readers of *Adventuring with Books* and indicate how to obtain these booklists.

American Library Association Notable Children's Books

The Notable Children's Book Committee of the Association for Library Service to Children, a division of the American Library Association, selects notable books each year on the basis of literary quality, originality of text and illustrations, design, format, subject matter of interest and value to children, and likelihood of acceptance by children. The complete list of Notable Children's Books appears yearly in the March 15 issue of *Booklist*, an ALA journal.

American Library Association Best Books for Young Adults

The Young Adult Library Services Association of the American Library Association each year chooses the fiction and nonfiction titles that best satisfy the criteria of good literary quality and popular appeal to young adult readers. The complete list is published each year in the April 1 issue of *Booklist*, or you may receive a copy by sending a self-addressed stamped business-size envelope to YALSA, 50 E. Huron Street, Chicago, IL 60611.

American Library Association Quick Picks for Young Adults

The ALA's Young Adult Library Services Association also publishes a list each year of books with high appeal to young adult readers who, for whatever reason, do not like to read. The complete list is published each year in the April 1 issue of *Booklist*, or you may receive a copy by sending a self-addressed stamped business-size envelope to YALSA, 50 E. Huron Street, Chicago, IL 60611.

International Reading Association

The International Reading Association each year asks children, young adults, and teachers to vote on a list of books recommended by recognized sources such as *Booklist*, *Horn Book*, and *Journal of Reading*. The complete list of Children's Choices appears yearly in the November issue of *The Reading Teacher*, the Young Adults' Choices appear in the November issue of *Journal of Reading*, and the Teachers' Choices appear in the November issue of *The Reading Teacher*. Single copies of any of the lists may be obtained for a charge of $1.00 from The International Reading Association, Order Department, 800 Barksdale Road, P.O. Box 8139, Newark, DE 19714-8139.

Notable Children's Trade Books in the Field of Social Studies

A Book Review Committee appointed by the National Council for the Social Studies, in cooperation with the Children's Book Council, selects books published in the United States each year that (1) are written primarily for students in grades K–8, (2) emphasize human relations, (3) represent a diversity of groups and are sensitive to a broad range of cultural experiences, (4) present an original theme or a fresh slant on a traditional topic, (5) are easily readable and of high literary quality, and (6) have a pleasing format and, when appropriate, illustrations that enrich the text. The complete list of these notable books appears yearly in the April/May issue of *Social Education*, the journal of the National Council for the Social Studies. Single copies may be obtained at no charge by sending a stamped (3 oz.), self-addressed 6" × 9" envelope to the Children's Book Council, 568 Broadway, Suite 404, New York, NY 10012.

Outstanding Science Trade Books for Children

Each year a book review panel appointed by the National Science Teachers Association and assembled in cooperation with the Children's Book Council selects a list of outstanding books for young readers that present substantial science content in a clear, accurate, and up-to-date way. Each book is also evaluated on its freedom from gender, ethnic, and socioeconomic bias, and on the quality of its presentation of material. The complete list of outstanding science books is published each spring in the March issue of *Science and Children*.

School Library Journal's Best Books of the Year

The Book Review Editors of *School Library Journal* annually choose the best among the thousands of new children's books submitted to the journal for review during the preceding year. Books are selected on the basis of strong story line, clear presentation, high-quality illustration, and probable appeal to young readers. The complete list is published each year in the December issue of the journal.

Lists and descriptions of other awards, prizes, and lists can be found at the front of recent editions of *Children's Books in Print*, an annual publication of R. R. Bowker.

Directory of Publishers

Aladdin Paperbacks. Imprint of Simon & Schuster Children's Publishing Division. Orders: 800-223-2336; fax 800-445-6991.

Annick Press. Distributed by Firefly Books Ltd. Orders: 416-221-4802; fax 416-221-8400.

Arcade. Distributed by Little, Brown. Orders: 800-343-9204; fax 800-286-9471.

Artists & Writers Guild. Imprint of Western Publishing Co. Orders: 800-225-9514.

Atheneum Books for Young Readers. Imprint of Simon & Schuster Children's Publishing Division. Orders: 800-223-2336; fax 800-445-6991.

Avon Books. Orders: 800-223-0690; fax 800-223-0239.

Barron's Educational Series. Orders: 800-645-3476; fax 516-434-3723.

Peter Bedrick Books. Orders: 212-496-0751; fax 212-496-1158.

Beech Tree Books. Imprint of Wm. Morrow. Orders: 800-237-0657; fax 201-227-6849.

Blue Sky Press. Imprint of Scholastic Inc. Orders: 800-325-6149; fax 573-635-8937.

Boyds Mills Press. Division of Highlights Co. Distributed by St. Martin's Press. Orders: 800-221-7945; fax 800-258-2769.

Bradbury Press. Imprint of Simon & Schuster Children's Publishing Division. Orders: 800-223-2336; fax 800-445-6991.

BridgeWater Books. Imprint of Troll Associates. Distributed by Penguin USA. Orders: 800-526-0275; fax 201-385-6521.

Browndeer Press. Imprint of Harcourt Brace & Co. Orders: 800-782-4479; fax 407-345-3075.

Candlewick Press. Distributed by Penguin USA. Orders: 800-526-0275; fax 201-385-6521.

Childrens Press. Division of Grolier Inc. Orders: 800-621-1115; fax 800-374-4329.

Clarion Books. Division of Houghton Mifflin. Orders: 800-225-3362; fax 800-634-7568.

Cobblehill Books. Imprint of Penguin USA. Orders: 800-526-0275; fax 201-385-6521.

Copper Beech. Imprint of The Millbrook Press. Orders: 800-462-4703; fax 203-740-2526.

Creative Education. Subsidiary of Encyclopedia Britannica Inc. Orders: 800-445-6209; fax 507-388-2746.

Crown. Division of Random House. Orders: 800-733-3000; fax 800-659-2436.

Delacorte Press. Division of Bantam Doubleday Dell. Orders: 800-223-6834; fax 847-768-7095.

Dial Books. Imprint of Penguin USA. Orders: 800-526-0275; fax 201-385-6521.

Dillon. Imprint of Simon & Schuster Children's Publishing Division. Orders: 800-223-2336; fax 800-445-6991.

Dorling Kindersley. Distributed by Houghton Mifflin. Orders: 800-225-3362; fax 800-634-7568.

Douglas & McIntyre. Orders: 800-667-6902 (west), 800-565-9523 (east); fax 800-263-9099 (west), 604-254-9099 (east).

Dutton. Imprint of Penguin USA. Orders: 800-526-0275; fax 201-385-6521.

Farrar, Straus & Giroux. Distributed by the Putnam Publishing Group. Orders: 800-788-6262; fax 201-933-2316.

Four Winds Press. Imprint of Simon & Schuster Children's Publishing Division. Orders: 800-223-2336; fax 800-445-6991.

Gareth Stevens Children's Books. Orders: 800-341-3569; fax 414-225-0377.

Golden Books. Orders: 800-558-3291; fax 414-631-7635.

Green Tiger Press. Imprint of Simon & Schuster Children's Publishing Division. Orders: 800-223-2336; fax 800-445-6991.

Greenwillow. Division of Wm. Morrow & Co. Orders: 800-843-9389; fax 888-775-3260.

Groundwood Books. Distributed by Douglas & McIntyre. Orders: 800-667-6902 (west), 800-565-9523 (east); fax 800-263-9099 (west), 604-254-9099 (east).

Harcourt Brace. Orders: 800-782-4479; fax 407-345-3075.

Harcourt Brace Jovanovich. See Harcourt Brace.

HarperCollins. Orders: 800-242-7737; fax 800-822-4090.

Harper Trophy. See HarperCollins.

Henry Holt. Orders: 800-488-5233; fax 212-677-6487.

Holiday House. Orders: 212-688-0085; fax 212-688-0395.

Holt Reinhart & Winston. Orders: 800-782-4479; fax 817-334-7634.

Houghton Mifflin. Orders: 800-225-3362; fax 800-634-7568.

Hyperion Books for Children. Imprint of Walt Disney Publishing Group. Distributed by Little, Brown. Orders: 800-343-9204; fax 800-286-9471.

Jewish Publication Society. Orders: 800-234-3151; fax 215-564-6640.

Kids Can Press. Orders: 800-265-0884; fax 416-960-5437.

Kingfisher. Imprint of Larousse Kingfisher Chambers. Orders: 800-497-1657; fax 800-874-4027.

Alfred A. Knopf. Subsidiary of Random House. Orders: 800-733-3000; fax 800-659-2436.

Lerner Publications. Orders: 800-328-4929; fax 800-332-1132.

Lester. Orders: 416-445-3333; fax 416-445-5967.

Listening Library. Orders: 800-324-8367; fax 800-454-0606.

Little, Brown. Division of Time Warner Publishing. Orders: 800-343-9204; fax 800-286-9471.

Lodestar. Imprint of Penguin USA. Orders: 800-526-0275; fax 201-385-6521.

Lothrop, Lee & Shepard Books. Division of Wm. Morrow. Orders: 800-843-9389; fax 888-775-3260.

Macmillan. Division of Simon & Schuster. Orders: 800-257-5755; fax 800-445-6991.

Margaret K. McElderry Books. Imprint of Simon & Schuster Children's Publishing Division. Orders: 800-223-2336; fax 800-445-6991.

Millbrook Press. Orders: 800-462-4703; fax 203-740-2526.

Mondo. Orders: 800-242-3650; fax 526-484-7813.

Wm. Morrow. Orders: 800-843-9389; fax 212-261-6595.

Mulberry Paperback Books. Division of Wm. Morrow. Orders: 800-843-9389; fax 212-261-6595.

North-South Books. Orders: 800-282-8257; fax 212-633-1004.

Orchard Books. A Grolier Company. Orders: 800-672-6672; fax 800-374-4329.

Oxford University Press. Orders: 800-451-7556; fax 919-677-1303.

Philomel. Imprint of The Putnam Berkley Group. Orders: 800-788-6262; fax 212-213-6707.

Picture Book Studio. Imprint of Simon & Schuster Children's Publishing Division. Orders: 800-223-2336; fax 800-445-6991.

Puffin. Imprint of Penguin USA. Orders: 800-526-0275; fax 201-385-6521.

G.P. Putnam. Imprint of The Putnam Berkley Group. Orders: 800-788-6262; fax 212-213-6707.

R & S Books. Distributed by Farrar, Straus, Giroux, an imprint of The Putnam Berkley Group. Orders: 800-788-6262; fax 212-213-6707.

Rabbit Ears Books. Imprint of Simon & Schuster Children's Publishing Division. Orders: 800-223-2336; fax 800-445-6991.

Red Deer. Distributed by Orca Book Publishers. Orders: 800-210-5277; fax 604-380-1892.

Scholastic. Orders: 800-325-6149; fax 573-635-8937.

Scribner. Imprint of Simon & Schuster Children's Publishing Division. Orders: 800-223-2336; fax 800-445-6991.

Sierra Club Books for Children. Distributed by Little, Brown. Orders: 800-343-9204; fax 800-286-9471.

Simon & Schuster. Orders: 800-223-2336; fax 800-445-6991.

Sterling. Orders: 800-367-9692; fax 212-213-2495.

Stoddart. Orders: 800-387-0172; fax 416-445-5967.

Tambourine. Imprint of Wm. Morrow. Orders: 800-843-9389; fax 212-261-6595.

Ticknor & Fields Books for Young Readers. Distributed by Houghton Mifflin. Orders: 800-225-3362; fax 800-634-7568.

Tundra Books. Orders: 514-932-5434; fax 514-484-2152.

Viking. Division of Penguin USA. Orders: 800-526-0275; fax 201-385-6521.

Walker. Orders: 800-289-2553; fax 212-727-0984.

Whitman. Orders: 800-255-7675; fax 847-581-0039.

Author Index

Illustrator Index

Subject Index

We have attempted to make this index as helpful to the classroom teacher and librarian as possible. Toward that end, we have included cross-references when it seems likely that a particular topic could be called by more than one name. The numbers refer to annotation numbers used throughout this book; the portion of the numeral before the decimal point refers to the chapter number, and the portion of the numeral after the decimal point refers to the particular book's position within the chapter. In a series of numbers, the first citation from a given chapter is highlighted in **boldface**. We include a list of the chapter numbers below so that you will be able to tell at a glance whether a particular citation is for the type of book you are interested in.

1. Books for Young Children
2. Poetry
3. Traditional Literature
4. Fantasy
5. Contemporary Realistic Fiction
6. Historical Fiction
7. Biography
8. Social Studies
9. Science: Pure and Applied
10. Fine Arts
11. Crafts and Hobbies
12. Celebrations: Fiction and Nonfiction

Title Index

Photo Credits

We wish to thank the following publishers for their gracious permission to reprint the photographs of book covers that appear on our photo pages.

Atheneum, an imprint of Simon & Schuster Children's Publishing Division
Gifts of Wali Dad: A Tale of India and Pakistan retold by Aaron Shepard. Illustrations © copyright 1995 by Daniel San Souci.
So Sings the Blue Deer by Charmayne McGee. Copyright 1994.
What a Wonderful World by George David Weiss and Bob Thiele. Illustrations © copyright 1995 by Ashley Bryan.
Where the Flame Trees Bloom by Alma Flor Ada. Illustrations © copyright 1994 by Antonio Martorell.

Barron's
Vikings by Fiona Macdonald. Copyright 1993.

Boyds Mills Press
The Always Prayer Shawl by Sheldon Oberman, illustrated by Ted Lewin. Published by Boyds Mills Press 1994, illustrations copyright 1994 by Ted Lewin.

Clarion Books, an imprint of Houghton Mifflin Company
Catherine, Called Birdy by Karen Cushman. Copyright 1994.
Cheyenne Again by Eve Bunting, illustrated by Irving Toddy. Copyright 1995.
The King and the Tortoise by Tololwa M. Mollel, illustrated by Kathy Blankley. Copyright 1993.

Crown, a division of Random House
Chin Yu Min and the Ginger Cat by Jennifer Armstrong, illustrated by Mary GrandPré. Copyright 1993.

Dial, a division of Penguin USA
Parents in the Pigpen, Pigs in the Tub by Amy Ehrlich, illustrated by Steven Kellogg. Copyright 1993.
Seven Candles for Kwanzaa by Andrea Davis Pinkney, illustrated by Brian Pinkney. Copyright 1993.
Soul Looks Back in Wonder selected by Tom Feelings, illustrated by Tom Feelings. Copyright 1993.
Snuffles and Snouts selected by Laura Robb, illustrated by Steven Kellogg. Copyright 1995.
Waiting for the Evening Star by Rosemary Wells, illustrated by Susan Jeffers. Copyright 1993.

Red Ribbon by Sarah Weeks, illustrated by Jeffrey Greene. Copyright 1995.
Walk Two Moons by Sharon Creech. Copyright 1994.
What You Know First by Patricia MacLachlan, illustrated by Barry Moser. Copyright 1995.

Henry Holt and Company
Fish Faces by Norbert Wu, photographs by Norbert Wu. Copyright 1993.
Happy New Year, Beni by Jane Breskin Zalben, illustrated by Jane Breskin Zalben. Copyright 1993.
A Moon in Your Lunch Box by Michael Spooner, illustrated by Ib Ohlsson. Copyright 1993.

Holiday House
The Goose Girl: A Story from the Brothers Grimm retold by Eric A. Kimmel, illustrated by Robert Sauber. Copyright 1995.
The Hanukkah Ghosts by Malka Penn. Copyright 1995.
The Three Princes: A Tale from the Middle East retold by Eric A. Kimmel, illustrated by Leonard Everett Fisher. Copyright 1994.

Houghton Mifflin
If You Should Hear A Honey Guide by April Pulley Sayre, illustrated by S. D. Schindler. Copyright 1995.

Jewish Publication Society
Raoul Wallenberg: The Man Who Stopped Death by Sharon Linnea, photographs by Thomas Veres. Copyright 1993.

Alfred A. Knopf
Sweet Clara and the Freedom Quilt by Deborah Hopkinson, illustrated by James Ransome. Copyright 1993.

Larousse Kingfisher Chambers
Kalinzu: A Story from Africa by Jeremy Grimsdell, illustrated by Jeremy Grimsdell. Copyright 1993.

The Lerner Group
Artistic Trickery: The Tradition of Trompe L'Oeil Art by Michael Capek. The Lerner Publishing Group © 1995.

Lester
Selina and the Bear Paw Quilt by Barbara Smucker, illustrated by Janet Wilson. Copyright 1995.

Little, Brown & Company
The Creation: A Poem by James Weldon Johnson, illustrated by Carla Golembe. Copyright 1993.
Dumpling Soup by Jama Kim Rattigan, illustrated by Lillian Hsu-Flanders. Copyright 1993.
Frida Kahlo by Robyn Montana Turner, illustrated by Robyn Montana Turner. Copyright 1993.
Grandma's Shoes by Libby Hathorn, illustrated by Elivia. Copyright 1994.

My Nature Craft Book by Cheryl Owen, illustrated by Cheryl Owen. Copyright 1993.

On Winter's Wind by Patricia Hermes. Copyright 1995.

Rainbow Bird: An Aboriginal Folktale from Northern Australia by Eric Maddern, illustrated by Adrienne Kennaway. Copyright 1993.

A Starlit Somersault Downhill by Nancy Willard, illustrated by Jerry Pinkney. Copyright 1993.

Tell Them We Remember: The Story of the Holocaust by Susan D. Bachrach. Copyright 1994.

Tracks in the Wild by Betsy Bowen, illustrated by Betsy Bowen. Copyright 1993.

Voices From the Fields: Children of Migrant Farmworkers Tell Their Stories by S. Beth Atkin, photographs by S. Beth Atkin. Copyright 1993.

Welcome Back Sun by Michael Emberley, illustrated by Michael Emberley. Copyright 1993.

Macmillan Books for Young Readers, an imprint of Simon & Schuster Children's Publishing Division

Coyote and the Laughing Butterflies retold by Harriet Peck Taylor. Illustrations © copyright 1995 by Harriet Peck Taylor.

Greek Myths by Geraldine McCaughrean. Illustrations © copyright 1993 by Emma Chichester Clark.

Pablo's Tree by Pat Mora. Illustrations © copyright 1994 by Cecily Lang.

McElderry Books for Young Readers, an imprint of Simon & Schuster Children's Publishing Division

Good Luck Gold and Other Poems by Janet S. Wong. Copyright 1994.

Millbrook Press

The Quilt-Block History of Pioneer Days: With Projects Kids Can Make by Mary Cobb, illustrated by Jan Davey Ellis. Copyright 1995.

William Morrow and Company

Pablo Remembers: The Fiesta of the Day of the Dead by George Ancona, photographs by George Ancona. Jacket photograph © 1993 by George Ancona.

The Woman Who Fell from the Sky by John Bierhorst, illustrated by Robert Andrew Parker. Jacket illustration © 1993 by Robert Andrew Parker.

Scholastic

Christmas in the Big House, Christmas in the Quarters by Patricia C. McKissack and Fredrick L. McKissack, illustrated by John Thompson. Copyright 1994.

Dreamer by Cynthia Rylant, illustrated by Barry Moser. Copyright 1993.

The Earth is Painted Green: A Garden of Poems About Our Planet edited by Barbara Brenner, illustrated by S. D. Schindler. Copyright 1994.

The Great Fire by Jim Murphy. Copyright 1995.

The Iguana Brothers by Tony Johnston, illustrated by Mark Teague. Copyright 1995.

Knoxville, Tennessee by Nikki Giovanni, illustrated by Larry Johnson. Copyright 1994.

Lift Ev'ry Voice and Sing by James Weldon Johnson, illustrated by Jan Spivey Gilchrist. Copyright 1995.

The Lion's Whiskers: An Ethiopian Folktale by Nancy Raines Day, illustrated by Ann Grifalconi. Copyright 1995.

Little Lama of Tibet by Lois Raimondo, photographs by Lois Raimondo. Copyright 1994.

Pass it on: African-American Poetry for Children selected by Wade Hudson, illustrated by Floyd Cooper. Copyright 1993.

The Story of Ruby Bridges by Robert Coles, illustrated by George Ford. Copyright 1995.

Two by Two by Barbara Reid, illustrated by Barbara Reid. Copyright 1993.

Charles Scribner's Sons Books for Young Readers, an imprint of Simon & Schuster Children's Publishing Division

Stitching Stars: The Story Quilts of Harriet Powers by Mary E. Lyons. Copyright 1993.

Sierra Club Books

African Animals ABC written and illustrated by Philippa Alys-Browne (1995) from Sierra Club Books for Children (ISBN 0-87156-372-X).

Viking, a division of Penguin USA

Math Curse by Jon Scieszka, illustrated by Lane Smith. Copyright 1995.

What Makes a Degas a Degas? by Richard Muhlberger. Copyright 1993.

Editor

Wendy Sutton is a professor of children's and young adult literature in the Department of Language Education at the University of British Columbia, Vancouver, Canada. She earned her advanced degrees at the University of California, Berkeley, and at Michigan State University, East Lansing, and is a former elementary and secondary school teacher, with teaching experience in Canada, Pakistan, and Tanzania. Active in the Council for over twenty years, Wendy served as chair of the Excellence in Poetry for Children Award Committee for six years and was a member of the Elementary Section Committee and the NCTE Nominating Committee. She is a past editor of *English International*, a member of the International Assembly and the Children's Literature and Literature for Adolescents Assemblies, and a reviewer for *Language Arts* and *English Journal*. Her most recent publication is *Only Connect: Readings on Children's Literature*, 3rd edition (Oxford, 1996), with Sheila Egoff, Gordon Stubbs, and Ralph Ashley.

This book was typeset in Palatino and Helvetica by Precision Graphics.
Typefaces used on the cover were University Roman and Palatino.
The book was printed on 50 lb. White and 60 lb. Finch by Braun-Brumfield, Inc.